OTHER WORLDS

OTHER WORLDS

Notions of Self and Emotion among the Lohorung Rai

Charlotte E. Hardman

BERG
OXFORD · NEW YORK

First published in 2000 by
Berg
Editorial offices:
150 Cowley Road, Oxford, OX4 1JJ, UK
838 Broadway, Third Floor, New York, NY 10003-4812, USA

Berg is an imprint of Oxford International Publishers Ltd.

Library of Congress Cataloging-in-Publication Data
A catalogue record for this book is available from the Library of Congress.

British Library Cataloguing-in-Publication Data
A catalogue record for this book is available from the British Library.

ISBN 1 85973 150 3 (Cloth)
1 85973 155 4 (Paper)

Typeset by JS Typesetting, Wellingborough, Northants.
Printed in the United Kingdom by Biddles Ltd, Guildford and King's Lynn.

COFRIN LIBRARY
28 DAY LOAN PERIOD

This item is due back on or before:

TO RETURN ITEMS:

- **during library hours**, bring items to the circulation desk on the Plaza Level or on the 3rd floor of the library
- **when the library is closed**, use the outside bookdrop located at the northwest side entrance by the Credit Union

FOR RENEWALS:

- call **(920) 465-2333**
- ask at the **circulation desk** (your ID is required)
- log into your **patron info** account through Cofrin Library Online Catalog

RECALLS:

- items can be recalled after an initial check-out of 14 days
- items not returned by the new due date will be subject to fines of $.25/day

IF THE ITEM IS OVERDUE:

- the **overdue notice** will be sent out via email, campus mail, or US mail the day after the item was due
- **NOTE:** if the item is **over 30 days overdue,** you will be **charged $60.00** for replacement and processing
- **fine or overdue dispute questions** can be made in person, by phone, or email (See below)
- payment of fines or fees is made in the library

FOR MORE DETAILS ON POLICIES:

- see **http://www.uwgb.edu/library/**

Cofrin Library
UW-Green Bay
2420 Nicolet Drive
Green Bay, WI 54311-7001
(920) 465-2540
circdept@uwgb.edu

for the Lohorung of Pangma
and for Henry and Diana

CONTENTS

LIST OF MAPS AND FIGURES

A NOTE ON LOHORUNG AND NEPALI WORDS

In this book, Nepali words are marked with a following N. and I transcribe them according to Turner's *Dictionary of the Nepali Language* (1965[1931]). I have simplified some transcriptions:ţ is t; ŋ is ng.
The transcription of Lohorung words follows my own phonological convention as shown in Appendix One. The glottal stop is indicated by a hyphen or a *k*, as in *miri–k* (tail). When the glottal stop opens a suffix it is represented by a hyphen on its own, as in *mi–wa* (tears). The vowel *ea* is represented by *a* and *ts* is pronounced as in 'lets'. The meanings of Lohorung words are offered as glosses in the text.

Key Lohorung terms used in the book can be found in the glossary below.

GLOSSARY

apikhuba	stingy, mean
bok	belly
bokshi	witch
bongsime, bongsik, bongchame	to lie, to be lied to, hence disappointed
bongbi	snakes of the underworld who choose shaman and local priests
bung	flower, genitalia, menstruation, vital essence
chap	ghosts, spirits of persons after death
chaptempa	world of the dead
chawa	ritual term for springs identifiedwith clans
chenchame, chen chen minuk	elated, pleased, like
chenchabokme	happy, content
chiksime, chiksik	disapprove,feel disgusted
chime	learn (a skill)
chung'lu	cold
chung niwa	cold–hearted
chungme	worship
chudel N	spirit of a young unmarried woman who has died, haunting her lovers, those she

	has loved or who have loved her.
dibu	beer
diha lengme	proud
dukka (N)	pain, suffering
essime, essik	lazy
ha'chak'wa minuk	excited, impatient
hang/hangma	king, queen
hangme	respect
hapme, habukmi	cry, weep
hekme, heku	be able
heme	hear
herem herem minuk	hungry, empty
hingchame, hingkrikpa	alive and flourishing
hoprek' pikhedu	empty
hongsiu	inside of house; innermost part of person
Kāhila N	fourth son
Kāhili	fourth daughter or wife of 4th son
kamnuk	beautiful attractive, nice, good
kamnuro mikuchini	feel unhappy, sad, uncomfortable
kanga yongpa	proud
khechimawa	irritable, itchy
khim	house
kisime	verb. to fear
kisimalu	adv. frightening
khimpie	house ancestor
khimtibungme	hold in mind, remember
kul N	lineage, the god within a person
labukme	respect
lamthing lamuk	jealous
langhangme	hope, wish for
lawa	wandering soul, animates the body giving consciousness of life
lawa kisik	shocked, terrified, soul loss
lemmang	ordinary reality
leeme, leeku	know, he knows

lemmang awake, ordinary reality
letokme learn (a fact)
lung stone
lungma heart/liver
lungchame like, love
lungma diha'l'le feel brave

maksa bear; kin term see kinship (Appendix 2)
mangpa/mangmani shaman, male/female
mangsuk household shrine
Maruhang Biksik clan king

Maruhang Biksik clan king
mehangkheda sulky
mi'bungdame, mi'bungdu remember
mi'chame/mi'lame homesickness, lovesick, sadness of separation, heart yearning for someone far away
minuk'wa'ruru leme feel like crying
minchame hope
mingkheme, mikheme forget
minukme, minuk feel
mitokme, mitoku remember

nabuk we'langdu hurt pride
namnungla'chi sun and moon people
nana elder sister
nenchame like, feel kind
ngenukme, ngenukmi quarrelsome, irritable
ngesime shy, ashamed, shame
ningbak' mesikme homesick, nostalgic
nisasi' lik fear (of water)
niwa chai'kheme feel hurt
niwa chuk'e'le feel generous, unselfish
niwa chume believe, trust
niwa entae feel relieved
niwa i'i feel moody
niwa kaise discontent
niwa kamnuk content
niwa kisik respect, awe
niwa makhara mad

niwa mi'chak'nga, huk yoktokni	homesick, lovesick, sadness of separation
niwa meding	irresponsible
niwa mak'chame	dizzy
niwa pime	trust, have faith
niwa tuguk	hurt, upset, sad
niwa yamuk	anxious, guilty, worried
naksubang	insane
panukha	energetic
pe–lam	corpus of myths, rites, knowledge, traditions relating to the ancestors and origins
pheguang	assistant to ritual officiant
phenni	forbidden, prohibited, wrong,
pima mikhuba	generous, giving
pudung	awake
sak/sage lubokme	hungry
sammang	spirits of powerful ancestors, ancestors, rituals to them
sapthame, sapthak	satisfied
saya	ancestor within, a psycho–physical force linking a person with ancestors and those forbears who established and maintained their traditions
saya dashi kheda	depressed, melancholic, demoralized, dispirited, (see *saya* in text)
semmang makme	dream, non–ordinary reality
sengkhara	drunk
sichame, sichak	dislike, hate, feel cruel
sinti'khema, sinti'kheda	angry, bitter
sirda yakchame	get angry
siri ledhangme	jealous
siri phongme	humble
siri tangpa	suddenly angry
sokma	breath
som	heart
som'chai'khenga	pity, compassion, sorrow, eat heart away
som'khepokme, som'khepok	angry (heart)
som'kheruk	feel, heart itches, feel jealous
som tuguk, tukung	heart hurts,compassion/love for someone close

tangpam niwa	individual mind, wishes, desires
tapnam yapmi	forest people, original people
tangpam yapmi	own people
temuku	frightened away
thamsik (thamsitingmi)	jealous
titepāti, (Artemis vulgaris)	Mugwort, St John's Plant: Used by Lohorung
tokma nenchame	feel grateful
tukchanie	sane
wai'mesime	thirsty
wairang	lower sections of the household shrine
waptokme, waptok	understand
yakta'khema, yaktampa	worn out, tired
yangsime.yangsima lu	fear (of height)
yatangpa	local priest, who journeys in an altered state of consciousness to diagnose and heal
yepmalitham hamalitham (also *Hepmalitham Yepmalitham*,)	the abode of ancestors and those of 'good' death
yik'bok'kheme	feel angry
yik'kheme, yik'ti'kheme	very unhappy
yin'keng	dejected
yongnukme	feel munificent
yongukme	possessed

PREFACE

Fieldwork for this book was carried out mainly from 1976 to 1978, and on shorter visits from 1978 to1980. I am very grateful to what was then the Social Science Research Council and The American Association of University Women for their financial support and to the Small Grants Committee at the University of Newcastle for theirs.

The experience of submerging myself in another way of perceiving and conceptualizing the world, living life as much as possible along with the people I was staying with, making mistakes and being corrected, exploring perceptions and being firmly socialised into the correct way of seeing things is still for me the process of understanding another culture. I was shown how to plant rice, though I was so bad at it they soon gave up on me; they showed me how to wash modestly at the spring, how to eat rice with my fingers, how to urinate standing up, without lifting my skirt. I ate as they did, drank as they did, rose when they did. The 'shock of otherness' was not so much while in the field, it was on my return to Europe. After years away Western ways seemed onerous. Travelling in London was a shock and I realized the extent to which I was not used to the speed or style of Western life: I was largely unaware of events that had taken place while I'd been away, and still partly operated in another framework. I had to learn how to avoid the pain of separation from those with whom I had shared so much.

To write analytically about my Lohorung friends became for a while a nightmare; how to put in language a sufficient description that could articulate their world and what I had experienced? It was like dissecting people one loves when every word is loaded with insufficiency. I felt I knew Lohorung friends and neighbors and yet the representations of them seemed insufficient, not close enough to the experiences to satisfy me. And maybe I had not gone far enough, or maybe I had gone too far. Edwin and Shirley Ardener had always advocated fieldwork in pairs, so that you can discuss issues and problems within your own idiom. I had taken the view that I had to immerse myself completely and that a partner would be a distraction linguistically, conceptually and practically. I tried to capture another framework.

There might be excuses for not being aware of biases we take to the field in a study of crop rotation but in studying the conceptual framework of another world I was constantly confronted by the limits of my own cultural make–up and also, of course, my own individual make–up. In studying other's emotions I had to look at my own; are my emotions biologically determined or part of my cultural clothing? Is my hot anger, fast arising and quickly disappearing, part of my genetic make–up or learned in the family home, or a combination? Are they sharing what I feel? What motivates them? How do they understand what it means to be a person? Fieldwork is a constant conversation between one's own culture and theirs.

It took me a long time to finally write about my experience of living and learning from Lohorung people in Pangma and neighboring villages. In one sense this fieldwork is now history. For example, the political system has changed. The Panchayat system no longer exists.The number of people, the number of houses has changed but their 'ethnopsychology' which is the core of this book has not fundamentally changed. I have to thank my publishers, and Katherine Earle in particular, for their patience.

I could not have written this book without the people I met in Pangma and elsewhere in the Arun Valley. I owe them an enormous debt of thanks. My gratitude goes to the Lohorung in Gairi Pangma, Dara Pangma, Loke Pangma, Tollo Pangma and other villages in the Arun. In particular, my thanks go to Hari Bahadur and all his family, to Sher Bahadur and Anumma, to Nanda and Rudra, Dachemma and all her family. They were all so generous, sympathetic and patient in teaching me what they could. They supported me in a way I shall never forget. Mark Oppitz helped me emotionally and intellectually from afar. And when I returned I could not have made it without the comments and guidance of Lionel Caplan, Richard Burghart, Christoph von Fürer Haimendorf, and particularly Paul Harris and Paul Heelas, whose insights and support were invaluable. My thanks too go to David Mylan, and my children, Sophie and Helen, who put up with so much, to Monica Stoppleman, Karen Chessell, Lisa Harland, Mick Sharp and Clare Roberts. Finally, thanks to Iain Edgar, for his reading and comments, and most of all his encouragement.

CHINA
Field work area
Kathmandu
EAST NEPAL
Khandbari
Bhojpur
INDIA
Dhankuta
0
150
Kilometres

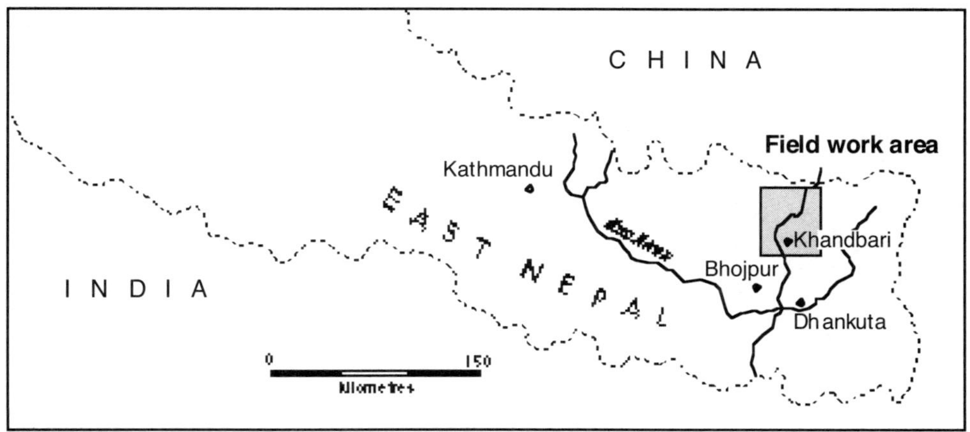

MAP 1 Location of Nepal

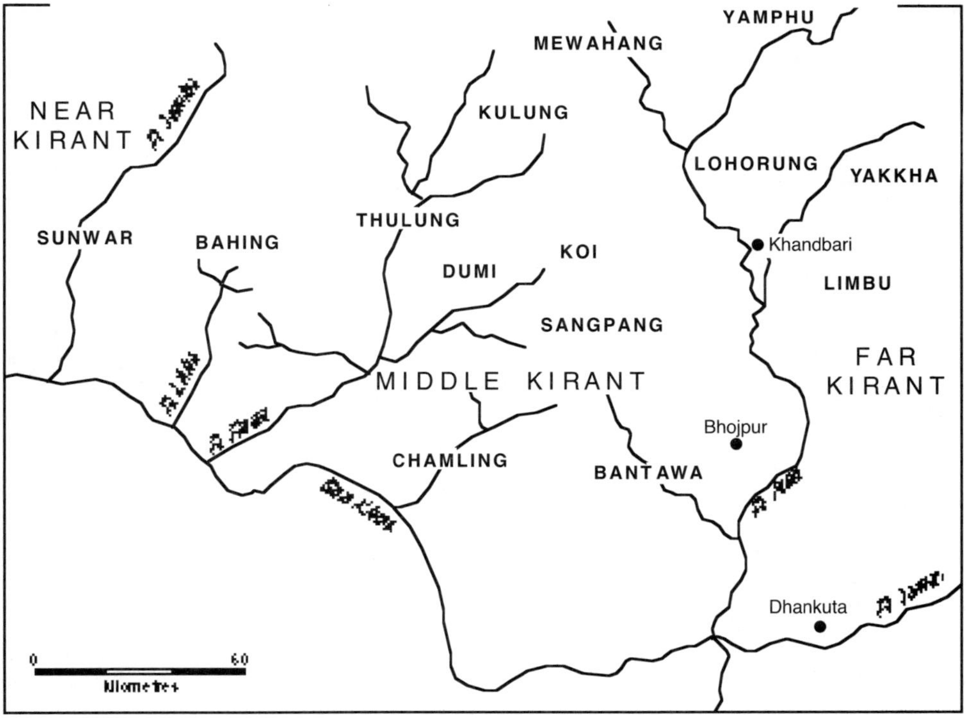

YAMPHU
MEWAHANG
NEAR KIRANT
KULUNG
LOHORUNG
YAKKHA
THULUNG
SUNWAR
BAHING
Khandbari
KOI
DUMI
LIMBU
SANGPANG
FAR KIRANT
MIDDLE KIRANT
Bhojpur
CHAMLING
BANTAWA
Dhankuta
0
60
Kilometres

MAP 2 Lohorung and their neighbouring tribes.

1
Theories in my Boots

I had been walking for days through the rounded hills of Rai country to the West of the River Arun. Lohorung country lay somewhere across from me. I could see how each side of the valley was isolated from the other by the turbulent and wide river, older than the Himalayas themselves, and by tributaries which, flowing into it, created their own smaller valleys, deep gorges and countless ridges. It seemed like a long trail leading from the riverbed up to Khandbari, the major bazaar town of the upper Arun, lying at about 4,000 ft. (1,200m), and then up even higher to the first Lohorung villages. As I walked up, the views constantly changed. My first impressions were dominated by the sight of the endless river, the patches of sienna clay earth, the rugged grey rocks and huge boulders, whose sculptured forms changed shape with the play of light. At times they emerged dark and stark against the lush shades of green, ranging from the verdant paddy–green of the flat terraced fields cut out of the gentler slopes, to the dark black purplish green of the jungle, the greenery of the primaeval forest. The dense sub–tropical vegetation of the lower slopes thinned out to reveal the cool blowing leaves of the plantain trees, the gentle sway of the slender bamboo, their tall growing stems bending against a vista of crag and snow–peaked mountain. What struck me first, before I had even met the people I came to know as Lohorung, was this rugged landscape and the variety of the natural world in which they live.

It's hardly surprising the topography of Lohorung country is so varied.

The terrain begins with the bed of the Arun river at 1,968 ft. (600m) and ends with the peak of Mount Makalu at 27,378 ft (8,345m.). Situated between the heights of the Himalayas and the middle hills of the Mahabharat range are the villages of Lohorung Rai. They lie scattered over a complex of interlocking hills and narrow valleys within a small area bounded to the West by the rivers Arun and Sankhuwa, to the east by the Sabhaya river, and to the north by the eastward swing of the Arun and an inhospitable region of rugged hills. Some 4,500 Lohorung live here.

It was fairly hot when I first came to Lohorung country in mid–April 1976. Later on, I learned how rain and snow can transform the landscape within a few hours. In the Himalayas in general, changes in weather, such as sudden rain, hailstorms, or fierce winds, are dramatic and often violent. In Lohorung country rainfall reaches an annual average of about 2,600 mm. (slightly over 100 ins.), and most of this falls during the months from June to September. I had chosen to work in an area often referred to as the 'wettest place in Nepal'!

The moist monsoon air from the plains drifts into the big open valley of the Arun

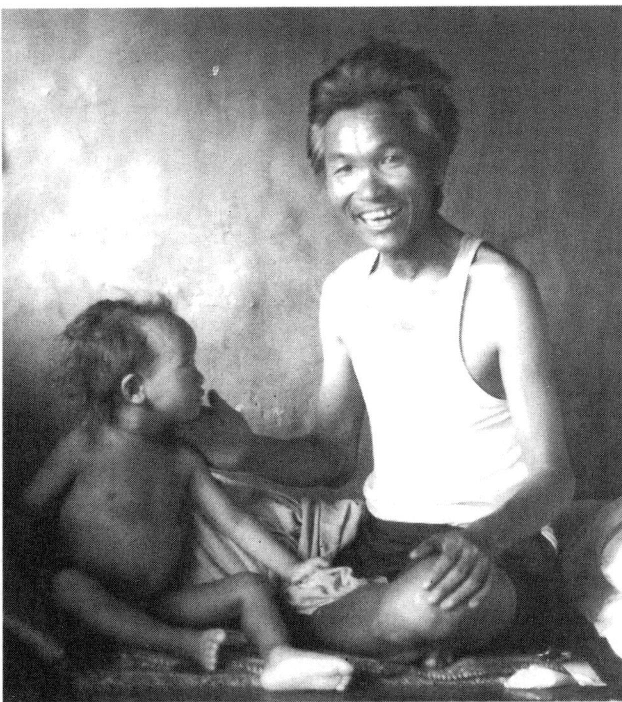

FIG 1 Sher Bahadur.

until it's forced to rise as it meets the steep gorges and mountainous area. Even though I'm used to English rain, I was amazed by the torrential downpours which made rivers and streams impossible to cross, swamped bridges, and flooded waterways. For three or four months of every year these downpours come daily, the skies and hills constantly shrouded in cloud. Mist descends every morning to swathe the houses, leaving its legacy of permanent dampness.

Sheltering themselves from these outside forces of nature, Lohorung houses stand clustered together in close–knit villages. In the Rai villages which I had become used to as I travelled to the west of the Arun, the houses were isolated one from the other, or at most clustered in twos and threes, separated from one another by fields or woods. The density of Lohorung villages means that almost all fields and house–gardens lie on the outskirts. All there is room for in front of each house is a small courtyard with stone walls which form the boundaries of the rocky paths which wind through the villages. Lohorung see themselves as closely related to stones, claiming their very name is related to their word for 'stone' (*lung*). The etymology is dubious, but with a glance at the visual landscape this began to make sense: huge boulders loom large inside villages and outside in the fields, natural focal meeting points and as I learned later, often shrouded in mythical history.

The houses themselves stand high on wooden stilts. Unlike other Rai groups, Lohorung Rai raise their living quarters clear of the rocky ground. This keeps them

FIG 2 Stone Walls and Rocky Paths.

above the monsoon floods and creates a covered open space underneath their hearths where they can house their animals. Land is highly valued for agricultural purposes and the stilt constructions enable Lohorung to make use of uncultivatable stoney areas. Fierce winds may disturb them more than houses built on the ground, but rarely does it cause great damage, for the stilt house sways with the wind. When earth tremors occur, the stilt–house is at a distinct advantage.

It was this style of stilt–house which the anthropologist Christoph von Fürer–Haimendorf found 'barely distinguishable from the raised bamboo and timber structures of the Assam Himalayas'. This led him to suggest 'at one time Mongoloid tribal populations of relatively primitive culture occupied many of the forested hill regions south of the Himalayan range' (1975: 108). Lohorung men confirmed this when they told me how they closely identified with a people called Mishmi in Assam and Arunachal Pradesh to the East. They described feeling at home with the Mishmi style of life, their rituals (such as to the snake deity and the house ancestor) and their communal houses which are built on stilts. Their connection to the Mishmi has developed as some Lohorung in search of waged work have for several years migrated to live with them.

Whatever the link might once have been between Lohorung and tribes of the Indo–Tibetan borderlands as far afield as Assam (and the fact that their Tibeto–Burman languages are related supports this) it's clear that after the dispersal of groups in the early centuries AD, rugged topography plus a strong tendency towards local endogamy has isolated these different groups, leading to linguistic and cultural differences.

It was the maintenance of cultural isolation, in spite of present–day proximity to other tribal groups, which struck me so forcefully on this first trip to Lohorung country. As I wrote then:

> Strange, only a few hours' walk away from the Newar bazaar town of Khandbari here is a village with a totally different feeling, with a self–maintained world of its own. Everyone communicates in a language of which I understand nothing. Somehow the place feels old, untouched. Surely that goes against the sociological expectation that cultural isolation and independence goes along with physical geographical isolation. What isolates these people? What keeps them so inward–looking? Their houses, all on stilts, thatched and with lattice–work bamboo sides huddle together, looking one over the other and not towards the fields, which are so completely the main concern of the other hill peoples. Why don't they live in their fields, like the Rai to the West? What are the things that motivate them? I've never seen a village with so many pigs – black pigs – roaming around as if unowned. Why pigs? . . .

With impressions such as these, and the incessant clamour that I had, a myriad of unanswered thoughts and a baggage of possibly useless anthropological theory weighing down my new walking boots, I climbed on and up to Pangma village, the first Lohorung village on the trail from Khandbari. Then on to the country higher up. Not far from Pangma the houses reverted to being at ground level, sheep and goats took over from pigs: I had reached the Gurung village of Sekaya. Further on there was nothing but steep, rocky paths, forest, and occasional wide–open spaces and Bhotia villages. Scorched trunks of trees and twisted branches indicated that slash–and–burn cultivation was still being carried out. After my hours of walking through almost uninhabited country, I suddenly came upon the houses of Num, another Lohorung village.

On the maidan above, children were playing in front of the school, a long tin–roofed building. The screams of a pig drew my attention to something that was going on in the fields below. Looking down, what I could see appeared more like a scene from Thailand or Burma. In a subtropical setting of huge bamboo groves and plantain trees, three constructions had been created from branches, leaves, and bamboo. Plantain leaves formed the base of two of them. A third, made out of bamboo poles, resembled a curiously low house. They seemed mere extensions of the forest, distinguishable from it only by the patterns and designs, combinations of the elements of the forest, evidence of human intent. On top of the central structure an inviting feast had been laid out. Looking down from the maidan, I thought these people were offering their most valued possessions: eggs, fish, chickens, drink in bamboo vessels, and this pig that was about to be slaughtered.

In the centre of the field a large pot of rice was cooking. Amid the green of the surroundings what I now took to be perishable 'natural' shrines struck me forcefully as 'culture', which I could only describe as 'green' and 'human'. It was completely at one with the natural world. There were no obvious images of anything superhuman, some distant power.

Imagine the scene: a forest picnic, hospitality set out for respected guests. An informal atmosphere. One man stands alone, chanting and shaking gently at the knees. Another man and a woman wrestle with a pig. Some distance from the shrines men and children cluster around two women making leaf plates. No one pays much attention to what is happening. A piercing scream fills the air. The pig lies dead, a bamboo rod rammed through its heart. The man who had been chanting – the *yatangpa* – moves slowly to join the group and stands with his hand on his son's shoulder in the dappled shade. Between me and them the heat of the Arun valley.

Later they explained to me they were making offerings to their ancestors, asking them for good crops. What struck me, apart from the strangeness of the subtropical atmosphere in the Himalayas, was the way the proceedings were unexceptional, matters of everyday life. No fuss or ceremony, no particular animation in spite of the fact they told me it was a *puja*, the Nepali word for ritual. And there was nothing particularly striking about the *yatangpa*. He was, if anything, rather more shy than the other men, an affectionate father, an easy, friendly man.

During the next three days I stumbled across two similar rituals on the path, routine daily events. As with the first, in all I had the feeling I was watching a regular communication with invisible beings, the same vitalization of a part of the shrubbery, the same atmosphere of hospitality. The old man performing the second *puja* was accompanied only by his young grandson and was totally uninterested in his unexpected audience, except to gesture with a wave of the hand for quiet. He went through the actions with the assurance of someone who has performed them all many times before.

> His focus of attention is a flat stone, tucked into the side of a hill amongst the roots of a *Chilaune* tree. Leaves and branches bunched together seem to grow behind the stone with thread intertwined between them. He selects flowers from a bundle he has previously collected and places them between sprays of leaves on the stone. He examines and chooses each one with the care of an artist for the right color. He takes a piece of wood from a fire kept alight by the young boy and places it on one of the bundles of leaves. He sprinkles water from a brass pot over the branches, leaf and flower shrine, and washes his hands, with deliberation. Orange paint is daubed on selected areas of the rocks and tree, and two live chickens are held over the shrine while he chants, shaking the croaking chickens in rhythm, occasionally punctuating his chant by spreading his arms wide as though ending a verse. One by one he slits the throats of the chickens and sprinkles their blood over the shrine chanting all the time. He cracks an egg into a leaf and cuts it into the fire along with the chicken livers he has removed. To the side of the stone slab some incense is burning. The egg and the liver is skilfully cooked and turned in the flames with a pair of bamboo tongs. Without any further communication he has gone. And what pathos. Looking at the arrangement that he had prepared so carefully, and which seemed so alive and elaborate in his presence, it now looks pathetic, neglected, dead and ancient. It has no further signifi-

> cance. In spite of the remaining egg–shell still placed in the leaves, tied with thread, everything now looks bedraggled and weeks old. The old man's presence and concentration drew me into something that was very much alive and important. Now only the smoking fire reminds me that something has really just taken place. (Diary 1976).

To me, of course, these rituals were not ordinary events and it was intriguing to see the nonchalance with which they were performed. Or was I misinterpreting what I saw? I had felt pathos, but what was the outcome for those involved? What had been the experience that the man had created for himself? What sentiments were supposed to be felt? What was the reality to which he had been addressing himself?

I came to learn that many of my first impressions were misconceptions. These perplexities which arose in the first few months of trying to grasp Lohorung ways derived from my application of false categories. In this instance, part of my mistake was to expect a distinction between the sacred and the profane. It took me time to understand how such activities could be everyday events. Another early mistake came from ignorance of Lohorung theories, their ethno–theories, such as their theory of emotions which, for example, tells them not to show fear when communicating with their ancestors. Initially, I was overloaded by my own theories and preconceptions. It was only gradually, from the way in which they talked about such ritual events and about themselves and their emotions, that I was able to understand how they organized and conceived their experiences.

This book is about Lohorung experiences, and their understanding of what it means to be a person. The questions which lay behind the kind of fieldwork I did were questions such as 'what kind of understanding do Lohorung have of 'human nature'; what powers do they ascribe to human beings, to gods or ancestors; do they have theories of 'mind'; how do they understand or classify emotions; how do they make judgements about other people's behaviour; is the 'human nature' they ascribe to themselves the same as the one they use to understand and explain the behaviour of other tribes; how do they conceive of 'the self'?

Some of the theoretical load that walked with me in the late 1970s, when I went off to do fieldwork, concerned a debate that anthropologists were just beginning to be interested in, and that has gone on ever since. It concerns the nature of personhood and the degree to which it varies across cultures. Mauss's historic essay on 'A category of the human mind: the notion of person, the notion of self' (1938) had had little impact in England until the 1970s.[1] Anthropologists began to pick up the major questions he had raised, such as 'does the contemporary notion of the person have equivalents in other cultures'; 'are there clear differences between the concept in modern western society and the concept in tribal societies'; 'is the notion of the "individual" a uniquely modern phenomenon?' These questions had been largely ignored in ethnographic work. One exception was K.E. Read who supported

Mauss's view that the construct of 'the person' is a uniquely modern Western notion. He pointed out that the Gahuku–Gama have no concept of the person, 'no essential separation of the individual from the social pattern; social roles and social status are not distinguished from the individuals who enact them' (1955: 276). Meyer Fortes later took the opposing view, claiming all societies have a concept of the person since it is in this concept that the individual and society are interrelated. According to him the key to understanding West African cosmologies was the realization that they are above all 'means of explaining, predicting and attempting to control the relationship between the individual and his or her society – ie "social psychologies"' (1973: 287).

Amazingly, interest in studying indigenous concepts of the person remained sporadic in the UK until the 1980s, but I found in the American culture and personality school a more sustained anthropological interest in the psychological; and indeed in their cross–cultural work lie the beginnings of what is now called the study of 'ethnopsychologies' and the nature v. nurture debate. Probably the first major piece of theoretical writing establishing the view of human nature adopted by the 'culture and personality' tradition was a paper given by Sapir, 'The Unconscious Patterning of Behaviour in Society' at a seminar in 1927 which later set the frame of reference for anthropological work in this area. The emphasis was on nurture rather than on nature. The thrust of the argument was that the fundamental organizations of individual behaviour, the 'personality', are moulded by a combination of cultural environment and individual experience and not by physical constitution (1927: 114–42).

The climate of opinion in the 1920s was that human nature was essentially malleable: 'human character is built upon a biological base which is capable of enormous diversification in terms of social standards' (Mead, 1939: x). Anthropologists, as now, began to doubt the strength of the human–nature thesis. Yet, at the same time as the supremacy of the biological and the innate was being resisted, popular theories about universal psychic states were being tested in the field (e.g. Mead 1935, Malinowski 1927) and psychoanalytic theory, an essentially pan–cultural theory, was being absorbed into cultural theories. Instinct was becoming a respectable word, and the 'psychic unity' of mankind was seen as at least an approximation of the truth. While the notion of universals in human–nature was being explored by, for example, Kluckhohn (1953), Hallowell (1950) and Kroeber (1955), others focussed on cultural differences in personality. The psychoanalyst Abram Kardiner (1939) and Ralph Linton (1945), an anthropologist, together developed the notion of 'basic personality structure'. If the experiences of childhood determine adult personality, then, they argued, 'basic personality structures' in cultures will vary according to the patterns of child–care. The assumptions they made about childhood determinism and the possibility of characterizing any society in terms of a personality type have been widely criticised and Bock (1990) does a fine job of summarising these.

What these culture and personality studies reported from the field is tantalising –

a potentially rich source for anyone like me interested in exploring notions about the person and emotion – but so disappointing because the views about human nature of the people they were studying were to them unimportant. Many of the authors were totally focused on reducing data on the person or culture to individual needs, personality types, or causal processes supported by psychoanalytic theory. There are exceptions. Jean Briggs's *Never in Anger: Portrait of an Eskimo Family* (1970) is set in the culture and personality mould and yet, by emphasizing the people's own interpretation of socialization and the need for control of emotions, she gives great insights into the people's own views about emotional development, the gradual acquisition of reason and understanding.[2] Gregory Bateson's *Naven* is another. Written with a 'rigorous taboo on teleological explanation' (1958: 288), he develops Ruth Benedict's notion of the 'configuration' of cultures as either Apollonian or Dionysian (depending on cultural emphases) into the explanatory concepts of 'ethos' ('the culturally standardised system of organisation of the instincts and emotions') and 'eidos' ('a standardization of the cognitive aspects of the personality of the individuals') (1958: 220) – concepts that are very useful as descriptions of processes of knowing and ways of arranging data, rather than as explanations of phenomena.[3]

What was the significance of the culture and personality school for this book? Of all the culture and personality writers, it was Hallowell's work which became the most pertinent to me and indeed to others writing about the self and emotion in the 1980s and 1990s. Few described more clearly the complexities of the mutual relations between self and culture, the interdependence of self and culture in their continuing existence, and the universality of 'self–awareness'. The notion of psychosocial reality being 'constructed' by our understanding of that reality owes much to Hallowell's concept of 'the culturally constituted behavioural environment' (1955: 87) and was developed later by Berger and Luckman (1967). Hallowell's concept is central to this book, emphasizing as it does the interaction of individuals with the external world, and providing a frame of reference, within which notions of self and emotion and notions about self and others must be seen to be bound up with other cultural and social phenomena and with the terms in which people themselves understand their experiences. We find Catherine Lutz also following Hallowell; 'we may ask about the behavioural environment of the emerging self. By the efforts and example of the socializing other, the child begins to construct a self. The acquisition of ethnopsychological notions is a process that can be observed in both verbal and non–verbal communicative acts' (Lutz 1988: 105). His work is also widely quoted in Heelas and Lock (1981). Hallowell stresses self in the context of the boundary between self and others, hence his comments on the universality of reflecting on human–nature,

> concepts (of self–image, self) are the major means by which cultures promote self–orientation in the kind of meaningful terms that make self–awareness of functional importance

> in the maintenance of a human social order. In so far as the needs and goals of the individual are at the level of self–awareness, they are structured with reference to the kind of self–image that is consonant with other basic orientations that prepare the self for action in a culturally constituted world (1955: 76).

How could all of this be of help to me in the field? The work of Margaret Mead, and many others of the culture and personality tradition, raised important issues. First, for me as a researcher in the field, was it important to examine the participants' viewpoint or not? Secondly, should I as a researcher be theoretically dogmatic? And thirdly, what were the different merits of the relativist or universalist approaches?

For myself, I knew right from the beginning that obtaining the participants' point of view was central to the focus of my research and it was in part frustration with 'Culture and Personality' studies which confirmed this. I needed to know how Lohorung conceive of themselves, how they understand their emotions; what kind of view of human nature do they work with? Inevitably, this kind of local knowledge is often unreflected, being more like common sense or obvious knowledge for those who own it. I saw part of my job to be the crucial process of coming to an authentic understanding of another point of view, taking that often implicit point of view and making it explicit, making sense of it by immersing myself and becoming engaged, not as a detached observer, but by participating in 'shared social experience' (Hastrup and Hervik 1994: 4, 92). More than this, I wanted to see how Lohorung ways of understanding themselves, their emotions, disruptions in their bodies, become systems of meaning, ways of interpreting their own experiences. Of course, I realised we couldn't completely share experiences. Even within ones own culture there are numerous ways of experiencing the same event. But we can involve ourselves in the lives of the people we live with and become 'socialized' into their culture and almost predict answers to questions; orient our bodies to move with their cultural expressions, learn their 'sense of shame', their feeling of depression, and this is what I wanted to do. Ots has described this kind of involvement as 'experiencing participation' (1994: 134). The notion of 'objective' participant observation is now even less of an ideal than it was when I went to live with the Lohorung[4].

Knowledge of the Lohorung's point of view could only come about as a result of understanding their representations and their ways of being in the world, that is their language or discourse and their experiences, agreeing with Csordas that 'language gives access to a world of experience in so far as experience comes to, or is brought to, language' (1994: 11).

This emphasis on 'the participants' point of view' was the theory that I took to the field. I took what in the anthropology of religion is sometimes called a 'fideistic approach'. It was to accept on faith Lohorung descriptions and explanations of their own experiences and to accept that their meanings could not be grasped if I applied too many rationalist explanations. It seemed to me that the problem for Mead and many others of the culture and personality tradition was that they were not concerned enough about the participants' point of view. Their observations were bound up with psychodynamic theoretical dogma which distorted their interpretations of field material. This emerges clearly in the Mead/Freeman debate about Samoa. In his devastating critique of Mead's work, Derek Freeman (1983) tried to displace Mead's interpretation of adolescence in Samoa by indicating the degree of stressful adolescence in Samoa. Though he has a point, Freeman's main aim was to attack the position of cultural relativists and defend his own position which stresses the importance of biological universals. Here is a warning about how not to be over–weighed–down by theory.

Whereas in culture and personality studies psychological functioning looked at cross–culturally was *assumed* to be a universal, I, like other more recent writers on self and emotion, have focused on what psychologists and anthropologists call the *emic* approach. In contrast to the *etic* position in which the analyst stands 'far away' from or 'outside' of a particular culture to see its separate events (Pike 1954: 10), the *emic* approach is 'an attempt to discover and describe the pattern of that particular language or culture in reference to the way in which the various elements . . . are related to each other in the functioning of that particular pattern' (ibid: 8). Indigenous terms and classifications have to be examined in their contexts.

Of course, following the logic of this, the term 'psychology', to describe a domain in another society, can only really be used as a heuristic device and should perhaps be avoided altogether, since other cultures do not possess the domain of 'psychology', embedded as it is in ideas of a Western science about the nature and functioning of the human mind. I use it because the term has now been used in 'ethnopsychologies' and 'indigenous psychologies' to delineate a particular area of study – a short way to describe 'folk models of personality, thinking and feeling' (White and Kirkpatrick, 1985: 5), 'cultural constructions of particular persons as well as of human nature . . . the way in which people conceptualize, monitor, and discuss their own and others' mental processes, behaviour and relationships' (Lutz, 1985: 36), those concepts, classifications, theories, assumptions, and figures of speech that are concerned with how a people understand human nature and ways of relating to the world, ideas that are reflected in social institutions, and contain 'advice or injunctions about the ways people should act, should feel and how they can find happiness and success in life' (Heelas, 1981: 3). The aim is to describe what people say and do in everyday life. This kind of commonsense knowledge provides insight into the culture's system for interpreting self, their experiences and others. This is the domain that I explore in this book.

I should point out that there are differences between the culture and personality tradition and 'ethnopsychologies' and between these and 'indigenous psychologies'. Those writing about ethnopsychology consider it important to avoid assumptions about the 'behavioral environment' and instead explore the different meanings and interpretations that other cultures use to describe personhood. Without totally rejecting the psychodynamic view of the culture and personality school, and the search for 'deeper' psychological processes, they assess persons and situations in their own social context and stress that before any assessment of these areas can take place, greater understanding is needed of other people's conscious interpretation: 'we find that we cannot *assume* we know the cultural significance of data on, for example, religious beliefs or styles of interpersonal communication' (White and Kirkpatrick 1985: 4). The main difference between most ethnopsychological studies and indigenous psychological accounts is the degree to which psychodynamic theories are accepted, although in more recent years more ethnopsychological studies could be described as constructivist rather than psychodynamic. They focus on the 'culturally constituted self', looking at how notions of self, person and emotions are constructed by people's own understandings, their own concepts and discourse, statements about the nature of the person and how they relate to the social world. Most of those who adopt a constructivist position do not deny the possibility that some psychological processes operate in a similar way across disparate cultures. The view that humans are in general self–constituting lies behind my own approach to the Lohorung. (See also Lutz 1985.)

There are different approaches to ethnopsychologies. Some accept that emotions have an essentially psychobiological basis and are hence universal (Kleinman 1980; Schiefflin 1985). Michelle Rosaldo (1980) and Clifford Geertz (1973) focus on the expression of symbols of the self and how they manifest in other areas, such as institutional life; they view concepts and theories about self and others as being part of the cultural system and as such being analytically distinct from social structure and individual psychology. As part of the cultural system they contribute to meanings in terms of which human beings interpret their experience and guide their actions, while social structure is the form those actions take. 'Culture patterns provide a template or blueprint for the organization of social and psychological processes, much as genetic systems provide such a template for the organization of organic processes.' (Geertz 1973: 216). For others, like Briggs, there is an emphasis on describing the details of an alternative ethnopsychology, whereas some are keen to seek to understand ethnopsychologies in terms of psychodynamics (Levy 1973); yet others want to argue the significance of experience – that cultural forms actually shape people's experiences (see Lutz 1985; Desjarlais 1992) rather than seeing people's experiences as independently constructed and simply viewed through cultural glasses.

The significant shift from the culture and personality tradition to indigenous psychologies is the approach of interpreting a culture through its own self conceptions. This owes much to people like Hallowell, Geertz, Rosaldo, Heelas, and Lutz. Clifford Geertz, often called the founder of 'interpretive anthropology', was one of the first to encourage the view of society as a text. He constantly outlined the problems for the ethnographer of interpreting some other culture as well as advocating `thick description' and actively analysed notions of self in other cultures.

What is important from what has been said here is the increasing number of anthropologists from Mead to Fortes to Geertz who have for one reason or another all encouraged anthropologists to look closely at how people understand themselves and to see their actions as in some ways the creations of those understandings. There is, for example, Geertz's seminal article 'The Native's Point of View' (1984) in which we see a view of the person as part of a total pattern of social life. The notion of the person is beginning to be revealed as important for understanding social behaviour, judgements, social relations in other societies – for understanding why people relate to each other in the way that they do and why emotions are being placed, along with the person, firmly in the realm of culture.

What I didn't know as I walked through the hills of Lohorung country was how the debate about the universality of emotions and the concept of person was going to develop to full force in the 1980s.There was an explosion of articles exploring the relationship between culture and self and emotion or affect[5]. The work was both theoretical and ethnographic though even by the end of the 1980s there were still few ethnographies specifically exploring conceptualizations of self and how they related to other metaphysical notions, moral notions, emotions and interpersonal relations. As I unfold the Lohorung world, and their notions of self and emotion implicit in them, I shall refer to these debates.

The disagreements between the 'universalists' and the 'relativists' continue: does human nature vary across cultures? To what extent are human beings biological products? To what extent are they socio–cultural products? Anthropologists and psychologists continue to be at variance and the answer, as this book will argue, I think lies somewhere between the two. It has in part to do with Hallowell's approach which is that of focusing on the 'culturally constituted self'.

The view that humans are in general self–constituting lies firmly behind my own approach to understanding the Lohorung. This book is concerned with how notions of self, person, and emotions, which have some biological basis, are also constructed by peoples' cultural understandings, the concepts, premises and discourse of the group they identify with, such as underlying assumptions about the nature of the person and how to relate to the social world. Most academics adopting a constructionist approach do not deny the notion of some psychological or biological processes operating independently of culture, but they downplay this. My focus, too, has been to look at how the experiences and worlds of people within a particular culture are constructed and shaped by their cultural concepts of self and emotions. Notions of self and emotion, seen by us as being derived from the human individual, can be conceived within different frames of reference which create other worlds. What I describe in this book is the frame of reference within which Lohorung beliefs and ideas concerning 'the person' and 'emotions' are embedded.

One of the main frames of reference used by Lohorung is one in which the 'natural' ancestral order, the original primaeval order, as recorded in their myths, has to be constantly recreated and the unity between nature, the superhuman, and the human reaffirmed. Failure to do this would lead to depression, increased sickness, possibly death, and ensuing chaos. In contrast, repetition of ancestral words and adherence to ancestral order acts like recharging the cosmos. It brings vitality.

Lohorung concepts of self, mind, and emotion reflect the necessity for unity. Owing to the inter–connectedness between nature, superhuman, and human, they do not divide up the world in the way we often do in the West. The post–renaissance model of the world of Descartes, Newton, and the industrial revolution has left us with a perception of humanity as outside nature, operating *upon* it for its own interests, exploiting it and exploring it objectively from a position of detachment. The Lohorung emphasis on unity and interconnectedness lies closer to the ecological or Systems worldview, Chaos or Complexity theory, and the new language of 'network dynamics' to explain the perception of a highly integrative system of life. This is a model developed from the works of Quantum Physics, Darwin, Einstein and also reflected in the works of romantic poets such as Wordsworth as well as in the works of Marx and Hegel who saw humanity as part of nature, within it and not outside.

For Lohorung the relationship between the superhuman, natural and human worlds is one of a natural unity – the unity being a oneness which underlies the vitality of all human beings, the well–being of ancestors, and parts of the natural and material world connected to primaeval beings. What they emphasize is the unity and order of the primaeval world. Ancestral order is seen in relation to the non–tribal order.

To follow Durkheim and distinguish between 'sacred' and 'profane' activities is, I shall argue, to misinterpret their conception of the correct way to relate to the world, though they can make this distinction. Equally misleading would be to describe their world as particularly 'sacred' in the way that Mircea Eliade (1957) characterized preliterate people as living in a 'sacralised cosmos' with an essentially religious attitude to the world. This approach is taken by Parish who writes about another Tibeto–Burman tribes', the Newars', 'sacred mind'. 'For the Newars of Nepal, mind, self and emotion are sacred and moral' (Parish 1991: 313). I shall argue that this does not apply to Lohorung: their representations of mental life are not 'sacred', holy, or awesome or separated from everyday life in any way. The opposition of sacred and profane has relevance in Western culture and in some other cultures but it should not be seen as a universal. For Lohorung, as we shall see, there is no clear binary opposition of sacred: profane. They do, however, see a clear distinction between 'ancestral tribal order' as opposed to 'non–tribal order' that predominates their framework. What this book is concerned with is the tribal view, characterized by an 'animistic' engagement with the world, which underlies their sense of self and emotions.

After the first few months of fieldwork I realized that any understanding of Lohorung experiences must entail grasping their notion of *sammang* (which I here gloss as 'ancestors'); and another more abstract notion *saya* which at first I translated as 'the ancestral spirit within a person' or the 'vital essence' of a person.[6] From the moment I began to understand these two concepts I was inevitably led to Lohorung notions of self and personhood; to their notions about mind, consciousness, the essential life–giving force of a person; and to what emotions mean to a Lohorung. Only by appreciating the complex workings and interconnections of these two concepts could I begin to make sense of such diverse things as child development, their conception of space and time, their houses, pigs, rituals, odd statements about flowers, trees, and crops, their attitude to the sexes, their interpretations of experiences, and their sense of appropriate conduct.

By looking at Lohorung from the point of view of their notions about the person and emotion, their statements about human nature and how to relate to the world, and by taking these seriously, I was led to appreciate the form and interconnections of their experiences. Learning how it feels and how they understand what it is for them to be shy, afraid, sad, or depressed led right away to appreciating a different way of being a person in another world. I suspect an analysis within more standard functionalist categories would not have made this possible. Some anthropologists still do take the position that social interaction, visible strategies and disputes, that is, the realm of observable social behaviour, is the substance of fieldwork. For them the verbal and mental framework within which social interaction takes place is a mere epiphenomenon of interaction rather than a determinant. In contrast, I saw the content of Lohorung beliefs, and adopting an 'in their terms' point of view, as key to my task. In Lohorung conflicts, in social interaction of an everyday kind, and in apparently arbitrary practices, I saw instances of the expression of cultural meaning, as understood from the way Lohorung talked about it.

Throughout my time with the Lohorung I attempted to interpret these moments in the light of my own developing knowledge of the society's conceptual framework. This knowledge depended on a gradual understanding of the interconnected network of concepts, verbal and non–verbal of the society in question. If the 'constitutive' position (e.g. Hampshire 1959) that conceptual systems are a determinant is too extreme, ignoring the interplay between mental frameworks and the sociocultural, I suggest we can at least say that verbal and mental frameworks – what people think and believe about their actions, their experiences and what they do – are worth studying. We can see that they relate to beliefs and action in a logical manner, provide philosophies of life, and are a way of sustaining the self with respect to the sociocultural[7].

Gradual understanding of Lohorung concepts came about in part from the slow process of learning the language. At times I thought I would never move out of the fog of incomprehension. Although I am not a linguist, with the assistance of many different Lohorung, and in particular one woman, Nanda, and two Gurkhas, Sher Bahadur and Hari Bahadur, I was able to write down a basic grammar and glossary of Lohorung and explore the semantic fields of concepts, their uses in various contexts, their metaphorical extension, and in what types of discourse they were acceptable. From just living among Lohorung I was able to find out the significance of concepts and experiences for the people themselves. I listened to how people described their experiences. I saw, for example, how concepts derived cultural meaning in rituals, how assumptions about human nature emerged in everyday discussions. These then helped to explain Lohorung motivations in diverse activities. One of the motivations for women to brew beer was that as a traditional activity of the ancestors any beer–brewing was seen as a repetition of the ancestral activity and was assumed to please them. Moreover, by a complex process to do with pleasing ancestors and raising the *saya* (the ancestors within) of the woman's household she could bring prosperity and well–being to the family.

Lohorung 'ethno–psychological' notions, such as their concepts of self and emotions, created an important frame of reference which shaped their values and codes of behaviour, the frames of meaning within which they worked. I suppose I looked to 'ethno–psychological' notions to explain behaviour in much the same way that some anthropologists have looked to subsurface or deep structure as a form of explanation.

Though some of these Lohorung concepts are not easy to grasp, they are, however, current in everyday discourse. They are commonplace Lohorung assumptions about what it means to be a person. These are the 'experience–near' concepts that Geertz talks about (Geertz 1984: 124). Not surprisingly, both the concepts and the assumptions feature predominantly in ritual. Their complex meanings are symbolised in objects and images throughout the ceremonies, and their affective significance is reflected in the behaviour of participants. What I want to stress, however, is that what characterizes these psychological concepts has ramifications in all kinds of areas of life, and not just rituals, and this helps to explain coherence and continuity as well as moments of conflict in Lohorung life.

To give a brief example, let me enlarge a little on that key concept of *saya* which I have already mentioned. Lohorung view the person as being essentially vulnerable. Every person must retain the correct bond with his or her ancestors – a bond which is internally represented in a person by *saya* (ancestor within a person). If a person's *saya* is in its correct position, associated with the head, he or she can be strong, protected, and therefore courageous and proud. The person's vulnerability however, is particularly susceptible to insults, demoralizing experiences, anger or the transgression of traditional ways. Any of these experiences may cause *saya* to fall. Unless the bond with ancestors is renewed a person can die.

The home is an extension of the person, a macrocosm of the male and female unit, and is conceived of as being as vulnerable as the human beings who live in it.

Various parts of the house have *saya*, just as people do. To experience and represent the protection that both need – the bond with the ancestors – there is a house shrine in every house which is a microcosm of the ancestral universe. This represents the presence of the past living members in the present. Rituals must be performed so that the living experience these relations. The temporal orientation of the Lohorung in this respect is to represent the nowness of ancestors. Real time and space are collapsed. As one Lohorung said, 'the way to keep *saya* high is to show interest in the ancestors'. The power of the emotion is believed to be such that it has to be managed, through rituals and through correct behaviour in certain everyday life situations. We shall see in this book how simply being aware of the ancestors, however, can bring them into everyday life and help restore *saya* – thus the importance of telling brief stories about them.

Lohorung are very clear that, sadly, everyday life does not allow the respect the ancestors should command: 'we cannot see them, so we can't avoid bumping into them, flicking ash over them.' Lohorung rituals can, however, compensate for everyday behaviour. They restore the link between ancestors, their traditions and everyday life, thereby raising *saya* and protecting the person.

Emotional and inner states are inextricably linked to the concept of *saya*. States which we variously describe as 'anger', 'depression', 'happiness', 'health' are connected to a person's essential state – his or her state of *saya*. *Saya* has to be protected and this can be achieved by what the Lohorung consider to be correct behaviour. Respectful behaviour and traditional behaviour reduces the extent to which people's vulnerabilities are attacked. Insults or anger on the other hand can attach to another person's body with the effect of lowering *saya*. Ultimately, this can be fatal. Lohorung thus place great emphasis on developing in their children the *niwa* 'mind, source of knowledge' that knows ancestral ways. Even *niwa* however, cannot always control such things as *kisime* 'fear' although they do talk about ways of living which can reduce fear. 'We live close together so as not to 'fear' (*kisime*): to live in the fields alone away from the village is *kisimalu* "frightening" ', and so on. We can begin to see here how the Lohorung notion of *saya* and the 'person' as essentially vulnerable shapes experiences, activities, and concepts in other areas of their life. Life in Lohorung society is shaped and institutionalized in numerous ways in order to protect the vulnerability of its members from the effects of a low *saya*, whether sadness, depression, hopelessness, loss of the soul, or death.

By disentangling notions of self, metaphysical concepts, and concepts of emotion within the context of everyday life and everyday discourse, this book explores the experiential aspect of Lohorung life; it looks at how their experience is culturally constructed. By looking at how Lohorung represent and describe their emotions, the situations that evoke those emotions and the expectations and institutions that accompany them, we are looking at some of the main forms through which they perceive and experience themselves[8]. If we can ever know what it is like to be Lohorung surely it must be in part through examining the frame of reference within which their notions of self and emotion are based, that is, by looking at their 'other world'.

Notes

1. Mauss's 1938 essay described the 'person' as a category of thought. He is not interested in the sense of 'self' – the sense that people have of themselves – but in the 'person' as a collective representation, a category that has passed through a social history of law and morality. He suggested that the Western notion of a psychological self derives from a developmenal sequence – the notion of the 'individual' being the uniquely modern phenomenon. See Carrithers *et al.* (1985) for a reprint of Mauss and related essays.
2. See for example Briggs 1970: 4, 111.
3. See Bateson 1958: 281.
4. The anthropological attitude towards 'objective' participant observation has changed as anthropologists have started tackling subjectivity and reflexivity in the ethnographic process (see Hastrup and Hervik 1994). Reflexivity, described as what must come after the 'experiencing participation' forces us 'to think through the consequences of our relations with others' (Okely 1992: 24) and forces us to acknowledge the conditions influencing our writing.
5. Heelas and Lock 1981; Rosaldo 1980, 1983, 1984; Lutz 1983, 1987 and 1988; Lutz and White 1986, Abu–Lughod 1986; D'Andrade 1987; Kleinman and Good 1985; Shweder and Levine 1984; Heelas 1986, White and Kirkpatrick 1985; Lynch 1990.
6. Allen (1976) found a similar concept, *seor*, to be the most problematic of the general terms he analysed. In an article on illness (1976c) he gives the Nepali words used by informants to translate the concept: these include *graha* 'planet', *karma* 'lot', *sakti* 'strength', at 'courage', *phap* 'growth, prosperity', *pitri* 'patrilineal ancestors', *kul* 'lineage' and 'the god within a person'. Allen suggests the term 'fortune' to cover the neutral and positive senses of the concept.
7. See Heelas and Lock 1981: 13–17.
8. For a collection of essays exploring the anthropology of experience, issues and problems arising from 'what has been lived through' see Turner 1985 and Bruner (eds.), *The Anthropology of Experience*, 1986.

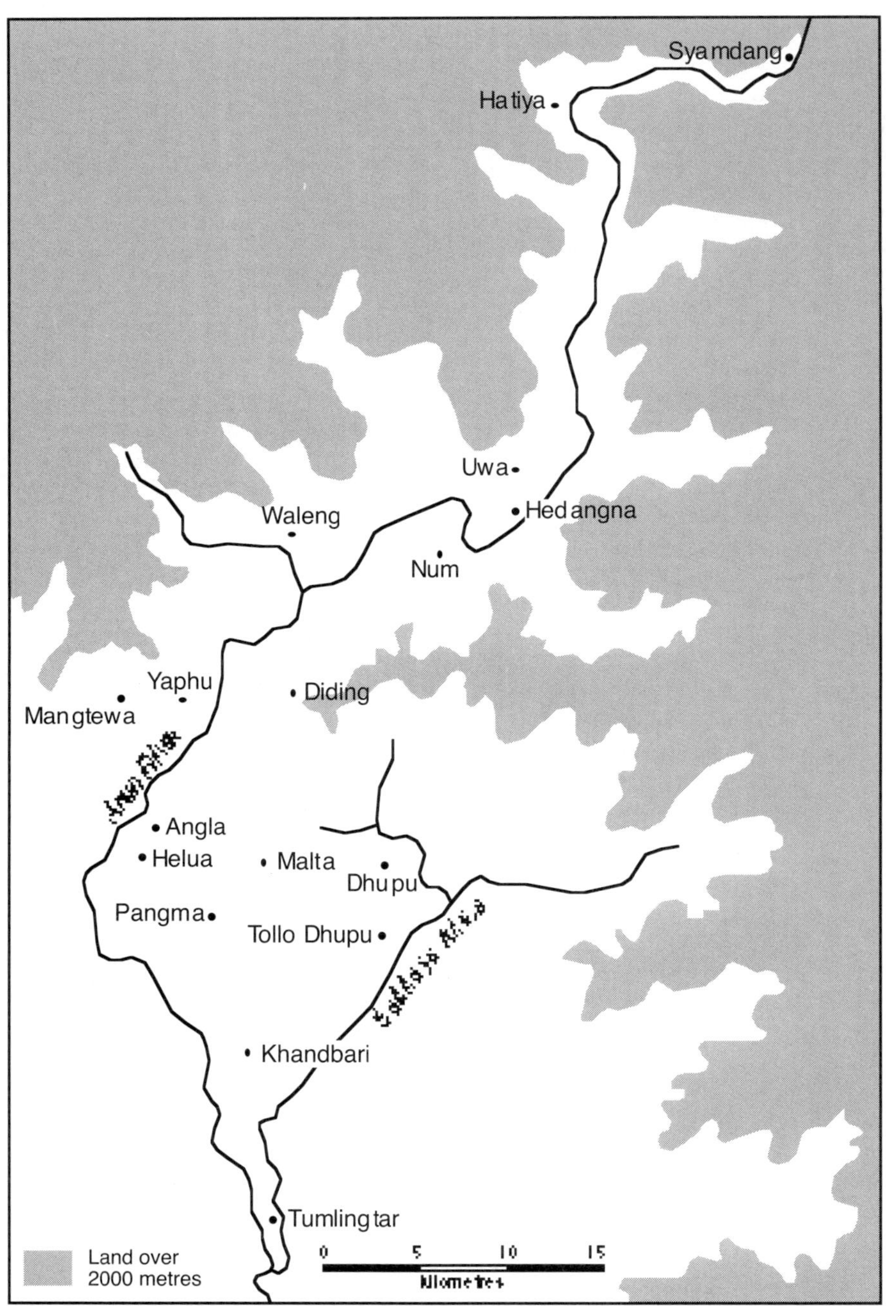

MAP 3 Map of Lohorung villages.

2
Pangma People

Pangma village settlements nestle into the hillside. The thatched rooves of the houses, patchwork rectangles almost hidden among the trees, lie in four main clusters with terraced fields stretching up and down. When I first arrived in Gairi Pangma I saw its giant pipal tree as a welcome rest after a hot climb. Very soon I felt this village was where I should stay and work.

But why choose here? Pangma was one of the main Lohorung enclaves. And Gairi Pangma was the largest of the four Pangma villages. It had 194 households and 900 or so Lohorung living there, often referring to themselves as *Pangmalichi* ('Pangma people'). Everyone I met claimed this was the oldest Lohorung settlement and the one where the most pure dialect of Lohorung was spoken. Pangma as a whole has expanded from 'Old Pangma' (*Purano Pangma*) or 'Upper Pangma' (*Gairi Pangma*) to the three other Pangma clusters, *Dara Pangma*, *Loke Pangma* and *Tollo Pangma*. (See Map 3).

The Pangma villages all straddle the higher stretches of the main ridge that slopes down to the broad valley of the river Arun on one side and the forested slopes of the Pangta river on the other. This area lay at the geographical center of the country lived in by Lohorung. At about 1,500 meters (5000 ft) the altitude was comfortable and when I arrived there first in 1977 there were only 17 non–Lohorung houses. They belonged to high–caste Chetri and Bāhun and Tamang and were located at a distance from their Rai neighbours.[1] I could not imagine an area more densely populated with Lohorung.

What finalised my decision to stay in Gairi Pangma, the oldest of the Pangma villages, was the hospitality and friendliness of one Lohorung woman who first gave me a meal by the giant Pipal tree. It was all so inviting: the density of the villages, the bamboo houses, the wispy clouds hanging in the open valley. But I still had to find somewhere to live. She told me there were one or two empty houses in Gairi Pangma but none had been lived in for years and she clearly saw them as uninhabitable. Sadly, by this time it was May and 'not the time of year to repair houses'. The high agricultural season had begun and everyone was in the fields. Mainly people were preparing the fields for transplanting rice and weeding the maize. House repairs would not be carried out until after the paddy and the millet had been harvested in December and January. Where could I live until then?

For a while I stayed in the nearby market town of Khandbari, a few hours walk away. During the first two weeks I walked up to Pangma almost everyday. But this wasn't satisfactory for the Newar family I lodged with. The Newar merchants look

FIG 3 Pangma people.

down upon Lohorung people as belonging to a class of 'Alcohol Drinkers' (*matwāli* N), making them ritually inferior. According to the first legal code (*muluki ain* N), and indeed until 1861, the Rai as a whole were classed as 'Enslavable Alcohol Drinkers', meaning that they could be punished by enslavement. Although this is no longer the case, Lohorung are still stereotyped as *matwāli* N (which is still legally correct) and as such are not permitted to enter Newar merchant kitchens. Only people from Chetri or Bahun families are considered their equals. The Newar family with whom I was staying in Khandbari made it clear they could not understand the attention I was giving these Lohorung.

> They cannot understand why I persist in my visits to Pangma nor why I look for somewhere to live there. N's father and friends talk of them as being boring, uneducated agriculturalists and, with the blindness which goes with ethnic superiority, see them as all alike. Young Newar boys are known to join Lohorung boys and girls who sit on the high ridges and sing to each other across the hills, but their parents disapprove. 'N's father this morning said, 'If you must talk to them, we can bring them here; they must come if I ask them to. You can't go and live there. Why not live here and do your work from here'. They think of them as being easily excited and often drunk, quick–tempered and sometimes violent. In some ways they seem frightened of them. (Diary 1976).

It would have been an interesting study to look at all the surrounding tribes from the privileged position of those living in the fast developing conglomeration at Khandbari but it was not what I had come to do. I persisted.

Suddenly, before two weeks had passed, the Lohorung couple with whom I had been spending time offered to build a small extra room on to their house in exchange for a monthly rent. Their house was unlike any other in the village and this household was unlike any other Lohorung household. It was that house by the giant pipal tree where I had eaten my first Lohorung meal; the first in the village coming up from the main trail; in front the large flat open space I had loved when I first arrived. It had been built without stilts in order to provide a small shop for the village. *Kāhili*, the fourth son, then stocked paraffin, mustard oil, a few dried spices, salt, matches, local cigarettes (and sometimes Indian cigarettes if he had managed to buy them in the market), Indian boiled sweets and their own home–brewed beer and distilled liquor. Protected by the overhanging of the enormous pipal trees the house stood out as a place of shelter from sun and rain, a haven after a steep climb from the fields. There were several places in the village where people gathered together and this was one of them.

My new residence in the shop made it easy for me to get to know many of the villagers without intruding into their homes and, as I learned the language, I picked up small pieces of information from casual conversations and could ask further questions. When almost all the other houses in the village were empty, deserted for daily chores, people still lingered around this house.

Kāhili, the wife of the fourth son, became a most patient teacher and interpreter. From the first time I visited Pangma we had an unspoken empathy for each other. I remember the loneliest feeling in the world when I arrived in Pangma, surrounded by strangeness, unable to really communicate with anyone. That first night I thought I had lost a treasured fountain pen on the walk up from Khandbari; I sat on the clay floor of Nanda's house and struggled to control my emotions. It wasn't the pen that I grieved for. I was suddenly aware of my isolation from any of the world I was familiar with. It was fear, loneliness, and grief for the people I had left behind. *Kāhili*, and another woman supported me as if they understood all these feelings. And later, I realized they did. They had had to make the same kind of shift when they moved from their natal home to their marital home, a home of strangers and a village where they knew almost noone. We became close friends. She spent more time at home than other Lohorung, looking after the shop and preparing the rice, maize and millet for food and drink for household consumption, for sale and for those labourers she and her husband could afford to hire. Her major tasks were husking, grinding, winnowing, preparing grain for fermentation or distilling it for liquor, laying out the grain to dry and keeping off birds and animals. I sat with her, at times to help, and at the same time I learned more Lohorung language. I asked her about the people who had visited, their customs and what had been discussed.

Working with her I began to appreciate one of the reasons why Lohorung women value daughters as much as sons – so long as there is at least one son. With only two small sons she had noone she could regularly rely on to assist her in the numerous, time–consuming food–processing tasks. The other five brothers, and their wives, lived in the land they owned in the Terai, leaving her and her husband to cope in Pangma.

She and I spent so much time together in the very beginning that people teased us with comments which ranged from the bawdy to friendly banter about the size of her new daughter, our difference in size, the way she treated her guest/sister/ daughter . . .. The bawdiest jokes were made behind our backs and filtered back. As a joke, since I am tall and *kāhili* small, villagers began to refer to us as *Hikdingpa Nāpchechi*. These are tiny, mythical people, so small they can't reach up to pick the fruit on a Hikdingpa bush. In order to *nāpme* 'knock down' its bitter fruit to make a much coveted chutney they each have to carry with them a long, thick bamboo pole. They live in villages 'down below', and go to sleep when Lohorung are awake, and wake when Lohorung sleep. 'When the sun goes from here it goes there.' My height made me an appropriate pole for the small *kāhili* who appeared even diminutive next to me. Thus when people saw us together the common refrain became, '*uh! Hikdingpa Nāpchechi tā'da'*, 'hey, look one of the little folk from down under with their pole has arrived'.

The more common name for me used by all Lohorung, was *nana kānchi*, meaning 'elder sister, youngest member of the family', or simply *kānchi*. One of the first things people wanted to know about me was my place in my family. While adults with children are usually referred to by a teknonym – the name of the first child whether male or female – it is common throughout Nepal to address someone by their position in the family. Once married, a woman adopts the female version of her husband's position. Similarly the terms *nana* 'elder sister' and *bubu* 'elder brother' are the Lohorung equivalents to the Nepali *didi* and *dāju* and, like them, may be used irrespective of actual kinship. In much the same way that French differentiate between madame and mademoiselle and between vous and tu, everyone in Nepal makes an important distinction between those who are older and those who are younger.

Though the time in the shop in Gairi Pangma allowed me an overall view of Lohorung life and an easy introduction to lots of people, I also realized that my identification with one particular wealthy family made it harder for other Lohorung to accept me in their homes and talk to me openly and freely. I spent my first ten months in Gairi Pangma and then moved to the neighbouring village of Loke Pangma. I was 'adopted' by two families. One built up a cattle shelter into a house for me. The other was the family of the man who had become my assistant and with them I ate all my meals. Sher Bahadur (known by his teknonym Anumpa 'father of Anu'), had been in the British Army. Now retired, he was willing to spend some time working with me. Moving meant I could live closer to Anumpa and his wife, Anumma, I could live in a less unusual Lohorung household in a remoter Lohorung village, and with a house of my own in Loke Pangma I could offer hospitality. As Mauss' essay on *The Gift*, has made all anthropologists aware, reciprocity is key in all cultures. People soon realised that in return for the tea I offered, what I wanted was words, their ideas, knowledge, to learn what was going on in their families, to discuss with them how they understood events that had happened, and answers to my endless questions. They knew that I wanted to hear stories – stories of any kind. It became a joke with some of my neighbours that I didn't need to be fed rice, just words.

One of these 'stories' told me that the 'Yamphu Rai' I had early on visited in the villages of Hedangna and Ala Oling (to the North of Pangma), were really Lohorung. They decided to call themselves Yamphu when neighbouring Limbu had laughed at them, scorning them because Lohorung eat buffalo meat. Instead, they became Yamphu Rai 'those ones who don't eat buffalo'.

So who are Lohorung? There were several answers to this. Depending on context, those in Pangma identified themselves as Pangmalichi (Pangma people) or as Lohorung. The 'Rai' bit of their name was important to their identity but mainly in spatial terms: 'We're not Khambu Rai – they live to the West of the Arun and there are lots of them: Thulung, Kulung, Khaling, Sangpang, Dumi, Bantawa, Dungmali, Chamling, Chheskam, Pelmange, Sotange; we're different. We live to the East of the Arun, like the Limbu but we're not Limbu. We are all *Kirānti*, or *Jimi*'.This view gleaned from two of the headman's daughters was locally general knowledge. The significance of villages in terms of identity (as in *Pangmalichi*) was clear in some names on their list; they gave names of villages which are also sub–tribes of Kulung, such as Pelmang and Sotang. Chheskam is one of the main Kulung villages but in fact not a sub–tribe. The two girls sub–divided the *Kirānti* into four groups; Lohorung, Khambu, Yakkha and Limbu, and this classification echoed those I had read before leaving for Nepal (Campbell 1840, Chatterji 1974, McDougal 1979) only Lohorung had never been mentioned as an exclusive category! Lohorung identify geographically as *Kirānti*, living in the hills of Eastern Nepal known as Pallo Kirānt, Far Kirant, and in terms of local legends which tell of *Kirānti* as the autochonous inhabitants of Nepal and as powerful kings who once ruled in Nepal and who fought against the Gorkha invasion of the East, finally falling to *Prthvi Narayan Shah* when he signed a treaty with the raja of Sikkim in 1774. In practice, the term *Kirānti* explained the kin relations between a vast number of tribes and sub-tribes, all of them able to inter-dine and inter-marry[2].

Lohorung Response to me and Mine to them

What puzzled many Lohorung men and women at first was how I could possibly leave and remain away from my own kin, mother and father, brother and sister, and in particular my 'husband'. I was initially taken aback by the frequency of certain questions. 'What kind of father and mother could let you, their daughter, go so far away;

didn't they want to see you? How could they manage without you? How are you going to have children?' The women in particular were concerned about my isolation from my family. Given the patrilocal pattern of residence, many Lohorung women come from neighbouring villages. They openly pitied me for my situation, which they recognised as being similar to their own when they had married. Whether for this reason or another, the Lohorung treated me from the very beginning with warmth, compassion and kindness, encouraging me to join in with their everyday activities, offering me hospitality wherever I went. They quickly accepted that I was there to learn their language and enjoyed testing my frustratingly slow improvements. It was noticeable that although at first they teased me for all my inadequacies, my inability to sit on my haunches, to plant rice or hoe, husk rice or carry a heavy basket on my head, and for my oddities, like my masculine dress and small breasts, the teasing was always tinged with affection and I felt as if I was being treated much as they treat their own children. For example, if they worked me hard in the fields for a short time they then prevented me from working any longer saying the sun was too hot, or that my back would ache. It became known that I had a child's-size appetite for rice and people often came to sell me eggs or offer them in exchange for medicines.

So, at first the Lohorung accepted me as a rather helpless child. Later, they had to tolerate me as a cognizant participator, someone who had begun to understand, who pursued questions, taped what they said and often wrote at the same time as talking and listening. And most of them did seem to tolerate me. When I walked around, villagers were always ready with quick repartee, jokes or the standard friendly greeting, '*Namaste, kānchi*, have you eaten rice yet? Come over here, come and help us pull up the weeds; come and chat to us'. When I visited people, the reception was generally warm and responsive. Occasionally when I asked questions they claimed ignorance and told me to see someone else 'wiser' or 'who knows a lot about it', and would change the subject to ask how long I was staying, about my mother and father or people I had met. Sometimes they talked to whomever I happened to be with, asking their latest news. In certain seasons the claim that there was no time to talk was obviously true. For the most part, most Lohorung wanted me to learn and write about them. They encouraged me to learn the language, to talk about their customs, present and old, and to find out more of their traditional stories. They were always ready to explore how their customs differed from those of the Khambu Rai or Limbu. They had no hesitation in discussing their crops, seeds and knowledge of animals and agriculture with me. Some people did become more dubious about what I was doing when I asked for figures of land ownership, production and income and others were unwilling to answer questions about members of the family, children or adults, who had died. 'What do you want to know that for, *kānchi*?' Initially when I tried to discuss rituals with them and in particular those connected to the ancestors called *sammang*, I received the same cautious replies and reluctance to talk. Often, I was warned not to raise such matters. In a few ritual situations some Lohorung obviously considered I was putting them in danger and then I knew there was some opposition to my presence.

Once, a Lohorung Gurkha, on leave from the army, became openly hostile when I tried to photograph him and several other men cutting up a water buffalo they had just slaughtered. His anger was explained to me later, when the explosion had died down. He didn't want anyone to see a photograph of him slaughtering an animal. Although this activity has no status implications in Lohorung society, his knowledge of other cultures had made him aware that among Hindus and even other Rai this picture could brand and demean him. Unwittingly I had humiliated him. For a Lohorung man to lose face was to risk the lowering of his *saya* – and risk the loss of his soul. The fact that these moments stand out so clearly in my mind is an indication of the extent to which I think the Lohorung accepted my presence in Pangma.

Lohorung women accepted me as a woman with male freedom. As one woman said, 'You are like a man, you go around wherever and whenever you want'. My lack of domestic ties as a woman puzzled them but didn't stop them from talking to me as another woman, nor from wanting me to become more of a Lohorung woman by wearing their traditional *lungi* (sarong–type skirt) and *cholo* (bodice). However, I did not associate solely with Lohorung women and female shamans. I gradually relied on several close male informants (among these the local priest, my assistant, and my neighbour). This seemed to make it easier for men to take seriously what I was doing. Some became more willing informants.

In spite of male contributions to my knowledge of Lohorung mythology, symbolism and perceptions of the nature of men and women, it was women who felt most comfortable talking about such topics. Most Lohorung men either were, or pretended to be, more interested in objective measures of economic and political status. I could say, as Edwin Ardener did (1972: 5) that 'symbolism in fact enacts that female model of the world which has been lacking, and which is different from the models of men in a particular dimension; the placing of the boundary between society and nature'. There was indeed a difference between the models of men and women, which was most obvious in their contrasting attitudes to modernity.[3] To be 'modern', when I was living in Pangma, was to minimalise the importance of mythology and symbolism and to emphasise politics and *bikās* (N), progress or development – a new school, growing orange orchards, and maybe one day having electricity. Some men were frustrated by my interests in the traditional: in rituals, customs, ways of saying things, folktales and myths. I heard these at times referred to as 'women's, or children's talk', or alternatively as 'talk of the *yatangpa*' and therefore to be avoided. If I had given priority to discussing local politics or the recent socio–economic changes in Khandbari, such as the opening of an agricultural bank, these would have been 'safe' topics. For me to focus on topics concerning the ancestors was considered 'dangerous'.

I never thought any Lohorung were particularly trying to manipulate what I was doing. Never did they ignore me. On the contrary – I was sometimes over–loaded with requests for medicines. At the beginning there were a few attempts to secure loans and gifts of local beer usually oiled such proposals. Ultimately, however, it was evident I could only lend very small sums and I followed local wisdom which was firmly against lending money, 'if you give, they won't pay back, and if you give to one, they will all come' and I was quoted a Nepali proverb, *tyo manche entay denko mula* (those men are as alike as a row of radishes) – or as we would say 'they'll follow each other like sheep'. Lohorung (like the Limbu and other Rai tribes) have lost much of their own ancestral *kipat* land to *Chetri* and Bāhun creditors.[4]

Rather than manipulate me, Lohorung drew me into their social world. This began with the primary protection of one household. My social contacts spiralled out from that one unit to their main relatives and neighbours in Gairi Pangma, consisting of several key households From those contacts I was taken beyond the village itself to the natal villages of the married women and the villages of married daughters or sisters, and so to the villages of lineages of the same clan. Gradually my network gained, as its central core, nine households, scattered over three villages, in which I was accepted. In those households they no longer bothered with all the formalities of traditional Lohorung hospitality. There were numerous advantages to being drawn into these Lohorung household units and their close–knit social world. There were also some disadvantages to this friendly response. For a member of a Lohorung household to be anti–social and unavailable, to withdraw from company, is an indication of ill–health. So too is sleeping late (later than about 6 a.m.), particularly if you are a woman, even if you've stayed up late the night before! The irritations of no privacy, lack of sleep, constant insect bites, worms and other ills are well–known to anthropologists. This does not relieve the personal pressure at the time and I quote one passage from my diary which reminds me that I was not always totally enthusiastic, not always full of patience and optimism, in tune with Lohorung ways and content with my own progress:

> My mind doesn't work properly. I feel alone, tired, inadequate and miserable and I'm beginning to weary of the struggle to keep going. How can I ever understand these people? I've lost my patience and my sense of humour, let alone any hope of sociological insights. Everything to me is grey. I enjoy nothing and nobody. Early this morning *kāhili* herself was feeling miserable and wanted to curl up beside me. I snapped at her and then felt even worse. I don't even know what to work on next, what to ask, although I feel as though I've hardly begun. There's so much to do. Everything is tasteless and boring, both food for thought and food to eat. I'm hungry but I can hardly face another meal of rice and pumpkin, and all I can drink is *dibu* (local beer). If only I could boil a cup of tea without half the village clamouring for a cup too. I can't stand the endless talk about shortages and people's suffering . . . It's the practical details that make me so low, like the fuss over tea. At least I've now found out the reason for my difficulty over names and family trees: the fact that

> it's an insult to use someone's name unless they're still children.
>
> . . . It's been dark for days. The mist never clears: it just moves around the houses. Now everyone has gone to the fields. Maybe I should have gone with them again. No. At the moment I just can't face being with them. All they talk about at the moment is what job needs to be done next, how much they suffer. So much *dukka* and how good life will be when food is plentiful again. They rarely leave the village these days. Can places like Hedangna, just a day's walk away really be such a mystery to so many of them?

Such moods came and went. A more consistent mood, and particularly as time progressed, was one of enthusiasm and sometimes amazement at how close to and caring I felt about so many of them. Of course, my response to Lohorung men and women was not uniform. Some I warmed to, others I found more difficult. Increasingly it was only the 'shocks of otherness' which reminded me of any gaps between us. I remember how I was rebuked for my careless behaviour when I wore a particular flower – they belong to *sammang* and should not be picked; when I poured out water backwards – a gesture to the dead. Other incidents stand out in my memory as being incomprehensible, such as when I heard a woman refuse her mother a loan of rice; when a stone removed from a field started a village row; or when I heard it said that an insult could be fatal. I struggled to understand ritual chants and the reason why *kāhili*, suddenly possessed, snatched fire and shoved handfuls of *titepāti* (*Artemisia vulgaris*) leaves into her mouth. The challenge of making sense of such moments kept me going when nothing but the toil and demands of agricultural life dominated everyday life. At other times, so many events or discussions took place that I had little time to digest or reflect on anything and amazed my Lohorung companions by remembering little of what they had told me only a few days before.

It would have been hard for me not to respond positively to those Lohorung men and women I came to know well. Although it makes little sense to generalize about a whole people, there was an ethos of egalitarian sociability. So many possessed good–humoured liveliness combined with a warm sense of hospitality. As we shall see, the person who is kind and has a 'big heart' is valued, as is 'dignity' – the sense of holding one's head high – combined with 'modesty' and 'respect' for self and others. These are important concepts and characteristic of the Lohorung ethos. The fact that many of them were endowed with these characteristics made them very easy people to be with.

My first impressions of them at the market in Khandbari was dominated by their appearance. It was impossible to overlook the colourful dress and jewellery of the Rai women of the various tribes – Lohorung Rai, Kulunge Rai, Khalinge Rai – who came from areas around Khandbari (see map 3, p.28). They wore brightly coloured cotton *lungi*, held firm by a length of differently coloured material wound several times round the waist. Their jacket tops, often in black or red velvet, were fastened with tags to one side, Chinese style. The long, thick head scarves twisted round their heads were woven in styles particular to the Rai and Limbu. Almost all went barefoot and wore numerous bracelets: some colourful plastic, others large heavy silver. Gold indicates wealth and each mature girl and woman had her left–side nostril pierced with a gold stud. Another gold ring hung from their nose and yellow gold earrings from their ears.Their necklaces, indicating marriage, varied according to the size of the twisted gold bar held around their necks by strings of green beads. Some of the older women wore heavy–looking silver bracelets on their ankles as well as their arms, and enormous round earring discs almost reached to their shoulders – traditions dying out among the younger women. Or rather, fashion is at work here too. None of the younger ones liked the gold bars on the upper front teeth which the older women wore; they thought the silver bracelets heavy and preferred smaller earrings.

The men, in contrast, were undistinguished in their traditional Nepali dress. They were differentiated from the Newars and Hindu groups only by their Mongoloid features, somewhat flattened noses and shorter, broader, stronger build. It was women in the main who carried to market the huge baskets which they supported on their backs by a thong going around their foreheads. What stood out about the Rai women in particular, but the men too, was how vivacious, and physically demonstrative they were amongst themselves. In part this was the atmosphere of the bazaar which Lohorung celebrate with large quantities of a specially brewed alcoholic drink called *saruwa*, for which they are renowned in the area. As I came to know Lohorung individuals better, I found this good–humour, hospitality and readiness to enjoy life was central to their general approach. To show one is coping with life that naturally involves hard labour and suffering is to indicate health and a harmonious relationship with the ancestral world.

Learning to Communicate

Language was a methodological priority for me throughout the time I spent in Pangma.[5] Based on my view that self and emotion are to some extent sociocultural constructs I had to come to an understanding of the verbal categories and key concepts involved in these constructs. Part of my understanding came from seeing how the constructs acquired meaning from the various contexts in which I came across them. For example, I looked at the way people talked in everyday life, the significance of certain concepts in ritual expressions, the actions which accompanied them, the way in which they reflected cultural values. But this was only part of the underststanding. The process of learning was neither easy or always conscious and part of the growth of my understanding came from being more totally 'socialized' by Lohorung friends. From close participation in Lohorung lives I was involved in the situations in which concepts emerged and took meaning. My understanding evolved over time. I was gradually able to experience and see what it meant to Lohorung to *ngesime* –

'feel shame': to hold the head scarf in a particular way to show that one possessed the sentiment, when it was appropriate to feel it, when it was unnecessary or almost inappropriate. Building up knowledge about concepts and situations I was gradually able to use them myself – making a comment that someone for example ought to feel *ngesime* from the way they behaved. Understanding was a complex interplay of the linguistic and the non–linguistic.

Much of the learning that we do in fieldwork is inevitably non–verbal as much as verbal and is gained through interaction with other people. Cultural learning comes from being with others as much as from specific learning. I agree with Bloch when he says:

> I believe that anthropologists who have done prolonged fieldwork have always obtained the basis of their knowledge about the people they study from informal and implicit cooperation with them . . . confirm[ing] what I already know to be right . . . because I have established in my brain non–linear chunked mental models. . . I then pretend that the linguistic confirmations of these understandings . . . are the basis of what I understand but this is not really so (Bloch 1991: 185).

Bloch supports his statement with evidence drawn from cognitive psychology which argues that children build up their understanding of concepts non–linguistically before being able to express them verbally. They have an understanding of 'house' before they can say 'house': 'studies . . . show that the acquisition of lexical semantics by children is very largely a matter of trying to match words to already formed concepts' (Bloch, 1991: 185; see also Boyer 1994). Though my grasp of the language was always lacking it was possible for me to get the gist.

From the very beginning of fieldwork I did make a conscious effort to learn and use Lohorung and to do this rather than to use Nepali, the national language of the Indo–Aryans and now the lingua franca in Nepal. I did not just want to interview and obtain knowledge through an interpreter. I wanted to soak up information and experiences, ways of doing things by being, hearing, listening, and learning. Since Lohorung life in the village was still largely carried out in their own language, to restrict myself to Nepali would have been to miss much of what happened. In–marrying women from other Rai tribes soon learned to speak Lohorung. Older people and women felt more at ease in Lohorung than Nepali. Nepali was mainly used to communicate with outsiders, non–Lohorung–speaking people. Thus, quite apart from any philological interest, in a practical sense learning the language of daily exchange was a necessity for understanding what was going on in the village.

Inevitably this approach meant that I restricted the kind of conversation I could have in the first few months of fieldwork. Moreover I had additional motives for persevering with an unrecorded language apart from the main aim of understanding key concepts. My attempt to learn the language was at first also an easy and genuine way to explain what I was doing. My wish to learn and record their language, as well as oral traditions that they themselves saw fast disappearing, made sense to them. Later on, when I could carry on hesitant conversations in Lohorung, both men and women seemed to find amusement in testing my abilities and a kind of pride in developing them. As I've said, many Lohorung had a great sense of humour – bawdy and witty – and not surprisingly therefore one of the ways in which they checked my progress was by confusing categories. They would ask '*cham ngidana*?', meaning :'have you cooked the rice?' but using a verb for cooking which is inappropriate for rice. The equivalent in English might be 'have you scrambled the rice?' When I answered 'yes', their peals of laughter ended only in yet more verbal jokes. The ease with which I was accepted might have had something to do with my entering the community in an idiom they respected – that is, their own language and verbal skills. Within their own traditions, verbal wit is one way to win a woman and in general a means of communication between the two sexes.

Learning Lohorung was illuminating in itself and neutral as a topic of conversation. As a means of developing friends and older informants, discussions about language was easy. Everyone was my teacher, both old and young, and since language inevitably leads to all areas of life, there was no limit to what could be asked. When questions were ignored it was often an indication that here was a topic to pursue at another time, or with different informants.

Lohorung is one of the eastern Kirānti languages in the Tibeto–Burman family. It is traditionally classified as one of the Kirānti group, or Bahing–Hayu nucleus, including about twenty different Rai languages, Hayu, Sunuwar, Limbu, and Lepcha a tribal language of Sikkim. Very little is known about the majority of these languages. Lohorung themselves use the term *yakkhaba khap* to refer to their language. The Limbu refer to theirs as *yakthungba*. The languages spoken by the various *Kirānti* groups are in general mutually unintelligible but Lohorung, Yamphu, Mewahang and Limbu share phonological and lexical similarities to a minor degree.[6]

Even within Lohorung territory there are local variations and dialects. Lohorung can immediately locate a person's village of birth from their accent and idiosyncrasies in their speech. The language of the Diding area, for example, has a much more lazy, lilting rhythm than the abrupt sound in Pangma. In Pangma 'where have you come from?' is *ha–tlo ta–dane*? with a glottal stop in the middle of the first word. In Diding each vowel is stretched out and the words are not divided up into crisp syllables: so they say *hābānā tādāna*? with a rising tone at the end of each word. Their second person ending is always a long *ā* instead of the Pangma short *e*, as in *malo kak ne*? as opposed to the Diding *māna kasanāa*? for 'what are you saying', which sometimes becomes *māntānāhi kāsānāa*? for emphasis. The Pangma for 'I' is *ka*, *kanga* or *kange* depending on whether the verb is transitive or intransitive, whereas in Diding the words *konenāhi* or *konanaahi* are used. The predominance of *ä* over a short *e* and *o* over an *a* significantly changes the sound of even very common words in Diding. The word *anne* which I had learnt in Pangma sounded like *ohna* and the word for rice *chohm* instead of *cham*. Details of all these local variations are not necessary here. My emphasis is on the importance of the immediate local group among Lohorung in terms of the framework of their traditions. Language is a good example of how a people can have variety without really altering content. The same can be said of beliefs, rituals and myths as well as concepts associated with self and emotion.

An increasing influence on Lohorung language, as on their ideology and ritual practice, is that of Nepali and Hindu ideas. The modernizing influences were not as strong in Pangma as elsewhere.[7] The scarcity of native Nepali–speakers in the immediate Pangma village clusters meant less pressure to alter their own traditions. In the case of language this was certainly the case. Whereas in Angla, Heluwa or Simle villagers sometimes mixed Nepali with their Lohorung, in Pangma this was far less frequent, even among the younger generation. To give a few examples, the Pangma Lohorung word for 'do it!' is *lete!* In Angla and Simle it is *banamuse*!, a combination of the Nepali word *banaunu* meaning 'to do' and the equivalent Lohorung word *mume*. Similarly, in Diding the Nepali phrase *ke bhayo?* for 'what's happened?' has influenced the vernacular *mang lisa?* to *mang bhayota?*

Even in the Pangma area, the region recognized as speaking the most pure dialect of Lohorung, Nepali loan words have crept into everyday conversations. There are three main reasons for this. The first and most obvious is that there is simply no native Lohorung equivalent; the second that the word or phrase was so frequently used in interaction with Nepali speakers that the Nepali word comes first to mind even among themselves. Good examples of this are numerals higher than three and measurements. The third reason was that Nepali is sometimes more precise. For example, though the Lohorung had a phrase which corresponds to the Nepali word *chimeki*, meaning neighbour, it was rarely used. The Lohorung term *tangpam yapmi* means rather 'own people'. This would have been incorrect for those few who for example have a Gurung or a Chetri as a neighbour. Examples of lacunae in Lohorung proliferate in such topics as local politics, schooling, land and its sale, or Hindu festivals. The lack of native Lohorung words for recent innovations such as the plough and other implements and activities associated with sedentary terraced agriculture was not surprising. What was more significant was the absence of a native word for 'gods' (*deutā*.N) and for 'worship', 'ritual' (*pujā* N). Lohorung talk about the Primordial Beings, who are mythical figures, by their names; *Paruhang*, *Somnima*, *Ninamma*, for example. There is also an abstract term referring to the ancestors, *sammang*. But whereas writers on Rai and Limbu often talk of their 'gods' and sometimes 'goddesses' (Sagant 1969, Jones, 1979, McDougal 1979), I think this is an over–hasty Western assumption. As we shall see the Lohorung pantheon is not full of 'gods and goddesses'. They have Creator Beings – unconcerned with the affairs of mortals –some like kings – some of animal form; they have ancestors, close and distant; they have spirits, shadows, ghosts of the dead; and they recognize the Hindu gods and goddesses.

Lohorung Villages

Staying in a Lohorung household I soon learned that the daily routine in the village was to a large extent dictated by life as agriculturalists in a terrain which was really hard to work. In spite of the long wet season, the lack of any developed irrigation system meant that they had to rely on sharing rivulets running through the territory. These dried out in the summer so second crops were ruled out. Other than rain, the main water supply for all Lohorung was created by the streams, swollen by melting snows and the perennial springs that dried up in the winter months. So, people had to work hard most of the year on the mountainous and rocky slopes to produce enough grain for their own needs. The main cereal crops they produced were rice, maize, and millet. Animal husbandry was less significant economically but still important. All households kept chickens and many had some black pigs, goats, sheep, or buffalo. That I was often frustrated in my attempts to find men and women who had the time to stop work and talk for any length of time during the day is not surprising. What the Lohorung had was a subsistence economy in which almost all of what they produced was consumed by those who produced it. Simple as that. Very little excess and therefore very little spare to make any cash profit but at least a sense of self–sufficiency. Quite a few Lohorung did, in fact, find ways of making some spare cash – by working as day labourers or selling their own products at market. Moreover, many Lohorung women gained status by adding significantly to the income of the household through their commercial liquor– making (Hardman: nd)

Household activities began early. Before dawn, two or more of the female members of the house started to complete some of the essential chores of the day, such as building a fire, fetching water from a spring, washing clothes, grinding maize or millet, or husking rice at the *dhiki* N 'footmill'. When I think back to those early hours all I can hear is the great stillness in the dark broken only by the thud of a *dhiki* or the rhythmic pace of a grinding wheel. Since there were no mills, all grain had to be husked and ground by hand. Once a week the floor was smoothed over with fresh mud and several mornings a week most households made distilled liquor. Each morning beer and snacks were prepared to keep people going until the morning meal. It was in the early morning hours before the first meal that the local priest was called in if someone was ill in the household. It was also a time (the other being at dusk before the evening meal) when households performed rituals. Daughters and daughters–in–law rose earlier than men. Sons in their teens tried to sleep on as long as possible, as did their fathers in the slack agricultural season. During these months, it was generally accepted that most menfolk do little before the first meal of the day except social visits, leisurely trips to the spring to wash or to streams in nearby wooded areas to defecate.

When I arrived it was in the heavy agricultural season, which lasts from May to the end of August (and again in December and January at harvest–time). Then everyone rises early. The family eat warmed–up left–overs from the night before or drink some thick beer and leave the house to fit in some work before the first meal of the day: weeding, preparation of the terraces, manure collecting, inspection of irrigation canals, fetching fodder or looking after the sheep and goats. The heavy work period of the day begins 'after eating rice'. Much of the agricultural work is done by labour exchanges called *parma* N. These groups are not kin–based but organized usually by women from different households within the villages. Parma groups usually consist of women only, although at peak agricultural periods, such as those for transplanting rice or harvesting, men and women join together. All the work of planting, carrying fertilizer, cutting and carrying wood, and weeding is done by these labour–exchange groups, first for one household and then for another.

I was amazed to find how much of women's time is spent almost entirely on agriculture and food processing. The difference in the work burden of Lohorung men and women is crucial to their sense of self. The kind of work carried out by men and women during the day is for the most part not rigidly assigned to either sex. However, after looking closely at the workload of men and women, I could see two main differences: first, men spend about eight and a half hours of a sixteen–hour day at work and women twelve and a half! Secondly, although gender–role division is not rigid, there was a strong association of particular work with a particular sex. In terms of some activities there were even explicit prohibitions. The crucial ones were that women should not plough, slaughter animals, weave with bamboo, or cook food during rituals. Men were forbidden to weave cotton but not *prohibited* from doing anything else.

In practice, men did the more 'public', high–status work; they took on the traditional political roles and involved themselves in the newer district–level politics, they tended to entertain guests while women cooked the meals; apart from ploughing they also looked after the cattle, sheep, and goats. Women looked after the hens and pigs. Male heads of household were rarely seen carrying heavy loads. It was women who did the work that involved a great deal of carrying – collecting wood, fetching water, or carrying manure. They also did the lengthy arduous tasks such as weeding, husking, winnowing and grinding. Men's involvement in what Lohorung themselves see as more 'important', public, more high–status or dangerous tasks was seen as making men more vulnerable than women. Given the work done by women this sounds ridiculous. But in Lohorung perception, men are vulnerable because they were more often exposed to insult, derision, failure in the eyes of the world, and because they perform rituals more vulnerable to the anger of the ancestral world. Women were protected from the dangers of the ancestral world, kept separate from shrines, because they are 'naturally' more easily frightened.

Work carried on until dusk, when everyone returned home to eat the second main meal. Members of the family talked about the day's happenings, received visitors or visited neighbours, and planned the work of the next day. Children and teenagers rarely stayed in their own homes after eating. Sometimes they gathered together in singing parties in the fields below or above the village or in one of their homes. Some parents tried to restrain the nocturnal activities of their children by insisting that they sleep in their own house. Many children, however, particularly boys, slept curled up together wherever they happened to spend the evening.

The Lohorung household is the key unit.[8] This is true in relations with the ancestors as well as economically. But households in a Lohorung village are not static. They pass through a cycle. Parents with their children form a nuclear household which becomes extended when the children marry and have children of their own.[9] This household remains extended until the grandparents die and all the sons with the exception of one, the youngest, have left to form households of their own. Everyone expects that a man and his wife will want to split away from the main parental household after the birth of their first or second child. Lohorung said difficulties always started when there was more than one wife in the home and quarrels started between them. Each son, therefore, tended to establish a separate unit of consumption, production, and decision–making as soon as he was able, while still maintaining close relations with the agnatic group (those related through the male line).

Timing and planning the split was a crucial issue for each Lohorung household. Traditionally, the eldest son and his wife build their house at the far end of the compound, or at least on available land furthest from the main house, while the middle sons choose plots lying between their elder brother and the parents. The youngest son remains in the parental home to look after the parents. At their death he takes over that house. Dividing the family inheritance can rarely be easy anywhere and here it is no different. When independent households are set up, the family inheritance has to be shared out. The principle of equality between male members is paramount. In these Eastern Nepalese hills the time when households are able to split tends to vary according to the wealth of the family. The poorer the family, the more likely they are to split. When land and produce are scarce, arguments about food, or about which couple and their children are eating most food, who is working hardest to produce it, reach an intolerable point. Tensions in Lohorung society prolifererated between brothers and their wives and were sometimes eased by one or more of the brothers leaving for many years to work in Assam, Darjeeling, or the Terai. The most common reason people gave me for the splitting of a household and the land was quarrels over rations and the ways they were shared.

Since men may spend several years away from the village working somewhere to make money, it is normal for these households to carry on with female household heads until the men return. A few men manage to obtain a place as a Gurkha in the British army. These men may spend twenty years or more away from the village, returning only sporadically for brief visits of two to three months, during which time children are usually conceived.[10] For such reasons quite a number of Lohorung households were neither 'nuclear' nor 'extended'. Apart from absence there were households in which one of the conjugal pair had died or had separated from the spouse. Separation was usually the result of the man bringing in a second wife. When this happens the first wife usually insists that she is given a separate, independent household, often created by dividing the single house into two. A thick bamboo wall coated with mud and plaster is built in the middle, and the rear end of the house is opened up to make a separate doorway.The two wives live back to back. Each has her own hearth. But relations between two co–wives were rarely easy and tensions existed. Fear of the husband's anger was said to be one of the few ways in which the emotions between rival wives is controlled.

In general each household occupied one single dwelling. As might be expected from the predominance of 'nuclear' families, the size of the Lohorung household was rarely large. There were seldom fewer than three members, and rarely more than ten in any one household.[11]

Although a dominant principle among Lohorung is that of equality and equal exchange, in terms of descent and inheritance, Lohorung households had a strong male bias. The basic principle of inheritance in operation was that each son inherited an equal share of the household estate.The assets of a Lohorung household were almost entirely bound up with their buildings and their land. Daughters had no claim to the estate, unless they were still unmarried by the age of thirty–five and even then only gained usufruct rights.

Whereas land was restricted to male inheritance, household utensils and livestock – that is, the movable property – were acquired or inherited by the female line as well as the male line. In each generation some movables were seen as being accumulated by the female line, an accumulation which was then divided between their sons and daughters, more going to daughters than sons. (For a full description of changes in land ownership in the eastern hills, see Caplan, 1970.)

In terms of understanding Lohorung notions about the self, descent is a strong principle. Lohorung households are organized into named *thar* (N). The tradition in the literature on 'Rai' groups is to translate this as 'clan'. Amongst Lohorung, all members of the same clan recognise descent from a common male ancestor, though his name is not known by everyone.The clans are localised and sometimes exclusive to one village: as, for example, the *cewa* clan of Khorunde. Sometimes a lineage branch of a clan forms a village of its own either nearly or somewhat distant from the other lineages that remain in the original village. *Dekhim* clan households, for example, are to be found in Gairi Pangma, though Loke Pangma was said to be the original home of *dekhim* and indeed consisted purely of *dekhim* households. Clans are often predominant in only one 'locality': the clans *lamsong*, *biwa*, *lumben*, and *dekhim* were concentrated in Pangma, the *heluali* and *themsong* in Helua, the *angla lamsong*, *ketra*, *tembra*, and *khaisong* in Angla. Each of these groups of clans are in fact 'brother clans' that have segmented and take on their own clan status. (The process of clan fission among the Rai is described in detail by McDougal 1979). The segmentation of clans over time in order to keep marriage within the locality is one of the significant features of Rai society. 'Marriage alliances for the direct exchange of wives tend overwhelmingly to be between descent groups of the same branch (of closely related agnatic clans) and within the same locality' (McDougal 1979: 155). The paradox of Lohorung society, which resembles that described by McDougal in Kulunge society, is that marriage does not unite its component segments but divides them. Instead of integrating the society, marriage reinforces bonds within one segment, and splits the society into insulated local units of 'brother clan' households.

The separation and dispersal of clans is central to Lohorung Rai social organization as a whole and to the development of Rai tribal groups which have formed over hundred of years. Some Rai tribal groups talk of separate tribes once being 'brothers', that Lohorung Rai were once brothers of Mewahang Rai and those who now call themselves Yamphu Rai are really also Lohorung Rai, but they had an argument and separated. `Brother clans' may also be far removed from the other brothers. Etter, working on a Bhotiya group living to the north of the Lohorung in the Honggaon, Hatia, and Syaksila area, says that 'one sPang dok clan, Lorunga, appears to be of Rai origin' (n.d.: 53). Could it be one local isolated unit, that never united with other segments, a Lohorung clan that remained when, as shifting agriculturalists, others came south? In a footnote Etter adds that

> The source of my statement that Lorunge was a *sPang dok* clan was an informant's statement, subsequently seconded, that Lorunga had been present in *sPang dok* at an earlier time. I still have the suspicion that there may be some Lorunga around, though I can't locate them . . . I stand by my statement that it is old Rai country; though as I indicated, this is only an inference based on stories about the distant past that lack any supporting detail (ibid.).

According to Etter, *sPang dok* also say they cannot marry Lohorung Rai because at one time they were all brothers and all *jimi*, a term short for *jimidar*, meaning landowner and more locally 'original settlers', – a name the Lohorung used to call themselves, rather than Rai, before the 1960s to indicate their status on the land. The *sPang dok* explain their difference from their 'brothers' in physical appearance as due to the rough country they live in. They add that they too would be cleaner if they had gone south, and point out that their houses are alike, except for the fact that they use wood all over and not bamboo. These people are agriculturalists, *shing–sa–wa* (field–earth–people), like Lohorung. They are unlike other Tibetans who roam around this border area who are nomadic herdsmen.

Clans are also adopted into a locality, as in the case of the *yangkhrung* in Pangma. According to Lohorung stories, the *yangkhrung* clan once all lived in Dhupu. There were many fights over land, especially with the *sibok–wachi*, a Kulunge Rai clan now living in Seduwa.The Lohorung clans in Pangma summoned the *yangkhrung*, who were good fighters, to come and help them. In return for their help they were given land in Pangma. The *yangkhrung* clan was, nevertheless, still identified as being somewhat diferent from other clans. Like the *heluwali* clan, for example, they were classified as being 'Tibetan', *tsampa*. This implied they come from territory now inhabited by Tibetans who call themselves 'Bhote', and who were characterized by the food they eat, namely *tsampa*. The *yangkhrung* were said to come from Honggaon and the *heluwal*i from Syaksila. They are fully accepted as being original Lohorung. Their Tibetan identification supports the notion that some Lohorung lived to the north of where they live now.

In terms of personhood clan names are significant.The clan name is inherited from their paternal line. Lohorung clan names endow a person with a history, and an identity connected to clan territory. They carry social images and imply geographical location and hence a particular dialect. Unlike an individual's personal name, which must never be used as a term of address, their clan identity, and the image it carries with it, is public knowledge.[12]

We can see the strength of clan names in the following story of the *tengsa* and the *khimpule* clans. They are famous for their antagonistic relationship.[13]

> The *tengsa* clan was reduced to one or two lineages. One of the *tengsa*, who only had two daughters and no sons decided to try to persuade two *khimpule* brothers (not of the original ten brothers Lohorung) to become his married–in sons–in–law, *khim maksa*, a position similar to the Sherpa *maksu*, or the Hindu *ghar–juwain*. The two *khimpule* brothers happened upon the village of Malta after they had been hunting and shooting two wild boar in the surrounding forests. At night they came to the house of the *tengsa* who had two daughters and no sons. After sharing the wild boar, the man persuaded them to stay as 'house sons–in–law' to marry his daughters and live on his land, thus adopting the *khimpule* as a new Lohorung clan. One of the brothers stayed, but one gave up, departed and disappeared. Others of his *khimpule* relatives arrived looking for him and accused the *tengsa* of stealing and locking up their brother, which he denied and explained his lack of sons. More and more arrived and many of them stayed and were given land. But then later on the *khimpule*, who now had far more houses in Malta than the *tengsa*, chased away the tengsa from their own land so that now there are only one or two houses left of *tengsa* in Malta. The branch of the clan belonging to the man with two daughters was chased away. Now they have gone up to Yuba. They chased them away from Malta to Yuba, poor things. That was what it was like at that time. Whoever could do things, did it like that' Later, the *khimpule* began to use the *yatangpa* (local priest) from Pangma, and the *khimpule* brought to the village all the leaves for the *sammang* (ancestor) rituals, and took them to the priest's helpers who lived in Pangma. The playful, teasing children who saw them always carrying leaves since they began to use the priest so much, said the *khimpule* were the 'leaf–bringing people' (*singbak tekhuba*). Soon they were being called by the name s*ingbok' kriwa*, *kriwa*, *singbok'krikpa*. *Krikpa* is the common suffix to indicate the category of 'insects'. The Pangma people then made them marriage partners, even though they were not of the 'ten original brothers'. Now they have taken on all the Lohorung customs and so we say they are of the 'ten brothers', but at first they had customs from the other side (of the Arun, i.e. West). We are *Yakkaba Rai*; they are like the *Khambu*. They still quarrel and fight with

Pangma people and the Malta *khimpule*: 'You *singbok'kriwa*, you *singbek'krewa*' the Pangma people shout at them and they reply 'you Pangma *bhegute*' (N for frog). 'You Malta *bayok*' (Lohorung for frog) the Pangma people reply.

The ease with which some clans seem to have changed their identity from *Khambu Rai* to Lohorung, or perhaps Lohorung to *sPang dok*, is an illustration of how similar these groups are, for example in terms of values, forms of livelihood, culture and concepts of self and emotion.

As we've seen, Lohorung Rai have a past typified by fighting over land between brothers and brother clans. Now they live in communities that value highly egalitarian principles, exchange, reciprocity, and hospitality. Beneath the surface there are tensions within households and between households and also in their relations with the superhuman beings.

Notes

1. The concentration of Lohorung was not reflected in the village district as a whole. Before 1991 the Pangma *panchayat* was the local administrative and political unit covering a large area to the North and South of Pangma villages (see map 2, p2). In the *panchayat* as a whole there were slightly more Gurung households than Lohorung and a significant number of Chetr_ and B_hun households.

2. *Kiranti*, or rather the older form Kir_ta, are mentioned in Yajurveda to describe the Mongoloid race living in the northeast, a cave dwelling people. In later texts (Mahabharata, Ramayana, Kiratarjuniya) they are described as wild forest and mountain people, prototype hunter people – fierce, warlike and handsome savage hunters.

3. For a discussion of social change amongst a Rai group see Allen (1972b) on the Thulung Rai.

4. Although about 50% of land in Nepal has belonged traditionally to the state, the Kipat form of land tenure is communal. 'A Kipat owner derived rights in Kipat lands by virtue of his membership in a particular ethnic group and their location in a particular area . . . limited to certain communities of Mongoloid origin, such as the Limbus, Rais' (Regmi, 1976: 19–20). The land belongs to the tribe. By 1886, however, in efforts to bring the eastern states under further control, the government of Nepal passed legislation prescribing that any Kipat land alienated to a non–tribal member could no longer retain its communal character and would convert to Raikar (the system of state landlordism). See Regmi (1976: chapter 6); and Lionel Caplan (1970) who describes the relationship between Limbu and the immigrant Brahmins in East Nepal and how Kipat land was lost over time.

5. When first in Pangma information on the Lohorung language was limited to a word list collected by Brian Hodgson, British Resident in Nepal in 1857 (1880). In 1987 van Driem published *A Grammar of Limbu*, in 1993 *A Grammar of Dumi* – one of the Rai languages.

6. Some informants said that the languages of the Yamphu Rai, Balali Rai, and Mewahang Rai are all mutually intelligible, differing mainly in pronounciation. One informant said that 'just as Lohorung, Yamphu and Mewahang were close brothers, so we were with Balali'. Support of this view can be found in Shafer, in a footnote on the Lohorung language says, 'Balali is the same language in a different locality' (1955: 102).

7. In terms of other mythologies and traditions the pattern has been for Lohorung to assimilate them into their own conceptual scheme. As Gaenszle has said, 'it is mutual "inclusivism": in the view of the Rai, the "great" traditions are part of their own – though somewhere at the periphery' (1993: 122).

8. See Macfarlane 1976 for his analysis of household and family structure.

9. Among the Lohorung, infant and child mortality are partially to account for the small size of nuclear households. From a sample of sixteen Lohorung women over fifty, the average number of conceptions was 5.25, of live births 5.12. The average number of children alive was 1.56 (male), 1.31 (female), that is, a total of 2.87. The fetal wastage rate was 2.48 per cent, the survival rate 56.05 per cent.

10. There has been a steady increase in permanent out–migration to the Terai, Darjeeling, and Assam over the last fifty years.

11. Further statistics on Lohorung households are to be found in Acharya and Bennett (1981) and in Hardman (n.d.). The aim of the Time Allocation Project was to assess women's contribution to the economy and especially in `productive' activities that met subsistence needs. We used the method of observing the activity of each family member, with random checks throughout the day and throughout every season.

12. Gaenszle's book (1991) looks specifically at the signficance of descent and mythology in the ethnic identity of the Mewahang Rai.

13. I have used some of my own phrases to shorten the text, but have adhered in every other way to the story as told me first by a woman in Pangma.

Fig 4 The Mangmani of Pangma

3

The Ancestors are Angry

I slipped on the wet stones by the house and broke three of the eggs I had brought from the neighbour. The house was unusually quiet. I took the eggs to the back store and then found *kāhili*. She started moaning as soon as I went near her. She seemed in agony. She said both her back and stomach ached. She moaned so much I was worried. Then she started writhing in pain, clutching her belly. She said she had no diarrhoea, no sickness, no headache. She seemed to be suffering so much, I eventually gave her a painkiller, but it didn't make any difference. I sat with her for hours listening to her and wondering what it could be. I thought of appendicitis, flu, cholera, but she had no fever. She was totally absorbed in her affliction, and her cries of pain, 'ai, aia, aiyaiya' never stopped. As time went on, I became really worried. From what I could see she was in agony; I saw no way to stop her torment and I thought she must at least rest: I gave her a sleeping pill. It had absolutely no effect on her. She went on groaning, and she was even worse if I went away. I remembered what she had said about Hem's wife's illness. She had simply said, 'women whose husbands have been away are ill for some time when their husbands return'. She said it as though the two simply went together, like I might say, 'people who go out in the rain come back wet'. I wondered if her pain had for her an equally simple explanation. It was hard for me at the time to dismiss the psychological. She said it came on as I was leaving for market – my first absence since I arrived – and she was insistent on my presence just as the previous day she wouldn't let me leave her side. So I simply sat by her, fanning her. I remember when everyone else came back from the fields they were annoyingly noisy and apparently uninterested. They certainly didn't seem to think it important for her to try to sleep. It was obvious to me she was in great pain and yet no one did anything for her.

After eating late, I was exhausted and she let me go to sleep but I was soon woken by her husband. He said she needed me again and now he was worried too. I sat and fanned and soothed her head while *kāhila* went to find the *yatangpa* (tribal officiant). They both arrived about an hour later. The *yatangpa* put six leaves on the ground in front of her. *Kāhili* had to sit up and I had to come away from her side. He put some uncooked rice and ginger on each leaf and spoke over them one after the other. Each one was apparently for a different *sammang*. It didn't take long. He said it was *pappamama'chi*, 'grandfather–grandmother' ancestor. It would need one pig, six chickens and twelve eggs to satisfy the hunger of this ancestor. The leaves were carefully wrapped up by *kāhila* in a cloth. *Kāhili* already seemed better. She had stopped moaning and could talk and drink a little *dibu* (millet beer).

In all seriousness they were talking about the ancestor's anger and hunger and how bad the pain is until they are promised the ritual. Prem, the neighbour, dropped in and he said he must see if perhaps it was *pappamama'chi* also making his wife so bad. He's been in the army and he told me that once he had tried to give up the *sammang* because he liked the idea of the goodness of the Christian God he had heard about in the camp. He never really trusted anyone, not even his father, and he thought it would be wonderful if he could trust in this God. It didn't work. As soon as he was back in the village he suffered acute stomach ache. He took medicine he had brought back with him but, as with *kāhili*, nothing had worked. He was in such pain he decided he must call in the *yatangpa*. Five minutes after the words had been spoken by the *yatangpa*, and he had been told that it was the *pappamama'ch*i ancestors, the pain went. He said he now knows that the ancestors do respond and that he can't avoid his relationship with them. He gave up all ideas of trying Christianity.

Kāhili was ill for another week and demanded my presence day and night. She quite often came to sleep on the space of floor by me. She revealed one evening, in one of the many long talks we had, that she had been 'in love' with her husband's younger brother. However, as Lohorung tradition goes, the elder brother has to marry first and when the mother of the two brothers was very ill and that family desperately needed extra female help, she was finally persuaded by her own family to marry her present husband.

The ya*tangpa*, the local healer who had diagnosed the hunger of *pappamama'chi* came several times and found 'the house ancestor (*khimpie*) was angry' as well as the 'grandfather–grandmother' ancestors. The *ojah* who deals with non–Lohorung spiritual beings and witches (*bokshi* N) also found a witch to be interfering with her, giving her cramps and diarrhoea. Witches work with poison and come particularly in the middle of the night when they're known to be most active.

There was no escaping the daily situations involving superhuman beings in Pangma. The episode just described occurred very early on in fieldwork. Lohorung related to them in the most human way, almost as if they were part of their living society. Superhuman beings have emotions and needs which have to be met; they explained how society came to be as it is, why people keep black pigs, why someone is depressed, the kinds of pain or illness people have. Answers to numerous questions were expressed in terms of these beings. Not surprisingly, I began to visualize a system of Lohorung relations which depended on invisible participants as much as on the visible.

Most of the time in Lohorung company I was acutely aware of my enormous lack of knowledge but not that there was any great difference between my general understanding of events and theirs. And yet increasingly, concepts and statements to do with superhuman beings called *sammang* and *chap* made me realise here were principles from a frame of reference that I was not used to. Other realities existed; the spirit world was all around. I realized that if I was going to understand Lohorung notions of self and emotion I had to fully appreciate who these superhuman beings were, the value that things in the external word possessed for them, what made them 'angry' or 'jealous' and how this affected the living. I would have to explore in particular the word *sammang*, which I here gloss 'ancestor'. The concept constantly occurred and at first it looked as though the Lohorung word *sammang* was the 'key to their philosophy'[1] In fact, as much as *sammang*, it turned out to be the closely related term *saya* ('internal link with the ancestors', 'vital principle'), their almost mystic sense of identity with progenitors and nature, which lies at the core of Lohorung philosophy. Nevertheless, it was in hearing about *sammang*, and in watching rituals to them, that I began to grasp aspects of the alternative reality within which notions of 'self' and 'emotion' are embedded.

At times it almost became natural for me too to interpret events and behaviour in terms of *sammang* and *chap*. I found myself behaving as though I was attached to a reality far greater than the here and now, which included ancestral beings. Anthropologists are not in agreement about the extent to which one should 'go native' and take seriously a belief in spirits.[2] My own view is that we should attempt to make sense of informants' interpretations of their experiences within their own framework which may include acting therefore 'as if' the superhuman reality accepted by Lohorung was true for me too, seeing how this worked in practice and affected my own experiences (as Geertz would say, seeing things from the native's point of view 1983: 56). We should also have what Wikan called a 'willingness to engage with another world, life or idea; an ability to use one's experience' that we should 'try to grasp, or convey meanings that reside neither in words, "facts" nor texts, but are evoked in the meetings of one experiencing subject with another' (1992: 463). At the same time we need to ask such questions as 'How do these experiences fit into the principles upon which these people live?' and `What are the concepts and practices in which those principles take shape and are expressed and how can we understand them?' This is to follow a social constructionist approach.

To take this view often meant little more than adopting a Lohorung habit or gesture, such as respecting the three ancestral hearth–stones, not sitting on the 'up' side of the fire, not stepping over someone's head, or flicking a few drops from any drink as a charitable act for the spirits of the dead. I sought the help of the *yatangpa* to help with a rash on my arm and he diagnosed a *boksi* (witch) and 'cured' it by burning a piece of cloth and rubbing leaves onto my arm. Sometimes it meant that as I experienced a stomach–ache I wondered which *sammang* might have something to do with it. I had been warned to keep away from talking and asking about *sammang*. I had been told how dangerous it was for me to enter into a relationship with them. I would have to maintain relations with them, respect them, keep them happy, follow their traditions, and treat them as Lohorung did. People were genuinely concerned about how I would continue to respect them when I returned home. And who, they asked, would be able to help me if the *sammang* became angry, hungry, or jealous and I became ill? There would be no one with knowledge, like a Lohorung ritual specialist, either shaman or local healer. If I was to initiate relations I would make myself as vulnerable as they are. From their point of view remaining an outsider was the only form of protection.

When it came to performing the *khimpie* ritual for *kāhili*'s stomach–ache both *kāhili* and her husband were insistent that I did not attend. They were frightened for her and for me. This *sammang* might be angered by the presence of a non–Lohorung and the ritual could be ineffective or, worse, *kāhili* could be in even more pain. Alternatively, they explained, these *sammang* might shift their focus of attention onto me and my interference would bring upon me, and possibly onto the household, the clan, or the village as a whole, disease and misfortune. They didn't know whether I had been accepted as a Lohorung or how the sammang would react to me. It was only some time later that I began to be allowed to attend these private household rituals. This was after an illness I experienced was diagnosed in terms of my relationship with the *sammang*, indicating that I had been acknowledged by them as a member of the community. From then on, though some Lohorung still sometimes complained, they no longer refused my participation in the dangerous or vulnerable aspects of their lives and instead concentrated their efforts on instructing me in the correct ways to behave so I would not anger *sammang*. I learnt one must never show fear in these rituals. 'Whatever you are really feeling you must not be afraid. *Sammang* want to respect us, not to see us afraid. Then they think they can take advantage.' I learned that only men possess the knowledge about what to put on the shrine for a *sammang* so they are the only ones allowed to cook in rituals.

From the episode with *kāhili* described above and other similar events, there was no doubt that superhuman beings are closely associated with pain or 'illness' experienced by Lohorung. Not necessarily all ill health had to do with superhuman beings, for, as *kāhili* pointed out, some may be merely connected to the return of a husband. It was unclear, however, what 'hunger' or 'anger' was for the ancestors, and what more exactly 'illness' meant to these people. 'Hunger', I later found out, when referring to the superhuman beings, is not so much to do with an exhausted sensation due to lack of food (as in *tungkhetu* 'fainting with hunger' which afflicts the living) but an indication that they need attention because they are 'angry' based on important local knowledge about the close connection between emotions and food which I shall examine in more detail later. (See Chapters Four and Six.)

All that need be recognized here is that Lohorung live in an environment in which the staple diet is rice and lentils twice a day. For those who cannot afford the rice it is replaced in one or both meals by a mush of maize or millet. Vegetable dishes are an occasional addition. In contrast dishes of meat or eggs and the addition of beer, particularly beer made from millet and offered in a *tongba* (bamboo vessel) drunk with a bamboo pipe, are a culturally recognised way of giving pleasure as well as show respect and hospitality. Such offerings are also central to the marriage process in which reciprocity between two families over many years gradually seals the bond.3 They are central too to processes of compensation and conciliation. The idiom of sociability and reciprocity applies to superhuman beings as much as to living kin, and generosity in its proper place is socially valued. Food as a relationship therefore needs rules about what to give which category of kin and these also have their counterpart in dealing with dead ancestors. However, only *yatangpa*, in contact with the ancestors, can say just how much food is needed to overcome the anger and satisfy the hunger. The 'hunger' is not for food as such since the dead, they say, cannot physically eat and digest. Food, however, is also a materialized emotion.[4] It indicates degrees of devotion. What the dead, like the living, can do is 'eat' through their noses and eyes; they become replete and happily reassured by seeing the degree of care taken with the shrine and its offerings of festive foods, closely associated with 'satisfaction' and 'happiness' (*chenchame*: lit. 'to eat strength') for all Lohorung, whether living or dead. (See Chapter Eight.) We shall see how ancestral 'hunger' is a desire for *chenchame*, this strength and satisfaction. When they are 'hungry' it is said 'their spirits need to be raised' (*saya pokmale*) which can be done by giving them respect and the sociability they are due in the form of offerings of food and drink.

What we would understand as 'illness' is understood by Lohorung as but one of a host of misfortunes and conditions, (including poor crops, landslides, death of animals, and depression) which may occur as a result of the anger of *sammang* or attack from one of the other superhuman beings. There is no abstract noun for 'illness' in Lohorung. Though they do know the Nepali terms *bethā*, *rog* and *bimāri*, the way Lohorung describe a sick person, in contrast to someone who is 'alive and flourishing' (*hingchame*), blooming like a flower, is to say they are *tukkha*, meaning literally 'in pain, hurting' or *tukpoka* 'pain erupted'. A 'sick person' is called *tukkhuwa* or *tukkha*. The verbs for 'to be in pain' *tukchame*, *tuksime* or *tukme*, all cover both physical and mental hurt. Thus a person with acute anxiety, or someone feeling hurt or insulted, whose *niwa* ('mind') *tuguk* ('hurts') is also in Lohorung terms *tukmawa*, suffering 'illness', whereas for us the term, standing on its own, tends to be restricted to a physical condition. Although a Lohorung 'illness' is most often an indication of the disruption of relations with the superhuman beings, the anger of some ancestor, Lohorung came up with other explanations, such as exposure to a human witch (*bokshi* N), the impact of someone's jealousy or envy, extremes of temperature, bad water, over–spicy food, or disruption of the planets. The actual physical symptoms of Lohorung 'pains' can also be described independently of superhuman influence. Hence they talk and diagnose such symptoms as fever (*dechikmawa*), diarrhoea (*khoklamba*), vomiting and diarrhoea (*tangpe yumpe*, literally 'upwards downwards'), breathing problems like asthma (*pisokma*), and shooting pains (*hupkhemimpa*).

Kāhili's illness raised all kinds of questions at the time. Why didn't the medicines work? In what ways do they conceive of the superhuman beings having a hold over their bodies? To what extent are they powerful agents? I found it hard to comprehend the way the family ignored her pain. Was it because they had themselves decided her illness was a sammang ancestor and therefore an inevitable pain to be endured? In interpreting the significance of her pain had they decided that this was 'normal' pain and therefore not in need of attention? How do they perceive and respond to pain? Should I be looking at pain as part of a wider concept of misfortune?[5] Later I realized how much my understanding was hindered by my automatic Western association of pain with illness and a malfunction of the body, and my expectation of finding the reason for the illness within the body. In the West pain is physical. Above all, this episode told me that if her pain was a manifestation of the anger of an ancestor, a Lohorung view of human beings, 'health' and 'healing' included a close relationship with ancestors in a way I had yet to fully comprehend.

The degree of involvement with ancestors was revealed in a second episode also concerning *kāhili*. The context, four months after her 'illness', was the family ritual to the ancestor *khimpie sammang*. Though her pain of the month of July had disappeared the household still had to fulfill the needs of this 'house' ancestor.

> The main *khimpie* ceremony was over and we all sat eating our special ritual rice and bits of meat and sucking at our *tongba* (bamboo containers full of millet beer). Everyone was fairly drunk and loud and the new *yatangpa* so shy he was hard to talk to. I had hardly finished eating when I heard *kāhili* moaning loudly from the corner. This was a strange noise. It sounded different and I thought she must be suffering badly again. Then I looked carefully and saw her with her back against the wall shaking and half singing in short phrases just like a *mangpa* (shaman). After a while she got up and began moving around with the slow shaking step of a *mangpa*. She became wilder and then with a sudden sweep of her hand knocked over the *tongpa* containers near the fire, picked up the hot iron tripod covering the fire, threw it into the corner, and began stamping in the hot ashes as if in time with her chanting. She didn't appear to feel any pain from the hot pieces of wood she handled. No–one seemed to know what to do. *Māhila*, *kāncha*, and *mamma* had never seen her like this before. The floor was now wet with beer and water. *Kāhili* had made her way to the yatangpa who was huddling in a corner with his *tongpa* beer. She splashed water over herself and him, calling for more and more water and for *titepāti* (N) leaves. Whereas she had been obsessed with the fire, now water was becoming more and more important. When she had used all the water in the house, she made her way down to the spring. She shook in the water, first standing and then sitting and then rubbed herself with water as if she was washing, her face, her body and her hair. The shaking took her over and she sat cross–legged, now frequently mentioning Satte Devi. *Kancha* (the one she had wanted to marry) was on his knees praying and asking forgiveness, saying he would give whatever was needed to free her. Suddenly apparently angry as she tore at the grass, *kāhili* threw away the bamboo channel for the water, started stuffing her mouth with *titepāti* (Mugwort, *Artemis vulgaris*) leaves and ripped open her blouse, baring her breasts to the air as she stood there shaking.

It was very strange: I half wanted to interrupt and comfort her, to tell her to cry on my shoulder or shout at me, to tell her to come inside and get dry. I saw *kāhili* in emotional distress, crying out for help. At the same time, I knew this was my own ethnocentric view, clouding the situation and completely misunderstanding that it was not a personal tantrum or fit of anger and sadness at her plight. *She* was not in control as far as everyone watching was concerned. This was not her but superhuman beings speaking and shouting in anger, directing her body and all her actions.

The next morning *kāhili* wept – unhappy with what she saw as her burden. The way she put it, she has *yompok* 'work' to do – to be a medium for the Creators, Hindu gods (and she used the Nepali word *deutā*) and *sammang*. They had been urging her more and more frequently to serve them and perform the *sammang* and other rituals. Satte Devi was one of the main 'guru' or teachers of the Pangma *mangmani*. Now she was calling *kāhili*. She said she didn't want to respond. She felt shy. On the other hand, she knew she might have to, since her grandfather, her mother's father, was a *yatangpa* and none of her brothers had shown any sign of being chosen. 'It's easier for a man, but very hard for a woman.' Some people, she said were scared of her and some people saw her powers as being those of a witch (*bokshi* N). It all began, she explained, when her head started to ache, and then her stomach around the heart and kidneys. The pain left as her shoulders and legs began shaking of their own accord. The *khimpie sammang* talked through her, angry that another medium had been brought in. She was afraid they would go on making her suffer until she attended to them.

Kāhili explained the ways superhuman beings communicated with her through intermittent pains, illnesses, and dreams, seeking to persuade her to become a shaman. Those Lohorung who had witnessed what happened to *kāhili* all explained it as ancestors and Hindu deities 'talking' and 'calling' her.

In both these two episodes other powers were accepted as being stronger than human desires. In the first episode Prem commented that in spite of his own wishes he couldn't give up his relationship with *sammang* and, in the other, *kāhili* was distressed that she would have to become a *mangmani*, a female shaman (male *mangpa*). Experiences, such as pains and dreams, were almost always interpreted in terms of a reality of intrusive beings so that in spite of their own individual inclinations, both found they were involved in an inevitable on–going relationship with superhuman beings. Belief in these beings was not the issue. Everyone knows they exist. The important question was whether they had to continue their relationship with them and if not at what cost. Both accepted illness, affliction, pain or spirit possession, as well as possible good fortune, to be strong experiences leading them to cherish the relationship. We might want to say that they understood superhuman beings as 'causing' them an 'effect' of pain.[6] But if we comprehend the Lohorung representation of their relationship with ancestors as being interdependent, to say this about ancestors might be misleading.

The communications between living Lohorung and their *sammang* ancestors was dominated by attempts to control the relationships, to prevent them going wrong and attending to the relationships when they did go wrong. It was not a one–way process in which the living were innocent, passive recipients as we tend to think of ourselves when we become sick. A person's relationship with *sammang* could be upset in all kinds of ways, as we shall see, and not only manifesting in what we think of as 'illness'. It showed in various kinds of misfortune, accidents, mental states like madness or others we define as 'emotions', (such as low *saya*, the inner ancestral force). In Chapter Four we'll see how the various categories of *sammang* constitute explanatory models not only of bodily states but also of social situations, when not one body but a whole household is out of harmony with the good ancestral order. We could say that their understanding of illness can be seen as confirming the social order in good functionalist tradition. Maintaining their society as opposed to maintaining an equality of status among individuals is a fundamental Lohorung value (see Dumont 1970: 9–10). But for Lohorung the key to understanding what we interpret as illness and emotions was not to be found in the patient's misdemeanors or breaches of norms because Lohorung recognized that it was in the nature of things to break tradition and for people sometimes to disobey. The key was in the concept of *saya*, the 'ancestors within' or 'ancestral spirit', their overwhelming connection with the founding ancestors, who established the harmonious good order upon which all their traditions are derived. As Allen says about the neighbouring Thulung Rai 'the health and fortune of an individual Thulung and his relationship to his ancestors are fused in a single concept . . . .health is only an aspect of a concept of good order which embraces the properly cooperative ancestors' (Allen 1976b: 510). Good health for Lohorung is certainly social as well as physical but the necessary sociality and hospitality must be directed as much to superhuman beings as to living neighbours.

The process of knowing *sammang* was complicated. It involved not just knowing how these beings shaped the way Lohorung acted and experienced life, it meant getting rid of the Cartesian split which dominates our thought, encouraging a mechanical view of the body, a bio–medical view of disease with 'a mistaken belief that our categories belong to nature, that disease as we know it is natural and therefore above. . . culture' (Good 1994: 53). It meant rejecting the supremacy of the scientific mechanical view of life and accepting a more fluid, related view of life, a more relational view of the human body. The body had to be seen as open to the emotions and thoughts of others. I had to accept that characteristics or emotions we place firmly only in mankind can exist elsewhere, in material objects for example. (See Chapter Five). It meant accepting the view of emotions as judgements and actions which inevitably affect others, so that the anger of ancestors was intentional and 'caught' (*lapme*) the body of a living being.

Lohorung understanding of illnesses may be understood better if we see them as the attachment to the body of ancestors' desires and anger. The ancestors themselves don't penetrate the body but their desires and emotions can. Preventive rituals can build up the strength of the boundaries of the body and pacify possible negative emotions by pleasing ancestors with the right kind of hospitality. Understanding how *sammang* and their bodies, their bodies and emotions, bodies and the material world are for Lohorung all intertwined also means addressing the possibility that 'disease is not an entity but an explanatory model. Disease belongs to culture... and culture is not only a means of representing disease, but is essential to its very constitution as a human reality' (Good, 1994: 53). That bellyaches, cramps and diarrhoea were seen as an 'illness'of angry ancestors or jealous witches made sense where bodies are open to the emotions of others, as did the form the pain took. This was often expressed as a burden, only eased by moaning, as if letting out an invading thought.

Mediating People

Since Lohorung 'illness' is often the unwanted anger and hunger, desires and feelings of ancestors and spirits affecting their bodies, then not surprisingly key figures in their lives are those who know how to communicate with these superhuman beings. Lohorung rely on various kinds of ritual officiants to interpret, appease and satisfy the hurt emotions of those in the superhuman world. The *yatangpa*, the expert in relations with *sammang* is the most important in Lohorung eyes. As one man said, 'the *yatangpa* is "big", "important": if there were no *yatangpa* no Lohorung work could be done'; they 'need' (*pabuk*) a *yatangpa* to perform the rituals at all such occasions as birth, marriage, death, in pregnancy, in the annual renewal of the house shrine, and the harvesting of first crops, all occasions in which the ancestors have always been involved. They also 'need' a *yatangpa* to maintain order, the correct state of life, health, and relations with other superhumans. Every Lohorung household must have access to a *yatangpa* – their doctor, priest, psychopomp, and diviner all in one. They cannot envisage life without one.

> When one dies another one emerges. You don't have to teach them. There's usually one for every clan. When the *dekhim* clan one died, the *mangsuk* (house shrines) of that clan began to go wrong. With no *yatangpa* the house shrines go wrong, and then people go wrong; they become mad, become blind, deaf, dumb. When the old *yatangpa* died, his older brother began to go mad: he would laugh endlessly, and then stop and talk like you and me, then suddenly he would cry. There was nothing anyone could do. He knew he had his father's elder brother's son in Assam, in Lakinpur, and wanted to fetch him. People persuaded him not to go, but when the relation from Assam did come, he began to shake and become possessed with spirits. He is now the *yatangpa* for Gairi Pangma village and the elder brother got better. It was the same with another *yatangpa*. When he died one brother became blind, another had a terrible wound on his leg, another lost the bottom part of his leg and he died,

and another clan member died after his wife took a thorn and popped a small growth he had on the top of his head'.

Yatangpa are different from the more ecstatic *mangpa* (female *mangmani*) shamans, the other main Lohorung officiant, and from *jhānkri*,[7] Nepali speaking shamans, and from ojah who deal with witches and non–Lohorung spirits and gods. *Mangpa* and *mangmani* deal with the broadest spectrum of superhuman beings – that is, Lohorung ones and the gods, ghosts and spirits of other tribes such as Tamang, Gurung, and Sherpa, and those of the Hindu Chetrā and Bāhun.

Lohorung describe their own tribal *mangpa* and *yatangpa*, the mediators between the spirit world and the human world, as *khangkhuba* 'ones who can see'. They have the ability to go into an altered state of consciousness at will and perceive what is for most human beings normally an intangible and invisible dimension, though all, they say, visit it in their dreams. This is the dimension where lost 'wandering souls' (*lawa*) can sometimes be retrieved, where ancestors can be encountered, where mediating officiants can communicate with natural phenomena like trees, mountains, or rivers connected to the ancestral world. At the heart of Lohorung ways of understanding this dimension is an acceptance of a mystical interconnectedness of phenomena in it – all are related, sharing a relationship to the primeval beings of the world, and having therefore a vital principle in the form of *saya*.[8]

One *yatangpa* explained that the power of 'seeing' lies deep in the belly, *bok*. He thought his power also came from deep in his *niwa* (memory, mind, consciousness). 'Seeing' was also explained in terms of *lemmang* and *semmang*. What we can see when awake – in waking vision (*lemmang*) is limited. In another vision (*semmang*) restrictions of time and space and the divisions of the world disappear. It is explored, I was told, by everyone in their dreams and by *mangpa* and *yatangpa* who have been chosen to 'see' that aspect of the world. Other human beings have lost this ability to 'see' and talk to this world. They were not talking about *another* reality, *another* world, since the realms are understood as co–existing and bringing each other problems. The ability to 'see' is accepted as a valuable and authoritative way of knowing the world.

For Lohorung, a balance of proximity and remoteness, unity and separateness at the metaphysical level, and disruptions of that balance, explain either prosperity or natural disasters, social order or disorder, well–being or inner pain. The tension in Lohorung society is between this fundamental balance and everyday behaviour, desires or events – which constantly create problems and upset the balance. For example, when Prem's mother was ill, he thought she should be carried to the hospital in Daran, even though it's a long journey. But the main worry was that taking her to hospital would be going against tradition, disrupting the relationship with the metaphysical world and drawing some *sammang* from their separateness, triggering the anger of perhaps the 'house' *sammang*, and that his mother would then become paralysed.

The close connection between Lohorung *yatangpa* or *mangpa* and superhuman beings is developed in the initial period of apprenticeship when superhuman beings are 'calling' someone. As in many part of Nepal, those chosen may fly, shake, dance, run away to the forest, or sit still for days on a stone or in a banana tree. At this time the person often shudders or trembles (*yongukme*): the body is being invaded by one or many *guru* 'teaching spirits' or their 'wandering soul' (*lawa*) has left their body to journey. One *mangmani* said her body particularly shook when someone died. Apparently during this initial period, if they eat 'forbidden' food, like 'goat' meat or somebody else's food remains (*jutho* N) all flying, dreaming, and shaking may cease but they might also become very ill. The uncontrolled shaking persists over a year or more. Once they have accepted their 'calling' the techniques of the *yatangpa* and the *mangpa* differ. *Yatangpa* either contact the metaphysical world by going on journeys or by being possessed.[9] They enter what appears to be a non–ecstatic but different state of consciousness (see Jones 1976: 1, Samuel 1993: 8) in which they can see and communicate with those in the *semmang* dimension. Their bodies tremble but remain in the same position. This is superficially different from the typical shamans' more intense shaking and dancing in many parts of the world.[10] *Yatangpa* hold no drum, sometimes a metal plate (*thal*), but usually only the particular leaves or branches required by the *sammang* ancestors. *Mangpa* or *mangmani* in contrast, are much more like shaman of the Tungus–speaking herders of Siberia (see Shirokogoroff 1935). They are possessed by tutelary spirits and capable of magical flights or journeys whilst in a trance. At times their performance is frenzied and they have elaborate equipment including drums, (*dhol* and *dhyängro*)[11] a headdress with such feathers as pheasant, peacock, and forest hen. They wear a long skirt called *sunna jama* to please the *sammang* and Original Beings. The tail and quill of a porcupine, and a tiger's bone are needed for the shrine construction (*than*), the horn of a deer to play the plate, two cymbals, a bell, waistbelt from which dangle wild boar's teeth and wild chicken feathers are needed as a weapon against 'enemies' when in flight.

At the age of thirty, the *mangmani* in Pangma began to shake and vomit wherever she went. She fell into 'dreaming' a lot and told me she talked crazy things. She had been chosen by one of the *sammang* and the ancestor of the house shrine (*bongbi*). Going on a journey to meet spirits or ancestors she said, 'My heart beats so much I begin to tremble until I can hardly bear it, until I can't bear it and the whole earth shakes, and when I touch a piece of cloth or a bit of rice my *guru* speaks to me. When they come my heart shakes more and then I begin to travel, to go on journeys to wherever they call, to Salpa Pokari, Koptane Pokari, to Kilika in Tibet'. On the journeys *yatangpa* or *mangpa* meet and communicate with the ancestors, spirits or Hindu deities. *The mangmani* confirmed the validity of her calling:

> At Salpa Pokari I dived into the lake. Inside there was a stone which looked like a man. When I tried to lift the stone it looked like a crocodile and it bit my hand and then disappeared. I saw Golbe Raja wearing white shoes and a hat. Dogs, ducks, pigeons all live

> under the water and maize, millet and rice grow under it too. And the biggest of snakes. I asked , 'if I am a real mangmani then let the waters dry up' And the water did dry up. I saw it. Then I said again, And if I am a real *mangmani* then let the waters come again'. And the waters did rise and I nearly drowned.

In terms of Lohorung understanding of self, the notion that someone can go on a magical flight to distant lakes, enter dreamlike states and shake, become possessed or relate to ancestors or the world associated with them is not strange. As we have seen, it's not so different from a form of 'illness' experienced by everyone. It fits in with their understanding of the inter–relatedness and the openness of their bodies to either being entered by spirits or to a part of them merging with the outside. They have a plurality of internal 'souls' (see Chapter Six) and even an adult's *lawa* 'soul' is soft and vulnerable, easily led astray, leaving the body to roam elsewhere, as it does in dreams. They have an 'ancestral soul', a vital principle (*saya*) which is a direct link with the ancestors and the person is least in control of these inner aspects, since they are most controlled by superhuman beings.

Interpretations

So far I have described *kāhili*'s painful back and bellyache, and her ecstatic[12] eruption, within the framework of the all–embracing interdependence of Lohorung relationships with superhuman beings. I saw it as the anthropologist's job to make as much sense of their world as I could from within their frame of reference and to make sense of what I began to see as their seamless world, where spirit and substance, mind and emotion, past, and present and many other of our oppositions are broken down.[13] Other worlds demand the respect that comes from their own frame of reference and the premise which shaped Lohorung frames of reference clearly had to do with a complex relationship with these beings called *sammang* and *chap*.

There is, however, an additional possible interpretation which I want to consider briefly. From my point of view at the time, it did seem that *kāhili*'s conduct might be in part a means for expressing individuality, and an acceptable means of expressing otherwise unacceptable emotions and behaviour. Or was this my own ethnocentric interpretation? I can think of many examples of women's 'illnesses' in Pangma, in which the social situation surrounding the illness was full of emotional tension. Prem's wife, for example, was constantly ill. She was not happy, having produced two daughters but no sons, and Prem was talking about whether she would allow him to bring in a second wife. Her father–in–law disliked her and had built himself a sleeping place on the side of the house saying he would not sleep in the same house as her. At one time he refused to drink the water she fetched or the food she cooked. Prem was a Gurkha and away most of the time. According to one informant the wife did most of her moaning and writhing in pain when Prem was 'on leave' in the village and able to watch. He then had to deal with her suffering (*dukkha* N), calling in *mangpa*, *yatangpa* and *jhankhri* (N) to diagnose her problem. It could be said in this case that her pains, experienced by her as connected to ancestors and spirits were both a source of discontent as well as a means for resolving discontent (see Jones 1975: 1).

This might be seen to follow the view of I.M.Lewis (1971), who argues for a sociological approach to ecstasy, suggesting that 'peripheral' spirit possession should be seen as the voices of the oppressed, as a socially accepted release of tensions and frustrations and as a means for gaining power and status in societies where women are subordinated and denied opportunities; that is, as 'thinly disguised protest movements against the opposite sex' (ibid:26).[14] But although spirit possession in Nepalese society in general and elsewhere was once understood as occuring more frequently among those categories of people, such as women, who are denied social status and traditional means for enhancement (Jones, 1976: 8), what I am suggesting is a less reductionist explanation. Lohorung women's possession by spirits and 'illnesses' cannot be reduced to responses to repression and attempts to redress status imbalance. After all, those who demonstrated possession were far from being those with the least status.[15] The view of possession as a response to deprivation, emphasizing women as excluded from public culture, a masculine preserve to which they can only react, does not fit with the strength and the agency of Lohorung women. Some of the Lohorung women who suffered ecstatic illness or possession were *de facto* heads of households; some were women who were gaining economic power for their households through economic activities like brewing and selling beer at market.They were not women without power. Moreover, it would be absurd to deny Lohorung women the reality of their experienced pain and underestimate the factuality of spiritual possession, and the complexity of the issues of agency involved. In possession we can, of course, see a meeting of the personal and the collective. The cultural form of possession allows the externalization of individual problems, passions and also intentions. Lohorung examples, however, pointless to desire for increased social stature or political power and more to individual pain and immediate emotional concerns. I saw women volubly and articulately expressing through their bodies the reality of individual emotions which otherwise remain unexpressed because of the cultural view of the power and the danger of emotions. Both illness and possession are embodied phenomena, and illness in some instances I saw as one idiom of possession. Possession in all its manifestations can be more clearly understood by looking at local theories of experience, and embodiment and local attitudes to emotions, which is what we shall be looking at in the chapters to come.

It is more satisfactory, then, to see these episodes, as Lohorung do, as a legitimate means to a certain kind of knowledge, and possession and ecstatic magical flight (or ecstatic illness) as culturally accepted expressions of the experience of contact with spirits, and as 'technique du corps' to express that relationship or extreme inner pain. One other 'illness' example made this poignantly clear for me.

While I had been away from the village, Ritu had flouted tradition and instead of agreeing to her parents' choice of husband had run away with a man from Dara Pangma who was already married. I was told Rituama, her mother, had been devastated and seriously ill ever since. I went to see her. She was lying stretched out on the floor, her husband fanning her from one side and her new son–in–law fanning her from the other. To keep her cool her top was bare showing her now limp breasts and emaciated ribcage. From her prone position she started shuddering; her legs and stomach quaked in shaman fashion. She stretched out her hands, tightening the muscles as if to try to stop the shaking. She had tears in her eyes. I felt tears in my own seeing her in this state and wanted to hold her hand but her husband stopped me saying that would only make her shake more. He said she had been like this for three months. It started with a fever, then headaches, then lassitude and the shaking. She had no desire to eat or drink. For two weeks she had lost her hearing. They had done every *sammang*[16] for her. The *mangmani* (female shaman) came every evening when she could. Rituama suddenly called for water to be poured over her head and chest, and Rituapa explained that she had frequent spasms of intense heat which she could not bear without water.

On my way back to my house I talked to Aitama, who seemed matter of fact about the shaking, saying Rituama always shakes when she is ill. She says Rituama is so ill because Rituapa's father used to do *chawatangma sammang* inside the house to get better crops, whereas Rituapa won't do it. *Chawatangma* is angry. Aitama therefore told Rituama not to take any Western medicines: they would only make *chawatangma* more angry. *Sāhili* (a neighbour) had a different explanation; she saw the illness as pain, her mind and heart hurting as a result of Ritu's sudden departure and marriage to a man who already has one wife. *Sāhili* suggested this was an emotional display of various emotions. She herself was venomous about Ritu, outraged that a girl should flee her parents' attempts to marry her well, and disgusted that she went to live with a man already married, who has two children from his other wife. *Sāhili* lived for a time in India and has more Hindu attitudes than anyone else in the village. Aitama was far more tolerant, saying lots of girls go off on their own.

Rituama herself was able to tell me a few days later that the three months after Ritu left had been very difficult. Her daughter had gone to a man who has no money, no fields. Her husband refused to fetch her back. 'She has gone of her own free will. She is not my daughter.' A special rite had to be performed before she could come back to the house. Then, with her husband, Rituapa, away, she had been left to do all the work of the house and land on her own at the same time as bearing a great sorrow. She herself saw her illness as a deep pain of sadness carried too long alone. Ritu had insulted her and her father by going against their wishes. She saw what Ritu had done as being very wrong and this had made her mother vulnerable to the anger of the *sammang*. They had done many *sammang* rituals but in spite of them she had become increasingly ill and weak. She had 'gone into herself" and had no wish to talk to anyone. For her, the emotional pain was 'an illness' (she used the Nepali word *bimār*) that she likened to the pain she had felt after the death of one of her twin boy babies. Sadness is rarely expressed and indeed to some extent one should not show it for to do so is to show vulnerability and attract possible attack from malicious spirits.

Here, as in the other examples in the chapter, there is no distinction between physiological and mental or emotional pain. The pain in the belly of *kāhili* is no different from this deep sadness in the belly mind (*niwa*). Sadness and feelings of rejection and insult require the attention of the shaman or local priest just as much as a stomach pain. Happiness and sociability are closely linked to health. Rituama's body was weary, overburdened with work and several emotions. She felt shame and anger that her daughter had disobeyed her parents, and sorrow that she had gone; and these feelings of deep sadness turning her inwards, away from eating and talking, are seen as dangerous. *Saya* (the ancestral link within) can all too easily fall if someone is insulted; the heart or the mind can hurt so much that the person can even lose *lawa* ('soul loss') which can lead to death. Health is intimately linked to relations with ancestors, and sociability with neighbours and kin, so that health has to do with emotional states just as much as physical states.[17] Lohorung themselves appreciate the emotional as well as the physical component of 'illness'. The emotional and the physical aspects are the initial triggers, opening up the body and taking away its defences against the demands of hungry and angry ancestors.

Possession and healing rituals have been seen by others as social safety valves for the underlying tensions of the social structure (see Firth 1996). Larry Peters suggests that Tamang 'curing activities involving shamanic healing are not exercises in the treatment of organic disease but attempts to treat disturbing emotional states and interpersonal relations' (1981: 65); 'that organic symptoms appear to be the result of tension and anxiety, hence the shaman is most effective curing the illnesses that are of a socio–psychological nature' (1981: 65). Peters stresses the social situation in which illness occurs and hence the need to appreciate the social context to understand the function of the shaman.

What I am concerned to show in this book (often ignored in more sociological or psychological approaches) is the complexity of the mental framework within which illness and possession occur and to emphasize their own theories about the nature of the person, relations with the world and what they themselves think and believe about such states and how rituals work. The rituals are not just standardized ways of 'controlling the unknown', making sense to the patient in their explanatory model of illness[18].The rituals are not just to be understood literally as feeding hungry ancestors to bring about desired events, working because they have in the past. Rituals for Lohorung are known to work if, and only if, they are performed correctly. Desjarlais argues that rituals heal through a process of changing how a body feels by altering what it feels. The 'cacophony of music, taste, sight, touch, and kinesthesia activates the senses' and wake up a 'spiritless body' (1992: 206) so that soul–calling rites can 'negate a sensibility bound by loss, fatigue, and listlessness and create a new one of vitality, presence and attentiveness' (1996: 208). Though in agreement that some healing rituals heal in this way, I think Desjarlais overstates the sensory element in Himalayan ritual. What is striking in Lohorung rituals (and others witnessed in Nepal) is the complete absorption of the practitioner in the performance in contrast to the relaxed and informal attitude of those attending, including the patient, whose attention is often only partially involved in the performance. What is important is that the practitioner performs *correctly* – the efficacy of the rite depends upon it, in much the same way that we require the *right* medication, even if a placebo, to achieve a cure. It is precisely the cognitive knowledge that the rite is being correctly performed that brings relief, not only some sensorial empowerment or '*feeling* of rejuvenation' though this may come too. For Lohorung what the rite achieves is a recreation of reality – it is an ideological shift [19].

The main problem with the sociological approach to possession illness as stressed by Lewis (1971) is that it undervalues the fabric of meanings in terms of which people interpret their experiences and manage their actions. This book looks at how notions of self, person, and emotions, which have some biological basis, are also constructed by people's own understandings, their own concepts and discourse, their statements about the nature of the person and how to relate to the social world. Indigenous psychological notions can be used to explore and analyse cultural patterns and symbolic structures. As I want to show in this book they can also be used to make sense of two other distinct domains, that of social institutions, marriage, rites, socialization and social life, and secondly, the domain of individual motivation, individual psychology, and experience.

The examples given here of relations between Lohorung and the superhuman beings can only offer a descriptive impression of the kind of experiences and situations I was trying to understand while among the Lohorung. Because of my emphasis on the view that humans are in general self–constituting, I resisted labelling and fixing their experiences in anthropological categories such as 'religion', 'animism', or 'ancestor cult'.[20] None of them fitted my ethnographic experience. Lohorung themselves never laid out their beliefs in any kind of systematic theory, they had no authoritative book or formal institution apart from ritual. The key frame of reference they used was in the mythical stories about the Original Beings which we see in Chapter Five and the rituals which we'll see in Chapter Four.

Inevitably, confusion and ignorance pervaded early fieldwork. The beings we see Chapter Four, however, provided the first particularly powerful set of images to explain all kinds of experiences, relationships, 'illnesses' as well as traditions and institutions. I began to see that Lohorung sense of order, their sense of well–being, as well as the chaos and complexity of the world, were to a large extent experienced and described through talk about ancestors and spiritual beings.

Notes

1. A term used by Evans–Pritchard (1956: vi) with reference to the words *mangu* for the Azande and *kwoth* for the Nuer.
2. Young and Goulet's edited book (1994) addresses the complexities of interpretation in the context of 'extraordinary experiences' such as powerful dreams, visions or the experience of other realities. In their conclusion they argue in favour of 'temporarily suspending disbelief, and attempt to take the accounts of experiences and explanations of our informants as seriously as possible' (ibid: 329). This does not necessarily mean accepting fully informants' explanations – of the source and meaning of experiences – for ones own experiences. Anthropologists aren't always consistent about how far to accept others' realities. Spiro has at times accepted the 'participants' point of view: 'The most obvious basis for religious behaviour is the one which any religious actor tells us about when we ask him – and, unlike some anthropologists, I believe him' (1966: 112). However, he is also psychologically–minded enough to reduce the ideas of gods, witches, spirits, and ghosts as being similar to dream images 'stimuli originating in the inner world are taken as objects and events in the outer world' (1982: 52). In a more extreme fashion Leach argued, 'nats' are 'nothing more' than a way of describing social relationships (1965: 182). But if spirits and the belief in them are no more than 'rationalizations' 'reifications' or 'expressions' of social phenomena, it's hard to comprehend the force of their role in social life.
3. Holmberg talks about an 'ethos of exchange' also among the Tamang, which 'shapes not only marriage but most casual and formal sociality including eating drinking, smoking, laboring, conversing, singing, and communicating among humans – siblings, spouses, affines, clan–mates, and others – and between humans and divinities and harmful agents' (1989: 53). It is an ethos which Lohorung recognize as being shared by some groups such as other Rai, Limbu as well as Tamang and Gurung but not by Newars and Chetri Bāhun whom they see as less giving, 'tight–fisted', grasping with their teeth under their armpits. Generosity is socially valued.
4. As Eagleton says 'food is just as much materialised emotion as a love lyric though both can be a substitute for the genuine article' (1998: 206).
5. See Helman's chapter on Pain and Culture (1990: 179–193) which underlines the importance of seeing the cultural context of pain.
6. For a discussion of the problems of 'cause' in interpreting apparently odd and apparently causal statements see Campbell (1989: 61–93)
7. Macdonald (1962) gives an account of *jhäkri* in Nepal; the edited collection of essays by Hitchcock and Jones (1976) points to the diversity and the similarities between officiants in Nepal and to some of the problems of definition; for Gurung officiants see Pignéde 1966; for Tamang specialists see Höfer 1981, Peters 1981, and Holmberg 1989.
8. The ability to see the interrelatedness of the universe in altered states of consciousness is said by modern Western shamans, such as Michael Harner, to be a universal human potential. In their conceptualization all things have a 'life–force', often described as an energy emanating from them and sometimes called an 'aura', which can be 'seen' and felt by those sensitive to vibrations. The Western scientific attitude has encouraged us to classify different states of consciousness into 'real' and 'unreal'. Dreaming and imagination are 'unreal'– ghosts and spirits are 'in the mind'. Western shamans and Pagans argue that it is only because we believe there is only one reality that there is. For descriptions of modern western shamanism see for example, Harner 1982, Doore (ed) 1988, Nicholson (ed) 1987, McLellan 1995, Lindquist 1997, or Tucker 1992.

9. See Allen (1973) on Thulung Rai journeys and Desjarlais (1989) in which the healing geography of Nepali shamans in Yolmo is described.
10. I do not wish here to enter the debate about the differences between spirit possession and shamanism. In my view the distinction has been exaggerated by the Western 'construction' of shamanism by Eliade 1964. The problem of how to approach the whole complex has a large literature. Is it a system for regulating psychological and social tensions (Shirokogoroff 1935), the origin of all religion (Eliade [1951]), a way of transcending social insecurities (Lewis 1971), a form of religious sensibility and practice (Vitebsky 1995), a quality rather than a role or office (Campbell 1989), a way of being in the world, and a type of knowledge (Humphrey1996)), a system of symbolic exchange between humans and the natural spirit world (Hamayon 1990), shamans as makers of worlds (Overing 1990), or shamans as the esteemed and despised sources of real power and knowledge (Taussig 1987)? Some of the best discussions on shamanism can be found in Humphrey 1996; Lambek 1981, Blacker [1975]1986; Hultkrantz 1978; Noll 1988, Yensen 1995; Peters and Price–Williams 1980; Vitebsky 1995;. Samuel 1993. For an understanding of the important relationship between the genre of ritual and theatre, and shamanism as performance see Schechner and Appel (eds) 1990, and Laderman, C. and Roseman M.(eds)1996.
11. Macdonald 1962 describes in detail the kind of costume worn by Nepali *jhankri*, very similar to that worn by Lohorung *mangpa* and *mangmani*. See also Allen 1976 for his description of Thulung Rai shamanism.
12. There is little agreement as to whether ecstatic and trance states are synonymous, describing a state of consciousness in which non–ordinary reality is accessed – or whether ecstasy is a separate state using trance methods. I would agree with Hultkrantz (1988) that trance is simply the medical term for the state, described in more mystical or theological language as ecstasy, which opens the way to the 'other' reality. Lewis (1971) and Eliade (1964) see them as synonymous.
13. Chapter Seven looks in detail at this inter–relatedness and the concept of self and personhood.
14. Lewis' theory is supported by several uthors arguing that possession is a means to gaining more powerful authority (see Bourguignon 1973, Firth 1964, 1996), Gomm (1975), Harris (1958), Messing (1959). They suggest possession is a safe outlet for protesting 'status deprivation' among women. In contrast, Boddy (1989) and Nourse (1995) suggest that Lewis' analysis overemphasises intentionality in women and underestimates the local power of women as well as the factuality of spirits.
15 The notion of women's status in Nepal is a complex issue involving a multiplicity of factors which have been discussed elsewhere (see Acharya and Bennett 1981 and Hardman n.d.).
16 The word *sammang* refers not just to the ancestors but also to the rituals performed for them.
17. This appreciation of the physical and emotional content of illness applies to other Rai and other tribes in Nepal. For example, Desjarlais (1992) describes illness among the Yolmo Sherpa. Though the "local rationality" may fail to note the link between illness and emotional distress, he says that `emotional tensions often seem to relate to incidents of "soul loss", for culturally shaped sentiments of grief, sadness, anxiety and despair tend to lie at the causal root of this dysphoric illness' (1992:22). Desjarlais shows how shamanic performance can bring about a change in the senses and emotions of the patient.
18. See Cecil Helman 1994: 239, 140.
19. Of relevance here too is Lévi–Strauss's essay on symbolic healing in South America in which he demonstrates the effectiveness of treatment through the use of images (1968: 197ff).
20. See Geertz 1993: 88, 122 on the unsatisfactory nature of these categories.

4

The Superhuman World and Knowledge and Illness

The Lohorung idea which lies at the core of their rituals and their understanding of themselves, and their environment, is the notion that every human being is closely bound to the natural world and to a world of spiritual beings. A dynamic and pervasive world of ancestors and spirits of the dead co–exists along with the world of the living. As we have begun to see, explanations of events, of cultural and social phenomena, of mental and physical states are commonly expressed in terms of superhuman beings or the natural world associated with them.

What the examples in Chapter Three cannot convey is the frequency with which Lohorung relate to the superhuman world and the complexity of the relations. The complexity of their experience of the superhuman is similar to that of the Tibetan of pre–Buddhist Tibet as described by Tucci:

> The entire existence of the Tibetan, his knowledge and desires, his feeling and thinking, is suffused and coloured by his experience of the sacred. His folk religion is not restricted to myth, to liturgy, or to a reverent attitude towards the numina . . .; it is also the living interplay of traditions of cosmogony and cosmology, genealogical legends of particular groups and families, rituals of magic and atonement, proverbial folk wisdom . . . . It is in short, an all–embracing heritage of the centuries (1970: 171).

The world of all Lohorung Rai is similarly affected by superhuman beings. The superhuman beings are as pervasive.

Classifying a Complex Pantheon

In describing the Lohorung pantheon I have restricted myself to what Lohorung themselves see as 'indigenous' and 'tribal', and have excluded Hindu deities and ideas because they are not essential to Lohorung constructions of self and emotion.[1] Any attempt to describe their classification has dangers and particularly in portraying coherence and clarity where they do not exist. Attempts to systematize become a Procrustean effort. Categories often had vague boundaries; they overlapped, and sometimes it was impossible to identify the one feature which defines a class in traditional Western philosophical terms. Moreover, inconsistencies were common, as others have found trying to identify classes of superhuman beings in neighbouring Rai groups.[2] Our own conceptions tend to be far more rigid and concrete than Lohorung ones and those of other Rai. So in the following description I shall mainly use the classificatory categories Lohorung themselves use.

The one Western term I use freely, 'superhuman beings', I chose with care, avoiding 'the supernatural' or 'the dead',[3] The 'supernatural'[4] implies that the beings are above nature, whereas for Lohorung these beings are very much part of the natural world. At one time the world of nature, the world of humans, and the world of the superhumans were united and part of nature. Human persons and tigers, bamboo and creepers and many other phenomena in their world are, as we shall see, ontologically related to them. Though spiritual beings are above human beings in the sense that they are more powerful, they are not above nature; they are not thought of as agencies above the forces of something separate called 'nature'. I've also avoided the word 'the dead' because it ignores the different Lohorung attitude to death and the dead. As we've seen, some Lohorung 'dead' are in some ways 'living' as much as human beings, coexisting on a different plane and in different places, but marrying and going on journeys, becoming hungry, angry and jealous, like living humans. Some of the superhuman beings are thought to have just disappeared and never properly died. Moreover, Lohorung have a word for 'dead people' – *sikhempa yapmichi*, or *singkripa* – to refer to those who have recently died. Unlike our dead those of the Lohorung continue to play a very important and active role in the human world. I also avoided the complications of the preconceptions and assumptions attached to words like 'god'or 'God', 'ghost', 'deity', 'divinity'. Instead I mainly use Lohorung category terms which will gradually take on their own more subtle meanings.

The term 'superhuman beings'[5] adequately conveys the Lohorung pantheon of beings, which includes a wide spectrum of colourful characters, with many human attributes, some considered to be hierarchically higher in the scale of beings than humans, and all, though ontologically related, possessing greater powers and capacities. They have two main advantages over human beings. First, those who wish to interact with human beings are not restricted by time or space. They are able to relate to different humans at what, to human beings, seem like the same time and in totally different places. For Lohorung their powers can be spread over a wide area – far wider than possible in any human interaction. At times this leads to great fear in the villages. The second advantage is that superhuman beings can see human beings whereas in general humans cannot see them. The invisible nature of the superhuman beings was explained to me in the following way:

At one time the living and the dead could see each other; and they also used to intermarry. One day one of the *hingkrikpa* (living species), who were very tall, insulted his wife and her relatives, the *singkrikpa* (having-died species), who were much smaller. He had been hunting with his wife's brothers. At the end of the day they shared out their game and all he was given by his brothers-in-law was the leg of a small bird. He was so angry when he arrived home, he threw the leg at his small wife. 'Here, look what kind of game your brothers catch!' 'Aiah!' cried his wife in pain when the leg hit her. *Hingkrikpa* was surprised the leg was strong enough to hurt her. His wife complained to her brothers. They were so angry they said,'Don't go back' This time the *singkrikpa* were not easily pacified, as they often were. Among themselves they said there should be no more marriages with the *hingkrikpa* and to make certain, they wanted to put up a barrier. They tried to separate themselves with a black cloth. They couldn't see any of what was going on. In the end, they covered themselves with a thin white cloth. Ever since, the ethereal veil has wafted between the humans and the superhuman beings: superhuman beings have become immaterial and invisible to humans, whilst the humans have remained both visible and material for the superhuman beings.

In a complex relationship of trust, anger, jealousy, and fundamental communion, it is the superhuman beings called *sammang* and *chap* who provide Lohorung with a key framework for understanding themselves, their emotions and their experiences. In this chapter I describe the chief characters articulating this frame of reference. As I came to understand it, any description of sammang has to focus on relationships, since the eruption of *sammang* anger is triggered by such events as the interruption, discontinuity, or violation of reciprocal relations between the living and the dead. What the *sammang* communicate through their anger (and the pain, misfortune, and accidents that are experienced) is their fundamental and inflexible commitment to traditional values as established by the original founders. As we shall see, each ancestor is committed to a particular area of traditional life, sometimes characterized by the way he or she died. Certainly the form of his or her death influences the way the ancestor relates to the living. The stories and the rituals performed for each *sammang* construct powerful 'images', symbols of this frame of reference, and I suggest it is through these well–established 'images' or symbols that personal experiences of sammang or chap are sensed, remembered, and given order. But also that the dynamics of illness among the Lohorung, whereby there is a changing focus on one ancestor rather than another, is built up through these 'images'.

As we meet the ancestors by name and character, their stories, and the ways in which they relate to human beings, we shall also see how from different perspectives they are thought to affect the consciousness, body, and everyday life of Lohorung. Images of *sammang* both help to create particular views of physical and mental states and are created by such experiences and the narration of them.

Sammang

The relationship with *sammang* is so interwoven into Lohorung traditional life that one might say it is the skeleton articulating Lohorung society. Such is the depth of this relationship that the few Lohorung, like Prem, who are known to have become skeptical about the *sammang*, were all soon drawn back into the traditional way of looking at their experiences when they encountered some serious illness or misfortune in their lives. I was told the story about a son of a *yatangpa* who tried testing out the efficacy of ancestral powers at the annual rite for all *sammang* called *iksammang*. He wanted to stop relating and, although his wife had made everything ready for him, instead of going to his field he started preparing the ritual in the back yard. Questioned by his wife on his odd behaviour he said, 'if they're real they'll come here just as well as to the field', and he sacrificed the chicken in the yard. That day in his rice field there was a big landslide.

Writers on the Limbu, another Kiranti tribe who share the term *sammang*, have introduced the notion of divinity, gods and even the Judaeo-Christian 'God' in their translations. The first to do so was Iman Sing Chemjong, himself a Limbu, who then adopted Christianity. For him, there was one *sammang* he translated as 'God, who is Omnipotent, Supreme and Eternal' (1967: 23). He considered one *sammang* 'to be the Supreme and the most powerful spirit of knowledge and wisdom . . . *Ningwaphuma*' and when the same spirit comes down to earth 'people regard him as their grandmother and call her *Yuma Sammang*' and it is 'He, who created the rest of spirits and other powers of fire, wind and water' (ibid: 23). The other *sammang* he described as the Good or first-class spirits and the bad or second-class spirits. According to Chemjong, the God *Ningwaphuma* loved human beings so much that he sent other good spirits to help them in their daily work. 'He sent *Heem Sammang*, a good spirit to look after the prosperity of the house of mankind; *Thoklung Sammang* to look after the health of mankind; *Nehangma Sammang* to give good energy and ambition to mankind; *Theba Sammang* to guide mankind at times of war; *Pung Sammang* to look after the good production of the field'. For him the word *Sammang* means 'the spirit of god'. 'The second class spirit is the evil spirit which is less powerful than the good spirit of the God. The head of the evil spirits is called the *Tamphung Sammang* which means the spirit God of forest.' (ibid: 22–3).

Philippe Sagant, also writing about the Limbu, describes all the *sammang* as 'divinité', with the land of the dead dominated by *Theba sam*, and *Yuma*, the most important as 'dieu céleste créateur' (1969: 107). The *sammang* have been referred to as the 'high god' of the Limbu, as their 'gods and goddesses' (R. and S. Jones 1976: 20); *Tamphungma Sammang* has been described as a 'spirit' (Jones, R. 1976: 33). Almost all the descriptions of what Jones calls the 'supernatural world' follow Chemjong and his translation of *sammang* as 'god' or 'deity' (1976b: 40–2). Höfer (1981) writing on the Tamang, who believe in *mang*, notes that the Tamang *mang* has no equivalent in the Tibetan language, but that it is 'etymologically related to Limbu *mang*, "*deutā*", "divine spirit" (Chemjong 1961: 205), Lepcha *mung*, "devil", "bhut" (Chemjong 1967: 259) and Gurung *moh* or *mxo*, "esprit", "ghost" (Höfer,1981: 23). Holmberg translates the Tamang term *mhang-mhung* as 'general term for evil spirit' (1989: n94, 240). In contrast, for another Rai group – the Mewahang – *mang* is closer to Lohorung *sammang*: 'all *mang* are ancestors, the term reflects the power of ancestral beings, who are divine and always exert a strong influence on the well–being of the living' (Gaenszle 1993: 214).

My own understanding from Lohorung is that, for them, most of the *sammang* are spirits of powerful ancestors – either their own or those of tribes with whom they were early on in contact; mostly beings from the remote primeval past, from the time when civilization (p*e-lam* or *mundum*) was being created and the strength of the natural order of the world prevailed. As we've already seen, at that time human beings had abilities they later lost, such as communicating with trees, rocks, animals, or breaking a stone with a feather. The 'shaman' (*mangpa*) at that time had wonderful magic and the spirits of those ancestors became clever *sammang*. All the *sammang*, however, are powerful coming as they do from the original order of things. Although there are *sammang* that affect the Lohorung as a whole, there are others that are localized. The *sammang* in Num village, for example, have slightly different identities from those in the villages of Pangma, Heluwa, and Angla. They all, however, give the same impression of being the spirits of worshipful ancestors rather than 'gods'. As a way of understanding the Lohorung notion of *sammang*, Chemjong's Christian gloss as 'spirit of god' with the idea of one God (also a *sammang*) behind it, is understandable given his conversion but not very helpful. It fits neither the Lohorung attitude to the *sammang* nor the characteristics attributed to them. Although perhaps the word could be glossed as 'gods', without any connection to any other superior God, or god, with its simple sense of 'What is worshipped by sacrifice; superhuman person, worshipped as having powers over nature and human fortunes' (OED), it is still not very satisfactory. As I have explained, the *sammang* do not simply have power over nature: they are part of it and own it.

Lohorung use the Nepali term for 'gods', *deutā*, or *dewa* to describe superhuman beings different from *sammang*. On occasions, to confuse matters, they may also use *deutä* to refer to the *sammang* – particularly if they are talking to non–Kiranti, simply to express the significance of their *sammang* to those for whom *deutā* is the most important category of superhuman being. For Lohorung themselves, however, the various *sammang* are more important and even more powerful than *deutā*. As one woman put it, 'In the face of the *sammang* the gods, *deutā*, are afraid'.

For us, the term 'gods' carries the sense of a non–mortal power, and not the notion that the beings were themselves once mortal and still share many of the characteristics of their mortal descendants.[6] *Sammang* are in many ways very human. Like human beings, they have *niwa* (mind, consciousness), and *saya* (sensitive link with protective ancestor/gods) which is affected like our 'hurt pride' or 'loss of face'; they manifest emotions of jealousy, fear, anger; they become hungry, hot and cold, excited, proud; they can be clever, stupid, childlike, impatient, crafty, quick to understand, or bored. Lohorung see them as being like children and treat them in part as needing the same discipline and direction, and yet recognize too the need to give them the respect that their greater age requires. *Sammang* are known to be sensitive to insult and disrespect which can lead to their 'hurt *niwa*', or 'lowered *saya*' and to a reaction causing disorder or misfortune in a family or community. The idea of the *sammang* as being closer to our 'ancestors' or 'ancestral heroes' than 'gods' is also emphasized by the Lohorung attitude that particular *sammang* 'belong' to particular clans or clan-groups or the tribe as a whole, even another tribe, so long as it is a Kirānti tribe; some are borrowed from the Limbu (*subba subbeni* for example), or from the Khambu Rai to the West (such as *ge'ereng me'ereng*); some are seen as relating to the whole Kirānti as the founders of Rai culture, from whom Lohorung see themselves as being descended.

The Christian concept of God includes attributes of omnipotence and of infinite goodness; God is almighty, omniscient, and infinitely benevolent. No Lohorung *sammang* are like this. There is no one *sammang* that is consistently more powerful than the rest. The power shifts depending on the relationships between the *sammang*, and between the *sammang* and the human beings. While I was there it was being said that the *cbawatangma sammang*, 'the forest *sammang*' had recently become very powerful whereas previously the *pappamamma'chi* had always been dominant. None of the *sammang* are simply benevolent: some of them will bring good fortune and general prosperity or long life to a household and its members, but it is always and only in return for special treatment. Lohorung talk of them as being 'eaters' (*cha'khuba*). Anyone who happens to be in their territory, whether Kirānti, Tamang or Hindu can be afflicted by them and Bahun and Chetri greatly fear them. Thus the term 'divinity' with its connotations of no negative attributes seems inappropriate.

Given their lack of common features, however, it's hard to generalize about *sammang*. Some are most obviously 'ancestors'; others have attributed to them so many capacities and noteworthy acts they seem more like 'heroes'. A closer look at each of the *sammang* and their relations with human beings will make clearer their significance in Lohorung lives and in particular in their explanation of events and human behaviour, and the Lohorung's understanding of how people act and react, and their idea of what is healthy and unhealthy.

Pappamamma'chi – The Guardian Grandparents

Pappamamma means 'grandfather-grandmother' (*chi* denotes plural). They are *sammang* and include all Lohorung's nearest and remotest ancestors – at least, all those who have died natural 'good' deaths. As the repositories of traditional wisdom, they

FIG 5 Shrine for *Pappama'chi*.

deserve even more respect than the wise and aged members of the living community whose qualities they share. They include the first powerful chiefs or kings, known as *hang*: *Paruhang*, for example, the very first, considered with his wife *Nayuma* (also called *Narima*) to be the Lohorung equivalents of *Siva* and *Pārvati*. He is thought of as having the same powers as *Siva* to destroy and to create, though there are also stories about *Paruhang*'s attempts to create people and the world, in which he keeps making mistakes. First of all he made people out of gold, but found they couldn't speak: only when he tried with ash and chicken droppings did they talk.

Paruhang is the Lohorung who first performed certain actions, found they made him strong, and thereby established them as 'custom'. One old man talked about *Paruhang* as follows:

> At his marriage *Paruhang* did it like that, he raised his *saya* first of all, to make him strong. So that's how we perform the action now as we plant the waiphoo tree. He gave us the words, so now at the house we call for his strength and use his words, saying to the groom, 'you oh, *Paruhang*, that's you!' It's *Paruhang*'s talk that we speak at the marriage. We talk the *pe-lam*, the *mundhum* (the story way). The Bāhun and Chetri way is different – not the story, song way. We go the story way because *Paruhang*, the youngest, did it that way. *Paruhang* was our first king. The day of the wedding we must do it the right way. We call the kings. The king and the *hanglisa* (Sister's son, Mother's Brother's son) are one, that's

> why we call him *hanglisa* – our own *hang* (king) now. The king, *hanglisa*, is needed at the wedding. It was so at first, so also now. We must make him like *Paruhang*. To invoke *Paruhang* we must kill a pig and we must do the *sikla* offering. Before that we should not drink any water. 'king respect, father respect, mother respect' it is called. That is the way of us ten Lohorung. Our king at first was *Paruhang*.

All the characters of the myths and stories of the *pe-lam* (or *mundhum*), some of which are included in Chapter Five, the 'culture heroes' as they might be called, are considered to be *pappamamma'chi*. The most important *pappamamma'chi* are called 'kings' (*hang*). Some of the earliest *hang* are the animals, who were man's brothers before divisions in nature occurred. *Tumnahang* is Bear, *Paknahang* is Tiger, while Man at the time was *Pomnakhang*, and Woman *Narinihang*. Other *hang* included in the *pappamamma* category are closely linked to specific clans, such as *Maruhang* to the *Biksik*, *Mirihang* to the *Dekhim*, *Sirihang* to the *Deksen*.

The *pappamamma'chi* guard and reign over a place called *yepmalitham hamalitham*, also called *chaptempa*, which is situated in the West. This world of the dead includes the sun and moon, explaining why those *pappamamma'chi* who are the culture heroes of the Lohorung myths are referred to as the 'sun and moon people' (*namnungla'chi*) and why Lohorung, as well as other Rai and Limbu people, carve a sun and moon into the resting places they build on paths in memory of a dead relative. It is the place to which those who die a natural death go, and forbidden to those whose form of death makes them unacceptable to the *pappamamma'chi*, who refuse them entry.

In what Lohorung call the 'ascending' season from February to August *pappamamma'chi* stay in their villages, but in the 'descending' season from August to February they travel South. During the month of *sāun* (mid–July to mid–August) no *sammang* ritual takes place, for the Lohorung say that the ancestors are too busy travelling with their own affairs to take notice of them and the rites would be ineffective. This is also the time Lohorung themselves are journeying to buy or barter salt and other provisions for the year. Nevertheless, as some Lohorung pointed out, you have to be particularly careful at this time since it is mostly when *sammang* travel North and South that they are hurt or become offended: 'we cannot see them, we mistakenly tread on them, bump into them, sometimes even spit on them or drop ash on them; when they see we are not doing things the way we should traditionally they are jealous or angry. Although they are old, they are more like children and are upset by very little things'.

Some of the *pappamamma'chi* are now very old, going back to the very first people and are portrayed in images which have them covered with moss and lichen, but still bearing the signs of their 'good death', the silver thong or white cloth to hold up their chin, and the money (*tikā* N) on the forehead. They have very long hair and also hair growing all over their body. The oldest ones, who lived in the forest before houses, or spinning and weaving had been established, are simply covered with moss and bodyhair. Their appearance is so frightening that children under ten are forbidden to attend any *pappamamma* ritual in case they catch sight of one and are frightened into unconsciousness from the flight of of *lawa* ('soul loss').

Of all the *sammang*, *pappamamma'chi* are capable of the worst anger. There is a special word to describe their anger, that is only applied to them and to young children. The word is *yiktikheda* (or *yikbokheda*, indicating its association with the stomach, *bok*). It is a verb similar to that for 'he has become angry' – *sintikheda*. Lohorung informants explained it to me as being 'the kind of anger that is very hard to counteract'. In this emotional state a child or *sammang* is unhappy and impatient as well as angry, displaying what we might call general discontent and irritability. 'They cry as well as shout.' Children have to be plied with something sweet or given the breast, while the *pappamamma*'chi have to be pampered with ritual offerings to distract them from their mood or the idea they have become locked into. In this mood, *papamamma'chi* sometimes team up with another *sammang* and work in league against a household or one of its members. Lohorung describe this as *sammang'chi tokchoktikheda'chi* (lit. 'intestines extended together') which they say 'joins their intestines to make one' (*eko thok lechi*). This image was conveyed by interlocking two fore–fingers together. When this happens it's known to be very difficult to appease either of the ancestors – as difficult as trying to separate two close friends or a man and wife who have joined together in a similarly close, intricate relationship (also described by Lohorung as *tokchoktikheda*). In this relationship, whatever one *sammang* does, the other *sammang* does too. They go everywhere and do everything together. Lohorung see such mutuality as the sign of real friendship and in human relationships its 'good' qualities are recognised but also the dangers, since if one died the other would die too, having become as one. Lohorung insist they must always try to separate the two. Such intimacy is too dangerous. When a household develops such a relationship with the *pappamamma'chi* or some other *sammang*, however, the bond cannot be broken. The relationship has to persist and the household must continue with its commitments to serve the particular *sammang* in the way it has agreed. If there's any hint of change it's said the anger of the *sammang* is felt by human beings in extreme ways. Misfortunes or severe illness are sometimes explained as the anger of a *sammang* whose close relationship has not been maintained. Such relationships never occur between one *sammang* and one individual, even though the ancestors may only display their anger by relating to only one person in the household. For the Lohorung it is households that relate to the ancestors, not individuals. I shall return to this point later.

Pappamamma'chi are considered to be the repositories of Lohorung lore and wisdom. What angers them most is the overt transgression of traditions, particularly those concerning ritual. Acute pain all over the body, but particularly in the stomach and head, is mostly experienced as *pappamamma'chi* angered by careless behaviour of human beings. *Kāhili*'s illness described in Chapter Three was a typical indication that the relationship with *pappamamma'chi* was not harmonious. *Pappamamma'chi* are sensed in a big way, not by some small pain. The semantic domain connected to them refers to morality – the 'anger' a response to seeing someone adopting new traditions such as smoking and drinking at the same time, or eating and drinking home–brewed beer at the same time. Older Lohorung insist these activities should be kept separate or they fight one another in the body, like people of different kinds fight. Though smoking, eating, and drinking *should* be separate – the problem is that nowadays people like mixing them together. Ignoring old traditions, like these, or adopting new ways, such as new fashions in clothing, can make *pappamamma'chi* very angry. If someone's mind (*niwa*) goes strange, as if 'mad', if someone begins to walk and talk strangely, it could be that the relationship with *pappamamma'chi* has gone seriously wrong. However, interfering with the workings of *niwa* is usually an indication of the anger of some other *sammang*. *Pappamamma'chi* are more like watchdogs over Lohorung behaviour, demanding a respectful *niwa* (*hangmale*) and that traditions are esteemed. *Pappamamma'chi* might well be called the Lohorung equivalent to the super-ego.

Deviation from traditional ways can become costly: the ritual to appease *pappamamma'chi* usually requires a large pig. If the mood-swing in *pappamamma'chi* has been misjudged and the pig is not big enough, their anger (usually of the *sintikheda* kind) increases very quickly, much like a child's tantrum, and the person in pain suffers an increase in pain to a corresponding degree. *Pappamamma'chi* even check the size of the pig, measuring it carefully with a piece of cloth! In spite of their volatile 'anger', *pappamamma'chi* are also characterized as being pliable and easily persuaded (*okningbak*). If they become 'angry' very quickly, they are also as quickly appeased. The drama and emotional displays are put down to strong desires combined with diminishing abilities, acompanying the loss of youthful and powerful *niwa* (mind, memory). In their indecisiveness and frustration it is said they become like children. The 'images' are vivid. If content with the offerings made to them, they cluster round the roof of the house with their weapons, men with hammers and *kukuri* knives and women with loom shuttles and sickles, brandishing them in the air, dancing and shouting to all the evil spirits lurking in every village to keep away and leave the house and its inhabitants in peace. If they are not satisfied, they congregate around the top of the ladder to the house and on the front verandah calling to other *sammang* to come and join them in their angry protest.

To avoid the 'jealousy' of other *sammang* when performing *pappamamma* rituals, Lohorung told me they also make offerings to the most 'jealous', to *ge'ereng me'ereng*, to *chawatangma*, *kuma*, and *yangli*. If they do not, these other *sammang* feel 'angry' and 'jealous', leading to yet more corresponding sickness and pain in human beings.

The relationship of Lohorung to *pappamamma'chi* is characterized by filial obligation and respect combined with compassion and firm manipulation. The following words (*sikhla*) spoken to them during rituals in which they are called to the house demonstrate well the attitude of the human beings to these ancestors:

> You dead grandmother, grandfather, maternal aunt, paternal aunt, elder brothers, younger brothers, elder sisters, younger sisters, all close relatives, from your place of origin rise and follow the sandy path, the desert path, the tree way, the stone way, along the windy way take a rest, protect your breath, do not wear yourselves out. Open your dreams, open your *lawa* and come to the vertical house pole . . . (long list of the parts of the house they should enter). . cross into the house, wash your feet and hands without embarrassment, don't be shy of the shrine, it is for you, we have called you. Now you have come, rest. If we have stepped over you without noticing, if we have stepped on you, even so don't let it hurt, do not be worried. Do not be angry. We offer you to drink and eat the spoils of the harvest toiled by the ten fingers of all your children and grandchildren. We offer you the new rice . . . (list of offerings). Come now, drink and eat to your satisfaction but this is not a general invitation. Come when we call you but not at any other time. If you come at other times the living will gossip about you. Did you know our troubles? Did you see our troubles? Do not let your niwa hurt, keep your *saya* an unending *saya*, give us strong *lawa*, give us long breath, give us strong *saya*. Keep away stomach pains, swellings, diarrhoea . . . (list of diseases), protect us from evil spirits. . (list of pan–Nepali spirits as well as Lohorung ones). Come, whatever we have offered, eat and drink. When you have finished, give up infatuation (for this place), wash your feet and hands and return to your place. Go and stay in your own place. Do not go astray.

FIG 6 Eat the Spoils of the Harvest.

As old grandparents, guardians of tradition but fading powers, *Pappamamma'chi* are addressed with a combination of command, cajolery, injunctions, and respect. The choice of offerings given to *pappamamma'chi*, as to other ancestors, convey this Lohorung respect and compassion as well as being coercive in maintaining the necessary measured relationship. They are coaxed to the house and also firmly told to return to their own place. Their *saya* must be raised and that of the household, thereby renewing the primordial link, and recreating primordial prosperity and the strength of the house. To please *pappamamma'chi* their shrine is built with sticks from a kind of chestnut tree called *waiphu* (*musure katuj* N *Castonopsis tribuloides*) – the wood used to build houses in the old days. When not available Lohorung use *chigaphu*, another kind of chestnut (*Castanopsis indica*). They make the shrine as if building a house, with four pillars and five, seven, or nine cross bars, the number Lohorung still use when building their own houses. The cross bars create a platform and on this they place pieces of the dark grey and white cloth, spun and woven by Lohorung women, representing the clothes traditionally worn by men and women. On the ground on a banana leaf are placed the offerings. The main item is the sacrificial pig, but the offerings must also include a hen and a cock, a minimum of seven eggs, two containers of beer, as many tongba (bamboo vessels filled with millet beer) as possible – but usually amounting to the number of participants. There must also be ginger, used for divination, and several leaf plates containing vegetables and chutneys. The *pappamamma'chi* are summoned to the shrine with a small bamboo whistle. In the most 'human' way, Lohorung offer what they themselves value most highly and like most to receive, namely, beer from a *tongba*, meat, poultry, eggs, some relishes and new clothes. These are customary treats that have never lost their appeal. Lohorung talk of being so 'close' to these ancestors that, until recently, the elders (*pasing'chi*) of each lineage could perform the ancestral cult without the help of the local officiant (*yatangpa*). Now, however, men are less well acquainted with the ritual language, some of them totally ignorant of the chants, and each household relies increasingly on the *yatangpa* to ensure their contacts with the *sammang* are carried out correctly. In any case, the other *sammang* are becoming increasingly clever and unpredictable; most people are now afraid to take on *Chawatangma* or any of the others, without the help of an expert.

Chawatangma – The Creative Old Woman of the Forest

Chawatangma is the most fickle and creative of all the *sammang*. She has over twenty names each indicating an area of her powers, an attribute or role, such as *bakhatangma*, owner/woman of the soil, *tapnamtangma*[7] owner/woman of the forest, *serepmotangma*, youngest one, *singtowatangma*, owner/woman of the trees, *lungtongtangma*, owner/woman of stones and rocks. As *khewama* she gave cotton to *mangpa* shaman; as *lilaoti*, *goanleni*, she is a village spirit, as *dewatangma* a mother goddess. Her proper name is *Yagangma* – but 'If we call her *Yagangma* she takes it as an insult but if we call her *mamma somnima* "grandmother *somnima*" [8] she is happy: it is her kin term. Only children who still enjoy eating soya beans with a millet leaf should be called by their proper name.' *Chawa* refers to the special springs, initially discovered and claimed by each clan when they first moved on to the territory in which it lies; 'our first watering place' as some Lohorung put it.[9] The name *Chawatangma*, indicating her ownership of the *chawa*, points to one of her greatest powers over human beings. Lohorung conceive of this ancestor as having direct access and control over the most valued place and resource of every clan, the waters of the *chawa* spring, which are thought to have special ritual powers.

Whereas *pappamamma'chi* ancestors rule over others in *yepmalitham hamalitham* (the land of the dead), *Chawatangma* is the 'owner' of most of the human world, the earth itself, and all that lives on or springs from it, the creatures, insects, plants, bamboos, fields, forests, springs, rivers, and villages. As *Somnima* she gave birth to all these and Man himself. Depending on her mood she lives in water, in the sky, in the jungle. She is referred to as the original creator of the earth, having taken over the task from her husband *Paruhang*, one of the *pappamamma* mentioned earlier, who was unable to do it. 'She is the creator of everything: she now creates radios and 'planes, those things you have, like watches, camera.' She can turn herself into a pig, a cat, many kinds of bird – almost any animal that suits her aim to tease, trick, and frighten human beings. At night, Lohorung blame *Chawatagma* when their bamboo torch is suddenly blown out, when the path is lost, or when boulders can be seen rolling down towards an unsuspecting traveller. If a buffalo blocks one's way, it is *Chawatangma*. She lurks by the side of the road at night in the form of a rat or mouse and throws dust or sand into people's eyes. In her trickster role she is known to bend down the top of a bamboo until it touches the ground, and as someone steps on it, she lets it free, sending her victim hurtling into the air as she runs away laughing. If angered she sends burning hot coals flying in all directions, like a chicken scattering earth when it scratches. Since she is known to corrupt or damage the *niwa* (mind, memory) of those who displease or neglect her, madness, anti–social behaviour, even the adoption of unusual modes of dress or mannerisms are attributed to *Chawatangma*. The *niwa* of children from age three to eight or nine are particularly vulnerable to the influence of this *sammang*. In her desire to play with them she lures them from their duties or play, out of the vllage and into the forest. She spoils their minds (*niwa*), turning them 'jungly' and as their memory for duties and relatives begins to decline, they start to wander off by themselves into the forest to follow her.

When *Chawatangma* takes the guise of *Yagangma*, or *mamma somnima*, the mother of the First Man and all the beings in the natural world, her breasts are so long they fall down her legs to her feet. When she walks she has to throw them over her shoulders to keep them out of her way. The advice to those who think they are being followed by her is to head for the nearest and steepest slope. While she struggles to keep her breasts from tripping her up, her victim can escape. It is interesting to note that Höfer mentions a similar spirit (*mang*) amongst the Tamang called 'Water/river Old Man Old Woman' about whom he writes,

> whoever comes into contact with the long emaciated breasts of the female Gemo is believed to lose his senses. If somebody feels persecuted by her, he can escape by running downhill, as her long breasts will hamper her in following him . . .Once captured, the victim – mostly a man who comes back from the fields after sunset – is dragged into a cave, and his limbs are severed from the trunk of his body. (1981:23).

Lohorung say *Chawatangma* can take on the identity of figures known by other groups by different names. The similarity of the Tamang and Lohorung story perhaps indicates that some of the numerous stories about *Chawatangma* are borrowed from other tribal groups and attributed to the eclectic *Chawatangma*. Though 'images' and descriptions of *Yagangma* abound, few admit to having seen her, except in the form of an old lady carrying a sickle and a basket slung from her head in the traditional manner, and a child tucked under her arm like a monkey. Some say she goes along cutting yams and because she's so small she can't run. Others say she's supposed to be treated like a mother and they threaten to beat those who don't treat her properly. Stories about her convey the image of her mischievousness, cleverness, inhospitality, and malevolence. They describe how she only stays one day in one place and can be in two places at once; how she cuts stomachs open, cleans the intestines and stitches them together again, people only knowing the pain afterwards. She gives rice from the back of her hand, an image conveying the antithesis of hospitable behaviour, and her milk is not sweet but like the water from washed rice. She typifies everything that is anti-social. *Chawatangma* is recognised as having once been the teacher of human witches (*boksi* N). They used to get their power from her and be very 'clever' with incantations and spells, whereas now they affect others 'with their eyes or thoughts' (*chohenha mitik'ma'chi*) or 'make stomachs swell inside' (*bok'homsi'mima'chi*). Human beings (even without the help of Chawatangma) are considered to have powerful emotions, like those of the *sammang*, which are not just internal feelings but can also enter or attach to someone else's body simply through their force and the power of sight, the 'evil eye' as we might say.

As owner of the forest and all trees, *Chawatangma* must be given offerings of beer before any tree is cut. 'Accidents' befall those woodcutters who omit them, splinters of wood flying into their faces and driving deep under their skin, or they lose control of the axe and chop off fingers and toes. Everyone becomes so clumsy no work can be done properly. Hunters also perform a rite to *tapnamtangma* ('forest woman') since she has powers to direct the animals of the forest in their favour, if she is pleased. For her, deer, wild boar, birds, all the animals of the forest are as tame as domestic animals. If hunters offer her nothing, she simply keeps animals hidden from their sight.

Chawatangma, creator of the order of the natural world, is also destroyer. She's amoral and greedy, jealous and often hungry. Known to reject traditional values and behaviour, she is the complete opposite of the *pappamamma'chi*, who represent moral perfection. Having created the natural world and the varieties of species, she now demands respect for her ownership and seeks revenge if it's not given. She's also isolated. Her only companion is *sikari*, the hunter spirit she is attached to, and from whom she must never be separated. When a ritual is performed for *Chawatangma*, offerings are always made to both of them. Unlike other *sammang*, *Chawatangma* can be persuaded (we might say 'bribed') to bring favours upon a household. In return for regular and lavish offerings it is said she will give the household plentiful crops of rice, maize, and millet, making them rich. Normally, her ritual is performed outside in an isolated bamboo grove or in the forest. When households start performing *Chawatangma* inside their homes on their own, without the aid of a ritual officiant, people become suspicious. As *sahili* said to me,'Those who want wealth do *Chawatangma* at home without *yatangpa* or *mangpa* and they don't let anyone'see the place or the things offered; they don't offer the meat from the ritual to anyone else – they keep it all for the family. They do it at midnight when everyone is asleep'. On another occasion a group were talking about Manjit whose grandparents used to do the secret rite to *chawatangma*:

> his grandmother used to do the rite in the store-room so noone would know. Every time they had new (batch of) beer, and also new rice, they offered to her before they ate or drank themselves. You may get much prosperity, but it's very dangerous. If she gets angry, she makes the fire spark, the house shake. The old *yumpang deren* (clan) woman in Gairi Pangma used to do it too. The family became very rich and always had so much to eat and drink. Then she died and the family stopped doing it. They didn't offer any more and now the family has dwindled to only one grandchild. All their land is under mortgage. His parents just gave it up, stopped doing it in the house and now they are dead and there is nothing but trouble in the house. Manjit's *niwa* (mind) doesn't work properly either.

Chawatangma attacks other parts of human beings apart from their *niwa* (mind). One of her most mischievous tricks is to entice away the *lawa* (essence of life, vital soul) of adults and children, putting her victims in danger of death unless the *lawa* is retrieved. Although *lawa*, as the 'soul' or 'essence of life' of a person, may wander from its owner of its own accord, as it does for example when a person dreams, no human can live without *lawa* for more than two or three weeks. Typically, *lawa* is lost through fright and this is what *Chawatangma* plays on. She frightens a child, the *lawa* leaves and she hides it under a tree, stone, at the top of a bamboo, in the depths of water or under the wing of a chicken. When she is simply 'angry' or hungry the human symptoms are sore eyes, nose, throat, or aching limbs and bellyache.

Irrespective of the well–being of the household, each one performs rituals to *Chawatangma* at the annual *iksammang* when the *saya* of all the ancestors are raised, thereby renewing village connections with the ancestors. Offerings are also made at least twice a year – one at the beginning of the 'rising season' (*thanglamba*) in about February, and one at the beginning of the 'descending season' (*yulamba*) in about August, as recognition of her importance and her powers to change people's lives for the better or worse.

While I was in Pangma one household was being talked about for suddenly performing a lot of *sammang* rituals and particularly *Chawatangma* rites. Their son had, it was said, 'lost his *niwa*'– that is, gone mad – lost his sense of right and wrong such that he had started eating his own faeces. Then he had lost his senses, his sight and hearing. Everyone suspected *Chawatangma*'s anger but there were those who suspected the number of rites were not just to cure the son but to do *Chawatangma* to get richer and 'to have forest meals', meaning just as an excuse to eat a lot of meat. Suspicion was aroused because the sick boy's father had done a ritual for *Chawatangma* on his own, without the priest, and this had to be to obtain good crops. The next day his son was in high fever and totally rigid, with his teeth clenched tight. When called, the priest told the man he had not done the ritual properly. With the help of the priest, the family then performed rituals for *Chawatangma* and for all the other *sammang*. 'They performed *Chawatangma* after *Chawatangma*'. If sickness or misfortune involves *Chawatangma* it is often said to be her anger, but Lohorung also talk about her acting maliciously, much like witches (*boksi* N) merely out of hunger, greed, or jealousy, and she will hold the household ransom until satisfied. However in this case, there was general disapproval and agreement that there was no real reason to perform so many rites to *Chawatangma* and that the household was just seeking excuses, as they had done in the past, to eat meat and obtain special favours from *Chawatangma* for better crops. Given the severity of the case people were also saying, 'If they truly worry and care about him, why don't they take him to hospital in Daran?' Western medicine is sometimes seen as being an important additional source of knowledge when they come to the limits of their own.

Khimpie and *Lataba* – House Ancestors; Woman of the Snakes, Lord of the Monkeys

Khimpie and *Lataba* are especially connected with the house (*khim*). In particular they protect the hearth and the household shrine, even though the shrine is not dedicated to them but to another couple who in turn protect household members. If anyone abuses the shrine, if non-Lohorung touch it, for example, it is said that that person will become deaf or blind. *Khimpie* and *Lataba*, the house ancestors, 'own' the house and are known to be 'jealous' and possessive about it, the possessions inside it, and the inhabitants. Non-Kiranti are discouraged (but not forbidden) from entering Lohorung houses for fear that they will offend *Khimpie* and *Lataba*. In the event of their anger, the corresponding symptoms include wounds, paralysis, or rheumatism in humans. The dangers of entering houses of another tribe, and possibly offending the house ancestors (*kul pitra*) is well known in East Nepal. Hence, the common occurrence of being invited to sit on the verandah.

When children are born they are considered to be outsiders until they have been introduced to the 'house *sammang*'. Boys are made known to *Lataba* in a ritual six days after birth and girls to *Khimpie* five days after birth, when all close members of the patriline are called to participate. This is seen as the most important rite in a person's life. It's the rite in which the child gains personhood – membership to a clan and the social world with all its rights and duties, and the beginnings of a moral and physical connection with the ancestors. The *saya* ('ancestral soul', 'ancestor within') is recognised and raised in this rite for the first time.[10] From this point onwards the infant is physically and mentally vulnerable to the morality (the code of conduct) and general health and success of the clan. He or she has become a 'person' which for Lohorung is inevitably linked to the fate of the clan.

Rites for these lineage ancestors can only be performed inside the house. Until recently, to prevent the hunger and anger of these ancestors the *Dekhim* clan had the responsibility of performing a ceremony for them once a year – this clan, because it is made up of the descendants of the youngest son and it is the youngest son who always inherits and lives in the parental 'big house' (*dya khim* from which their name arose). In the past the *Dekhim* offered an ox, but in about 1972 they finally had to accept the government ruling about not eating beef and began offering a large pig instead. The sacrificial pig stands on the ground by the stilts of the house under the hearth. A rope tied around the pig runs up into the main house and is threaded into a small bamboo house made for *Khimpie*. This made sense when I realized that *Khimpie* and *Lataba* live in the watery underworld and have to be led up out of the depths by the ritual chant.

As the Pangma story goes,

> *Lataba* and *Khimpie* were an old couple. *Lataba* was a hunter and one day he went off to catch some meat. He wandered and wandered and first reached Rambeni, a place in Limbuan. He went on and reached Change and then Ameni. He hunted on, killing and eating the game as he went and dropping the discarded bones on the ground until he reached Tumling Pokari, a pond in Limbuan near Milke. From there the game became more and more scarce as he went on to Umling Pokari, at that time a lake. There he was so tired he hung up his bow and arrow in a tree and leant over to take a drink. As he drank he fell into the lake and drowned. After many days had passed, his wife said to her mother-in-law, 'mother, your son has not returned home. I'm going to look for him'. Her mother-in-law replied, 'Why do you go on your own I'll go with you.' So they went searching everywhere; here and there they found the discarded bones of the hunter's kill, and then finally they came to Umling Pokari; they saw no more bones and they saw his bow and arrow

> hanging on the tree. 'My husband is here', said the woman, 'lo, so if he is here, so I will be here too', and she jumped into the lake to join her husband and drowned.

Some say that he did not drown. Realizing he was unable to kill any more game and being a clever shaman (*mangpa*) he climbed into a tree and became a monkey, eating what monkeys eat. Other versions describe *Khimpie* as being pulled into the lake by a big snake. The Pangma ritual corresponds with the version in which *Lataba* becomes a monkey, for in the chant *Khimpie* is addressed, among other things, as 'owner/woman of the snakes' *sipumatangma*), and *Lataba* as 'Lord of the monkeys', '*mangpa* of the tree–tops', as well as 'eldest *mangpa*' (tumbumangpa). Some informants said that *Khimpie* was also known as *sāp dew*[11] (Nepali for snake god) and *Lataba* as *bandar dew* (Nepali for monkey god). In agreement with the initial story above, both are now considered to live in the water.

Most Lohorung understand talk of people turning into animals, birds, or rocks without scepticism, particularly when those talked about are people from the remote past. Even in the recent past humans are thought to have had much greater powers than they are now endowed with. As we've seen, every human being is thought to be closely bound to the natural world and some closer than others; shamans (*mangpa*), like *Lataba*, are known to develop the ability to become attuned to various species. I heard many stories about very strong men, and about especially clever shamans. One story about a recently living relative who could turn into a tiger was met by most of the audience without disbelief. They were sure it could happen if you were a clever enough *baidangi* N, a term which Turner translates as 'physician' (1931: 459). The idea of *Khimpie* turning into a snake and *Lataba* into a monkey is thus merely in keeping with the exceptional abilities of beings from the remotest past. There is nothing totemic about it.

The connections of *Khimpie* and *Lataba* with the lake can be clearly seen in the ritual. Their recognized dislike of cold water is said to be what prompts the Lohorung to perform their ritual in a warm place near the fire of the house, which is cleaned with cowdung. In the lake the fish became their competitors and so it is said they delight in feeding on them. The Lohorung therefore give fish: a small kind of fish called *lichenga*; crabs (*khobek*); and small foul-smelling smoked and dried fish called *sidra*, brought especially from the South because they say the ancestors like the smell so very much! 'It is their favourite chutney.' In addition they give any other fish they can catch. No fish bought at market can be given, just as no eggs or chickens from market can be offered – only what is raised or caught by either the household or another tribal member. What raises the *saya* of *sammang* is their share of what belongs to the house. To *Lataba* and *Khimpie* the Lohorung also offer *kinnama* made of soya bean and ash from the fire and dried 'until they putrify like dead bodies', and many different kinds of leaves as well as the more usual meat, eggs, and beer. When a large *Khimpie* ritual is performed, the Lohorung make a small effigy of her and a house for her and hang it above the fire or near the hearth. To please her they hang around her neck a copy of the old kind of heavy necklace made of silver, which they make out of leaves so thick that their inside is likened to flesh, and put flowers in her 'hair', made of bamboo leaves. These are in part to show it is a woman. Lohorung find it hard to conceive that somebody wearing no jewellery, or flowers as a substitute, is really a woman. When they saw photographs of my mother, who was wearing no jewellery, it took time to convince them that it really was a woman. As with other *sammang* the Lohorung try to give them what they are known to like best to appease either their 'anger', their 'jealousy' or their 'hunger'. Only if they are content can the relationship with them be renewed and re-strengthened.

Informants agreed that the old couple suffer in the cold water: when they are feeling neglected, people develop sympathetic symptoms like knee-ache, backache, rheumatism, swellings, and loss of appetite. Occasionally, when *Khimpie* is feeling particularly angry, hungry, or jealous, human beings find they have a strong desire to run away to the jungle, to jump into rivers or off precipices. At times the changes in human beings involve their senses, such as losing their sight, or they lose the use of a limb or their mind goes strange. Paralysis of the knee, leg, or hand, or illnesses which come out in boils are also attributed to *Khimpie*. She is considered to be as dangerous as the *pappamamma sammang*, if she is not kept happy or given what she wants. Like them, she at times requires a pig to satisfy her. Whereas rituals for her husband *Lataba* can be done by the family alone without an officiant, this has never been the case with *Khimpie*. When these rituals are performed, the house is closed off from the outside world. Only close relatives of the patriline are invited to participate in the rite. Though married-out daughters are not invited to attend a *Khimpie* ritual, when *Khimpie* is enraged or insulted the area of repercussions can extend to all Lohorung as well as to women who have married non-Lohorung and their offspring up to twelve generations.

So far we have seen the relations between the Lohorung and three of the most important *sammang*. These three cover the three worlds that constitute the Lohorung cosmos. The *pappamamma sammang* reign over the upper world, *Khimpie* and *Lataba* rule the watery lower world, while *Chawatangma* resides over the world between with its forests and springs. Yet none are bound by these territorial associations since they are all known to travel, and anyway space and time have no meaning in the world of superhuman beings. Nevertheless, such associations give humans a sense of the order of the world. These are the main ancestors who helped create Lohorung society and continue to protect it and with whom relations must be maintained. Well–being and prosperity depend on the satisfaction and happiness of these ancestors, and these in turn depend on the effectiveness of rituals in raising their *saya*, the complex state tying natural and social processes to the Lohorung's own emotional states and development of the self.

Waya Warema – The 'Flower Way'; A Brother and Seven Deaf Sisters

Some say *Waya Warema* are not original Lohorung *sammang*, but came to them when they adopted the *yangkhrung* clan. *Waya* was the son of the family, *Warema* the name for the seven daughters. Everyone knows the story.

> The brother and all his sisters went for a picnic in the forest. While the brother went to play in the trees, the sisters stayed together by the stream to cook little breads. One sister poured oil into the large pot but the pot was so hot that the oil exploded in the pot and went up in flames. One by one the sisters tried to stop the fire, and in turn instead burnt alive. Their burnt bodies disappeared upwards with the smoke of the fire, up to the sun. Because they were taken so far away by the smoke and were also made deaf by the burning, the *yatang-pa* or shaman has to shout to them when performlng their ritual. The brother, who could not find them on his return to the cooking spot and innocent of the fact that they had all been burnt alive, went in search of them; he wandered from river to river trying to follow the trace of where they had gone by looking at the flowers, becoming weaker and weaker he eventually drowned.

Of all the *sammang rituals* this one is most like a re-enactment of the mythico–historical event, at least as performed by Pangma Lohorung. As I wrote after I had attended one *waya warema* rite,

> The atmosphere of the scene was like a re-living of the picnic in which the seven sisters and their brother died. I kept to the women. Everyone says it's dangerous for women and children. The men are the cooks for all *sammang* performed outside and the women gather to one side, making leaf plates or spinning to keep their hands busy. By the time we reached the clearing, the men had already started building the shrines. Two households, the families of close lineage brothers, were performing it together and there was the excitement of an outing, and the enjoyment of friends gathering together, but there was also a seriousness about the business. There was work to be done and it had to be done correctly; the shrines had to be finished and the meal cooked. There was some anxiety about my questions, particularly about all the flower names and I promised to keep them for later. Visually it was a perfect spot for the theatrical recreation, and I was told that all *Waya Warema* take place there. It was hidden, tucked away in the forest with a stream running through it, with a wide stage area and hillocks on two sides on which we women sat – yet still only a short distance from any of the four villages. The flowers had been collected earlier in the day. They are all flowers that, at any other time, cannot be picked since they belong to the ancestors and not to the human beings of the present. They were sorted into ten bundles, nine placed on the shrine, and one extra for the *mangmani* (female shaman) to hold. The 'flowers' (*bung*), most of which looked to me more like leaves and some of which never have flowers in our sense of the term, need further explanation for two separate reasons; first, the way in which they are central to the *Waya Warema* ritual and secondly, the way they relate to a complex metaphysical notion of the Lohorung. Looking at the first, 'flowers', bung, are for *waya warema* what particular trees or types of bamboo are

FIG 6 Shrine for *Waya Warema*.

> for other *sammang*. They are their 'weapon', as Lohorung told me, meaning also their source of strength. Every human being and every 'ancestor' (*sammang*) has some tool, which is for them the most useful and important thing they own, from which they gain both security and identity; it is something they are so familiar with they know all its uses, potentialities, and powers. Knowing more about it than others it gives them power and therefore protection. A woman's 'weapon', for example, is her weaving shuttle and sickle, a man's his kukri knife. They told me mine was my pen. For the 'house ancestor' *Khimpie* it is the largest kind of bamboo called *sakbaphu* (*Tama bāns* in Nepali), one of the most important components of house-building; for *Waya Warema* it is *bung*, all those 'flowers' which are chanted in pairs in the rite, and placed in bamboo containers on their shrine. One of the ways in which these *sammang* are angered is if these 'flowers' of the forest are picked.

The significance of these *bung* 'flowers' made more sense when I learned that they are closely connected to the Lohorung notion of the person. Lohorung conceive of each person as having a *lawa* (gloss for the moment as 'wandering soul'), relating them to and identifying them with particular flowers, which also 'have *lawa*' in the land of the ancestors. Some of these 'flowers' never die and it is with these that each person's *lawa* must identify. *Lawa*, however, tend to identify with and relate to the flowers with the same condition as their own human host. If their own host is psychologically and physically in a healthy state, the flower their *lawa* is attracted to is blooming, or 'undying' as the Lohorung say, which we call evergreen. When the person is sick or unhappy the flower their *lawa* is attracted to may be wilting or dying. It is dangerous, however, if a *lawa* wanders to a weak flower for if the *lawa* manages to return to its host he or she will soon manifest the same characteristics. If the *lawa* doesn't return, the person's life is in danger. 'Soul loss' is a serious condition and if diagnosed the performance of *Waya Warema* is one of the ways in which the 'soul' *lawa* can be returned. I'll look into this in more detail in later chapters. All that need be noted now is the significance of the flowers for *Waya Warema* and for every person in that their vital aspect, that is their *lawa*, must remain with the strong 'flowers' protected by *Waya Warema*. In the story of origin, the brother used flowers as a means to find the existence of his sisters; so too the Lohorung healer can use flowers to find the whereabouts of a lost *lawa*.

The healer is understood to be able to find a lost human *lawa* in a *Waya Warema* ritual because it includes a version of *bung chokme* 'flower extending/pushing', in which a person's life can be lengthened. For the full 'life–extending' ritual the household has to offer a forest sheep and four chickens to *warema* and two to *waya*, and the healer has to remember a much longer list of strong, eternal flower names than he does for a normal *Waya Warema* rite, in which the aim is either to retrieve a lost *lawa* or to strengthen the general health and prosperity of the local lineage group. The other full version of *bung chokme*, not involving *Waya Warema* is rarely performed because it is so difficult and said to be fatal if incorrectly performed. A similar Limbu ritual is described by Chemjong:

> an expert priestess sings or recites the whole of the creation of flower and its use and compares such inanimate object to human life in such a way that she particularises the mentality of a certain man to that of the stage of that particular flower. She then diverts the stage of that flower from freshness to withered condition. At the same time the particular man who was compared to that particular flower would also become slack and senseless. Now when the priestess refreshes the flower the man also would regain his energy and become fresh and active again.(1967: 26).

The *yatangpa* Lale explained how he finds a lost *lawa* using *bung chokme* in the *Waya Warema* ritual:

> First I have to say all the flower names, without dropping any of them, in the right order and these take me in my mind (*niwa*) to an enormous forest, *Emalitham Demalitham*, in the North. Then I make myself wings with the flowers, the wind catches in the flowers and flies me to *cheksokhim*, a place like a boundary between earth and the place above called *Yepmalitham Hamalitham* (where all the well-integrated ancestors live). There is nothing in *cheksokhim* but when I reach *Yemalitham Hamalitham*, I can see many people – all the dead, the ancestors; the women on the left, below, on the lower side and all the men to the right on the upper side. They wear clothes, the traditional kind. The house is long, very long like your 'rel'. I go inside and ask the way but nobody speaks; they just signal to me

where to go. I come out from the eastern door, where the sun rises. The house is with the sun in the west (*namkhe'ma khim*). When I come back I put the flowers back with words and in my *niwa* onto the shrine, saying the *samek* (ritual name) of the sick person without a *lawa* and the *samek* name of the flowers. As I say them the person's *lawa* comes back, and I put it back onto the flowers with a little water. (The *mangpa* blows it back, but he can see it whereas I can't; I know in my *niwa* that it's back and I place the water), and I show what we are offering to the *sammang*.

It's very important that the *yatangpa* collects all of the correct 'flowers'. If he misses some out he's in danger of leaving behind the *lawa* he is seeking. We see here how the ritual is effective if it is carried out correctly since 'in its very carrying out, the order of the world is reproduced and maintained' (Herrenschmidt, 1982: 26). The right order of the ritual assures the right order of the world. *Waya Warema* is performed by some Lohorung once a year whether or not members of the household have suffered headaches or giddiness diagnosed as *Waya Warema*. The ritual is conceived as being one of the best for maintaining a strong and healthy *lawa* and *saya*, for it directly handles the 'flowers' of those participating, which for Lohorung is like the substance supporting the core, or the individual soul, of the human person, apart from their 'consciousness', *niwa*.

Sammang Summary

Central to this account of *sammang* lie numerous Lohorung assumptions about human nature and 'illness' to do with the workings of mind, soul, emotions, motivations, and their mystical union with ancestors. The way Lohorung talk about *sammang* and represent them in ritual is closely linked to their understanding of 'the person' and their representation of emotions as key factors in devastating the unity and balance in relations with other living beings and with ancestors. From their view, the stability of their society depends on maintaining the balance of relations between humans, superhumans, and nature. To understand how Lohorung view this destabilizing power of emotions is one of the aims of this book.

So far in this chapter we have seen how Lohorung knowledge of what it is to be human is extended to include *sammang*. Ancestors are human even though they are dead and as humans they become depressed, feel lonely, their *saya* falls, and their *niwa* (gloss 'mind') hurts when they are insulted, ignored, or forgotten.[12] They understand ancestors to have emotions, in particular 'anger', 'jealousy', and 'hunger' which are not just recognized as emotions but seen as having an impact on the phenomenological world around them. The impact on humans often takes the form of what we might call 'illness' or misfortune.

What I found among the Lohorung could be interpreted as a full-blown ancestor cult, rather similar to ancestor cults found in China, West Africa, Assam or the Naga hills.[13] Initially, this was a possible interpretation which might have supported my argument that, in relation to the Lohorung material, 'religion' is not an appropriate interpretive framework (Hardman 1996). Some anthropologists have long maintained that the beliefs and practices of ancestor worship do not constitute 'worship' in the strict sense but institutionalized reverence for elders; that is, attitudes normally directed towards living elders are simply extended to the ancestors (Tylor, 1871, Driberg 1936, Kopytoff 1971). Following this view, ancestor worship could hardly be considered a system of religious beliefs and practices. However, although Lohorung society might be described as an 'ancestor-worshipping-society', I don't see the category 'ancestor cult' as being any more helpful than 'religion' as an interpretive framework. As Geertz says, categories such as ancestor worship usually tell us little more than the obvious, for example that 'ancestor worship supports the jural authority of elders', and in fact detract from the vitality of what is actually going on. 'The individuality of religious traditions has so often been dissolved into such dessicated types as "animism", "ancestor worship" and all the other insipid categories by means of which ethnographies of religion devitalise their data' (1993: 88,122).

Much of the material concerning Lohorung ancestors comes to life when we see that one of the key problems underlying Lohorung attitudes to themselves and their world is how to deal with the power of emotions – their own and those of dead ancestors, and those who did not have a 'good' death[14]. Anger, jealousy, 'hunger', greed, longings, and fears as well as the unconscious workings of *saya* and *lawa* all have the power to upset the delicate balance within the cosmos, the household, village, or person. The emotions are made manifest in sickness, misfortunes, bad crops, or landslides. Lohorung frames of reference are largely rooted in an interrelatedness between human beings, nature, and superhuman beings, and what a study of self and emotions highlights is the force of this interrelatedness.

Rather than looking at Lohorung's 'ancestor cult', I see the Lohorung attitude to *sammang* as being part of a more complex set of ideas about what it means to be human in a world with different ideas about how emotions work, and different notions about how selves develop, and where order has to be constantly restored and refreshed. Ancestors are not just revered elders, they are also irresponsible child-like beings whose *niwa* have diminished, whose *saya* fall and have to be renewed, beings who suffer and are angry, capricious children and destructive tricksters. The general motivations, the mind and temperamental nature of *sammang* are seen essentially as being a mixture of the very young and the very old put together. Their likes and dislikes, their 'anger', 'hunger', 'jealousy', and erratic volatile behaviour encapsulate Lohorung knowledge about the domineering, blundering tyranny of elders, who try to maintain the attention of those around them using the power of their age, along with other knowledge about the helplessness and wilfulness of young children, constantly needing attention and desiring to play.

Realizing the extent to which Lohorung appreciate the mental states and motivations of their *sammang* ancestors, I could begin to understand the attitude of compassion towards them. I could also make sense of the very 'human' rituals, in which Lohorung cajole and tempt *sammang* with food, drink, and sometimes cloth or some other material object – whatever they like best – because ancestors fit into their own social ethos of hospitality, generosity, and exchange.[15] In every aspect of social life Lohorung share and reciprocate. This is institutionalized, for example, in a form of gift-giving called *huksok* (see Chapter Eight) in marriage exchange and the marriage dialogues, in songs, and in labour exchange. There is a 'functional interdependence' between groups of all kinds; unlike everyone else the aged and the very young have to be pampered with gifts of food and drink to gain their co-operation: so too do the *sammang*. And this is particularly the case when the delicate relationship of trust has been broken and *sammang* are outraged.

By explaining illness and behaviour in terms of the 'anger' or 'hunger' of the *sammang*, human behaviour which is out of character, or for which there seems no obvious reason, may be explained as *sammang*. This is not to say that Lohorung always resort to *sammang* as an explanation. *Sammang* are named to explain sudden and usually serious changes in a person's physical or mental state, or serious events or disasters, and not to explain everything unusual or incomprehensible, or even every physical affliction. Each *sammang*, as we've seen, is associated with particular behaviour, mental and physical states or symptoms:

pappamamma	acute pain, dizziness, strong *lawa* and *saya*, long life, protection from other superhumans, good crops
Chawatangma	burns, boils, paralysis, stomach pains, limb abnormalities, blindness, loss of *lawa*, *niwa* (mind) problems eg. madness, anti–social behaviour, abundant crops and wealth with secret rites
Khimpie, *Lataba*	wounds, paralysis, debilitating and consumptive sicknesses, colds, rheumatism, protection
Waya Warema	fevers, dizziness, swellings, eye–ache, blood from nose or mouth, long life, strong *lawa*, *saya*, *niwa*

Members of households who know they have not paid attention to particular *sammang* for some period of time may become worried about their relationship with *sammang*. Each household expects to perform the ritual for each *sammang* at regular intervals, some such as *Chawatangma* very frequently, others annually, others every two years and others every five years. When I asked why wealthier households performed more *sammang* than others I was told that their way of life, such as frequency of visitors, the presence of 'outsiders' hired to work on their land is more likely to anger or attract the notice of the ancestors. 'Preventive' rites can be performed, if a household knows that the time is due for a renewal of the relationship.

Particularly in the case of *Waya Warema*, this is done by some households. But in the case of other *sammang*, as we saw earlier in this chapter, such rites can be misinterpreted as a bribe for favours, such as plentiful crops. Neighbours talk unless there is some visible reason for performing the rite.

How The Rituals Work

Lohorung rituals to *sammang* and the shrines are shaped and formed by forceful 'images' of particular *sammang*, by their knowledge of *sammang* behaviour and emotions. But how do the rituals work?

I want to look at how they work from a Lohorung point of view before going on to the view of some anthropologists who have suggested ways of interpreting sacrificial ritual more generally. Rituals to the ancestors for the Lohorung are about restoring the general order of society, regenerating vitality (by raising *saya*) and giving sacrificial gifts to placate angry ancestors. Their notion of order comes from the original order of things (see Chapter Five) as created by the original 'Culture Heroes' of the *pappamamma'chi*. As recorded in mythology all the main species of animals and plants and the First Man were either born from Somnima (*Chawatangma)* or all arose from their primeval dwelling place, the Primal Lake, and sacrifice is established as the essential institution for emergence.[16] As the story goes, the various Rai tribes, described as 'brothers', emerge and migrate 'from Khuwalung' carrying the 'sisters' they have divided between them. The elder brother tricks his younger brothers into thinking he has gone through the forest a long time ago by leaving signs in the form of notches on *kālo bohori* N (*Reevesia pubescens*) trees which go black when cut and by planting quick-growing plantain trees. He then tricks his brother again.[17]

> 'Oh! brother has gone; long gone. Where has he sheltered? Where has he gone? Oh, I will turn back,' said the youngest brother. He returned to Meche Koche. First of all of them the eldest brother came. He made an offering of that black bird named *kālo jureli* (N). He cut that bird and offered blood and then he crossed over here. Our second great grandfather came. The eldest told our brother to stay behind.'Our brother you stay over there. We cut our sister's finger and we offered her [blood]. Then we crossed over here. But he lied. That eldest brother forgot his language. (From the eldest come Khambu, from the second come Lohorung, and from the third brother come Limbu and the youngest turned back). Then our brother, he took his sister from his small basket and he said, 'Oh sister, eldest Khambu has gone. He cut sister's finger and he offered blood and then he crossed over there. We'll cut your finger just a little bit', he said and he cut a leaf from a grass called *semphu* (*amliso*, N *Thysanalaena agrestis*). He cut her finger just a little bit and when one drop fell down they crossed over. But when they had crossed over the sister developed a fever and her wound was painful. They caught up with the eldest brother who admitted he had cut the black bird and offered the bird's blood. 'That is how we crossed'. The younger brother

> said, 'if you hadn't told us such a wrong thing we too would have cut the black bird and offered its blood. Now we've cut our sister's finger and now our sister is seriously ill. Now our sister might die. This is a sinful path (*hi'wadam*)' Then the sister said, 'oh! brother you go and don't return back. Do not look back'. So they walked on up and eventually arrived above. 'Why shouldn't we look back?' So they looked and saw their sister. They saw her body being licked and eaten by a nanny goat and saw that she liked eating their sister. So now we don't eat goat.[18]

We can see here that the second key element to these rituals lies in the sacrifice. It's taken for granted that offering blood is the effective way to initiate the exit. By offering blood, human beings achieved their desired goal. In the myth the bird took the place of the human blood offering, birds being mythically the closest and 'natural' substitute for humans. In Lohorung, Thulung Rai, Mewahang Rai and Dumi Rai mythology human characters are at times represented as birds – that is, as part of the natural world and not separated from it. The characters are as human but have other 'natural qualities' which make it clear they are bird-like. Reflecting this identification with birds, each clan also has a bird that it cannot eat – the bird that is seen as an identifying feature of the clan. The black bird *kālo jureli* mentioned in the extract above, known in Lohorung as *kerokpa*, is not eaten by the Lamsong clan, *yangkoama* not eaten by Yangkhrung, *lelo'wa* by Dekhim, and so on. Now, just as human beings are not sacrificed, neither are these birds. They are represented instead by chickens and pigs, domesticated animals living alongside humans, who made a pact with the ancestors as they migrated on their way. As one man explained,

> Chickens and pigs are given you know in our place. *Sammang* rites had to be done as they migrated, and it was with chickens and pigs that they made a promise. 'I'll go in your place' said the pig and so did the chicken. In place of human offerings we took their blood instead. In order to become well we cannot offer birds to *sammang*. We stopped offering them when we made a promise never to offer birds again. It was same as offering our sister. Goat is also prohibited because goat was despised for eating our sister.

We can begin to see Lohorung sacrifice as the ritual killing of substitutes as a way of ensuring contact and communication with ancestors. They employ the symbolism of killing, the shedding of blood in minute quantities, to bring about rebirth of the original order and revitalization which in turn will raise the *saya* of all concerned. The efficacy for them lies in two things, the appearance of blood and not watery saliva (*makwa*) which will placate ancestors and in the correct performance of the communication which along with the offering has the regenerative effect of raising *saya*.

For Lohorung the original effective rite was a blood sacrifice laying the model for later rites which work by communicating with the ancestors with the appropriate blood offering. These Lohorung rites can be compared with Vedic and classical Indian sacrifice, in which every act of sacrifice refers back to the creation of the world: 'every sacrifice may be said to replicate the primal act of Prajapati who produced creation by the sacrificial dismemberment of his own body . . . Any sacrifice then . . . maintains or repairs the cosmic order . . . It therefore represents a renewal of time'(Parry 1982: 77; see also Eliade 1964: 11). The effectiveness of the communication which is linked to its correct performance is similar to the Brahmanic tradition in which 'in its very carrying out, the order of the world is reproduced and maintained. The right order of sacrifice is, and assures the right order of the world' (Herrenschmidt 1982: 26).

There is a key sense in which the effectiveness is accounted for in the way in which the order of the world is linked explicitly to and maintained by sacrifice and the visibility of just a few drops of blood (see Herrenschmidt ibid: 25). If the sacrificial chickens are very small their heads have to be chopped off to produce the drops of blood. Larger chickens produce drops of blood from the mouth when killed by hitting them hard on their spine with a stick. Blood doesn't flow in any great quantity in any indigenous Lohorung ritual (see also Chapter Five): what is important is just a few drops. If we look at the way in which the order of the world is linked to sacrifice, the key to it is in the myth but also in the notion that blood is connected to the vital force (*saya*). The order of the world is maintained and restored to balance when the correct sacrifice and correct ritual chant, re-enacting the original ritual, are performed so that *saya* is raised. Sacrifice is an act of universal regeneration. The restoration of a mystical union through sacrifice was of course also one of the key elements to sacrifice noted in the anthropological essay by Hubert and Mauss.[19] The order of the world is based on a mystical union between living and ancestors in the form of *saya* and links explicitly to sacrifice since correctly performed this is how *saya* is raised, and the connection accounts for its effectiveness.

Hubert and Mauss also conclude in their essay that sacrifice is both useful and an obligation, reiterating a theory of sacrifice going back to Plato, that sacrifice as a form of gift creates an obligation 'if he gives it is partly in order to receive . . .. Disinterestedness is mingled with self-interest. That is why it has so frequently been conceived as a form of contract' ([1899](1964: 100).[20] Lohorung have expectations that the offering of their own domestic chickens or pigs, symbols of the of the original sacrificial victim, will placate the ancestors. Such gifts are about re-affirming relationships just as they are with living relatives and involve a contractual element. The efficacy of sacrifice in Lohorung eyes also has to do with the importance of gifts in controlling emotions. I shall look at this aspect of ritual more closely in Chapter Eight (see section on *huksok*).

The controlling aspect of rituals is central to the theories of René Girard and Walter Burkert who both see ritual sacrifice as controlling, channelling, and repressing human violence so as to allow for ordered social life[21]. We could see Lohorung rituals as controlling what is described in the myth, namely a tendency of Lohorung males to violence or the need to outwit others. Maurice Bloch, similarly seeking an explanation of the symbolism of violence present in so many rituals, suggests that rituals act out a denial of the transience of institutions and human life by symbolically sacrificing the participants so they can become part of the transcendental. For this to happen, he argues, a double violence or 'rebounding violence' has to take place – 'the need for the violence of expulsion of the native vital element and the need for the successive violence of the consumption of external vitality' (1992: 21). Relating this to the Lohorung material we can see the former in the violent sacrifice of the chickens or pig, substitutes for humans, whose death (revealed by the blood) releases the animal's 'breath' *sokma* – the vital element to the ancestor. To sacrifice, the shaman or local healer symbolically loses his or her 'native vitality' by going into an 'altered state', in which he or she goes on a ritual journey following the path of the particular ancestor. For *Khimpie* they travel the lower route along the Sabhaya Khola and Southwards, whereas for *Waya* they travel from Salpa Pokari leading eventually to Khembalung mountain. The second part of the ritual amounts to a feast, the consumption by the participants of the sacrifical animal, also seen as revitalizing – what Bloch calls the 'consumption of external reality.' Vitality is raised (*saya* raised) as the blood offerings are made to the ancestor in question and as the meal is consumed by the participants.

Bloch's theory is particularly helpful in focusing on how the renewal of vitality in ritual sacrifice through 'rebounding violence' is also political, that is, to give support to actual violence or at least potential conquest. The sense of full vitality, high *saya*, or head held high was clearly politically important in the role of Rai 'chiefs' and is still important in the role of the male head of the household (see Sagant 1985). Philippe Sagant described violence among the neighbouring Limbu as 'the concrete expresssion of a religious concept, the vital force, for each household chief. It is that part of *Nahangma*, the war goddess, which each man has within himself, in his right shoulder or on top of his head. Violence is life' (1985: 202). I would also say that violence is central to Lohorung sacrifice as a means of recovering the kind of vitality they envisage as essential to well–being and in the past saw as preliminary to territorial conquest or inter–tribal warfare.

From the description in this Chapter of the main *sammang*, we have been able to see how the concept operates in interpretations of people's experiences and behaviour. In trying to understand why Lohorung perform *sammang* rituals my emphasis here has been on context and on the view that Lohorung ideas about human nature and ancestral nature and their practices in ritual are rational as well as 'symbolic'. Given the essentially human Lohorung view of ancestors I cannot say, as Beattie does, that ritual should primarily be seen as expressive behaviour and that the tenets of myth, magic and religion 'are not scientific propositions, based on experience and on a belief in the uniformity of nature, and that they cannot be adequately understood as if they were' (1966: 72). Lohorung statements about *sammang* and their 'hunger', statements about 'flowers' representing a person's *lawa*, are not symbolic statements. Undoubtedly, their rituals include symbolic action. The shrines are symbolic representations of their houses, there are numerous symbolic or mimetic qualities to the enactment of past events as in *Waya Warema*, the sacrificial animal is symbolic but the activity is operative. The *yatangpa*, *mangpa*, and participants perform the ritual because their knowledge of the *sammang* and the symptoms of the person indicate to them that relations with a particular *sammang* have become unbalanced. Experience and divination tell them that this person's acute pain and dizziness is an indication that *Pappamamma'chi* are enraged. In part involved in a web of reciprocal obligations, in part feeling compassionate for those ancestors they have hurt, in part trusting the sacrifice will satisfy, based on their own theory about how ancestors work, those performing the rituals know the ritual will be effective and regularized relations will be restored, so long as the ritual is correctly enacted and the diagnosis was correct.

Mistakes are made. The paralysis may indicate that *Khimpie* is responsible when, in fact, it is *Chawatangma* playing tricks trying to look like a *Khimpie* paralysis, just like a person playing at being ill to express individuality. Diagnosis goes wrong, but there is always a reason, whether based on the complicity of the *sammang* to mislead the *yatangpa* or the inability of the *yatangpa* that day to 'see'. When diagnosing they say, 'It is *Khimpie*' or '*Chawatangma* is hungry' or 'she is angry' or 'the *niwa* of *pappamamma* hurt, we must raise their *saya*'. They know *sammang* have *niwa* from the evidence that they 'feel' and have 'wants', that require *niwa*. The word they use for the superhuman beings is *luchakmi*, meaning they have desires, feelings, and in particular wishes for the possession or presence of something or somebody, needs, or we might say 'wants'. The human equivalent is '*minchakmi*' with much the same meaning: 'wanting to do/eat something,' 'to feel like something', 'to feel . . .'. *Sammang*, however, 'feel' and 'want' (*luchakmi*) in a more selfish, dramatic way than adult human beings. They compare the wants or possessiveness of the *sammang* with those of children in their sudden intensity, using this to explain the sudden onset of certain illnesses. The rituals work by satisfying the *sammang*. Even those who are sceptical find themselves drawn back to performing the rituals.

I here argue against the view that rituals for Lohorung are essentially expressive and crucially different from 'practical' action in the way suggested by Beattie (1966), a view that tends to support the validity of Durkheim's division into sacred and profane. Rituals are, of course, 'showing' and 'saying' in all kinds of expressive ways exactly what the ritual is enacting. But what the ritual actually did and meant to the participants, I found was based on firm notions about how ancestors and humans behave, how they respond to coercive offerings, how anger can be counteracted with satisfying food, and how *saya* rises when compensations ease the insult. Once *sammang* have been satisfied, Western medicines will bring the most speedy cure in humans. The focus in the ritual was always on bringing about a change in the feelings of *sammang* and thence restoring the relationship between humans and ancestors. Illness associated with *sammang* was always understood as requiring a restoration of the balance between the living and the ancestors by raising *saya*. As with pregnancy, one cannot be 'a little bit ill from *sammang*'. If *sammang* are involved, the relationship has to be addressed but once that has been done it is recognized that Western medicine can sometimes be very effective in dealing with other levels of the illness. Without initial ritual sacrifices, however, the Western medicines cannot work. Some did, however, say that taking Western medicines could be dangerous if it increased the anger of the *sammang* involved.

If we leave indigenous definitions and approach the rituals using non–indigenous criteria, many different interpretations are possible. Desjarlais was particularly interested in understanding how one particular shaman's soul-calling rites in Yolmo worked to rejuvenate spiritless bodies (1992: 206). He rejects intellectualist and symbolist approaches: in the former, rituals help patients to think differently about their condition and in the latter, rites work by 'provoking transformations either of the worldview held by a patient or of the symbolic categories that define the experiences of that patient' (1992: 207). Though 'transformation of experience' is part of the answer (208) the rite works because the shaman 'changes how a body feels by altering what it feels. [The] cacophany of music, taste, sight, touch, and kinesthesia activates a patient's senses. This activation has the potential to "wake" a person, alter the sensory grounds of a spiritless body, and change how a body feels. A successful soul–calling rite recreates the sense of "presence" intrinsic to Yolmo experiences of well–being' (206). My own sense is that this may be an answer for some patients but what it ignores is that the focus of most rituals in Nepal is not on the body of the patient. It is not the patient who has to be convinced but the superhuman beings. The reasons they 'work' from our Western point of view may have to do with catharsis, externalizing problems, resolution of social conflict, or transforming experiences – and Desjarlais has usefully added the sensory dimension to the social and psychological dimensions already suggested (see Csordas and Kleinman 1990; Schiffelin 1985). My uncertainty about placing too much emphasis on activating senses, at least in terms of the majority of Lohorung rituals, is the degree to which many patients are ignorant of the ritual terminology. Much of the style of presentation, obvious to the ritual officiant, is lost on the patient and audience who are not specialists.

Those *sammang* I have not dealt with in depth, namely *ge-ereng me-ereng*, *subba subbeni*, *yangli*, *khuma*, *dechapa* and *dhankutte* are those with whom the Lohorung have a less intense relationship, and whose rituals are performed at *iksammang*, an annual harvest-time rite, but less often on their own. The other ways in which the *sammang* contribute to Lohorung indigenous psychology, I shall discuss further in Chapter Seven.

Let me now turn to the *chap*, the other most important category in the Lohorung pantheon.

Ghosts of the dead: Chap

All the *sammang* are *chap*, but not all *chap* are *sammang*. *Chap* is a collective term referring to what we might call 'ghosts of the dead', or 'spirits of dead ancestors', whether they died a 'good' natural death or a 'bad' unnatural one, whether recently buried or far back in time. Interestingly, when asking a fellow Lohorung which clan he belongs to a man asks '*mang chap ro*?', that is, 'which are your dead ancestors?', and the man answers with the name of his clan. (A woman is asked 'whom do you belong to?', 'whose are you?'*mang mi' lo*? and the woman answers with the name of her father's clan, in accordance with the patrilineal, patrilocal emphasis of the society).

If a person is about to die, in the last few weeks and days his or her *lawa* goes to 'the *chap* side', increasingly following the chap path. In his or her dreams the person sees the dead relatives more than the living. Human beings are said to have died when the 'soul' (*lawa*) has left the body for too long for it to be returned, and the breath (*sokma*) has stopped. The *lawa* goes to the household shrine (*mangsuk*), wanders and meets other *chap*. Then the 'soul' of the person is thought of as *chap*. For three days after the breath has stopped and the person described as 'dead', their *chap* wanders freely and may 'attack/strike' (*tusikme*) anyone before it is finally persuaded to join (*tongtimale*) the other *chap*. It may try to take the *lawa* of another person for a friend. Children are very frightened during the three days after someone has died. When his grandfather died, the little boy in the house in Pangma I was staying in would not sleep. He had heard so many stories about what can happen.

The *chap* are only called to visit the living at funerals and at *nuagi*, the ceremony to renew the household shrine. Otherwise, the Lohorung's actions are to keep them away. At the funeral they are called to escort away the newly dead. They are tempted with food, offered to them by the graveside and in the house. It is interesting to note that the *chap* are always given cooked meat or raw fruit and vegetables, never uncooked meat or the blood as the *sammang* are. The *sammang* are said to need the smell of the blood to 'know' there has been a sacrifice made, to 'know' that something special has been 'given' from the human household. The *chap* are 'hungry' rather than 'angry' and want to have the food they normally eat. To show they respect the needs of *chap*, Lohorung adults do not eat any new cucumber or pumpkin, rice, or millet before offering them to the *chap*, at Saune Sagratti (a Hindu rite) and then at *nuagi*. Lohorung, however, are not interested in maintaining relationships with *chap*, but they do need to be controlled and this is achieved through feeding them. When offering food to the well-integrated chap Lohorung avoid attracting *sammang* by avoiding blood. As we have seen above, these well-integrated *chap* are known to give no trouble to human beings, and Lohorung consider they relate well (*tonguk*) with them. They are called twice a year as *sikhla* to be offered food and drink and that is considered to be sufficient to keep them 'happy'.

The problem for human beings comes with the unintegrated *chap* whose form of death precludes them from entering what is sometimes called *chaptempa*, the land/place of the *chap*, or the superhuman place known as *yepmalitham hamalitham*. Their relationship with these *chap* is more complicated. The kind of death considered to form these *chap* is unnatural or premature, whether from childbirth, falling from a cliff or tree or other high point, from drowning, burns, being attacked by dogs, cats, or some other animal causing or immediately after their death, or suicide – usually by hanging – each one a separate category with its own name. On the occasion of a 'bad' death, the other *chap* are not called. The shaman, *mangpa*, is needed to keep the *lawa* away from the family and protect the household. If the *mangpa* is not called, the fear is that a member of the household will fall sick very quickly and the *chap* will come at night as a *chudel* N – one of these fickle spirits who look female in front and are hollow in the back and who move at great speed. For twelve years it will disturb the household doing whatever harm it can. After twelve years it loses all its power and strength and never returns.

Forbidden to join the other *chap*, these *chap* are destined to roam forever. Inevitably they become hungry, thirsty, lonely, or sometimes cold and it is these needs which Lohorung see as forcing them to attack. In general, Lohorung do not think of them as malevolent even though their 'attacks' have the effect of producing various kinds of physical symptoms, which may be summarized as follows:

harikmang, mammam lam (death in childbirth):	stomach–ache,sweating, severe cramps
dinchaimpa (corpse touched by animal):	headache, limbs and chest–ache
hongma yongpempa (death by drowning):	cold body, stomach–ache from navel up, cramp
damsimpa (death from falling from cliff): limbs	body–aches especially head and
mie (death from burns):	high fever, body very hot
keng sikhempa (suicide):	neck–ache, respiratory disease

When the 'soul' of a woman who has died in childirth 'attacks/strikes' (*tumsiha*) they say someone has collided with *mammam lam*, 'the path of mothers'; when it is *dinchaimpa* 'attacking', it is described as *kaise lam* 'the bad, difficult path'; when it is any of the other four categories, it is 'the thin, dried up path', *sukha lam*. None of these *chap*, it is said, can follow the 'good, happy, easy nice' path of the well-integrated *chap*, for they do not get on with the *pappamamma'chi* who rule over that path. Although Lohorung talk of themselves as being 'attacked' by *chap*, their attitude towards them is, in general, compassionate. Though some are known to be malicious it is mainly in the form of wishing to tease, especially when they are thirsty and hungry. Lohorung conceive of only a few as being malevolent. This contrasts strongly with the Hindu *lagnu* spirits of the dead, who are generally accepted in the hills as being 'evil' and malicious. The compassion of the Lohorung is exemplified, for example, in the way women relate to *harikmang chap* 'women who have died from childbirth' and destined to roam alone unless they find another of their own kind. When women go to the spring to fetch water many of them flick some water into the air from the top of their water pots, as I myself learned to do, which they say is 'for *harikmang*'. They sometimes do it for other female *chap*, who cannot themselves get water from the spring to quench their thirst. Unable to drink from the spring they are said to take dew from leaves. We can see the same compassion in the Lohorung habit of flicking into the air some of the liquid from whatever they are drinking before starting to drink, and placing some of the cooked rice from their plate 'for the *chap*'. There is an element of self-protection in these activities as well as compassion.

If the *chap* of one of the 'bad paths' does attack and a person falls sick, it can usually be dealt with by a relative by burning a piece of cloth and calling to the offending *chap*, 'You, bad-death-person, you have attacked. We know you, and tell you to go away.' Only if it becomes severe does a household call in a shaman or priest, who performs what is known as '*tse tse*' with flowers and sometimes small elephants and horses made of earth, different kinds of seed, rice, maize, and millet on a leaf, which attracts the chap. The elephants and horses lure them into believing it is a place other than where they have been making trouble. The noses of *chap* are known to be very sensitive and smell the smoke from the burning rag. They also have *niwa* ('mind') and 'know' as well as 'feel' (*luchakmi*). Lohorung say they know they have *niwa* because if they are near enough, they understand when they are told they must go away. The fact that they attack at all is also said to be an indication of their *niwa*.

Most *chap* tease. They are never encountered before sunset or after dawn. Lohorung sometimes describe them as being like leaves flapping in the wind, 'first you hear them near, then far away. When you look where you thought you heard them, there's nothing there: the ear finds them; but the eye has nothing to see, like words'. Sometimes they slam doors or blow out fires, or someone finds their feet standing in a pool of water. *Chap* try to take wood from people's fires, or strips of bamboo, especially the kind of bamboo called *yong baphu* which is use for carrying the dead. When fires suddenly fall into a new position this is said to be the work of *chap*. The following is tyical of *chap* stories:

> Chitra was at home alone in their house up on the hill. Dhoje wasn't there so he made rice and lentils, ate his own share and put Dhoje's on one side. He tried to go to sleep. 'As I lay there I heard children's feet going this way and that way, as if running between two houses, and they were crying. But there are no other houses nearby. I called out "Who's there?" and went to look outside. There was nobody there so I went back and lay down. I heard it again, the hurrying feet and the crying, and again there was nobody there when I went to look. I lit a fire, then the wood ran out and I tried to sleep again. Sleep wouldn't come, only

the teasing sounds. I was sweating, trying not to feel frightened.' The next morning he found out from his sisters that a child had died on the path going past his house nearer the village that afternoon. The sounds he had heard that night were all the chap children going to meet the new spirit that had joined them in the afternoon.

After sunset and before dawn Lohorung are careful about moving around the village and usually carry a flaming torch, or a glowing piece of wood from the fire and, if possible, some Mugwort (*titepāti* N, *Artemisia vulgaris*) tucked somewere into their clothes to keep away the *chap*. Almost nobody wanders outside the village after dark unless forced by circumstances, and then with a companion and always 'trying not to be afraid', an essential form of protection.

There are individual *chap*, however, who do more than tease or attack from hunger and are certainly conceived as being malevolent, and it is the stories circulating about these *chap* which encourage Lohorung fear of *chap*. One such *chap* was called the Heluwali *chap*, named after the village of the dead man, but he was also called Marga Devi. It used to wander around all the four Pangma villages as well as Heluwa, Angla, Malingtar, the main Lohorung villages in the area. It mainly attacked women, cutting off their nipples, although it also attacked a man in Heluwa slashing him in many places without actually killing him. In Gairi Pangma, my next-door neighbour's face, disfigured by a large scar, was said to have been attacked by the Heluwali *chap*. It fought with another neighbour who says he saw it and at first it was a small being; they fought and both fell down the house ladder to the ground. 'Then it looked like a very tall and white person, as tall as if it reached the eaves'. He also has a large scar on his face. The following is what I was told about this *chap* one evening by a boy:

This *chap* is a Heluwa man who went off hunting with only his gun as his companion. As he went off singing, his gun went off on its own killing him. His chap began troubling people soon after and none of the *mangpa* shaman could catch him. When it wanted to fight women it took the form of a woman; when attacking men it became a man; and it moved so quickly it was already attacking another person when a first victim started calling for help. The Tibetan *lama* eventually caught it with mantras and a small kind of prison. The *chap* cried and cried but it couldn't escape from the prison: it was trapped by the mantras. When they do a rite for Marga Devi to keep it quiet they can't do it inside the *lama*'s 'prison', only outside. It needs pigeons, chickens, goats, everything but nothing can be taken home to be eaten, it must be eaten there. It took off the ear of Dhan Bir too in Angla. Hearing us, Rekuama said we should stop talking about it or it might hear and return tonight. She was genuinely a bit frightened, though she was trying to hide it, because everyone says the only way to keep them away is 'not to be frightened'. People come with news of *chap* who have come to the locality, warning what their teasing tactics are so that others can be prepared. In my first few months in Pangma someone came with news of a *chap* who calls out to people in the night. It was said to have reached Dara Pangma, and everyone was warned not to answer to anyone who calls in the night.'If you answer you too will die. Two families have been finished in a village near to the Arun. It is possible to see her; she is a young girl, her

> front is normal but her back is hollow. If you answer she says, "come to me in six hours". We know it's a chap because she doesn't make any sense, like human beings do. Sometimes she comes to boys in their dreams and makes their semen flow. She comes night after night and the boy gets weaker and weaker until he dies. One has just died and now she is maybe looking for another'.

Sainli explained that in spite of the many chap stories Lohorung don't become too afraid if they know they have kept good relations with the *sammang*. On the whole, she considered Lohorung are well protected by their *sammang*, far better protected from the *chap* than the Chetri or Bahun. '*Chap* are afraid of *sammang*. They say, 'those people (Lohorung) have so much gods, lots of beer, *sammang*; those people can drink a lot of beer, they have *sammang* who look after them, we had better be careful, we must fear these ones.'

What we've seen here is that *chap* solve several metaphysical questions for Lohorung, such as explaining what happens at death to a person's *lawa* and *niwa*. They distinguish between *chap* who are predominantly 'hungry' as opposed to *sammang* who are 'angry'. The living need to be in control in relation to these superhuman beings, and particularly those who are not well-integrated, for whom they feel compassion but no trust. *Chap* may do anything. In general, however, in return for being fed most *chap* comply with Lohorung reminders that they must keep away from the world they used to inhabit. It is only a few of the unintegrated *chap* that remain troublesome.

Khammang *and* Yimi (Yumang, Yimang)

The superhuman beings of the previous two categories are represented as being essentially human, with fluctuating needs and emotions, and many with colourful personalities. Lohorung are forced into fairly constant consideration of the state of their relationship with them. In contrast, the couple *Khammang* and *Yimi* are almost entirely represented in abstract terms, with few human characteristics. They come across as being more distant than either *sammang* or *chap*. Yet, the relationship with this couple is of extreme importance to every household and is given particular attention at least once and often twice a year in an annual ceremony called *nuagi*, which I describe in detail in Chapter Six.

The couple, most commonly known as *Khammang* and *Yimi*, are also known as *Khammang* and *Yimang* or *Yumang* and are closely associated with *mangsuk* the household shrine. Lohorung emphasize they are not *sammang*. Obtaining information about these superhuman beings was always difficult and the information often vague. The most concrete information collected concerned their existence as a couple. Strangely, however, it seemed to me at first, although *Khammang* and *Yimi* were also always talked about as a complementary couple, that the couple were sometimes referred to as brother and sister and sometimes as husband and wife.

One of the old men of the village tried to explain the confusion by telling me a brief story involving several brothers and their sister. He said *nuagi* was for worshipping sisters of the house 'to bring back out-married sisters and to let them know that we do not want to lose them'. The story behind it, he said, involved three brothers who had to cross a river to take their sister to the man she was to marry. They didn't know how to get their sister across the river safely. All the brothers loved her very much. One brother suggested putting the sister into a basket and carrying her across and this is what they did. Half way across, however, she fell out of the basket into the river and drowned. The brothers were left with no sister. The story didn't explain the discrepancy until *kāhili* told me one evening about nuagi and mentioned that, of course, *Khammang* and *Yimi* were brother and sister, as well as being the husband and wife that they are presented as being in the rite. I questioned her more and she explained they were the first incestuous couple. *Khammang* and *Yimi* were the first couple to 'break the bones' *sekowa pokme*, that is, marrying someone of one's father's clan before the prohibited seven generations have elapsed. She explained that originally a brother and his younger sister became husband and wife; they had intercourse, but the wind blew violently, it began to hail; p*ap lagyo* (sin in the Hindu-Buddhist sense) and both became ill. They couldn't hear, see, or speak. It was because of this that people knew brothers and sisters mustn't have intercourse. A brother must have another woman apart from his sister. To make the brother and sister healthy again they had to place all the different kinds of food and drink that is given now at *nuagi*. After everything had been offered the brother and sister could see, hear, and speak again. *Nuagi* is to remember this. If people sin (*pap* N), what happens is that we become deaf, dumb, or blind or our minds stop working. That's why in *nuagi* we ask them 'don't stop our minds working properly; stay in your own place'. *Kāhili* said this is not the explanation of *nuagi* usually given by the *yatangpa* priest, but it is what she has heard from other people.

Marriage with classificatory clan 'sisters' is prohibited. The intermittent transgression of it, however, is in fact an essential part of Lohorung social structure, as well as that of other Kiranti groups. It is one of the identifying features of their culture. As Charles McDougal, writing about the Kulunge Rai, has shown, *hadphora* 'breaking the bones' marriages are expected in order to maintain local endogamy. As he says, 'the Rais "want to have their cake and eat it too". Rather than give up a sister to another man in order to obtain a wife, the Rai solution is to marry the "sister" – i.e. a clan woman'. (1979: 155). And though, as *kāhili* said, 'nobody wants to talk about it', it is nevertheless recognized that as a result of several incestuous marriages many Lohorung clans have split. In this way Lohorung men have been able to carry on marrying, exchanging women within a small locality, and very rarely marrying across the river Arun, or with the Yamphu Rai who live to the North or the Yakka Rai and Limbu who live to the East. Four of the six main clans living in Pangma villages today, the *Lamsong*, *Bi'wa*, *Dekhim*, and *Lumben*, are 'brother' clans, having separated as the result of 'breaking the bones' marriages. Marriage within the Pangma locality is both preferred and a statistical fact (a high percentage of married women in Pangma were from houses in the locality: from Pangma, Heluwa, Angla, Dhupu, Chewa, Khorunde, Malta, Apurdam, Malingtar, or Diding.) The story of the three brothers and their sister began to make sense. Perhaps it's saying 'to marry sisters to someone across the river, to another tribe, is the same as seeing them drown. Either way you lose them'.

One of the significant aspects of *kāhili*'s story (one that was later acknowleged by others) is that it represents *Khammang* and *Yimi* as being the innocent creators of an important structural feature of Lohorung life. Signficantly, though *Khammang* and *Yimi* were transgressors of what is morally correct, they are now seen as being the guardians of spiritually and morally correct behaviour. *Niwa* learns what is 'correct', but *Khammang* and *Yimi* – both the terrestrial manifestations and the superhuman couple – 'know' (*lekuchi*) what is morally correct. Unlike *sammang* who are easily enraged or insulted, the only time the relationship between humans and *Khammang* and *Yimi* lacks harmony is when some important moral rule has been broken. Usually the relationship with human beings is one of protection. If a household is healthy and prosperous their relationship with *Khammang* and *Yimi* must be good.Their *saya* must be high. We will see more of this aspect of *Khammang* and *Yimi* in Chapter Six.

Finally, it should be said that *Khammang* and *Yimmang* are connected to all three cosmic zones, the sky, the earth, and the watery subsoil, though their names identify them particularly with the earth. *Mang*, as we have seen, may be glossed as 'spirit'; *kham* is 'earth' or 'soil'. *Yumang* is less obviously an earth spirit. It seems very likely, however, that she is the Lohorung equivalent of the neighbouring Limbu spirit *Yuma*. Chemjong, a Limbu himself, writes about Yuma as being the earthly version of the Supreme Good spirit *Ningwaphuma*, 'the most powerful spirit of knowledge and wisdom' (1967: 22) The Lohorung *Yimi* or *Yumang* is an authority on traditional lore and wisdom and closely connected to people's *niwa*: the Limbu *Yuma* is the 'mine of knowledge and wisdom' whom 'the Mundhum addresses by the name of *Ningwaphuma*' (ibid: 22).The association of *Khammang* and *Yimi* with all three cosmic zones is clear in the representation of the Lohorung house shrine. I could look further here at these superhuman beings and their shrine, but their significance in Lohorung life makes much more sense if considered alongside the important ritual in which their shrine is renewed. I've therefore delayed a more detailed discussion to Chapter Six when I look at the Lohorung house and the *nuagi* rite.

It's impossible to give a full overview of all the various superhuman beings, but I have tried to cover the main categories. It's worth now emphasizing several features that have emerged. One of the most obvious features is the lack of One God, The Creator and Almighty, who is personal, transcendent, and holy. The Lohorung pantheon is polytheistic, not monotheistic. Even to enter into this terminology to describe their superhuman beings seems semantically incorrect for, as I have explained, Lohorung do not have any indigenous word for 'god'. What Lohorung mean when they do use the term *deutā* (Nepali for god) is that *sammang* are their nearest equivalent to, and are as important as, the Hindu *deut–*. For them, the two concepts *sammang* and *deutā* are two different mental constructs with their own individual signification and intelligible properties. The *sammang*, the *chap* and *Khammang* and *Yimi* are closest in signification to 'ancestors', perhaps 'divine ancestors', not 'gods' or deities.

I found it inaccurate to think of Lohorung relations with their *sammang* as a system of 'belief'. Lohorung relate to ancestors on the basis of mutual dependency, trust, and reciprocity. This is much the same way they relate to living relatives and neighbours involving other systems of reciprocity and trust, such as the form of gift exchanges called *huksok*, or the availability of women for marriage in a system of reciprocity between villages. It's as if the principles of social life are extended outward to include relations with superhuman beings. In return for respect shown to their traditions and their property superhuman beings are trusted to offer prosperity, health, and protection. Grammatically, the construction is one of 'if angry . . . then corresponding pain' suggesting a 'functional dependence' relationship (see Campbell 1989: Chapter Four). The vital link between ancestor and living is *saya*, the 'ancestor within' which I'll come to in depth in Chapter Six. The illness that occurs in humans is the identity of a *sammang*, hence the relationship between *sammang* stories and the illnesses or misfortunes connected to them. *Sammang* afflictions are manifestations of *sammang*. It would be incorrect to interpret the actions of *sammang* as punishment. There is rarely blame unless private rituals for personal gain have been performed. It's recognized that the living cannot help upsetting the dead. The rituals offering blood sacrifice pacify the ancestors, restore the balance in the interdependent relationship, and raise the *saya* of superhuman and human being.

The third feature of significance that emerges concerns the characteristics of the superhuman beings. With the emphasis in Western thought on a good God we are used to the idea that the most important superhuman beings are noble, gentle and good and above all mysterious. The characteristics of Lohorung superhuman beings, as we have seen, are in striking contrast.They are essentially 'human' and non–mysterious. There is a wide spectrum of colourful characters, authoritarian spirits of older ancestors, majestic spirits of past kings, fickle spirits, mournful desperate spirits of ancestors who died unnatural deaths, ones who protect, those who stand incarnate for the maternal and paternal line and most of them beings who have to be placated like children, so that the humans become 'fathers' to their ancestors. There's little that is inexplicable about them: their whims are well-known. It would be hard for beings, who closely interconnect and penetrate Lohorung institutions and everyday life in the way they do, to remain mysterious. Of course this is known to be a common feature in societies involving ancestor worship (see Fortes 1959, Hsu 1949 or Ahern 1973) but for me the pervasiveness of ancestors and other superhuman beings in Lohorung life, as if part of their own society, was unexpected. They were there wherever I looked.

Lastly, I want to emphasize the Lohorung consciousness of their trust in their ancestors. Contrary to Horton's argument that people from a closed system cannot have consciousness of their own system (1967), many Lohorung have clear insights into both the 'Lohorung system' and what keeps people from giving up the trust in the ancestors. They sometimes describe themselves as having 'blind' trust. Explaining this, they recognize a trait in themselves; to be very ready to trust others, even to the extent of being naive, (and they quote how they were so in their land transactions with the Hindu Brahman and Chhetri people). Their trust in their traditions and the *sammang*, in *Khammang* and *Yimi*, and in their priests (*yatangpa*) and shamans (*mangpa*) is not always based on knowledge, since much of that knowledge has disappeared over time. Their great–grandparents 'knew', but because they are illiterate much of it has gone. So now they say they 'blindly' trust. For Lohorung 'trusting' linguistically entails doing what and being where the mind trusts (*niwa chume*), or where the mind feels responsible. For them mind, niwa, should be directed by parents and ancestral traditions, so if 'mind trusts' their actions should be the right ones. It is in part 'our *niwa*', they say, that will not allow them to escape from their own system.

Fear also prevents Lohorung escaping their own system. A few, such as Prem, have thought about avoiding their relationship with *sammang*. The attraction of the Christian God, presented as a deity who is never angry, gave a vision of fewer pains and sickness; but *sammang*, they say, are so powerful – more powerful than Hindu or Christian gods. When the intending convert meets misfortune or illness the explanation is always in terms of angry *sammang* who will not let them go. That's why Lohorung were worried about me. I had been claimed by the *sammang*. I must have been or *chawatangma* would not have been angry and I would not have been ill. What was I going to do in the West where there were no priests or shamans to deal with them? In Nepal they know how to pacify them, feed them, and give them the beer they like. Who could contact them, who could go on the ritual journey to meet the *sammang* and pacify them, who in England could raise their *saya*?

The *chap* are no different. It's for Lohorung a certainty that they will one day become *chap* and, so long as they have a good death, will be fed and given offerings by the living. The implications of not having any children and in particular male children, who will look after the household shrine, *mangsuk*, to which they are called, are perhaps hard for us to appreciate. We can, however, see why a wife's barrenness is seen as the worst curse, depriving a man and his wife of being direct lineal ancestors. As far as Lohorung are concerned those who think differently about death, such as the Tibetans who believe in re–incarnation are simply 'wrong'. Lohorung accept Tibetans as just different people, with different and 'wrong' ideas. Some other Rai groups don't treat their *chap* properly either. Lohorung find the Khambu Rai custom of putting their dead in the field close by the house almost incomprehensible. *Chap* should be buried outside the village. Any other way of treating *chap* is 'disgusting'. Lohorung also express disgust at the Khambu Rai custom of feasting after a person has died: 'how can you cry and eat at the same time? We Lohorung say the close family should eat only a little rice or some *ghiu* (clarified butter) for three days.' Ideas about the correct way to behave, so as not to insult or offend, are as crucial in relations with the dead as they are with the living.

We have seen here how the frame of reference within which the Lohorung notion of the self is shaped and constructed is one in which a unity between the superhuman and the human is constantly recreated and re–affirmed. In Chapter Five I look at the oral traditions that lie behind the relations between the living and their ancestors, and we can see how the unifying principle binding Lohorung to their ancestors binds them too to the natural world.

Notes

1. Hindu and Buddhist deities figure in Lohorung lives. To separate off the tribal from that which is Hindu or Buddhist, as I have done, might be seen as a crude simplification. Lohorung have undergone innumerable changes in the process of contact with other societies. However, since Lohorung themselves did not see Hindu or Buddhist deities as central to their traditional world view and since they are not essential to the construction of self and emotion, I have not dealt with them here. To name only a few, Satte Devi, Visnu, Shivaji, Sansari, Ganesh, Bhume are all understood as part of the superhuman world with which they relate. Incorporation is a principle in Lohorung human relations, as in the adoption of clans. The same principle is at work in the superhuman world. Thus when a woman from another Rai group or from another tribe marries a Lohorung, she also brings with her the ancestral beings of her group. Through this process the number of superhuman beings acknowledged by Lohorung has expanded to include those of, for example, the Limbu, Khambu, and Yakka Rai.
2. See Allen 1976b; Gaenszle 1992. In one case it seems that the only common feature uniting the members is the fact that they are said to belong to the same class. A further problem is that each Lohorung category contains various beings or sub–groups of beings with different attributes and characteristics, to whom the Lohorung express different attitudes. Therefore, rather than adopting some Western category distinctions, which might roughly correspond to those of the Lohorung, I shall retain the Lohorung term in the text, with brief glosses where the indigenous term alone may become too confusing for the reader.
3. Writing about the Mewahang Rai, a group linguistically and culturally close to Lohorung, Gaenszle comments on the difficulty of finding a term that is appropriate for all the beings; he uses the term 'ancestral types' (1992: 198) as a general term and distinguishes between divine ancestors 'while others are spirits of more recent origin' (ibid: 198).
4. Åke Hultkrantz (1967, 1981, 1983) argues that religion is fundamentally rooted in belief in the supernatural. For objections to the 'natural'/'supernatural' dichotomy see Hallowell (1976).
5. Anthropologists usually address material about superhuman beings in terms of the 'religion' of the people. In Asia religion is often discussed in terms of either the 'great traditions' of Hinduism and Buddhism or the 'little tradition', or 'folk tradition' of the villages (See Marriott 1955 who contrasted Indian village religion with the Hindu textual tradition of Hinduism). Lohorung Rai would

have been identified as a 'little tradition'. In Nepal the 'religious' activities of people in the middle hills, like the Rai, have mainly been understood in terms of `spirit possession', in terms of priests and shamans (Hitchcock and Jones 1976, Peters 1981) and the duality in the role of the ritual specialists (Fournier 1978, Pignède 1966, Höfer 1969, Sagant 1969). Some studies have analysed particular aspects of ritual as reflecting larger principles of the society as a whole (Sagant 1973, Paul 1979, Holmberg 1989).

6. Those writing on ancestor cults often describe problems in defining the beliefs and practices as constituting `worship' in the strict sense and argue rather they are the extension of attitudes towards elders, see Newell, 1976.
7. See Sagant's article on the Limbu spirit *tangpungma* 1969, for close parallels with chawatangma.
8. In Mewahang Rai mythology Somnima drinks Paruhang's semen and eventually becomes pregnant giving birth to all living beings (see also chapter four). Gaenszle describes her as being `not the object of any cult' among the Mewahang (1992:201).
9. Gaenszle tells us that the related Mewahang Rai term *ca:ri*, once the impersonal force of the ca:wa, manifest in an ancestor stone sakhewalung, which has now become identified with more personalized spirits of local ancestors, and notably a female 'owner of the *ca:ri*', who is also seen as 'owner of the crops' (1992:205–7). Lohorung understand *sakhewalung* as the stone representing the ancestor of the mangsikhim clan, who mainly used to perform rituals to her, though at one time all four Pangma villages used to make offerings of a pig to her to make the rain come. At one time they used to offer one female and one male calf. Lohorung tell a story about how the mangsikhim clan died out but what is significant is that 'They offered to sakhewa just as we do now to our *Chawatangma*'.
10. See Hardman 2000: 209 and Chapter Seven for a more detailed description of the birth rite.
11. Gaenszle mentions that Mewahang's Lù^kwamang is also called sapdew 1992:205.
12. During Desain, a pan–Nepali festival, Lohorung make sure *sammang* do not become hungry or feel ignored or jealous by putting four leaf plates aside for them.
13. See for example Granet 1922?, Elwin 1958, Fürer–Haimendorf 1954, Hutton 1921.
14. My use of the term 'ancestor' remains somewhat problematic: a gloss for the wide and complex pantheon that I have been talking about in this Chapter. In what follows, however, I do distinguish between the Original mythical Beings, the Culture Heroes, who are both procreators and associated with the creation, and later ancestral beings. All, in Lohorung eyes, are human progenitors.
15. Holmberg describes a similar ethos among the Tamang. 'Not to exchange and share stifles well–being. To hoard, to leave out, to be tightfisted or closemouthed, to crave wealth, or to exploit without return for personal enrichment all are violations of the principle of exchange and are the traits of harmful agents who swarm the village groves and regional forests' (1989: 54)
16. Allen, in his recording of a much more detailed but similarThulung Rai myth, calls the place of Origin, the Primal Lake. The 'Rai subtribes, emerge from their original dwelling–place by means of a blood offering, sometimes that of a bird, sometimes that of a human

    Then Khimci came out from there. 'I did it by making a Blood Offering', he said, (for) he had sprinkled the blood of a *le pikpuri* bird. After he had done so the Door closed again. 'How did you get out, elder brother?' asked (another brother). 'It was by making a Blood Offering' he replied. But the other misheard him, and thought he had said that it was by killing his younger brother. So he sprinkled the Door with the blood of his younger brother and came out. (Allen, 1976: 144).
17. According to Allen, one Thulung version suggests that the younger brother misheard his elder brother and this led him to sacrifice his younger brother rather than a bird. Allen says that the basis for the misunderstanding is the closeness of the Thulung for younger brother loak and the ritual expression for blood offering *loakbe bukbe* (nd:144). Gaenszle found a similar story of trickery among the Mewahang Rai. Mewahang was deceived by his elder brother Khambuhang into killing his sister (1992: 204).

18. Most Lohorung do not eat goat. No ritual officiant may eat it or any adult member of a household. The Dumi Rai also have a myth – somewhat different – explaining why certain people cannot eat goat (see van Driem 1993: 317–8).
19. The classic study of sacrifice by Hubert and Mauss suggested sacrifice is a procedure which 'consists in establishing a means of communication between the sacred and profane worlds through the mediation of a victim, that is, of a thing that in the course of the ceremony is destroyed' (1964[1898]: 97).
20. See Girard, 1972 and Burkert 1983; also Robert G. Hamerton–Kelly ed 1987.
20. Sacrifice has been seen in terms of various theories; for Sir Edward Tylor (1871) sacrifice was seen as a gift from man to the gods to gain their favours; for Sir William Robertson Smith, sacrifice was communion in which the God and the worshippers share the flesh of the victim (1889); Sir Edward Evans–Pritchard distinguished between collective sacrifice and individual sacrifice, the former accompanying rites of passage and the latter rites of affliction to appease the spirits and concerned with moral and spiritual, not natural crises' (1956: 200). Unlike Hubert and Mauss, Evans–Pritchard emphasised that for Nuer since 'Spirit is always dangerous to man' sacrifice has to do with separation rather than fellowship (1956: chap VIII). Victor Turner (1966) focusses on the cathartic aspects of ritual sacrifice, integrating the individual and the social externally and internally, through communitas.

5

Knowledge of the Past for the Present

Pe–lam: The Present and the Past

In Chapter Four, I examined the nature of the Lohorung superhuman beings who lie at the core of their indigenous traditions and their understanding of illness, misfortune, and prosperity. The myths, language, and special knowledge pertaining to these beings is the subject of this chapter. We shall see how Lohorung conceive of the strength, support, and protection of their society, and the individuals within it, as coming from the primeval past, from the Original Beings and Ancestors, and from the indeterminate power that was invested in the natural original order of the world.[1] Those who do not have this strength behind them, though they may appear powerful, in fact have more to fear and are said to be turning towards the traditions of the Lohorung ancestors in order to overcome their vulnerability and face life as it is. The recent adoption by Brahmain and Chetri households of ritual sacrifice to Lohorung ancestors are explained in this way. The significance of the ancestral world to the Lohorung themselves is such that one of the first acts to be performed when a Lohorung has been absent some time from Lohorung society is to restore the connections of that individual with the ancestors. Knowledge about this ancestral past and the means to maintaining it in the present are contained in what Lohorung call *pe–lam* or *mundum*, from now on to be referred to as *pe–lam*. In this chapter, I convey what is meant by *pe–lam*, how the Lohorung view it, and how it affects their lives.

As a phenomenon, the *pe–lam* or *mundum* clearly links to a wider tradition existing among several hill tribes of the Himalayas, as well as having similarities with the *sgrung* ceremonies of pre–Buddhist Tibet (see Tucci: 1980). It is generally accepted that all the various Kiranti tribes have some form of *pe–lam*. The *mundhum* of the Limbu, for example, is said by the Lohorung to be 'compatible with' (*tonguk*) their own *pe-la*m. Lohorung use the terms *pe–lam* and *mundhum* interchangeably. The term *mundhum* is not to be found in Turner's Nepali–English dictionary, but as Macdonald notes (1975: 159) it is explained by Kajiman Kangangba in his Nepali-Jan-Sahitya (Kathmandu 2000, B.S.: 103) as containing traditions about the creation of the world and that they are sung by *dhami*, *bijuwa*, *phedangma*, and *baidanga*.The term is, however, most connected to the traditions of the Kiranti tribes of East Nepal and in particular to those which one Kiranti man has described as 'scriptures', dealing with Kiranti religion (Chemjong Limbu-Nepali-English Dictionary, 1961: 126). In another book Chemjong gives a fuller explanation of the meaning of the word *mundhum* for the Kiranti people: '*mundhum* means the power of great strength and the Kirat people of East Nepal believe it to be true, holy and powerful scripture' (1967: 21). Chemjong's work on the *mundhum* is based largely on manuscripts written in Limbu script, which is why he is able to use the term 'scripture'. This is, however, unsuitable as a translation for the essentially oral *mundhum* of any of the other Kiranti tribes.

It's not only Lohorung and Limbu who possess a corpus of lore and knowledge. Lohorung generally accept that every Rai tribe has myths, rites, and traditions relating to their own ancestors and origins, and that some of these overlap with their own, especially relating to the stories of origin concerning the First People and the dispersal of tribes. For example, the story of how Lohorung ancestors first came to live in the Arun valley is the same as that recounted to me by the Mewahang Rai, a 'brother' tribe of the Lohorung, living to the North. Since research has yet to be carried out on the mythology of most of the twenty or more different Rai tribes, it is hard to assess the nature of the similarities and differences in their oral traditions. Nevertheless, Nicholas Allen's collection of myths from the Thulung Rai (1976) and Martin Gaenszle's study of Mewahang Rai mythology (1991) reveal themes and stories strikingly similar to the Lohorung tradition. This re–affirms the local view that there exists a proto–tradition linking together a large number of now dispersed and differentiated tribes in East Nepal.[2]

Pe-lam, in terms of content, includes those Lohorung customs, habits, traditions, rituals, and myths, which they conceive as belonging to their own ancestors. In this sense, *pe-lam* is what distinguishes them in their own eyes from other tribes. As one man put it, it is '*tangpam, jat*' (our own tribe). Thus the *pe-lam* gives Lohorung cultural identity and 'unity'. It is one of the key ways Lohorung maintain their boundaries and express and experience their own distinctiveness in relation to other groups. It sets them particularly apart from Hindu groups and brings them closer to neighbouring Kiranti, who are conceived as sharing many of the same traditions. The *pe-lam* is quintessentially 'tribal', much of it spoken in ritual language. Lohorung culture is inevitably involved in the complex process of Hinduization but if we ask what is left of their own culture, undiluted by Hinduism, it is the stories, myths, concepts, and rituals of the pe–lam that stand out. (See Allen 1976a: 258; Gaenszle 1991: 246.)

Lohorung sometimes refer to *pe-lam* synonymously as *riti-lam*, using the Nepali term *riti* meaning 'custom, ceremony, manner, or way' (Turner 1931:537). The term *pe-lam* incorporates the meaning of both the 'way' of performing a ceremony or ritual, the paraphernalia, the occasion, the form of the ritual chant, as well as referring to the ritual itself. *Lam* in Lohorung means 'path' or 'way' in our sense of 'course of action or line of conduct' as well as 'footway'. Thus, *pe-lam* is the way of the *pe*. *Pe* has no separate meaning that I know of in Lohorung, except as linked to the verb *pe:me* 'to speak, warn'. More obviously, however, one is drawn to the Tibetan *dpe*, meaning pattern or model; parable, example, or analogy; also symmetry, harmony, book (Jäschke, 1975: 327). *The pe-la*m is precisely this: (the way of) patterns or examples to be repeated, the past acting as a template for the present. Stories and songs (*gtam-spe*) in pre-Buddhist Tibet seem to have had a significance similar to the *pe-lam* of the Lohorung, as we learn for example from Stein when he writes that:

> The stories and songs . . . were supposed to 'protect the kingdom', like the rites of Bon, through their religious powers. They express the wisdom of the elders and their trustworthy nature lends its sanction to the social and world order, the structure of the environment and that of the group inhabiting it. . . . These accounts are frequently called *gtam–dpe*, a term whose second syllable combines the meanings of example, metaphor, maxim, tale and book. During the colloquies, 'sayings' (*dep*) of the elders are cited as authority. When describing the 'religion of men', the different parts of the lion's body are used as a pattern or metaphor (*dpe*) for different types of tradition. By conforming to the patterns and precendents laid down in the time when things originated, we take our place in the order of the world and thereby help to uphold it. (1972: 198).

The idea of stories and songs (or ritual chants), associated with elders or ancestors, as being a form of protection, as ratifying and upholding the social and world order if one conforms to their example, is as familiar to the Lohorung as it appears to have been for the pre–Buddhist Tibetan.

The ancestral past for the Lohorung is neither myth nor history: that part of the past is an intrinsic and ever–living part of the present, acting as a constant reminder, an image or consciousness of the knowledge, morality, and correct order of nature and society, which has to be respected and maintained in order to ensure the continued strength of their society. The 'consciousness' is altered by generations and brought alive and made present by those who speak the words of the *pe-lam* and perform the ritual acts they accompany. It is full of symbols that evoke life as it should be. To understand the full impact of the *pe–lam* it must be said that reality for the Lohorung is not necessarily what they can see, the world is not as presented to them by ordinary experience, it is not physical and material reality. Reality for them consists of what they know to have been the order in the past, in the world of their ancestors, and which still exists in the present. Things that are not part of the *pe-lam* lack ultimate reality. It exists in the present both in the separate world of the ancestors in *Hepmalitham Yepmalitham* and also in the world as known by the living. Its presence is manifest everywhere, in any place, any happening, and in all things possessing *saya* within them. Thus, for example, crops, springs, and material objects possessing *saya* could, in the time of the ancestors, talk to ancestors who could understand them. Although at the present time men and women can no longer hear or understand the speech of these phenomena, many Lohorung believe they must act as if they did. The order of things at the time when they were heard is recorded in the lore and legends of the *pe-lam*, which acts as a model or template in terms of which

Lohorung conceptions of the world, self, and relations between them are given a definite form.

Although *pe-lam* functions as a charter, it should not be forgotten that its connection with the origin of things is predominant in its semantic range, which will become obvious in this chapter as I describe the contents of the *pe-lam*. The ancestral pattern, the template of the *pe-lam*, was laid down in the time when things originated and were established. Thus when attempting to explain the status of a particular activity the Lohorung might interchangeably describe it as being part of their *pe-lam* or as part of their *poktham-yeptham*, the place/time of rising, originating – the place/time of settlement, establishment. *Pok:me* is the Lohorung verb with the most general meaning of 'to rise, to get up from a lying position' while *yep:me* means 'to stand, remain standing, maintain a standing position' with a sense of 'standing firmly'. The Nepali term *utpatti* with the meaning of 'creation, production, origin, source, parentage, pedigree, beginning' (Turner, 1931: 48) was used to explain to me their own notion *poktham-yeptham*.

The significance of the origins lies in the Lohorung belief that the repetition of the stories of origin, linked with the Original Beings and Ancestors, or the performance of rituals in their name, as well as the duplication of activities such as hunting, fishing, weaving, or house–building, which are considered 'civilizing', act to commemorate and bring to life again the power of the primeval time. In particular, the recitation of any part of the pe-lam gives new strength to the society: the mention of the ritual name, the original names for things, raises *saya*, thereby strengthening the tie between the living and the ancestors. The importance of maintaining connections with the origin of things seems to have been equally significant for the pre–Buddhist Tibetans.

> The recitation of a myth of origin has the meaning of a restoration of a primitive state; this evocation of the origins (even if it only lasted for a brief moment) gave new strength to society and to the family dominating it, through the function innate within the ritual of making a connection between the three worlds (the heavenly world, the intermediary world, and the world of men). The three worlds were brought together in the ritual in a unity which in daily life continually deteriorates and which is, consequently always in need of renewal. (Tucci, 1980: 233)

For the Lohorung the three worlds whose unity should be maintained comprise the world of the living, the world of the ancestors above, and the world of the ancestors in the sub–soil. In primeval times these were as one, and it is these roots of existence which are the source of energy and identity. (Even the original trials of success and failure act as warnings to indicate correct behaviour and the right path to follow.) If we think of the imaginary rope, figuring in the *Khimpie* house ritual, that connects the head of each Lohorung and their *niwa* to the ancestral worlds, we could say that the recitation of the *pe-lam* strengthens the rope, renewing the lines of communication between the separate worlds and allowing better understanding and mutual support. The repetition has the same kind of force as the renewal of an old memory – a memory which whether good or bad brings back into existence a moment of the past. Time past is vitalized and brought vividly into the present. Proust aptly describes the force of this combination of past and present, which derives its strength in art from a realization of an essence. In the recitation of the *pe-lam* it is the essence of things too that is recalled and recreated, given a new existence. Proust's description helps to appreciate this process:

> . . . the noise – to be mirrored at one and the same time in the past, so that my imagination was permitted to savour it, and in the present, where the actual shock to my senses of the noise . . . or whatever it might be, had added to the dreams of the imagination the concept of 'existence' which they usually lack, and through the subterfuge had made it possible for my being to secure, to isolate, to immobilise . . . what normally it never apprehends: a fragment of time in the pure stage . . . this being (reborn with a sudden shudder of happiness when I heard the noise) is nourished only by the essence of things, in these alone does it find sustenance and light. In the present it languishes (1972: 228).

As we shall see it is the essential identity of the Lohorung, the essence of man as a hunter, woman as a weaver, the relationship between man and nature, man and superhuman, for example, that is conveyed in the *pe-lam*. We also see described the shared essences deriving from the community of origin, and the ultimate nature of things. It is because the *pe-lam* is so closely linked to the Lohorung sense of their own identity, their own cultural heritage, and their own ancestors that it is often understood as being 'that which the *yatangpa* (tribal priest) deals with' as opposed to the *mangpa* shaman, whose guiding spirits and gods come from a variety of sources, rather than from the line of Lohorung heritage .[3]

The path of the *mangpa* is mixed with non-*pe-lam* elements. It is the *yatangpa*, as seen in Chapter Four, who deals with the well-established ancestors, following the path of the lineage ancestors connected to the household shrine – that is the *bong-bi–lam*, the path of the *kul* N. To simplify a little, the main concern of the *yatangpa* is to maintain the order of Lohorung society. He deals with the life–cycle rituals, rites concerning the fertility of the soil, the protection of the crops, the house, the village, the clan; he retrieves lost *lawa*, he propitiates the *sammang* ancestors and performs the rituals to them when he has diagnosed their anger or envy as the cause of a person's sickness. In contrast, the *mangpa*, who never performs during the day, in the strictly *mangpa* role, deals almost exclusively with the forces of disorder, with the spirits of those who have died unnatural deaths, when there is some misalignment between a person and the planets, when there is general misfortune or sickness within a particular household, or there is lack of harmony between household members, or he may be called to kill the fire spirit thought to be threatening a house. It is the *yatangpa* who is primarily concerned with order and the ancestors of their own lineage, as opposed to the *mangpa*'s function to control disorder, which makes the *yatangpa* so closely linked to the *pe-lam*, though the *mangpa*'s performance does also include many references to the stories of the *pe-lam*.

The different techniques of the two officiants reveals the more local tradition to which the *yatangpa* belongs, and the wider shamanistic traditions to which the *mangpa* is a part. While the *mangpa* possesses an elaborate range of magical powers, including the shamanistic techniques of trance and possession, the powers of the *yatangpa*, as his name suggests, 'mouth alone', derives largely from the power of the ritual words of the *pe-lam*, words that can only be understood by ancestors of the Lohorung heritage and not from any other heritage. As one Lohorung explained, one particular ritual part of the *pe-lam*,'*sammang* ancestors have their *lam* (path) which is the one the *yatangpa* follows, and knows about, and which we don't know about. It's dangerous for us to know. It's dangerous for him too but he knows how to control it. He knows the weapons – the leaves and flowers, and the words – how they should be spoken.'

Memory, action, and performance are central to the *pe-lam*. Without some conscious memorization and action, the *pe-lam* as the Lohorung know it would die. And indeed, some of it is disappearing as the old who knew it die and as the young lose interest in the myths. Rituals remain central in Lohorung lives and the texts are recalled by ritual specialists, and incompletely by some of the older men and women. Even so, one 'life–prolonging' rite is now no longer performed. It is said that exact memorization or word–for–word reproduction was needed; the ritual terms for numerous flower names had to be recited in exactly the correct order or the ritual would be fatal for the patient. Now it is merely part of the collective idea of what priests used to be like when they were more powerful. Perhaps the rite always had this status. Other rituals requiring good memory still persist, such as *chokho* or *waya warema*, mentioned in Chapter Four. It also requires a memory for flower names; if one flower name is omitted, 'people become frightened and there is a possibility someone will die.[4] Most ritual chants have a particular formula,'path', or journey which fits the ancestor involved and clearly acts as a mnemonic device.[5] The 'path' can be listed. The path of *Khimpie sammang* (house ancestor), for example, goes first to the *chawa* (the ceremonial spring of each clan) of the household, then to the *samek* (ritual name of the clan) and follows the 'Arun river path', *Salpa pokhari*, *Irkhuwa Chirkhuwa*, *Maha Kulung*, *Khempalung*, *Maha Chin* (*China Rajam* country), *Kumbu Karna* country, *namdama lam* (setting sun path), *nam ketam lam* (rising sun path), *sunnaliyo lam*, *rupaliyo* (the easy, pleasant path), and back to the *chawa* and the house and the parts of the house possessing *saya* and ritual names. This is the mountain path (*wasri-ma lam*) which is very difficult, so many go the lower path along the S*un Kosi*, the *Dudh Kosi*, to *Halesi*, that is, the *Chenge khasukma khaya-ma* path. The route almost always starts and finishes in the house, and with a detailed listing of all the parts of the house that possess *saya*, and therefore need their *saya* raising. Apart from 'paths', there are other types of aids to performance, such as repetitions of phrases particular to each ritual; '*sahe!*' constantly appearing in *waya warema*; or 'saying words', that is, meaningless words, repeated after ritual phrases such as in the above *rupaliyo* to go with *sunnaaliyo*. These 'saying words' constitute a ritual language and are seen as the 'proper' way to address ancestral beings. Similar ritual languages have been found to exist amongst the Thulung Rai, Mewahang Rai, and the Kulunge Rai. (Allen 1978: 237–55, Gaenszle 1991 and McDougal 1979: 92–3.)

We can see, then, that each *yatangpa* has an outline within which he can compose his own performance. In the recitation of the *pe-lam* he remakes the tradition and remakes it personally, making additions and omissions and changes in order. Thus, although there is a continuity of tradition, there is also a wide variety which retains the pattern and essential meaning of the ritual or myth but each time alters the text. In the telling of the myths no one complains about personal additions. Ritual chants have a more rigid structure. *Yatangpa* communicate with the superhuman world and Lohorung express fear the rite might anger the ancestor involved unless carried out properly, so people complain about *yatangpa*, distressed that they did not say the words correctly or that they did not know enough of them so that the ritual was rushed. Just as we complain about our doctors and have our favourites so inevitably, certain *yatangpa* are favoured. Each household tends to stick to the one they trust to perform the rites in the 'correct' fashion.

The ritual chants have survived better than the myths; the myths have no immediate prophylactic function in the way that the rites do, and are mainly of interest at weddings and to those Lohorung who are concerned about their heritage.

Let's now look more closely at Lohorung attitudes towards the *pe-lam*.

Lohorung Dispositions towards the Pe-lam

Pe-lam is central to the Lohorung sense of identity, continuity, and their psychological and physical well-being: it acts to maintain the strength, support, and protection of ancestral traditions and those who are their living executors. It provides them with the history of their own identity (there is no clear distinction between history and myth) and provides the categories through which they conceive of themselves, giving order and meaning to their universe. Men and women are destined to be linked with the condition founded in primeval time, when the world was taking shape and ancestral beings were making it habitable, humanized, and civilized, when the relationship between man and nature, man and the natural species was established. The inevitable nature of the link is reflected in the Lohorung notion of *saya* which acts as a kind of ancestral connection between the living and everything originating at the time of the Original Beings and Ancestors. Everything mentioned in *pe-lam*, including Man, has *saya*, an indestructible life–force, or ancestral substance.

This raises the issue of whether Lohorung regard *pe-lam* as 'sacred' or 'holy'. My hesitation in using the term lies in the implication of a separation of categories 'sacred' as opposed to 'profane', whereas Lohorung see these as almost inextricably intertwined. They do make a distinction between *lemmang*, the reality which is graspable and perceived by the waking consciousness, and *semmang*, the reality reached in dreams or trance, neither bound by space or time. And there is the reality which is the perception and meaning of things as derived from the *pe-lam*.Things that are *pe-lam*-marked (sometimes ritually marked, but not always) have a particular valency in Lohorung life owing to their connection with the ancestors. On the other hand, Lohorung dispositions towards the *pe-lam* are not always what we would understand from the word 'sacred'.

The dispositions closest to any notion of the 'sacred' are evoked at times of the more formal recitation of *pe-lam*, such as at the *sammang* ancestral rites, explained as being a combination of respect *hangmale*, fear (*kisimalu*), and excitement (*chencha:me*). The fear is because there is danger.

> The *sammang* ancestors come: they are called to the place. If they are angered by someone's behaviour that person may become ill, they may even die. Like Prem's mother who can hardly move. They were doing *Khimpie* (the house ancestor), and they didn't use the good beer. It was a little sour. Before she was a bit stiff, now she can hardly move.

Women and children, spinning, making leaf plates, or delousing each other sit in a relaxed and lively group somewhat distant from the shrines, which can only be made by men. Men are the active participants in the rite, performing all the necessary functions such as cooking and aiding the *yatangpa* priest. It is said to be too dangerous for women and children to relate to the ancestors by taking an active role in the rites or even by sitting close to the shrines. Their *saya* is *michupa* 'small', *lulo* 'relaxed, bending, easily persuaded', or *niphero* 'weak, fragile', and cannot protect them against the possible anger, envy, or jealousy of the ancestors. Some *sammang* ancestors, too, are said to like to tease and try to tempt away the *lawa* (the wandering spirit or soul) from women and children, not necessarily maliciously, but simply for want of a companion. The *saya* and *lawa* of men are *nithuri* N 'cruel, ferocious, powerful'; they are *chenchen* 'firm, strong' and keep the *sammang* at a distance.

Although I have glossed *kisimalu* above as 'fear', a better interpretation of it, in the context of rituals, might be 'fearsome' or 'awesome', the propensity to evoke fear, rather than the emotion itself, particularly since Lohorung emphasize the prohibition of fear during *sammang* rituals.

During *sammang* rituals, *phenni* 'prohibition' rules control behaviour so that people conform to ways of behaving pleasing to the *sammang* involved. *Phenni* has a general sense of 'it is wrong, bad, worthless' as in 'if you are ill, to drink beer *phenni* – wounds appear', 'this water pot *phenni*, it leaks' or 'to kick a cow or sister *phenni*, you will be cursed and develop wounds or die'. In the context of *sammang* rites the meaning is perhaps closer to 'it is forbidden'. It is *phenni*, for example, to eat or drink once the main leaf of the shrine has been laid down, and until the sacrifice has been performed and the offerings given to the ancestors. It is *phenni* to have any communication with any person other than those in the group; performing the ritual. The special place for the ritual, whether in a secluded spot in the forest, or the garden behind the house, or in the house itself, is 'shut off' from contact with the outside world. In the case of the house ritual the house is literally boarded up. This action of cloistering is classified as a *nep:me* 'prohibition' or 'restriction', similar to the *phenni* rules.[6] Some Lohorung 'restrict' Tuesdays: they go no where, receive no guests, and exchange no goods. Certain rituals, such as *iksammang* (also known as *bali puja* N.), require a 'prohibition' of work on the following day. If people work, they say, the crops fail. Those who are *yatangpa* have food 'prohibitions'. They cannot eat the category of food called *sung-sa*, including goat, and mountain sheep.

The Lohorung take these *phenni* 'prohibition' rules seriously. Any breach of the rules is said to lead to chaos, failure of the ritual, and sickness or death amongst the participants. Either the ancestors become jealous of those taking food and drink, or they are enraged by acts which are interpreted as demonstrating lack of respect. Such behaviour would obviously be counter–productive to rituals performed to assuage ancestral anger and to indicate that ancestors and ancestral ways constitute the body of authority in Lohorung society. Thus, at one level, rules are followed to convey to ancestors that the household or lineage have the correct attitude towards them.

At another level, the *phenni* rules – and especially that of prohibiting contact with outsiders – reflect the extent to which the Lohorung regard rituals of the *pe-lam* as being efficacious. They are effective not only in curing particular individuals, but also in transforming the state of all the participants and the objects involved. During the period of many indigenous tribal rituals, such as *Khimpie* or *waya warema*, the participants are brought into contact with the ancestral world and become transitional beings, in much the same sense as neophytes do in the rites described by Turner (1966). As liminal personae they have no social reality – no property, no heirarchy, and no social identity. For the rite to be effective the participants must maintain this non-social status. The Lohorung say that the most destructive form of contact with someone outside the ritual would be to be called by one's name, to be asked for a loan, or to be asked to join in some agricultural labour, i.e. to be recalled into one's status in the world of the living. Not only is the ordered, social everyday world of the living dangerous for the ritual group, the transitional state of the ritual group is also a danger to the outside, and therefore to be avoided. Other occasions when houses or villages are said to be isolated, such as at times of epidemics or incest, are perhaps more obviously dangerous and polluting. But from the Lohorung point of view it is just as dangerous to be taken by the recitation of the *pe-lam* words into ancestral space and time and feel the presence of ancestors called to the shrine. For the participants themselves, the liminal period – if conducted correctly and without interruption – results in the raised *saya* of all concerned as well as of all ritual objects.

In contrast to the moods and attitudes considered appropriate at the *sammang* ancestral rituals, there are those expressed in response to the stories about the *namnunglachi*, the 'sun-moon people', the Original Beings. Few Lohorung admit to knowing these stories in any depth. Mainly, I heard them from older women (three in particular), who had learned them from other women when they were young. Snippets of the stories accompanied respite from labour in the fields. 'As we sat to rest, we all used to gather round mamma, drinking our *dibu*, beer, and eating our snacks. She used to make us laugh. We used to say "mammo, tell us some more about *Yechakukpa* and *Chumling Chongma*." We didn't know they were our *uptpatti*, our origins.'

The stories were always repeated to me with considerable laughter and dramatization; demonstrations of the tricks and misfortunes involved in the story were a necessary part of the recitation. Certainly there were no *phenni* restrictions on drinking or on any other behaviour. Just as at all times when men were not present, the women were carefree with their dress, posture, and comments.

Men rarely admitted they knew these stories, though their evident embarrassment at the very mention of them indicated that many of them did know about them. Rather, they were ashamed to admit or re-tell the stories, some of which in the eyes of the modern day Nepali, seem childish. Women agreed that 'men are ashamed (*ngesimalu*) of the stories. They pretend to be big and important and not to know. They want to talk about the *panchayat* (local village council). But it is our *pe-lam*, we should respect it.' From this, it should not be concluded, however, that men disregard the stories of the *pe-lam*. That is far from the case. Many men regarded the stories as essential for understanding who the Lohorung are, and even encouraged me to discover those more particularly concerning the origins of tribes. The shyness and hesitation on the part of men had more to do with the ever–increasing pressures on Lohorung to devalue the tribal aspects of their society – such as their own language, the Rai headmen, the ownership of the jungle, their traditional dress and ornaments, their house style, their tradition of hunting and raising of pigs – and instead to adopt Hindu and pan–Nepali traditions.[7] The young are naturally more eager to learn Nepali songs than *pe-lam* stories and to go to school rather than hunt and weave. There is nothing'sacred' about these stories and yet it is widely recognized that many Lohorung traditions and institutions are founded on them. Respectful attitudes displayed at rituals has to do with the danger involved in activities which open up the means of communication between the living and the ancestral world.

Ironically, although the present social milieu detracts from the significance of the *pe-lam* stories in the lives of Lohorung (in the sense that the *pe-lam* has to compete with the modernizing ways of Hinduism), at the same time the milieu creates increased motivation for them to perform ancestral rituals, since contact with the outside world merely emphasizes the extent to which they are vulnerable. And the one way Lohorung know how to counteract vunerability is by raising their *saya*, by performing the rituals of the *pe-lam*, thereby strengthening their contact with ancestors, renewing their vitality, and coming to terms with change. *pe-lam*, for the Lohorung, is thus one of the main ways of coping with the modern world. The imbalance of the present (in terms of their own knowledge, status, and prestige in relation to other groups) can only be neutralized by the power of their own ancestral bond and the vitality within it. *Saya*, as we shall see, as the source and indicator of collective well–being and vitality, acts as a central institution in Lohorung society dealing with the tensions that arise between individual motivations and public expectations.

Pe-lam, *Man, and Nature*

The *pe-lam* spells out the relationship between man and nature, between man and the natural species, as being one in which man is regarded in many ways as part of nature, bound by psycho–physical ties and those of kinship. One of the most striking statements I kept hearing from the Lohorung was the assertion that 'We are the brothers of tiger and bamboo'. I should like to look here at how this statement is embedded in the *pe-lam*, and to tease out exactly what it does mean to the Lohorung. One of the stories I heard that included the statement went as follows:

> First of all there was only water, rain and ponds, only water. Then a rainbow came and earth and sky – earth became the mother and sky the father. The child's name was *Ninimaremma*. *Ninimaremma* was filled with, had intercourse with the wind, and *Ninimaremma* became pregnant. *Niniyama* was born. *Niniyama* asked her mother where she came from, and her mother told her 'The wind came into me and I became pregnant.' Having heard her mother's words, *Niniyama* went to the spring and called to the wind. But the wind indeed did not come. She called again and still nothing happened. *Niniyama* returned home; 'Why didn't the wind come to me?' she asked her mother. Her mother replied, 'the wind is your father. You must look for a husand in the sky.' *Ninimaremma* had heard about *Sukra* (N) (the planet Venus). She gave money and beer to two *jogio* (*tse perekwa*) birds telling them to bring *Sukra*. Off they went, but on arriving there they found that he was not there. *Bryaspatti* (N) (Jupiter) was there. So the birds said to *Bryaspatti*, 'you must come with us.' 'I won't go to that place: they don't like me.' *Bryaspatti* you see had an ugly goitre. The birds insisted and they all went off to *Niniyama*'s. When she saw him she obviously didn't like him. He saw this and he became very angry and he decided to go back. *Bryaspatti* said (to himself), 'When I get back I'll make the sun very strong. Everything will dry up, all the water will dry up. And when *Niniyama* is thirsty the *jogio* birds will give

> her my urine from a leaf. And some of the dried droppings from the birds' tails will fall on her mouth.' He told the birds that when *Niniyama* cried out in despair they should give her his urine. The birds dipped their tails into the urine put in the hollow of a tree and shook them over her mouth. The birds gave it to her and she became pregnant – all the species began to grow and from her was born the thorny creeper (*chiching*), bamboo (*baphu*), the tiny black fly, (*busunna*), bear (*maksa* or *Tumnahang*), monkey (*pubbang*), Tiger (*kiba* or *Paknahang*), and man (*Pomnahang*) – the Kiranti. We are all brothers, our mother the same.

There was some disagreement among informants about whether it was a rainbow or thunder and lightning which had initially joined the earth and sky. Some people also talked of the initial creation as deriving from a great and circular motion, like weaving an enormous *pira* (N.), a round woven rush mat, or from the movement of leaves blown into a spiral by a strong gust of wind.[8] They all, however, accepted the power of the elemental forces, such as the rain, the wind, rainbows, and thunder and lightning. There were variations too in terms of the original plants, a few more sometimes being added, but there was always a clear progression from the simplest forms of life to mankind. Lohorung say that they have a reputation for looking like tigers because the brother closest to them – to the Kiranti – was a tiger. Another version of the creation story was given to me by a shaman.

> First from *Niniyama* came the thorny creeper, the reed, the small cane, the large cane, and bamboo – all the different kinds. These were created, then Bear, then Tiger, then Man, a *Yakkaba* like us. You know him – *Yachakukpa*. For ten months he was in *Niniyama*'s womb. With him a bow and arrow, a shield and sword. We are all descendants of that part of creation. Our rising place is the same, all of us brothers. The destination was not the same. Some of them went off into the forest: Tiger, Bear, and Man remained in the same place as their mother. When they were grown up they began to quarrel. The place was not big enough for all of them. Tiger, the eldest son, went off to kill birds, the main source of food that was available. Bear tried to catch some in a trap. He was not very successful. *Yachakukpa* (Man) became important with his bow and arrow; he shot many birds and Tiger didn't like it. One day, Man and his bamboo bow and arrow went off with tiger into the jungle. Man had no clothes, at that time, you know, he had only strips made of pliable, dried grasses intertwined. While hunting he noticed Tiger looking at him: 'will my brother try to eat me?' he asks himself. Next time, *Yachakukpa* went hunting on his own, leaving behind Tiger and Bear with their mother. Now, nothing that Tiger had hunted would he share with his mother. All the birds that he caught, he ate himself. And that was all the meat there was to eat. However much he caught, it was only enough for himself. . .When *Yachakukpa* returned he found his mother dead. Tiger had starved her to death. He went to look for Tiger but looked in vain. Later he found Tiger and told him to go with Bear and bury their mother. But after some time he came across Tiger and Bear again, lying asleep by the pile of bones of their mother. They had eaten their mother. *Yachakukpa* sent them off into the jungle.

It is clear that one of the main themes of this part of the *pe-lam* is dispersal.[9] First, some of them go off into the jungle, but even so the place is not big enough for the remaining few. This strikes a familiar key. Lohorung sons and their wives soon find the parental household 'not big enough' when they begin to have children and wish to make their own decisions. There is obvious rivalry in the story just as there often is in reality. In the end *Yachakukpa* separates himself from Tiger and Bear, once more dispersing the original brothers. It is pertinent that certain species are not mentioned as 'brothers'. It is as if birds, trees, stones, springs, fish, insects, and flowers always existed. There is no part of the *pe-lam* which deals with their origin as species and Lohorung surprisingly seem uninterested in their origins. They are, however, much concerned with how particular types within these species came to look, smell, or act as they do now. Stories proliferate about why, for example, different birds cry out and behave as they do, why insects have different shaped bodies and wings, why some flowers of the same type have two colours, why one kind of frog is likened to a bird, why man cannot walk soon after birth like other species with legs. Lohorung are thus here interested in how a type becomes differentiated within a species, defined by them as such. And this, I suggest, is also the concern of this section of the *pe-lam*. It is explaining how the original species dispersed, and how Lohorung man came to have different kinds of 'brothers'. Tiger or Bear represent one kind of brother and Bamboo another. While still remaining 'brothers' Tiger and Bear must be somehow separated from Man and sent off into the wild. In contrast, Bamboo in the form of bow and arrow is the brother who cannot be set aside; the one who, transformed from a natural state, becomes in culture the brother accompanying man in his domestic space.

In the myth, the plants leave for their destination in the forest. The only one to figure later is Bamboo in the form of the bow and arrow. It is the destination of Bamboo to live alongside Man, in solidarity with him, just as do the brothers of his lineage, who fight with him and work in collaboraton with him. In contrast, Tiger and Bear begin in the same place as Man, until he finds that between them they have killed and eaten their mother, after which they are then sent off to the jungle. It is significant that it is the two elder brothers who depart and the youngest who stays, a replica of the way in which brothers traditionally set up their individual households; all but the youngest leaving the parental home to build their own, the youngest remaining to look after the parents and inherit their house. The *pe-lam* acts as the template for the present.

Let me first look at the 'brother' role represented by Tiger and Bear and then that of Bamboo. Tiger and Bear must be seen, I suggest, in the context of a large number of tribes to whom the Lohorung consider themselves related and with whom they have apparently little in common except a vague notion of being 'brothers' (*dajyu-bhai*) – a Nepali term combining the respectful term 'elder brother' and the more general casual term 'younger brother' or 'brothers in general'. The Lohorung do not use their own language to describe these 'brothers' since the brother tribes all have languages of their own. The lingua franca, Nepali, is used instead. As mentioned earlier, 'brothers' for the Lohorung include all those they call *Khambu* living to the west of the Arun, all the *Yakthumba* (or Limbu), all the *Yakkha* as well as the *Mech-Koch* and the *Dhimal* of the Terai. Lohorung also accept as 'brothers' a clan called *Lohorunge* of the Tibetan–speaking Lhomi of the upper Arun, whom they refer to as *Syamdang'chi* after the village Syamdang. They sometimes use the term *tsampa'chi* (that is, those Tibetans and Sherpa who eat a kind of porridge called *tsampa*), which has abusive connotations to infer a people who rarely wash their clothes and even less frequently their cooking vessels and plates, preferring to lick them clean after use, a people completely different from themselves. Nevertheless, they still refer to them as a 'brother' clan.

An appreciation of the meaning of 'brother', from the Lohorung point of view, must be seen in connection with their system of descent. One of its most important features is a dual process of clan fission called *sekowa pokme* (breaking the bones) and clan separation due to migration. Although the Lohorung claim that originally there were 'ten Lohorung brothers', I was able to collect the names of thirty–five clans.

As Figure 8 illustrates, the proliferation of clans within one branch is the result of either clan fission or the adoption of a clan which has migrated from another locality. In the diagram some branches are shown as having sub–branches of three or four clans. This is the result of a series of fissions on two or three occasions but in which the sequence of separation has been forgotten. The Yamdang brother exemplifies the division of a tribal branch by the process of migration and physical separation, as the following brief story documents:

> Two brothers were travelling south and found good land in Syamgang. After some time one brother decided to leave. First he went to Dhupu and (later) he stayed in Pangma. The other brother Lohorung stayed in Syamdang. Then the Lhomi came. And now his great-grandchildren and his great-great-grandchildren (i.e. his descendants) have become just like the Lhomi.

Lohorung say they never marry with the Syamdang Lohorung because 'we are brothers', and the rule of clan exogamy is still applied by these two different sections of what was a clan unit. The Syamdang case helps to understand this part of the *pe-lam* by emphasizing that differences in physical appearance customs and habits do not discount brother relations in Lohorung classification. I suggest that brothers Tiger and Bear of the *pe-lam* are not just representing the brothers who are physically unrecognizable as 'brothers'. They also stand for the brothers who caused the first clan fission. The *pe-lam* states that the brothers Tiger, Bear, and Man all have the same mother. Even though the father is not expressly mentioned, they are of one clan. According to Lohorung, and Rai tradition in general, segmentation of one clan

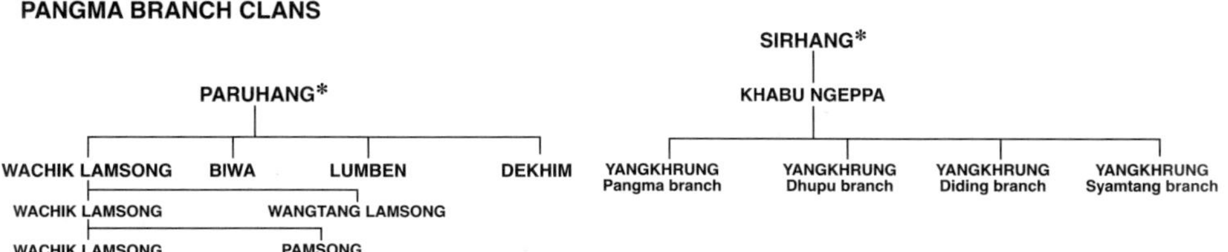

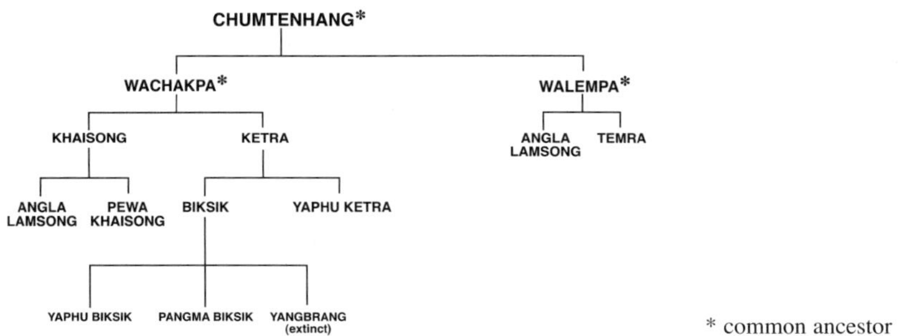

* common ancestor

FIG 8 The Ancestry of Clans in Pangma

into two separate clans is achieved by 'breaking the bones' of the clan.[10] The patriline, 'the bones', is split by means of an incestous marriage between members of one clan. Genealogically speaking, marriage within the clan is prohibited for seven generations. If in the eighth generation however, a union takes place between members of the same clan, the clan is broken into two, and rituals are performed to formalize the event. This form of division is accepted and even encouraged so long as the requisite eight generations are thought to have lapsed. For Lohorung the idea of sharing is important. People should share what they have with others, and especially with brothers. Men or boys, for example, who go hunting or fishing are expected to share their spoils with their closest lineage brothers. Although in general sharing women within the clan is prohibited by the rule of clan exogamy, clan fission after eight generations makes it possible.

The three main components involved in 'breaking the bones' of a clan are an incestuous union, separation, and the ideal of sharing. All three components are present in this section of the *pe-lam*. Eating, *chame* in Lohorung, has connotations of desire and especially of copulation (*hokchame*). *Chame* can also mean to defeat or overcome. When Man and Tiger go hunting together and Man wonders if Tiger will eat him, I have understood *chame* to mean 'eat' because Tiger was obviously so hungry or greedy that he refused to share any of the hunting spoil with his mother and had eyes on Man. The 'sharing' component is clear. The sexual connotations in the myth are blatant when Tiger and Bear 'eat' the flesh of their mother (the matriline), leaving only a pile of bones (the patriline). As we have said the typical way for the Lohorung to talk about the matriline or the patriline is in terms of flesh and bones. It seems likely that this episode represents the incestuous union precipitating the fission of the clan. When Man finds Tiger and Bear licking their paws, he sends them off in different directions, thereby splitting up the group and bringing to mind the separation of the clan. It may be more than just a coincidence that the Lohorung names for tiger *kiba* and bear *maksa* are similar to two kin terms. *Maksa* is the term to refer to daughter's husband, brother's daughter's husband, younger sister's husband, younger sister's daughter's husband, sister's daughter's husband, and *ki-bu* refers to elder sister's husband and his brothers, that is, men who may take or have taken women from ones own clan (see Appendix 2 for kinship terms). It seems likely that what links *kiba* and *ki-bu* is that they both provoke fear *ki* (as in *ki-malu* 'I feel fear'); *kiba*, fear from that one, *ki-bu* fear/frightening brother. And the Lohorung do indeed treat both with awe and respect.

Bamboo contrasts with Tiger and Bear as a brother. In part, it is separated from *Yechakukpa*, taking its place in the wild with the other plants. Yet its place in culture, as opposed to nature, is elite. It stays alongside Man as an indispensible tool. Most Lohorung material culture comprises bamboo in one form or another. Bamboo provides the Lohorung and most other Kiranti groups with the material means for self–sufficiency. A study of its uses leads almost inevitably into almost every sphere of their lives.[11] They know best and use for numerous purposes ten different varieties ranging from the small *dingmik* (*malingo* N) which can be 6cm (2.5 in.) in diameter to the giant *sakbaphu* (*tama bans* N) growing large enough to act as supporting poles of a house. Depending on how the ubiquitous bamboo is treated it can be pliable or strong, flexible enough to weave baskets and mats, sharp enough to be an arrow. Watertight and hollow bamboo makes good water canals, drinking vessels, or pipes. It is so elastic and yielding it makes a perfect natural swing or a bow. Shaved finely, bamboo can be used as a brush or a toothpick. The young shoots of certain varieties can be eaten. It is the thin supple exterior which is used for making baskets, after it has been soaked in water and put in the sun to dry; the strip beneath the exterior is slightly thicker but even more flexible and is used for mats. The inner strip is wide, more resistant, and used for fencing. Bamboo is the main material which accompnies a man when he goes hunting or fishing, and as he builds his house, protects his fields. Stripping, splitting, and weaving bamboo is an ancient Rai tradition belonging exclusively to the men of the society.

Man is envisaged as being born with bamboo in his hand, reflecting the Lohorung view that they, and indeed other Rai, are archetypal bowmen, bowmen by tradition and by nature. Though less frequently called upon to use bow and arrows, except for ritual purposes and shooting small game, Lohorung men are still considered to possess the stereotypical qualtities of the hunter. Men are seen as inevitably *ichhuba* 'mean, crafty, and strong' (both physically and mentally) and essentially *hacha'wa* 'excitable and vital' as well as *chake'le* 'brave'. Hunting is said to bring out all these qualities and also increase them. Most men talk with enthusiasm of the time when they really could hunt, when the forests were full of game, and they repeat the stories of Lohorung fights with neighbouring tribes and the long excursions into the jungle followed by enormous feasts when all the game was shared out. Many Lohorung men have been to Assam and they claim 'there it's still like that – among the Mishmi' – the people with whom they most associate and identify. Lohorung think of the bow and arrow as man's natural and most important weapon. It is widely known that the Rai are essentially bowmen and they are characterized as being aggressive, hot–tempered, violent, excitable, and fierce. The image is so commonly held that until recently Brahman, Chetri, or Newar, forced to walk through Lohorung territory to go to market, would take circuitous routes in the hope of avoiding a confrontation with one of these Lohorung. This was apparently particularly the case in the early 1970s when there was a violent feud between the Newars of Khandbari and the Lohorung of Pangma.

That Rai males have the reputation of being bowmen is reinforced by the versions of the Tiger myth collected by Nicholas J. Allen among the Thulung Rai. In some versions the conception of man as bowman is very explicit. For example,

> Ph: 'Mini Rai possessed magic powers, and was a skilled bowman . . . (Mini) made a slight movement. Down below, seeing the shadow of his younger brother, Tiger pounced. At that moment Mini shot him.'
> On another telling Ph mentioned that Mini was born with a bow in his hand, and with the power to steer and call back arrows.
> Mj. 'Mini was armed with a bow, and later on he killed Tiger. That is why Tigers are afraid of us' (1976a: 53–4).

For Rai as a whole, I suggest, the first man is conceived as being born with a bow and an arrow, a shield and a sword. Man, just equipped with his natural disposition, could not survive. The bow provides the medium for man to gain protection and for him to attack; it is his weapon for survival. The bow is conceived as representing those qualities which are valued in a man – the bamboo bow is his strength. Man should approach life ready for hunting and warring, for the protection of the lineage. Men should have the qualities which will ensure its continuation and to achieve these aims he is aided by bamboo in his right hand.

The inner force and potential power of a bow is intrinsic to bamboo in general, the visual symbol of inner strength and vitality. In its link with the ancestors, bamboo always has potential power as the following illustrates:

> Dhupu *ngeppa* (chief) had the intention of plundering Yuba and killing *Thanaba* and *Thudak*, the kings of the two clans *Pakpusa* and *Rungbangsa*. The kings agreed to help the

> Yuba *ngeppa*. On their return from Yuba with their new ally they stopped to rest on Batboteni Dänra. *Thanaba* blew some grains of rice as offering onto the plant of a *dingmik* (*malingo* N) bamboo. Immediately one shoot of the bush started shaking 'tirrirri' 'tirrirri'. *Thanaba* picked that shoot and crushed it into a pulp on a stone, and thereby made himself a weapon and gave himself strength to fight. *Thudak* said to *Thanaba* 'Your strength is now made, what can I do?'

The Dhupu *ngeppa* was killed by *Thanaba* and *Thudak* and for this reason the *Yangkhrung* clan, descendants of the dead man, are forbidden to use or eat the shoots of *dingmik* bamboo.

Bamboo is the brother of man and not woman. Women cannot weave or work with bamboo: all activities with bamboo are done by men. Women weave with cotton and similarly this is forbidden to men. If a man were to weave with cotton he would become impotent and if a woman worked with bamboo she would be infertile. Bamboo has to do with virility and superstitions flourish. Lohorung say they must slit bamboo into *singka* (fine strands) before the maize is planted or the maize will have thin stems and few cobs – their virility cut. Women are forbidden to cut the delicate edible bamboo shoots.They have to call in a man to do it. If they do it themselves one of their children would surely die. The life of the family is partly maintained by the constancy of the relationship between man and bamboo. At the time of the first ancestors houses were totally made out of bamboo and it is now the most consistently used material in rites to ancestors for making their houses on the shrine. If man has bamboo by his side he has the tools for their protection, the weapons and the strength to fight and the virility to procreate. Bamboo is 'brother' to man as that which stands by him, like the brothers of his lineage.

While bamboo is the symbol of male virility and vitality; the symbol of man the hunter with enthusiasm for life, crafty, strong, and essentially excitable, *saya* is the concept expressing this inner state. We can begin to appreciate why the *saya* of men has to be raised more often than in women. In the ancient ancestral order of things it was men who needed the strength and vitality to hunt and make war with neighbouring tribes, whereas for women *saya* and the link with ancestors was mainly to do with self–protection.

Inner strength and potential power is intrinsic to bamboo, the visual symbol of vitality. Because of this and its link with the primeval age bamboo is a natural medium between ancestors and living beings. One obvious expression of this is found in the tradition of carrying the dead on a bier made of a particular kind of bamboo – *yong baphu* the name derived from its function (*yong:me* meaning 'to transport, carry'). Only other kinds of bamboo can be used on the shrines to ancestors where it is used extensively. It is also used by *mangpa* shaman during night–long seances in which they act out part of the *pe-lam*. *Gungring* (*phurke* N) or long bamboo wands with shaved frills like fronds at each end are used by shaman as a weapon in the same sense as a bow and arrow is for man.

Chawa *and* samek

Apart from *saya* two other concepts closely bound man to nature. They are *chawa* and *samek*.[12] The two concepts are essential to the Lohorung notion of 'the person'. These concepts are crucial to their relations with the superhuman world, the natural world and, in certain specific cases, with members of their own society. *Samek* is the 'original' or proto name which identifies people, clans, and objects in their relations with the ancestors. The name relates a person not to a clan but to the original clan–group. *Chawa* is both the 'first clan watering place' and the territorial name which identifies and binds together a clan, identifying the spring to which the clan first spoke when its members claimed the land. It therefore links the 'person' through an identification with the clan to a particular area or territory.

Samek and *chawa* relate to each other and together they locate people in relation to a collective group and to a particular locality. No individual has his or her own *samek*. Individuals adopt the *samek* name of their clan–group, thus relating a person to a group beyond his or her own clan to the original clan-group. When clans split and take on new independent clan names they still retain their original *samek* name. For example, all the four 'brother' clans in Pangma have the same *samek* name – *dekhaba* for the males and *dekhama* for females. The *yangkhrung* clan has separate branches in Pangma village and Dhupu, but they are all identified for ritual purposes, in their relations with the ancestors, as *kechaba/kechama*. Their 'ancestral' name identifies them as they were in the past before any splits occurred. Their *chawa* gives them the reference of their locality. A few *samek* groups have more than one *chawa* because branches of the proto-clan have claimed territory independently. So, whereas all the original four Pangma clans have the same *chawa* and the same *samek*, the *biksik* clan has two *chawa* and one *samek* name, because one branch of the *biksik* stopped and claimed land in Dhupu while the other branch went on to claim territory in *Pangma*. Lohorung clans and their respective chawa and samek are as follows:

TABLE 1 Lohorung Clans, their *Chawa* and *Samek*

Clan	*chawa*	*samek*
Bi–wa Lamsong Lumben Dekhim	*lamawa* or *lambuwa chawa* (Pangma)	*chiksaba/dekhama* or *dekhaba/dekhama*
Wangtang Lamsong	*tamuwa chawa* (Yaphu)	*yukchami/yukhama*
Bik–sik	*tumbuwa chawa* (Yaphu) *tumbokma chawa* (Diding)	*chiksaba/chiksama*

Clan	*chawa*	*samek*
Yangkhrung	*pittuma/pi-tukma chawa* (Pangma) *dara pani* (Dhupu)	*kechaba/kechama*
Yangkhe–la	*pungben chawa* (Malta) *tumbuwa chawa* (Yaphu) *yoktokwa chawa* (Apurdam)	*kechaba/kechama*
Heluwali Themsong Karduwali	*sing–bongma chawa* (Heluwa) (Heluwali Lamsong)	*yungkhaba/yungkhama*
Angla Lamsong Ketra Khaisong Tembra	*minchi–wa chawa* (Yaphu)	*yungkhaba/yungkhama*
Che–wa (Chukhuwa)	*khamle–wa chawa* (Arbote)	*rungkhaba/rongkhama*
Khimpule	*hangchuwa chawa* (Malta)	*yungkhaba/yungkhama*
Deksen Hangkhim	*chokawa chawa* (Mangtewa)	*wachihang/wekhama*
Pakpusa Tsanka	*yimua chawa* (Num)	*yungchaba/yungchama*
Rumbangsa Lumbangsa	*yimua chawa* (Num)	*songsaba/songsama*
Kesa	*yimua chawa* (Num)	*kechaba/kechama*
Kikura Kakura Nikura Menaba	*kheksuwa chawa* (Num)	*kechaba/kechama*
Drikhim	*chonglama chawa* (Pangma)	*kekaba/kekama*
Tengsa	*mingchiwa chawa* (Yaphu)	*yungkaba/yungkama*

Clan	*chawa*	*samek*
Deren Lamsong	*lungkowa chawa*	*yungkaba/yungkama*
Yumpang Deren GairiAngla Deren	*lungkhukma chawa*	*yungkaba/yungkama*

Samek, however, does not only apply to clans. Many other phenomena also have a *samek* name. All of them are conceived of as originating in ancestral time. The *samek* name is the ritual name, the *pe-lam* name, and everything that is mentioned in ritual must have a ritual name. One old man trying to explain samek, put it as follows,

> Everyone has a *samek*. We can't do without it. At marriage time we ask 'is it permitted? or is it forbidden?' If the *samek* name of the girl and the boy is different then we know it's all right; if it's the same then we must look more. We should keep the *samek* name of everything. Everything has some name – all trees, leaves, *singlung* 'nature' have a name. That is 'green grass', that is 'stone'. We are 'man'. We became rich by grass and stone. Once it was free, freehold. But now that green grass also has *samek*. It is owned. Everything has a *samek*, making it a separate kind; fire has *samek*, door has *samek*; we call maize *lingkhama*, rice we call *rungkhama* and millet *wekhama*; money is *pekhama*.

My informant was here trying to explain to me the classificatory aspect of *samek*, based on ownership by the ancestors, who discovered something and claimed it, naming it with a *samek* name. The name now makes it recognizable in the catalogue of the ancestral world and allows it to be named in ritual. The name may identify individual objects or animals or it may name a classificatory group.

A female shaman (*mangmani*) added another aspect by saying: 'If there was no *samek* people could not say anything. With the *samek* we can call the ancestors, we can relate to the things in their time. *Samek* is the same as a name; without a name we wouldn't be able to experience anything or do things. Everything needs this name. Then its *saya* (vital force, ancestral substance) can be raised and strengthened. If there is no name then nothing.' Thus *samek* identifies and gives substance and existence to things for the ancestors and for those wishing to communicate with ancestors.

Samek names are also supposed to indicate something about the order of creation, the migration of tribes, the order of arrival of tribes. As far as clans are concerned they indicate who settled first. *Pekhama* denotes the eldest, *wekhama* the first settler and *dekhama* the second, whereas *yungkhama* is said to be the one that was allowed by the others to settle on their land. In general, Lohorung say millet is the oldest known crop, *pekhama*; rice was the first to be settled in this area and so that is *wekhama*; and maize is *dekhama* because that was the next one planted. For some reason my informant said money was also classified as *pekhama*, the oldest, but didn't explain why.

Samek names are essentially ritual names to identify all the paraphernalia, the participants and places mentioned in a rite. All must have a *samek* name. They are also all said to have *saya*. All the objects used in ritual with *samek* names are vehicles for the ancestors. They perpetuate and immortalize ancestral time and by repeating the *samek* name the vitality of the object, person, or plant is renewed and their *saya* is raised. The objects are not personified; they are the homes or seats of ancestors. Pillars of the house, the stones of the hearth, particular plants, trees, and bamboo, water pitchers, the ladder of the house are examples of the places to which the ancestors are called, the places where they come and sit. Everthing with *saya* and a *samek* name is tribal, traditional, and ancient. They are the continuation of ancestral time, thereby ensuring its immortality.

The fact that these objects and places, plants and animals all have a 'vital ancestral link', a kind of soul called *saya*, might encourage us to consider that Lohorung thereby endow them with personhood. For Lohorung, however, the attribute of *saya* functions metaphysically as the transcendent unity with ancestors and the primeval past. *Saya* acts as a kind of energy. Objects like the hearth stones exist and have *saya* because they were brought into being by the creators of society, and were a necessary part of its creation and its continuation. We might liken *saya* to a life-force or a subtle emanation linking the ancestral heritage into an eternal and dynamic whole. Trees, plants, birds, animals, and springs (all the things possessing *saya* and a *samek* name) used to speak and understand each other at the time when ancestors were still establishing clan territories. When they lost these powers they left only the *yatangpa* and *mangpa* to act as mediums.

In terms of the Lohorung concept of the person, the concept of *samek* is revealing. In relation to the ancestors, the person is essentially part of the clan group and only individually differentiated by the addition of a piece of the person's clothing added to the paraphernalia of the ritual shrine. The concept also binds the person closer to nature, closer to ancestral beings, and closer to the society of their creation, not society as it is. The person is part of an interconnected whole whose elements are mutually dependent on each other. This unity of reality might be called spiritual monism. Here we can see the significance of human beings living in harmony with the other elements in order for them all to survive, all vulnerable to the unbalancing behaviour of human beings, enraged ancestors, or the random acts of the dead not properly integrated into the ancestral world. We shall see more of this in Chapter Six.

The second name *chawa*, like *samek*, links the person through his or her identification with the clan to a particular area or territory. *Chawa* is probably etymologically related to the Tibetan *chu for* 'water' and *wa* for 'water channel' (Jäschke 1975: 157). Identifying the spring to which the clan first spoke when they claimed the land, it is always a spring that never dries up and its name is often related to how it was found by the clan. Thus the *Heluwali* and *Themsong*, two brother clans, both relate to *singbongma chawa* 'tree fallen spring', so-named because the tree fell down and the spring rose from its roots. The special ritual spring of the *Yangkhrung* in Pangma is called *pi-tukma chawa* 'cattle squashed spring'. It is said that when some cattle squashed it with its feet, water arose. Claiming rights to the chawa by making offerings to the spring settlers simultaneously claimed rights to territory attached to it. The water from these springs is used in ritual, and chawa is the name that always accompanies that of a *samek name* – so that, for example, any member of the *Yangkhrung* clan is known for ritual purposes as *kechaba* or *kechama* of the *pi–-ukma chawa*.

From what we have seen here, it is clear that *samek* and *chawa* give the individual an important spiritual adherence to their clan group and the clan territory, giving him or her a line of continuity with ancestors.[13] The names give a sense of solidarity with other living clan members and those parts of nature they claimed as their own. They represent one of the significant ways in which Lohorung history and tradition are transcendentally internalized by the individual. They are indispensible to the living in their relationship with the ancestors but also in understanding the historical pattern of their relationships with other Lohorung clans.

Pe-lam *and the Establishment of Culture: the Story of* Chumling Chongma *and* Yechakukpa

We have seen how *pe-lam* upholds the past as an intrinsic part of the present through concepts which mystically links the person to the ancestors. The person is also bound in more pragmatic ways to particular ancestral ways and traditions through their creation as described in *pe-lam* myths. The most apt examples of myths creating traditions are the Lohorung stories about the mythical figures *Chumling Chongma* and *Yechakukpa*. Of all the myths they are the most well known among the Lohorung and the ones to which pan–Rai institutions relate. Nicholas Allen's work on the myths of the Thulung Rai (Allen,1976a), those of the Dumi by van Driem (1993), and those recorded by Gaenszle (1991, 1993, 1996) from the Mewahang Rai support local statements about the prevalence of these stories among Rai groups. The Thulung versions relate to *Jaw*, *Khliw* and *Khacilik*, the Mewahang to *Khewa*, *Lakca* and *Khakculukpa*, the Dumi to *To:ma*, *Khe:ma* and *Khopsi-Likpa*, and Lohorung to *Chumling Chongma* and *Yechakukpa* or sometimes to *Tawama Khewama* and *Khakculukpa* or *Khakchrukpa*. The first part of the myth goes as follows:

> *Chumling Chongma* and *Yechakukpa* were brother and two sisters. Their mother and father were angry with each other and always fighting. Their mother were hitting each other. One day their mother called out, 'my husband has beaten me so heavily. Oh! *Changlang*! Come here. Come and take me away!' *Changlang* came and took her away: off they flew, the two

of them. *Changlang* means perhaps *chap* (spirit of a dead ancestor). Anyway, after they had left, the three children decided to look for their mother. As they were searching they called out to their mother, 'mother where have you gone to? Where are you?' On their way they met a woman weaving at her loom. 'Weaving woman, Oh elder sister, you haven't seen our mother, have you?'

'Help me to finish weaving this and then I'll tell you where your mother is,' said the woman.

'There, that's done, now tell us where our mother is. Where is she?'

'No, no, go down there to that spinning woman's house. The spinning woman will tell you,' she said to them.

'Spinning woman, you haven't seen our mother, have you? Have you seen her or not?'

The spinning woman was making a round ball. 'Look, you see this, roll it and follow it, throw it and follow it wherever it goes,' she said.

'Mother, mother,' called out the brother and sisters, rolling the ball of thread. 'Hoi, hoi,' cried out their mother, who very quickly then appeared. Her new husband *Changlang* was not there apparently. As quickly as possible their mother cooked rice and then closed them into a *bekbi* (a small round woven basket without a handle). 'Stay there and be quiet,' she said to them. A little later *Changlang* came home, and sure enough, he sniffed and called out, 'I smell living, it stinks here of living man!'

'But there's no-one here. I'm the only living person here,' his wife said to him. A little later *Chumling Chongma*, the daughters I mean, cried out, 'ouch! ouch! heh! *Yechakukpa* is pinching us! ouch! ouch!' Immediately their mother tap, tap, tapped the basket, tap, tap.

'What is it?' asked her husband.

'We have some mice here', she said, and quickly she added, 'I dreamt a good dream today, you should go and hunt'. And so truly, just like that, off he went.

The mother turned to her children *Chumling Chongma* and *Yechakukpa*. She cooked rice and a side dish as quickly as possible and gave it to them to eat. Then she said to them, 'Now, children quickly, quickly you must leave. That *Changlang*, don't you see he is a *chap* (spirit of the dead) and he will catch and eat you. I ran off with *Changlang* so I must stay. You go. On your journey avoid the *siksikwara* paths, follow the *bekbekwara* paths. A *bekbekwara* path means the path is wide, easy and pleasant, *siksikwara* means a path through forests and over cliffs, and ugly path always to be avoided.'

Off they went and of course *Chumling Chongma* set out leading *Yechakukpa* along a *siksikwara* path. 'Mother told us to go on the *bekbekwara* paths, didn't she? *Yagangma* (mischievous female ancestor) will catch us and eat us if we go on this path. That's why she said to go on the *bekbekwara* path', said *Yechakukpa*.

'No, no it was on the *siksikwara* path that mother told us we wouldn't meet *Yagangma*', replied *Chumling Chongma*. So on they went on the *siksikwara* path. Down below them *Yagangma* was in the midst of cleaning some intestines. *Yechakukpa* caught sight of her. 'Oh no! Sisters, look, down there, that's *Yagangma*; it must be', he said to his sisters.

'There is an old woman, indeed,' said his sisters; 'Grandma, *Yechakukpa* says you are *Yagangma*. Are you?' they asked.

'No, no my child, I am your grandmother. Come down. Come down here, all of you,' said *Yagangma*. And so they were led to *Yagangma*'s house. That night *Yagangma*'s daughter asked *Yechakukpa*, 'Where do you want to sleep?' 'I'll sleep in the attic under the beams, I'll sleep near the tray above the fire. I'll catch some sleep in the corner by the door', he said. 'She is preparing to kill me,' he thought. He picked up a big wild potato (*khi-wa chabuk*), you know, the bitter kind, and then up in the attic he cut it into pieces and laid it out on the floor. Then, *Yechakukpa* went to sleep. *Chumling Chongma* slept alongside Grandma. Later that night *Yagangma* and her daughter took out a metal rod and set about spearing *Yechakukpa*. *Yechakukpa* found it difficult to find a safe place. Finally they speared some wild potato, speared it and then licked it, speared more and tasted it again. Of course it was very bitter. 'Goodness! *Yechakukpa* is a bitter one. Well we must eat *Chumling Chongma* then' they said. They speared them and ate them, the two of them, mother and daughter. The next morning *Yechakukpa* came down. 'Oh! people were saying *Yechakukpa* was dead, but it seems you are still alive,' said the daughter. 'Heh! Where are my sisters and where is your mother?' asked *Yechakukpa*.

'They've gone off to work.' The daughter then gave Yechakukpa rice and a side dish made of the fingers and toes of his sisters *Chumling Chongma*. At the same time as he was weeping, Yechakukpa did as if to eat, putting the meat instead into a string bag. Like that he sat there crying and stayed sitting there.

Later when they found that whatever they did they couldn't kill him, *Yagangma* said, 'Let's go. I'm going anyway. You kill *Yechakukpa* and fill the container for pig food full of his blood.' She said to her daughter, 'Look for his lice for him and as you look for the lice, kill him.' But *Yechakukpa* heard this. The daughter heated the oil and began to delouse *Yechakukpa*. 'What beautiful hair you have!' said the daughter to *Yechakukpa*. 'I have heated the oil. I must pour some over your hair and then it will be very beautiful. That's what my mother told me,' she told *Yechakukpa*. But when the oil was thoroughly heated *Yechakukpa* tipped it over her, and *Yagangma*'s daughter died.

Yechakukpa then dressed up in *Yagangma*'s daughter's clothes and pretended to be her. He put blood into the container for pig food, and hung her intestines on the door to dry in the sun. *Yagangma* came home, talking to herself about how she would slowly eat and enjoy the blood of *Yechakukpa* and his intestines and so she came home. She ate the intestines slowly and she drank. She ate the guts and drank the blood and the blood made her drunk. Saying to herself she would roast the flesh, and how she would eat beans with it, and rice and maize and millet, and how nicely ready everything was for her feast, she fell asleep. Upon which, *Yechakukpa* plastered her eyes with the sticky white of an egg and hid the rest of the egg.

Some time later on, *Yagangma* woke up. 'Where is she? Where have they gone? Perhaps *Yechakukpa* isn't dead. No one is here,' she thought to herself. Then she thought to herself 'Goodness! Maybe he has killed my child.' She scraped and scratched at her eyes, but whatever she did was to no avail, whatever she tried did nothing. She looked inside but there was no one. 'He has killed my child. I must catch that *Yechakukpa*. I won't miss any chance to kill him', she said, following him. *Yagangma* scraped at her eyes with a large sickle, and called out, 'Oh! Grandson, come down here, come down here!'

'All right, all right, grandmother', he called, running away as she started to follow him. She looked to select some rice: 'So that *Yechakukpa* has stolen my rice, millet and my store of *khausuk* [rice grains broken in husking]. So that's how he can run so fast.' And again she ran after him, and never ceasing to call out 'hoi' she ran and she ran. As she drew close to him he threw a feather and a large, large mountain rose up in front of her.

'What kind of path are you going on, *Yechakupo*, *Yechakukpo*.' Looking for the path was now difficult, up the stoney mountain path, but she never ceased calling out 'hoi!'. . . . .

Yechakukpa used all he was carrying to keep her away. In the end there was only the egg left. As she came close to him, he threw the egg and as it rolled, it burst and the outside became the hills and the white of the egg became a river, a big wide river. Then *Yagangma*, still searching, came to the river. 'Grandson, what kind of path are you going? By this big river? Wait for me, *Yechakukpo*!' she cried.

'Grandmother, take off your waistband; I tied my legs and hands together, and then I just rolled across. You do the same,' he said. She did and the river took her away. After the egg had broken, *Yechakukpa* went to his mother's brother's house. His uncles were fishermen. It was as they were casting their nets that they caught *Yagangma*, that same grandmother in one of the nets. They took her home. She complained 'that *Yechakukpa* he took this and that, he did this and that, he killed my daughter, and all this he did to try and kill me . . .' she said to his uncles, who then spoke, 'there, there, we must make peace between you, you must stop quarrelling.' They wove two baskets. In the basket for grandmother *Yagangma* they put dog, tiger, cat, bear – these things they put in her basket. In *Yechakukpa*'s they put cow's hair, ox hair, sheep's wool, goat's wool.

'Don't open them! Go off both of you. Only when you reach grandmother *Yagangma*'s house should you open them,' they said. As grandmother *Yagangma* was carrying her basket, tiger and bear jumped out and ate her. As for *Yechakukpa*, the hair and wool turned into cow, ox, sheep, and goat.

There is some uncertainty as to whether *Chumling Chongma* is one sister or two. In some versions *Chumling Chongma* is clearly only one person and in terms of the action in the myth they always act together as one. Most narrators, however, and audience were insistent the there were two sisters. This agrees with the Thulung cycle and the Mewahang version. There is a further uncertainty about the identity of the characters. From the phrase 'off they flew' it sounds as if their mother and *Changlang* are birds. This fits in with the Lohorung love for stories about birds, with the importance of animal actors in oral literatur,e and again with the Thulung version in which the sisters are conceived as birds. The Lohorung, too, conceive of birds as having performed the human tasks and roles before the world was inhabited by humans. Moreover, the Lohorung conceive of birds as mediators between heaven and earth, between the abode of the living and that of the dead. This interpretation, thus, accords with one theme of the myth, that is, relations between the living and the dead. The Lohorung find nothing strange about relationships between animals and humans; after all man is the brother of Tiger and Bear. As was explained in the previous section (see pp 121–125), Lohorung conceive of themselves as being very much part of the natural world. There are, however, no further references to the characters as birds and the flying may equally be referring to the powers of the spirits of dead ancestors (*chap*) who can appear nearby and then far away the next minute, or transform themselves into other animals at will. The narrator tells us that *Changlang* is perhaps a *chap*, and later the mother warns the children that he is a *chap*. Shortly after, there are echoes of Jack the Giant Killer's 'Fee, Fie, Foe, Fum, I smell the blood of an earthly man' (or 'English man') as *Changlang* smells the three children and indicates a chap-like quality – a desire for living human flesh. At the time talked about in the myths, everyone had powers that they no longer have; they could, for example, converse with springs, trees, flowers, and birds. Put in this context *Changlang* and his new woman can be bird, and human.

The myth is about the relations between the living and the dead, but particularly about *Yagangma* and *Yechakukpa*, both important figures for the Lohorung. *Yagangma*, the old woman, who is the weaving woman and the spinning woman, is the ancestor *Chawatangme*, the fickle, trickster ancestor. The story concentrates on her. Instead of the spirit of a dead ancestor, Changlang, eating the children, it is *Yagangma* who eats the two daughters and tries in every way possible to catch *Yechakukpa* too. This Grandmother ancestor, as we have seen in Chapter Four, continues to plague the Lohorung: they explain much sickness, pain and misfortune as being the hunger, anger, or viciousness of this old woman, in different guises. Her powers are many: for example she teaches *boksi* ('witches') and she chooses many of the present-day shamans and gives them certain of their powers. *Yechakukpa* is generally accepted as the first shaman, the first of the Original Beings 'clever' (*ichhuba*) enough to outwit the trickery of the old woman ancestor. It is from *Yagangma*'s own stores that he steals the equipment to overpower her, echoing the situation that shamans derive power from their 'guru', who are also among those they are called to control. *Yechakukpa* uses his cleverness and the material he steals, the feather, the egg, to alter the landscape and defeat *Yagangma*. Feathers and eggs are part of a shaman's standard equipment. Their headgear is made of feathers: in Pangma, the old woman's headdress had amongst others, feather's from a peacock's tail (*Taraiwa* in L *mujuur* in N), pheasant feathers (*daphe* in N), forest hen (*chi-wa* in L), feathers of a bird called *sangma* or *binguma* in Lohorung and identified as being *Heterophasia capistrata* (Black–capped Sibia), feathers from *Marangma* in Lohorung (*kalchora* in N), said to have been the *mangpa* (shaman) when there were no people, and robin feathers (*dhobi* in N). The dhobi bird is said to have been the first *yatangpa* (local priest). Shamans are known to be able to 'throw' feathers as cutting instruments and, in general, they are also used as weapons against an enemy. They keep away spirits of the dead (*chap*). Wild chicken feathers (*wasang*) are used by both Lohorung shamans (*mangpa*) and local priests (*yatangpa*) to stop an enemy flying to attack them. It is said that if the feather *wasang* is used by one shaman, for example, to kill another, then the attacking shaman must die too.

Eggs are used in divination: the insides of patients can be examined by looking at the inside of an egg. If there is a dark brown or red spot, then the patient is healthy. If the spot is white and long, then the person will die. One informant said, 'the spot is like the white flag that is carried after a dead body'. The stickiness of the egg is like the *liso* (bird lime), a grey glutinous substance, made from pounded leaves (*kaulo*

N), used by shamans in their seances to attract the gods.

The mother's brother has a role in the myth similar to that in present Lohorung life – that of giving assistance to the sister's children and particularly to nephews, who are compensated for not being descended from one of the sons by a gift of goods, cattle, or even land on marriage. It is appropriate that *Yechakukpa* is given cattle and sheep and goats.

Before any further comments, let me add two other related narratives. The first is about *Yechakukpa*, given me by a male informant.

> Long ago there were two daughters in a certain family and one son. The oldest sisters' names were *Chumling*, *Chongma* and the younger brother's name was *Yechakukpa*. Neither their mother nor their father was alive. While they grew up they stayed all together in the jungle. But one day when the two sisters had grown up and their brother was sleeping, the two girls ran away. The younger brother was left in the jungle, alone and helpless. But soon he made a small house for himself in the jungle and lived in that. Even so, now there was no provision for food for him as there had been before: now there was only yams and wild bananas, forest potatoes, and so on. Then later he learned how to make fire with one piece of wood and one piece of string. When he was a little older he knitted a fishing net for himself and began to fish and caught fish in the net for food. Then he became a hunter. He was not going to be (ambitious to be) a hunter, but he had to become one because living in the jungle there was no other means of living. So that's why he became a hunter. With a bow and arrow he killed birds and other wild animals. So that was how he obtained his meat. He also caught fish in his net and thus obtained another food.
>
> Then he began to slash and burn down some of the forest and made the land ready for planting. But there was no seed to sow in it. One day the young boy *Yechakukpa* killed a dove and in the dove's crop he found grains of rice and millet. Although he didn't realize what kinds of seed he had found – he knew neither rice nor millet – yet he planted them. People say he was the first one to grow our rice (*cham*) and our millet (*panke*). And thus *Yechakukpa* lived – in such a way.
>
> One day *Yechakukpa* set out to fish with his net. Usually he caught many fish in his net. Compared to other ways of hunting, catching fish was good: it was plentiful and easy. Day after day he had been able to kill fish, until this day he caught nothing. From the beginning of the day all that turned up was a small stone. He threw it away, but even when he threw the net into another place he caught the same stone instead of fish. He went to yet another river and cast his net. And again he caught the same small stone and no fish at all. He tried another river further away, but still he could catch no fish, only the same small stone. Sadly, he put the stone in his bamboo woven basket for fish (*tutuk*). But before returning home, he cast his net once more. And this time he was able to catch fish, many fish.
>
> Later that day he went back home to his house in the jungle and placed the stone he had caught in the basket hanging above the fire (called *mukdang-ha* or *keng-kengma*).
>
> The next day he went out hunting. In the evening when he returned home, he found all the food had been prepared and was ready for eating. He was surprised. But he divided it in two. And he called out. But nobody came.

The next day the same thing happened and he was cross thinking about it. He wanted to know who it was and why he did it. He tried everything but still he couldn't find out.

And so it came about that one day an old woman, or some say a *goanleni* (female ancestor), passed by. And *Yechakukpa* asked her.

'Who is it who comes to me?'

'You must do as I say,' said the old woman. 'Hide the winnowing tray, hide the sieve [for sorting out the chaff], and hide yourself. If you do that, when she comes to find the winnowing tray and the sieve, you must hold onto her right hand and say three times, "I won't let you go!" '

And he did just as the old woman told him. He hid himself behind the winnowing tray and the sieve. A moment later the stone dropped down from the basket above the fire, making the sound 'bung!' and it turned into a beautiful girl. She went to take the winnowing tray and the sieve, and he held her right hand, 'who are you? Why have you come here? Why do you do this work for me?' he asked. She said, 'Don't hold me . . . I came into your net in so many different places, but in every place you threw me away. Don't hold me now.'

Then *Yechakukpa* remembered and said three times, 'I won't let you go! I won't let you go! I won't let you go!' Three times he swore that he wouldn't leave her. So from then on they became husband and wife. It is from those two that the Lohorung are born. This is why they say the Lohorung come from a stone.

Another version given by a female informant changes the names and goes as follows:

Tawama Khewama were *Khakchrukpa*'s elder sisters. When *Khakchrukpa* was young his mother and father died. After their death the child had to be fed and looked after. *Yagangma* came to hear of it and then comes the story about the grinding stone, about *Nagelungma*, who was *Khakchrukpa*'s wife. But first, well, the two elder sisters left, and he grew up on his own. He planted plantain trees, and then lived in one, lived at the top of one. The rest of the time he spent catching fish, casting his net, casting it into the water – you've seen it, I expect. One day he threw in his net and what he caught was a grinding stone. He threw the grinding stone back into the pool. He cast again and he found it again in his net. He threw it back, went to another pool and again the grinding stone came in his net. What had happened, you see, was that *Nagelungma* was menstruating and she felt shy it seems to stay around her natal home. *Ses-nag* (the king of the serpants) was the head of her natal home. She went to see *Yagangma*, 'Oh! what shall I do? This is how I am', she said. *Yagangma* said to her, 'all right, go down there. There is a fish pool. Go into it until you are better. Go and stay ther,.' said *Yagangma*.

It was at that time that *Khakchrukpa* was going fishing everyday. *Nagelungma* became a stone, which is why she's called *Ngagelungma* (*nga*/'fish' and *lungma*/'stone'). We also call her *Narunglema*. Anyway, everyday he went fishing and he used to take with him a bamboo woven basket for fish and into that he put the stone which kept coming into his net. After that every day when *Khakchrukpa* went fishing the grinding stone jumped down, she mudded the floor of the house and cooked the most delicious rice and side dish. 'Who is preparing these meals and mudding the floor' asked *Khakchrukpa*, and then he remembered what *Yagangma* had told him to do: 'One day in the afternoon when she has done all the work go in and take hold of her.' So this is what he did. After he had been fishing and she had made his rice and side dish she was about to climb back when he jumped out and caught her, 'You', and he took hold of her by the arm, 'you can't go. You can't go. Who are you?' he asked. She waited quietly and then said, 'let me go, let me go. ouch! ouch! previously you threw me away in the pond, the lower one, then you threw me away in the upper pond. In the upper you broke my head, in the lower you broke my shoulder. In other places you broke my back, my knee, everything in my body aches. Let me go! Let me go!'

He let her go but he wouldn't let her leave. So they became husband and wife. They built a house and what they did to build the house, they cut down the wood for the main pillars. At first they did not know how to cut the pillars. Then one day *Ngagelungm*a saw a *Gechikwa* (*Cibe cari* N. King-Crow or *drongo*) with its divided tail[14] and she said, '*Khakchrukpa*, you see the tail of that *Gechikwa*, you must bring pillars which are forked like that.' So all the *khamba* he made like that from then onwards. On the day of placing the main pillar *Ngagelungma* was carrying their small child on her back and was explaining how to lift up the pillar. Then just as *Khakchrukpa* raised the main pillar, the child fell from her back into the hole and was crushed as the pillar went in. That's why now we say children must keep away when they put in the pillar. Since the child had fallen they didn't bother to bring any more pillars for the roof, *Khakchrukpa* made a cover. Then he said, 'we must have a house warming' (*ghar painchha*). So *Khakchrukpa* went hunting – and he saw small doves, caught them, killed them, and found in their crop rice seeds, barley, wheat, and millet. They sowed the seeds and when there was grown rice they said 'we must do the house warming.'

'If we do that you should ask your sisters *Tawama Khewama*. Where are they?' *Khakchrukpa* wondered if they were dead." We must look for them. They are needed.'

So first they sent a louse, but the louse couldn't find them, so they sent a flea. It could not find them either, so they sent a bed–bug. He looked and did not find them. Then they sent a cock which flew from hill-top to hill-top crying out and crowing.

'*Khachrukpa ghar painchho! Khachrukpa ghar painchho!*' He found them weaving at a loom: the sisters were weaving a mat. 'What's he saying? Our brother *Khakchrukpa* is dead. What is that son of a bitch cock saying?' they said and threw a shuttle at the cock. It missed so they threw again and went on throwing the shuttle all the way as the cock led them to *Khakchrukpa*'s house. 'Eh, so it seems my elder sisters have come.' And they performed the *ghar painchha*. They did it indeed and that is why we now have to seek out our sisters at *ghar painchha*. Sisters are needed for it. Long ago they said, '*Tawama Khewama, gheu! Tawama Khewama gheu*', and saying it they circle round the fire stones three times. Now we still do.

This informant went on to recount yet other incidences between *Khakchrukpa* and his wife. As in the first version, in these too the son was left to fend for himself. *Yechakukpa* and *Khakchrukpa* were a metaphor for all men: vulnerable since sisters leave to marry, but comforted and strengthened by 'culture', by building a house, making fire, fishing, and hunting. His bow and his arrow are by his side. He fishes, hunts, and performs all the necessary agricultural tasks as if by instinct. Even though he has no seed he knows that the land has to be prepared. This both creates and supports a Lohorung notion that they are hunters and agriculturalists by nature: that is, essentially cultivators and owners of the soil. The Lohorung of today generally conform with this tradition. The tradition as shown in the myth has superficially changed only in the sense that over the last 250 years or so, they have shifted from their lives as hunters and gatherers, slash–and–burn cultivators to a more fixed life as sedentary agriculturalists, with hunting and gathering as occasional activities.

The son, whether *Yechakukpa* or *Khakchrukpa*, continues his relationship with *Yagangma*. Unknowingly, he is caught in a trap to capture his wife. This episode gives sanction to the Lohorung institution of marriage by theft. The tone of the formalized Marriage Talk, a separate part of the *pe-lam*, suggests a kind of pretence capture even in arranged marriages.[15] The elders from the bride's side, for example, pretend they do not understand why gifts are being laid out in front of them.

> 'No! It can't be. Why have they come to lay out gold and good cloth. We were only going to give them somewhere to sleep. They said they were looking for the rivals on the border they had quarrelled with. Now, what are they doing?'
>
> The Groom answers, Father, mother do not pretend you do not know. I could not scrape from the ground or dig out either the *suwa* [*bhyakur* N. a kind of creeper, the roots of which are eaten] or the *warek* [*githo* N. roots of which are also eaten], so I took the *nam-hi* [*bantarul bhyakur*, the wild version of the *suwa*] and dug out its white part and took away its seed. I have followed the path, I have held the pole [by the ladder of the house], I have made the *suksukma* [area of the house for the house shrine] listen, I have made the *Kengkengma* [the basket above the fire] listen, the sun I made listen, I made the gift carrier for the groom carry, and I made the gift receiver for the bride receive.'

In reply to the parents' pretence that they do not know what is happening the groom says that since he could not bring the *suwa* (the father) or the *warek* (the mother) to his side, in the end he took the inside of the *namhi* and took the seed (the daughter) of the mother and father. Although marriage by theft is less common than it used to be it still occurs. In brief, it relies on capturing the girl on her way to the bazaar or distant fields, usually the former. With the help of some conspiring relatives of the girl, who approve of the relationship, and some friends of the boy, not necessarily relatives, they waylay her on the path. The *pe-lam* narrative thus acts as a template or charter for *khume biha* ('theft marriages') but also contributes to the evidence suggesting that even in *ngakme biha* ('request, i.e. arranged marriages') there is an enactment of the mythical capture. In his discussion of the Thulung myth Allen comments, 'With reference to *Khakcilik*'s capture of *Wayelungma*, both *Kam* and *Karb* remark on the conventional protestations of contemporary brides when taken to their new homes.' Presumably they had in mind also the traditional 'marriage by capture' (1976a: 121).

The same myth is also enacted at the Lohorung wedding as the cooks come back from the fields and sing,

> *tawama khewama* have come! *tawama khewama* have come! Today, oh *tawama khewama* have come to the pillars of the house, to the beams of the house, to the main front door, to the side door, to the three hearth stones [the two 'upper' and the 'lower' apex stone], to the clan spring, *tawama khewama* have come!

When the Lohorung build a house they still call in the close out-married sisters, who come with gifts of beer and circle round the hearth four times in a clockwise direction and recite the above section of the *pe-lam*. The sisters are given rice and beer, as they are in the myth. By performing this small ritual the Lohorung say they raise the *saya* of the new house, the *saya* of the beams, the pillars, the hearth, and all those parts of the house that have *saya*.

The interpretation by my female informant of *Nagelungma*'s parentage as *ses-nag*, and her menstruation as a reason for entering the pond, are interesting additions and a renegotiation of the meaning of aspects of the myth. Here we see clearly how Hindu elements enter the tribal. *Nag* and *nageni*, and *ses nag* are Hindu snake gods. My informant is perhaps confusing or conceptually binding them together with the Lohorung *bongbi* 'water serpents', who, like *chawatangma*, 'choose' shamans, protect the hearth and are considered to be very significant in the creation of the world. That *Ngagelungma* would be shy about menstruating makes sense in a Hindu household, where menstruating women's activities are curtailed. Few Lohorung women have in fact adopted the Hindu attitude and continue to work as normal when menstruating. My informant, however, is one of the few who has adopted a more restrictive attitude to her menstruation. This is a good example of personal additions to the myths. Here one woman has added her own explanation as to why *Ngagelungma* ended up in the pond. Most of the other Lohorung and Thulung versions do not offer any explanation for her presence in the pond. Two Thulung versions offer brief accounts, as Allen records:

> Later, Wayelungma's mother, whose name I don't know, said to her daughter: 'You don't listen to what I say, you take no notice. Go and jump in the water'. So she went and jumped into the water and became a stone. The Tingla version of this episode included a dialogue between Wayelungma and her mother. The daughter says she wants to visit the home of her mother's brother, and is told that it is down in the Primal Lake. (Allen, nd: 101).

Ngagelungma – a fitting combination of 'fish' *nga* and 'stone' *lung* – also sometimes called *Narungrema*, teaches *Khakchrukpa* how to build a house, the style of which is still used today. The myth explains the origin of hunting, fishing, some crops, slash–and–burn cultivation, and certain continued customs such as inviting sisters to the 'house warming' and 'Theft Marriage' as well as forbidding children to watch housebuilding.

The main point of these particular *pe-lam* myths is to act as a charter for social action, to establish precedents for prescribed actions and institutions and thereby validate the culture. I have concentrated more on the mythical aspect of the *pe-lam* in this chapter since the ritual aspect receives attention in both Chapter Four and Chapter Six. What becomes clear in the myths and the ritual chants is the power of the superhuman beings and the extent to which they created order and now interfere with the lives of the living expecting the order to be maintained. The characters in the myths are mainly dealt with collectively in ritual in the *pappamamma'chi* rites. *Yagangma* is given special attention as is *chawatangma*. Only by ritual action can they retain the original order, which is constantly in need of renewal. A 'consciousness' of the ancestral past and ancestral order is found in living humans, in the superhumans, and in everything mentioned in the *pe-lam*, be they animals, plants, or parts of the house. This animating consciousness, which brings man to have a close affinity to nature is *saya*, the concept which links the living to the the ancestors and which will begin to make more sense in Chapter Six.

Notes

1. The power contained in the natural order of the world is linked to the Lohorung understanding that the Original Beings created the natural world along the lines of an eternal and ideal pattern or groundplan. The world of spirits, men and natural phenomena are all inter-related and bound to this ideal. The same cosmological perspective is familiar to anthropologists looking at non-industrialised communities (Morris 1996: 26) but it can also be seen in Plato, and Greek thought. Morris describes the three central tenets of this attitude to the universe as being the view that the world consists of a totality of inter–related things; that nature itself is permeated with spirit, or mind and is a living entity; and that 'there is no separation between man and nature, or between the individual and society – but all are encompassed in a spiritual order where every–thing has its place or purpose' (Morris 1996: 28).
2. Thulung Rai refer to their body of traditions as *diumla*, the Chamling as *dum la*, the Mewahang as *muddum*, close to the Lohorung *mundum*, the term *mundhum* is Limbu.
3. See Sagant, 1973, for a description of the difference between the two Limbu priests, the *phedangma* and the *bujuwa*, whose functions are complementary at a symbolic level, and made clear with an analysis of household space organization. See also Fournier (1974).
4. Hitchcock describes a similar ritual being performed by a Matwala shaman, in which over 100 local flowers, bushes, and trees are mentioned.'The *deutā* is conducting his soul among the plants named in the song, for somewhere among them the soul is hiding' (1973: 170).
5. Allen 1974 suggests that the ritual journey is a useful ethnographic category in its own right and puts the notion of `shaman' into a wider context by looking at the different 'ritual journeys' of the Thulung Rai. See also Desjarlais 1989 and 1992.
6. See Macdonald 1957 on cloistering villages, in which he reveals the widespread nature of this kind of solemn prohibition over Asia and Southeast Asia. What is interesting is that for the Lohorung the unit of exclusion is the household, the main social unit, rather than the village.
7. Some recent development work by KHARDEP (Kosi Hill Area Rural Development Project) is reversing the trend. It has encouraged the economy of the Kosi hills by giving support to weaving, basketry, and the traditional use of the indigenous nettle *Girardinia diversifolia* to produce cloth similar to cotton and tweed. (See Dunsmore, 1985.)
8. A similar version to this creation myth is given for the Thulung Rai in Allen 1976a and for the Mewahang Rai in Gaenszle 1991: 200.
9. Compare with similar stories of origin in Allen 1976a and in Gaenszle 1991: 252ff.

10. See McDougal 1979 for his detailed analysis of the process of clan splitting, 'splitting the bones' among the Kulung Rai.
11. Klaus Seeland (1980) examines the significance of bamboo in the Arun Valley.
12. These concepts among the Mewahang Rai are *same* and *ca:ri* (see Gaenszle, 1991: 81 and 129sq.). Gaenszle describes the *same* of the Mewahang Rai, as 'a common ancestral soul' (1991: 205) while 'the same group constitutes a kind of proto-clan' (1991: 215). Their concept of ca:ri is described as referring to both 'a delimited and named territory' and 'the spirit of the local territory'. The territory 'is linked with the first Mewahang settler who occupied the land and established a ritual bond with the spirit by being able to deal with it in the proper ritual language'. The myths tell us of previous clans trying to settle being frustrated or killed by the curse of the spirit of the territory (1991: 134 and 1994: 2).
13. For a more detailed discussion of the relationships between clans and their *chawa* see Gaenszle 1991: 120–47.
14. Similar myths in which the King Crow acts as an inspiration in house-building exists among other Kiranti – the Thulung Rai (Allen 1976), Mewahang Rai (Gaenszle 1991), Khalinge Rai (Toba 1983) Limbu (Jones 1974). I am grateful to Mark Oppitz for pointing this out.
15. See Allen 1975: 168 where he discusses a narrative text in Thulung ritual language, and his article 1978 on Thulung ritual language.

6

Lohorung Houses: *Saya* and *Nuagi*

I've said that this book is about Lohorung experiences and what it means to be a person in Lohorung society. Well, I began to have a particularly strong sense that the house was fundamental in Lohorung understanding of the person while watching one particular ceremony[1] called *nuagi*. It went on in the Pangma villages for two weeks. The old traditions of the *pe-lam* were still very much alive in Lohorung society.

What I want to explain here is how the house and personhood were intimately linked – the house and the ancestral house shrine were both essentially extensions of the body. The house should be seen as embodied self. The house rather than the person is the central unit of agency. So Lohorung experience of the body became key to understanding how they order the world, their houses, and their interpretation of the unity underlying the complexity of the world.[2] This is the same kind of knowledge about personhood as our own knowledge of genes, evolution, and our ancestral heritage – knowledge which effects the way we interpret behaviour, our experiences, our environment and our relations with nature.[3]

At the heart of the Lohorung view of a unity of house and personhood lies that elusive concept of *saya*. As we saw in Chapter Five, reality for Lohorung consists of what they know to have been the correct order in the past, in the world of their primeval ancestors.The powerful presence of that ancestral identity can reveal itself in any place, person, and object possessing *saya*. Its power of reference affects Lohorung thinking about the nature of culture, the nature of nature, and their existential situation as cultural beings.The human body, the dwelling house, and the local environment are just different worlds embodying and providing support for that power, *saya*. In this sense, as we shall see, persons, houses and the natural environment are united by and diffused with, the power emanating from the primeval mythic domain.The *nuagi* ceremonies I watched showed how humans are intrinsically a part of nature, and essentially linked to it.

I'm going to suggest that *saya* can be seen as an institution in Lohorung society, acting as a symbolic code, a model of behaviour, an experience and a practice of male personhood, and a pattern for tradition. I think we should question the appropriateness of standard anthropological categories such as 'religion' as an interpretive framework within which to understand this Lohorung material. The problem with the box 'religion' is that it distorts the force of inter–relatedness which the notion of *saya* highlights. It implies that life is either 'religious' or 'non–religious', 'sacred' or

FIG 9 Lohorung House.

'profane', when for Lohorung and many others this distinction simply cannot be made.

The House

The *nuagi* ceremonies, held annually by every Lohorung household (and bi–annually by some) took place inside Lohorung homes, and as I watched one after another what struck me first of all was the way every house had a similar structure, in spite of superficial differences. In fact, to be a 'proper' Lohorung house it had to be build in a particular way. Houses are closely connected to the ancestors and to the myth in which the first couple are said to have built a house. As you may remember from Chapter Five, house-building was discovered by *Nagelungma*, who instructed *Khakchrukpa* to choose forked trees to make pillars for the house (see pp. 132–3). This couple are two of the founders of Lohorung social institutions. Lohorung described how they transformed Lohorung from *jungal*i, 'barbaric' beings, into civilized people – a role shared by the protectors of the house, *Khammang* and *Yimi*, who by their very incestuous union established a structural feature of Lohorung society. The house and the beings associated with it are emphasized as being a 'civilizing' factor in Lohorung personhood. This is reflected in the Lohorung opposition

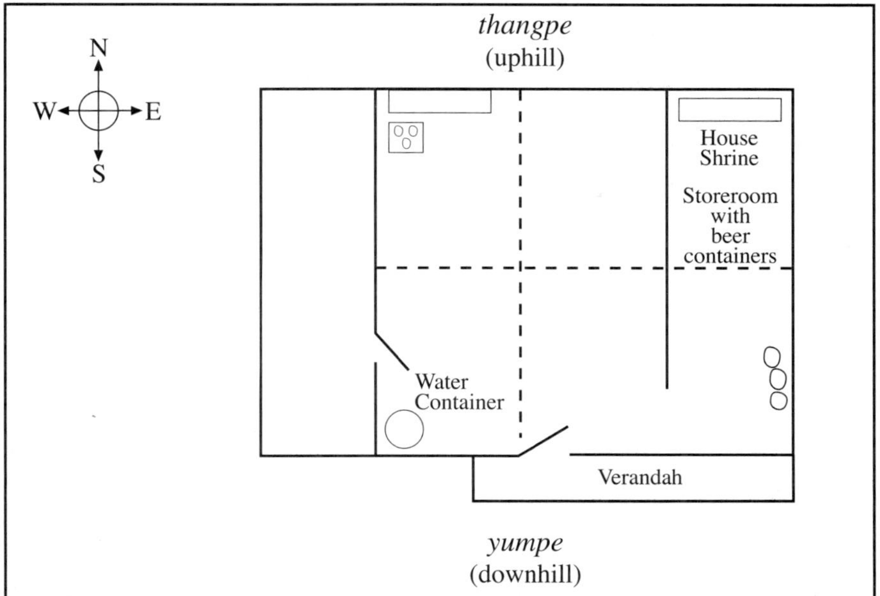

FIG 10 Layout of Lohorung House

house v. forest (*khim v. tapnam*). Whereas they were previously all 'forest people' (*tapnam yapmi*), now they are 'house people', with a 'husband' (*khimtangpa*) and a 'wife' (*khimtangma*) in each house. When they were in the forest they had few customs and no restrictions, called *phenni*. Stilt houses of the kind they live in today are conceived as being introduced at the same time as the first wedding, funeral, and house-shrine. These are the things that for the Lohorung mark the beginnings of their civilization. The way a girl is complimented for closely adhering to good manners and traditional knowledge and ways of behaving, in terms of posture, walking, sitting, talking, and serving, is to say, 'how house-shrine like she is!' ('*kho ettano mangsuk le*!', meaning how civilized she is!).

The Lohorung house (see Figure 8) is single-storey, raised on stilts, with latticed bamboo wattle walls, thatched roof, and one or two external verandahs. As can be seen from the diagram (Figure 9), part of the central living area is usually partitioned off by an internal wall to make the *beng'towa* space used for storing grain and other household implements. The roomy upper loft (*talletu*) provides further storage space. The *omphoo* or verandah at the front has a mudded floor like the rest of the house and is sheltered by the thatched roof. It's the counterpart to the storeroom at the back.

Whereas the storeroom and the main living area (*lumkhanda*) are *hongsiu* (inside) and considered to be private, the front verandah is public. It's the place where family, friends, and visitors sit, talk, and work during the day, and often sleep at night, during all but the coldest months. The side verandah and side entrance are more specifically, though not exclusively, the domain of women, since it is the area where dishes are cleaned, and where women often give birth. All the cooking vessels, plates, implements, spices, huge pots containing fermenting grain, and other provisions, are kept in the 'back', some of it in the 'storeroom', and this 'back' area is also conceptually associated with 'female'. This area between the storeroom and the central pillar is where women prepare meals and beer. In contrast, the 'front' (*lumpanke ge-ereng*) of the house, from the central pillar to the ladder, is the area associated with that which is 'male'; that is, with the hearth, the front door, public talk (as opposed to family talk). At meals, the male head of the household sits near the hearth at the very front of the inner room. The female household head sits opposite her husband on the other side of the hearth, on the 'back' side of the house. In spite of this conceptual division into male and female areas, unlike the Kulung Rai, there are no sex restrictions on movement within the house.[4]

Inside, the house is conceptually divided into four with the central pillar as the junction of four rectangles. One side of the interior is considered to be 'uphill' (*thangpe*) and one 'downhill' (*yumpe*) and this is seen quite clearly in the way people address each other in the house. The verb 'to come' differs according to where the person is coming from. If two people are on flat ground and one says to the other 'come here', the word to use is *dabe*. I tried using this word early on to a young girl in my house and was amazed when I was corrected for using the wrong word! Instead, I was told that the verb 'to come up' (*kare*: come up here) is used when the person speaking is in that part of the house which is 'uphill', particularly if they are also near the hearth.[5] The hearth is always in the 'front' part of the 'uphill' side, that is, to the left or right of the main door, depending on whether the door is placed on the side facing in a rough easterly or westerly direction.

The household shrine to the house ancestors (*khammang* and *yimi*) which is renewed at *nuagi*, should be located on the 'uphill' wall hanging behind and above the hearth. And some still locate it on this wall on the floor above, in the attic. Most houses, however, place their shrine on the 'uphill' wall of the storeroom at the back. Many Lohorung find it out of place, but less dangerous to have it situated at the back. Non-Rai visitors can anger the ancestors and since Rai and non-Rai (apart from untouchables) can enter Lohorung houses, Lohorung say it's safer to keep the shrine 'back', 'inside' hongsiu, even though few visitors are in fact invited anywhere but on to the verandah. The place for visitors to sit inside is always on the 'downhill' side. It's a bit like we ask visitors into the sitting room but rarely into the bathroom. As Mary Douglas has shown us in her classic *Purity and Danger* (1966) there is 'danger' in people or things that are 'out of place'. For Lohorung, as for us, everything has its place. The rules of order in Lohorung houses have to do with ancestral ownership and ideas about what is dangerous.

For Lohorung each object in the house that has *saya* is valued because associated with some part of a *pe-lam* story, and owned by the Original Beings and the ancestors. When superhuman beings are called to visit the living, the superhumans are said to rest in those places that they recognize as belonging to them and which are addressed by their ritual, *samek*, names. The 'doorways', 'beams', 'hearth-stones', etc. in each Lohorung house represent and replicate the mythical beam, central pillar, and hearth stones easily recognized by ancestors. The *saya* within them might be thought of as a 'sensitivity', or 'consciousness', that is particularly responsive to ancestral presence and the treatment of ancestral property. The presence of *saya* gives to the object a potential for vitality, strength, but at the same time a sensitivity to insult and weakness.[6] However, Lohorung would never attribute 'mind' (*niwa*) to these objects. What they all possess is a common relationship with ancestors. Thus *saya* gives a relational unity to various parts of the house and also links them to plants, animals, and everything else that has *saya* including the ancestors, and the living.

It's not only in ritual that this unity is expressed. The hearth, the doorways, the beams, and the pillars are always regarded with respect. This is expressed in the careful way they are treated, by the order in the house. Nobody abuses the hearth or the doorway: no one can sit in the doorway or flick ash or any debris into the fire. 'The ancestors are angry if we do not treat the house with respect', was the standard response to questions about the way the house is treated. Convention and danger rule the order and rules. Abuse of the house has its consequences. Lack of respect for those parts of the house associated with the ancestral order in the past can affect a household member either psychologically or physically. The ancestors identify so closely with the house that they are known to take revenge just as if they themselves had been mistreated. One's own lineage ancestors honoured at *nuagi*, *Khimpie*, the house ancestor, and the Original people like *Yechakukpa*, are particularly upset if the house is mistreated. It was only later, when I understood *saya* better, that the ancestors' response to mistreatment of the house – to do with maintaining their power – could be more completely appreciated, as we shall see later in this chapter. During fieldwork, I knew that if ancestors are angered by treatment of the house, they swiftly let you know about their anger – by *mangringma bopsime*, a condition in which the head turns dizzy, limbs tremble, and victims fall over.

The House Shrine

The household shrine (see Figures 11 and 12) is called *mangsuk*. *Mangkringma* are those represented in the shrine and includes all the *pappamamma'chi* and all the past kings and queens. *Sukme* is 'to climb' as in 'to climb a tree'. The name of the shrine, *mangsuk*, is related to the idea that the *lawa* (the 'wandering soul', 'life principle') of

FIG 10 The house shrine.

a dead person climbs the *mangsuk* and from there ascends to the residence of dead ancestors, called *Hepmalitham Yepmalitham*. The shrine *mangsuk* should perhaps be glossed 'soul ladder' – the five or seven bamboo fronds being the rungs of the ladder. After death, it was said, the *lawa* of a woman goes first to a white cloth, on which her body is carried to the grave, the man's to his white turban, and then both climb the *mangsuk*, a man's going then to the right and a woman's to the left of the shrine. An unmarried woman's *lawa* goes to her father's *mangsuk* onto the left side, a married woman to her husband's left. So long as the person has had a 'good' death, their *lawa* joins the spirits of dead lineage ancestors. A few women said that women's *lawa* go to the three hearth stones and not the household shrine, but men were always adamant that all *lawa* go to the household shrine.

The main idea behind the shrine has to do with communication between the various layers of reality, or as Eliade (1972: 492) puts it 'that communication between heaven and earth can be brought about – or could be in *illo tempore* – by some physical means', whether rainbow, bridge, stairs, ladder, vine, cord, or mountain. All these symbolic images of the connection between heaven and earth are merely variants of the World Tree or the *axis mundi* (see Eliade, ibid.). The notion lying behind the shrine is the same as that behind the Lohorung stories telling how mythical and early ancestors did not die but merely disappeared into the sky in smoke, as did those seven sisters remembered in the *Waya Warema* ritual. The rope is represented, for example, in the *khimpie* 'house ancestor' ritual. The notion of the soul climbing may be compared with ancient Tibetan beliefs about the way the first kings did not die but dissolved into the sky by way of a rope (*dmu* rope) (Stein, 1972: 203). More generally the ascending soul may be compared with numerous shamanistic myths and rites, in which gods descend to earth or shamans ascend to heaven, facilitated by a rope or ladder (see Eliade 1972: 487ff.).

To define themselves and explain many of their rituals, the Lohorung say '*kangka das bhai mim Lohorung-mi, kangka hang labukingka, mangkringma tengkingka*' (we ten brothers Lohorung, we respect the 'kings' and maintain the 'souls, spirits' of the dead). The pronoun *kangka* expresses 'we, excluding others', and stresses their separate identity as a social group in the way they respect the spirits of their dead ancestors. Clan and lineage ancestors, the Original Beings, those *hang* 'kings', *khammang* and *yimi* gain an immortality and presence in each house through the ritual recreation each year of the *mangsuk*. The ritual allows them to retain their power.

The shrine acts as a representation of a basic principle of Lohorung society: respect towards those older than oneself – and in particular the old, those who will naturally die next or have died most recently. The order in which each household *mangsuk* was renewed was determined by the most recent death in the immediate lineage, whether mother, father, elder brother, grandmother, or grandfather. The day was remembered in terms of numbers of days before or after the full moon.

Constructing a *mangsuk* was described as being exactly the same as building a house. The basic structure is very simple, as can be seen from the diagram (Figure 12). The upper part consists of two horizontal 'beams', called *upmalitham*, and three short vertical 'pillars', called *yepmalitham*. The ends are called *khapmalitham*. One of the names for the abode of the dead, as we have seen, is *hepmalitham yepmalitham*. Ritual officiants, *yatangpa* and shaman *mangpa* always have extended 'upper storeys' with one further house or room formed with an additional vertical beam. This was to accommodate the primeval snake (*bongbi*) also referred to sometimes as *ses-nag* (N), 'water serpent', who choose the officiants.[7]

Some households build a lower section, called *wairang*, attached to the wall below the upper section of the *mangsuk*. It consists of five separate long, vertical bamboo pillars, two of them placed behind the other three, diagonally to the two outside and crossing over the centre pole, thus creating a central axis (see Figure 12), the same as the central house pillar, and the World Pillar. The ends are said to be 'like the roof'. It is significant for the Lohorung notion of the person that the houses in

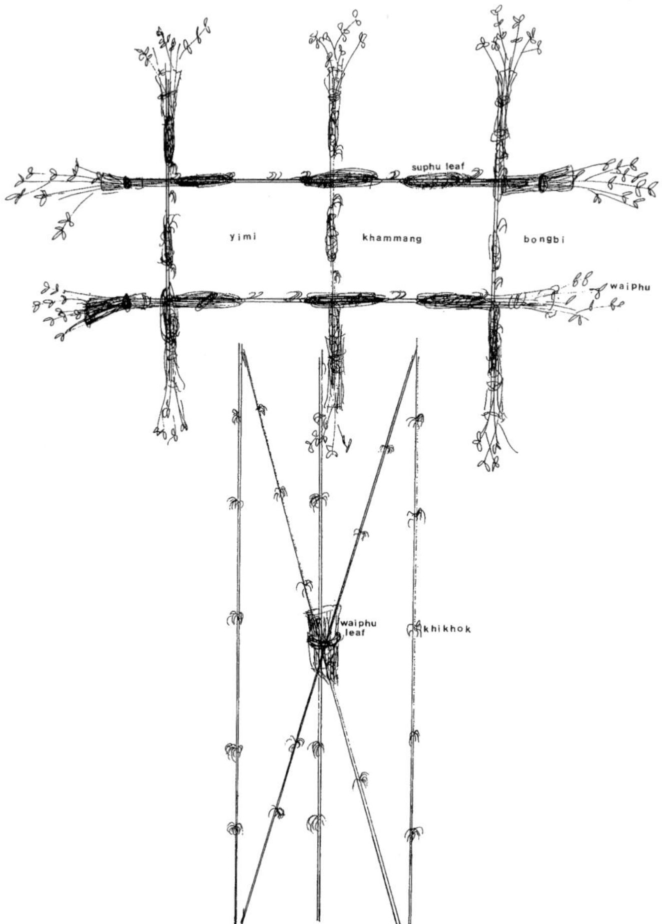

FIG 11 *Mangsuk* and *Wairing*.

which these *wairang* were constructed belonged to the 'Rai' headmen of a clan (or local clan group), the local *yatangpa* and *mangmani* and the 'head household' or household chief of each lineage – those for whom *saya* was most important – the people and households with the most responsibilities and who must therefore keep their *saya* raised.

The political implications of *saya* will become clearer as I describe *nuagi*. It's important to realise that similar concepts exist for all Rai and Limbu.[8] Look, for example, at how Philippe Sagant describes the neighbouring Limbu concept of *mukumā sām* or 'vital force' which he says is central to the old social organization of the Limbu,

> The state of the vital force belongs to each house, showing itself very concretely. To carry one's 'head high' (how can this be said in Western terms?) means to be at the top of one's

> form, audacious, full of happy aggressivity. You become successful in everything. Fearlessly you throw yourself into political action. When hunting the game springs to your feet. . . you are prosperous . . . influential, well supported by your allies, powerful and feared. . . The state of the vital force differs from one house to another . . . It's the thing in life the least fairly shared . . . In such a society, the powerful are the best integrated, socially . . . Social order depends on the game of vital forces (1985: 210–11).

For Lohorung too the *saya* of the house and that of individuals within it are united – represented in a concrete sense by the presence of a *mangsuk*. The shrine acts as a physical manifestation of the ancestral primeval power. It may be strong in a house or weak. A house without a *mangsuk* is not considered to be a Lohorung-house – even if it is being lived in just like a house. It could only be seen as a kind of cattle-byre. Cutting off ties with ancestral beings is to ignore crucial social relations. And social relations are a key to health, prosperity, and vitality. The *mangsuk* is one of the identifying marks of being Lohorung: to omit it would be tantamount to a denial of Lohorung identity. Those who *have* to exist without a *mangsuk* in everyday life, like an old man who insists on living in his fields, or anyone in the army, always belong to a household with one in their own village and attempt to return to the home of their *mangsuk* for the *nuagi* ceremonies. The closeness of other Kiranti tribes is sometimes judged by whether or not they have a *mangsuk*. On this basis, the Dhimal of the Terai, for example, are said to be closely related to Lohorung.

During the ritual both the shrine and the house clearly become microcosms of the universe. The common element in all three versions of the shrine is the presence of three storeys, created by the two horizontal beams, echoing the three storeys in the house. It became clear during *nuagi* that the shrine is more than just a structural replica of the house. In performance both the shrine and the house clearly become microcosms of the universe, both of them independently representing the three cosmic zones, the subterranean world, the world of the living (the earth), and the sky – reflecting too the shamanistic aspect of Lohorung tradition.[9] Here was their variant of the *axis mundi* or World Tree, for as Eliade says, 'The pre-eminently shamanic technique is the passage from one cosmic region to another – from earth to the sky or from earth to the underworld. The shaman knows the mystery of the break-through in plane. This communication among the cosmic zones is made possible by the very structure of the universe . . . [the] three cosmic regions, which can be successively traversed because they are linked together by a central axis.' (1972: 259). In the Lohorung case, the central axis is clearly portrayed in the *wairang* and *bongbi* constructions, and still adhered to when building houses. On the shrine the emphasis on three is made clear by its continuous repetition; the three *suphu* leaves, the three vertical main branches, the three storeys in the 'house' for *khummang* and *yimi*, and the three compartments into which offerings are placed. Significantly, also, it was said that although there are usually five 'flowers' made on each branch, it could also be three, seven, or nine, the numbers typically associated with the Cosmic Tree, The Axis of the World (Eliade, ibid: 274). The number of pillars that a Lohorung uses to build a house is always in multiples divisible by three: twelve, fifteen, twenty-one.

The lower part of the shrine, also, points to the importance of the central pillar, indicated by the one central *suphu* leaf. The central pillar takes on its significance in the *nuagi* chant when it becomes the central axis of the world, and therefore one of the routes the *yatangpa* can take to the world below and the world above. These routes are needed in most rituals. It should be remembered for example, that the main house ancestor, the *khimpie sammang*, turned into a snake, and has to be called from the lake below the sub–soil up to the hearth. In the ritual to *khimpie*, there is an offering placed under the hearth, with a rope running from the offering up into a small bamboo house, *bongkriwa*, made for *khimpie*, and placed by the hearth.

Lohorung understand both the renewal of the shrine and the building of a traditional house as renewing and representing acts of creation, which in themselves become rituals or acts of 'restoration'. They are valued most highly because they are acts which restore the traditional order that ultimately sustain the Lohorung world and Lohorung society, and maintain the sanity of those who live in it. As explained in Chapter Five on the *pe-lam*, Lohorung conceive of the strength, support and protection of their society as coming from the primeval past: from the Original Beings and Ancestors, their lore and traditions; and from the indeterminate power that was invested in the natural order of the world.

Nuagi

So it's not surprising that Lohorung consider *nuagi* to be the most important of all their rituals – although, as many wryly put it, there is never enough to eat and drink: too little beer and not enough chicken meat for too many visitors. No Lohorung would consider omitting the performance of *nuagi*; voyages away are never taken at this time and those who are absent try to return. The value placed on *nuagi* is a reflection of what I consider the commendable obsession of Lohorung society with maintaining itself. It gave many of them what I took to be a nonchalance about modern influences, so when roads were built, for example, they soon reverted to the old paths; while some took to modern Indian cloth, many still wore homespun cotton.

As the *nuagi* celebrations began and I became involved in the ceremony, I felt I was caught up in an event showing me how superhumans lived alongside the living in this society. The ceremony itself involved much social visiting both within the village and to others nearby. For two weeks every year the whole community is taken over by a ceremony, which perhaps most significantly, from the outsider's point of view, renews the *mangsuk* in each household. For Lohorung, however, the crucial aspect is the revitalization, or the 'raising' of the 'ancestral spirits within', the 'vital force, energy' (*saya*) of the house, the household members, out-married sisters, the ancestral couple, khammang and yimi, and the lineage ancestors of the house, in which each ritual takes place. As we shall see, in the *nuagi* ritual chant the parts of the house are addressed by their ritual (*samek*) names. That in itself is said to be sufficient to 'raise their *saya*', to refresh their powers.

Initially, *nuagi* made me realize the significance of the house and the household in Lohorung relationships with the superhuman beings. The house stood out as being frequented by the protectors and defenders of the values and traditions of the *pe-lam*. Later, when I understood *saya* better, I could see that the significance of the house as a political institution was derived from its very link with *saya* and that *saya* itself could be seen as an institution, a code of communcation, and a model of behaviour, as well as being linked to an emotion (see Chapter Eight).

The more *nuagi* was explained to me, the more I was led into Lohorung understanding of the nature of man's being, and this complex concept of *saya*. By maintaining *saya* Lohorung are able to maintain their society and the strength of each household. The main purposes of *nuagi* is to raise *saya*, strengthen *lawa*, and clear *niwa*. Understanding what that means to the Lohorung is one of the main aims of this book. We shall see this emphasis on *saya*, *lawa*, and *niwa* in the ritual chant. To fully understand the ceremony I had to have a clear grasp of all these complex notions, how they inter–relate as parts of a functioning human being and whether they are thought to be controlled by forces outside of the individual, such as by superhuman powers.

I shall begin to look more closely at the psychological, metaphysical, and ontological questions raised by *saya*, *lawa*, and *niwa* in the latter part of this chapter. First, I want to give you a feeling for *nuagi*. This may seem extended – with descriptions of the general atmosphere of celebration and a close look at the long ritual chant, and at *khammang* and *yimi*, the couple associated with the shrine – but I do this because it's both the informality of the gathering, and the formality of the words and actions which give the ceremony meaning. The notion of *saya*, which, so far I have tended to gloss as 'ancestors within' or 'vital force, energy', became alive, embedded in complex links between *nuagi*, *saya*, the house, and individuals.

Imagine you are there. Come with me into Pangma village. I'm sitting in the midst of a complex of household activities. The whole village is full of new faces and excitement, and the poor *yatangpa* already looks as though he needs a rest, although the rituals only began two days ago. But *kāhili* did say that everyone likes to have the *nuagi* performed either near the beginning or near the end of the fifteen days, so the rush may ease off soon. She was laughing a bit just now when she said, 'People think the ancestors will feel unimportant if left to the middle, that they'll listen more near the beginning or near the end, but it's silly – you must do it on the same day of the week as the last death of the house, the same day that mother, father, grandmother, or grandfather died.'

Everyone is so concerned to have their *nuagi* performed with as many relatives as possible. Each household 'calls' all the 'sisters' of the house, (including father's sisters, their daughters and husbands and children, father's brothers' wives and father's brothers' daughters, mother's sisters, brothers' wives and *their* sisters, the sisters – and husbands and children – of the wife of the house), and as many children of the village as possible, although the children are all collected after the *yatangpa* has finished chanting and offerings made. Children just come and eat: you can hear people in the morning saying, 'Today is our *nuagi*. Come over and eat and drink.'

It's that part of this intense activity that makes the word 'potlach' seem apt— that feasting and ostentatious gift-giving which allowed Kwakiutl or Chinook Indians to show off their wealth and reaffirm their social status. All Lohorung know that their household gains status if lots of adults and children attend the household's *nuagi*. Apart from 'sisters' there must be at least five, preferably ten, elders of the village present to say the *sikla* words to the dead. A 'big' *nuagi* signifies a healthy and wealthy house. A prospe rous, powerful, influential house will hold a 'big' *nuagi*. *Kāhili* explained,

> The *nuagi* is a bit big – with many people – if the house is strong and wealthy; so everyone wants to *look* as if it's big . But if it's big, then you have to feed lots of guests and give them enough to drink. You want to have lots of people, but sometimes you can't have too many because it costs so much and there isn't room. That's why children are good to ask: they can be squashed together, so it looks big but they don't expect anything to drink.

To bring this ritual alive I'd like to add here some paragraphs from one of my field diaries. Yesterday, Prem's aunt, his father's classificatory sister (his second cousins wife), a widow, was threatening not to go to her 'brother-in-law's' *nuagi*. Since her mother's brother is dead, she has only her late husband's brothers to rely on to look after her and it's the brothers' duty to look after the widow of a clan brother. There are frequent disagreements between them. But if she refuses to go to Prem's father's *nuagi* that will be considered more than a great insult. She would be 'throwing away the nose' (*nabak we'langme*)[10] of her *bubu* (elder brother), to whom she must show respect. And that is dangerous. Everyone agreed. *Nuagi* is all about raising *saya* of ancestors, sisters and household heads. Such a travesty of convention, such a pointed insult might make her own *saya* fall, Prem's father's *saya* fall and his uncle's. Once *saya* has fallen it can mean death.[11] Prem is certainly quite worried. Sometimes his aunt does talk nonsense when she's drunk. Today he hoped she'd be more sensible. Let's see.

This morning – another *nuagi*. As we waited for the *yatangpa* to arrive, the women were still busy making leaf plates and chutney and the *pheguang* (the ritual assistant) was working on the new shrine. Any mature man can take on the job of being *pheguang*, but if his wife is pregnant he doesn't, because the job entails killing animals and if a man kills an animal when his wife is pregnant they say the child will either be still-born or will die soon after. We were still waiting when suddenly Ram B. laughed and said, 'It doesn't matter if Lale doesn't come up to do *nuagi*: we can use *nana kanchhi*'s "tep"!' – of course referring to the tape recording I had taken of the *nuagi* yesterday. Ram took my tape recorder, held it in front of him, and began shaking like the old *yatangpa* in front of the shrine. It was a very good imitation of the old man and everyone was in stitches – even Chimeki, though she cried out 'stop it, *phenni*, you mustn't, it's wrong!'

People started talking about the competence of new and old *yatangpa* priests and shamans: Ram B said that once, when his wife was sick, her body and feet swollen, the *yatangpa* had first said it was one *sammang*, but then when she never got better, he tried another *yatangpa*, and he said, it was a different *sammang*, but it still didn't work, so he went back to Lale, who said

'Ah yes, now I know which one it is!' and it was a different *sammang* again. And she did get better.

'He's a good *yatangpa*, it just takes him a long time now he's old'.

'We need a young one. If the old die, nobody is short, why don't the old die? So many young die and all the old are left – Dambar Bahadur's wife, the one who is paralysed and can't see.'

'Don't talk like that. That's what *majha khim*'s mother used to say, "If I die then nobody will be short", then other people suddenly began to die; "it's all her fault" they said'.

'Perhaps if the "snakes who choose the *yatangpa*", the *bongbi*, keep coming on my *babbang* (uncle), we'll have a new *yatangpa* anyway. He's already stopped eating goat's meat'.

Everyone agreed,'*yatangpa* and *mangpa* are better when they are new – then they are really in touch with the other worlds and they can travel there easily. It's not the same with Jyotishi, the Brahmin astrologers. They are better the older they are'. Chimre, who had been looking for some crushed chilli she had left somewhere, suddenly shouted out and began to giggle. She whispered to her neighbour who laughed out loud. At the risk of stereotyping I should add that Chimre is what I have come to think of as one kind of typical Lohorung girl: within a few moments she can turn from being the most shy and demure daughter to being raucous and bawdy. This afternoon she was being very funny: 'I won't leave that "janto-sitter" (the boy sitting on the grindstone) alone until I've burnt off his sexual organs! And we can do without the chilli!' (meaning she would turn the wheel with the boy still sitting on her chilli, which would be very hot and painful on his sexual organs).

I'm so aware here how compartmentalized our own lives are in comparison to Lohorung. I often feel trapped by the rational, my almost instinctive drive to label the 'religious'. Here is what most anthropologists would immediately call a 'religious' event. But that label doesn't fit. What's happening here is so incorporated into daily life and humour that it's hard to tell what is part of ritual reality and what is mundane reality. All the humour and socializing is all part of 'raising *saya*'.

Narbong, who was walking by, looked up as he heard our laughter. I thought he looked very angry and his cheek was very swollen, apparently the result of a fight with Tinsule, who jokingly used the Nepali word *tan*, the inferior 'you' form, with him. When Narbong, in return, became very abusive and finally insulted him with 'you are your mother's husband', Tinsule hit out. Narbong has been going around today saying 'I'm going to find him: if I find him and leave him alive, I'm the son of a bitch!' Fights like this happen fairly regularly, men and women trying to injure the dignity and reputation of someone else if they feel they have been mis–treated in some way. And this is only one way in which people's *saya* falls.

I didn't know anything about Narbong, and people began explaining his *niwa* ('mind') won't work properly anymore, since the death of his parents. Sometimes he can't work, he has become very quick-tempered, easily hits people, and argues all the time. One moment he's rushing around making so much noise no one can sleep, the next he won't say a word. To me, it sounded rather like bereavement grief – somebody who was upset, confused, and angry about the death of his parents. But Lohorung explained his behaviour in terms of his household's *mangsuk*. They said that since his parents died his *mangsuk* hadn't been working properly, or as one said, 'his *kul* (N), lineage, *mangsuk* connections have gone wrong'. One explanation was that his parents had done the *chawatangma* ritual inside instead of outside the house, without any *yatangpa* or *mangpa*. People say that's the way to get much money, lots of paddy and millet but it's very dangerous. The *mangsuk* can't work against the powerful force of a secret relationship with *chawatangma*. That's why his *niwa* was not working well.

Your mind can go wrong if connections with your lineage are in disarray. Each individual has *saya*, each house has *saya* and both are connected to the shrine and your very sanity. *Saya* is an institution, it's a way of living, a mode of existence; it involves necessary rules of behaviour, it indicates the wealth and well-being of a house and of an individual, and indicates a household's relations with its ancestors. It's deeply bound to the being of man, the being of the world and the ontological link of personhood with all primeval objects and beings. It's not something that men and women *accomplish* – it has to do with the way people relate to each other, to ancestral beings, and to the world around them. You can't achieve a healthy *saya* on your own since it is based on accord, affinity with others. It's rather a mode of communication. And *nuagi* is the event of communion. To put it bluntly *nuagi* is the way to survive, to ignore it is unthinkable. In terms of personhood it points to the essential nature of relations with living and dead kin.

At a household level,and at a lineage level, *nuagi* is the time to support each other in a way Prem's aunt was threatening to disrupt. It's a time when lineage ancestors are given support, shown respect, and invited to visit their descendants to unite with them to eat the new crops. At a wider level, *nuagi* unites separated social units, separated sisters, emphasized by the arrival and departure of Lohorung women from villages in other valleys.

As we were talking, the assistant had destroyed the old *mangsuk*. He took it in a basket with a piece of lighted wood from the fire to a place in the forest, where no one walks, and burnt it. No member of the household can either make the new shrine or burn the old one. After all, the household is supposed to keep open the lines of communication, not destroy them. The *pheguang* had also been making the new shrine. He had split a length of bamboo of the largest *sakbaphu* type, (*Tama Bans* (N), *Dendrocalamus Hamiltoni*; Turner 1931: 279), the kind used a great deal in house-building and also in the other main house ritual *khimpie*. Having split the lengths of bamboo, he shaved them and made five fronds on each of the five pieces, attached a branch of *waiphu* (*masure katuj* N) *Castonopsis tribuloides*; Turner ibid: 68) to each bamboo strip at both ends and had wrapped five *suphu* leaves (*sal* N. *Shorea robusta*; Turner; ibid: 602) around each end and in three places in between. Each of these he had tied together with bamboo strips.This was all for the top part of the shrine.

'See, this is just like building a house: the three up/down branches are the pillars or t*oklang*, (*anglak khim* in ritual) and the other two are the beams (*surak khim* in ritual).[12] The ends of the branches are like the roof' or *ta'prawa* (*miring pokling* in ritual language).

He made the lower part of the shrine by splitting another length of bamboo into five, and shaving five more fronds on each piece. When he fixed the shrine onto the wall he added a leaf of the *suphu* tree to the centre. The long, bamboo legs of the *wairang* are like the stilts of the house. They take the house into the earth and the 'flowers' are said to be in honour of *khammang* and *yumang*, sometimes also known as *yimi* or *yimang*, the beings specifically identified with the shrine, and the generations of male and female Lohorung, whom they represent. Their 'houses' are the left- and right-hand cubicles on the top part of the shrine, the male *khammang* to the right and the female *yimi* to the left.

As soon as the *yatangpa* arrived he was led to the *mangsuk*. Appropriate offerings had been placed on a banana leaf. Sixteen different things must be offered, including the essential ginger, rice, chickens, lentils, and millet in the form of beer. The millet beer must not be touched by anyone except the female head of the household who makes it. It's always stored in a special place in the house until the day of *nuagi*.The other items must include some milk or yoghurt, cucumber or pumpkin, banana, parched rice, eggs or fish, cooked sweet breads, raksi (alcohol), mustard or radish greens, salt, chilli, mushrooms, potatoes, and various other available fruit and vegetables. What's important is that they are given food they recognize. So garlic, onions, pepper, or maize should not be offered. 'We give them what they used to like to eat: the first things; the things they used to eat when they were alive.'

The arrangement on the banana leaf was divided into two, each half a mirror image of the other. There were two *tongba*, wooden beer containers, each with its bamboo straw, covered by a leaf, with some ginger and rice in it, and two gourds containing prepared millet beer, two copper water pots, and two copper bowls containing the raksi liquor, two sprigs of the ginger plant and two leaf plates of cooked lentils. The other leaf plates containing the other edible items were placed in their twos on either side of the banana leaf.

The floor of the house had been specially cleaned with red mud and cow dung. The other day, catching the chickens for *nuagi* had been very difficult and the women of the house had commented, 'it's always like this; they know when the house has been cleaned and prepared like this, it means death'. Sacrificial chickens must be raised from birth in the household or village, never obtained from an outsider.

The *yatangpa* stood in front of the shrine holding two chickens, one under each arm, the cock under the right and the hen under the left. Almost immediately he began chanting.

[The Lohorung text can be found in Appendix 3. The words really are chanted. To allow the flow of the chant I've given the explanations to the chant after the text.]

'pillars of the house, oh, beams of the house, large bamboo parts of the house, small bamboo parts of the house, I call upon you!

Oh! oldest of all kings, oh! strongest of all queens; oldest of all queens, strongest of kings! (1)

the dried up deserted way, the desert sand way, yes that one (2)

the path of the separated birds Jalewa and Jakhewa, yes, that path (3)

ha:y! yes, the path of the plantain leaf placed at the foot of the shrine, the path of the low valleys, that one,

ha:y! the path over *Khempalung*, yes the path over high places (4)

a:y! a:y! the path of the rivers, yes, that one, the path of the setting sun (I fly), yes, that one,

a:y! the path of the rising sun, yes, the main door the beautiful way, yes, the way of the side door,

a:y! pillars of the house, beams of the house, oh! parts of the house made of the large bamboo *chiba*, parts of the house made of the small bamboo, *den*,

a:y! yes, this is a house made of *sakbaphu* (bamboo), this is that kind of house, yes, this is a tied together house

ha:y! the path of *waiphu* trees, ha:y! we follow the path of the *pheguang*, everything on the leaf laid out below, the shrine laid out by hand, the ginger, the turmeric laid out by hand,

a:y! ha:y! ha:y! the essence of the pitcher, the copper bowls, this is the main door, the beautiful way, this is the way of the side door,

ha:y! we follow the deer, yes, this is the way of the deer and the Indian elk,

ha:y! the way of the *ghoral* in the high hills (we follow),

a:y! ha:y! we offer water from our *chawa*, first spring,

ha:y a:y! we offer beer and liquor of all kinds; this is the *lawa*, this is the piece of clothing belonging to *khammang*, the household head, ha:y! this is a *wekhama* [female member of *hangkhim* clan] speaking! (5)

ha:y this is the piece of *khammang*'s clothing; even if you don't feel like eating and drinking, eat and drink; this is a *wekhama* speaking.

ha:y! the descending season, the path to the plains, this is now the path of this *wekhama*.

ha:y! on the path of the piece of clothing, on the path of soft cotton,

ha:y! a:y! make clear (people's) consciousness, their *niwa* daydreams, tell (me) and make clear the paths of my dreams, give well-being and good fortune! give comfort and fortune, this is a *wekhama* speaking.

ha:y! give *lawa*, give long life (to this house); give wealth, give rice, give enough.

ha: y this is a *wekhama* speaking, raise their *saya* as high as the snowy mountains ha:y! this is a female settler, a *wekhama*, if our *saya* has grown small, make these *saya* tall! ha:y! I mean *saya* oh! queen.

ha:y! this is a *wekhama*, protect us from the evil spirits, ghosts, spirits of dead ancestors, from bad gods who give diseases, from male witches,

ha:y! this is a *wekhama*, protect us from the *sehe* (N) and *shrindi*, the evil spirits of the Sherpa, protect us from rivals, save us from the bad omens of chicken-tears or nose-dribbles,

a:y! oh you! whoever it may be! this is a *wekhama* speaking,

ha:y! protect us from evil noses, from evil eyes; this is a *wekhama*, this is a *wekhama*, protect us from itching, protect us from coughing; this is a *wekhama*, protect us from shooting pains in the head, and from terrible restlessness, protect us from burning pains inside, from throbbing pains, this is a *wekhama*, save us from blindness, from being unconscious, protect us from swellings, swollen bodies and swollen bellies, this is a *wekhama*, hold back vomiting and dyssentry, stomach pains, yes, this is a *wekhama*, protect us from drying up fevers, from losing consciousness, protect us from colds, protect us from coughs,

ha:y! protect us from dying, yes, indeed, protect us! save us from becoming dumb, from long disabling diseases, protect us! protect us with creepers, with wire creepers like an iron fence, with creepers made of gold, with creepers made of silver, from the left and from the right protect us as with peacock's feathers, you will protect and make well, won't you! protect (us) small children as with peacock feathers.

protect us and make us well, won't you, father,

ha:y! father, ha:y! *saya* of ginger, *saya* of all the things laid out on the leaf under the shrine, and the *saya* of the ginger again, yes the *saya*, yes! *saya* of the deer, *saya* of the Indian elk, *saya* of the ghoral, *saya* of the *raksi* liquor, *saya* of the beer, ya:y! ha:y! (we have) protected and enclosed the *saya* of the chicken, oh yes, up until now we have! the female hen and the male, the chosen ones, we have covered (them) with a basket, yes, we have protected them. now one held by the left hand, one held by the right hand.

SOKMA: 'The Breath' to *khammang* and *yimi*

[The cock is hit on the back and killed, then the *yatangpa* continues]: the chickens are hit (with a stick) and killed; make the blood from the chicken's mouth fall into the middle of the *raksi* liquor; take it! take the blood, take the chickens, take them; (it is) the descending season, yes! now (we follow) the path south; this is a *wekhama* speaking, from today onwards make clear our day–dreams, our consciousness, make clear our dreams, give health, give good fortune, give well-being, give wealth, give rice, yes give us all these!

[The hen is killed, similarly by a blow on its back with a stick].

UMCHA 'The Final Plea'

protect us from ghosts, and spirits of dead ancestors, protect us from evil spirits and gods who send disease. Protect us from the *sĕhe* (N) and *shrindi*, the evil spirits of the Sherpa; from today onwards take away bad omens, tears coming from the chicken, water from its nose; protect us with the splayed-out peacock's tail, surround us with it, protect us; from your place in the earth, come! you are welcome! from your place in the sand, come! you are welcome! come the path of the river Arun, (to) the pillars of the house, the beams of the house, come to the offerings on the leaf placed under the shrine, come! to the ginger, to the copper bowls, and pitchers, come to the beautiful offerings, come! you are welcome! come guests to the middle, come! come to the left, come to the right; old men and old women come, you are welcome! come to (eat) meat and fish. Come to (drink) beer and our spring water! Come to (eat) the new rice, you are welcome! may your *saya* be raised! come and keep away the bad omens, give us good (be kind), come! give us good *niwa* , protect our day–dreams, make open our consciousness, raise *saya*, bring *lawa*, bring long life! We worship you!!'

Comments on the chant:

1. The priest uses the ritual names for *khammang* and *yimi*, addressing them as *hang* which may be translated as 'king' and 'queen', indicating their power and status. Some of the older villagers agreed that in the past it was the female *yimi* who was called first, whereas now the *yatangpa* always calls *khammang* first. 'They used

to call, "*Yiminayo, khammang nayo; chungchimayo, chongchi hango! lolihango!*"' There used to be eight or nine names for the woman, and the same for the man.

2. The emphasis is on the 'deserted' places, whether they are at the highest or the lowest altitudes.

3. The birds emphasize the loneliness and desolateness of the path.The reference is to a well-known song.Two birds, one male, one female are separated from each other: *pari malewa, wari jalewa royi, royi, yuta biha ye*. ' On the far side, the female, on the near side the male, in spite of their marriage, the fate of *malewa-jalewa* is decided at night.' All day long they are together in one place, but at night they have to separate, one remaining on one side of the river, the other on the opposite bank, and throughout the night they can be heard crying to each other across the river. Women were able to explain further that in 'women's talk', if a woman dies in her natal home before the final marriage rites have been undertaken, i.e. when she and her husband are already sexual partners and companions, but are separated by the location of her death, she becomes a *jalewa* bird, fated to be separated from him.

4. *Khempalung* is for Lohorung, and many other groups in East Nepal, a special mountain, the paradise and residence of gods; their name for mount *kailas*, 'The mountain on which the gods dwell'; especially the location of the heavens of *Siva* and *Kuvera* (Turner 1931: 105). According to one local shaman, it's the abode of *Varuna*, *Vishnu*, *Shiva*, and *Zema*, the four main Hindu gods, (though others say it's where all the gods of the world live). They sit inside the palace of *Khempalung*, guarded by a female guardian with a golden complexion. 'They sit on four continuously rotating, golden seats. The palace is lit with amazing light, like electricity, and golden flowers are everywhere. Also in the palace are seven golden horses, and many cows and chickens, all golden. The people who live there never do any work and live a very long life; the gods grow the medicines for the cures the mangpa shamans make, and which they collect by "flying" to *Khempalung*.' entering through a door in a rock leading to the other world. *Khempalung* is the legendary kingdom equivalent to the Tibetan *sbas yul* or *Shambhala*, built on top of a mountain, a place of peace and prosperity, where kindness, compassion, and wisdom are the characteristics of the rulers and the ruled.

5. This version of the *nuagi* chant is in fact not that of Lale, the *yatangpa* of Gairi Pangma, but of the female *mangmani* of Loke Pangma. She is a member of the *hangkhim* clan and *wekhama* is the *samek* for females of the *hangkhim* clan. The men of the *hangkhim* clan are called *wachihang* in ritual, not *wekhaba*, as one might expect. When Lale *yatangpa* is identifying himself he says, 'I, a *chiksaba* of the *lamawa* spring' as he does in the ritual chant that follows, thus identifying himself as a member of the Lamsong clan. *Chawa* and *samek*, the ritually identifying features of a clan, have been described in Chapter Five (see p. 121–125). Since *chawa* names the spring found on land claimed or conquered by a particular clan, the water is considered to be the most suitable for offering to ancestors (see Gaenszle 1991 for

Mewahang Rai and their 'transcendental' link with the divine forces of the *ca:ri* – their notion of *chawa*).

As soon as the *yatangpa* had finished chanting, the older men gathered around the hearth. Squatting on their haunches, their hands clasped together, just as we would in prayer, they began to chant or mumble the *sikla*, depending on how well they knew the words:

> You of the *lamawa* spring, dead grandfather, grandmother, great-grandfather and great-grandmother, dead married-in aunts, married-in female cousins, brothers and sisters, nearest and dearest, you are called. Get up and come from wherever you are, from your sleeping place, from your standing place, from your sandy place, your place in the earth, your tree or stone. (If) you come with the wind, catch your breath at the resting places, rest your body if you come the upper, sky way. When you come, bring food and drink; make open [risk, expose?] your *lawa*, expose your long life, your dreams, your day–dreams. Come, cross over to the pillars of the house, to the beams of the house, to the main door, the side door, to the three hearth stones. Wash your feet, wash your hands, and do not be shy, do not hesitate to come to the ginger, to the plantain leaf under the shrine having left the place you have been standing, sitting for twelve months. We have laid out for you on the leaf the new rice, *tongba* (bamboo container) of millet beer with its bamboo straw, beer from the clay pot, turmeric, egg, meat from the chicken, fish, soya beans, food to go with rice; a copper bowl with water, beer, spirits. You dead grandfathers, grandmothers eat enough to satisfy, drink enough to satisfy, come and drink and eat with your close relatives. Did you know about our troubles, have you seen our troubles? If you did know, do not be anxious, do not worry, I, a *chiksaba* of the *lamawa* spring, ask for your blessing; give a strong *saya* (to) this *saya* grown small, yes, a *saya*; yes, give a *lawa*, a long-life *lawa*. The swellings, the dysentery, the stomach-aches, if they come – give protection. Protect me from witches, evil spirits, bad gods who give diseases, thieves, epidemics, ghosts, the evil spirits of the Sherpa. Help us with our affairs [administration], our ruling, help us manage our own people and our enemies. From all (the things) like the snake without a tail weakening us (from which we could die), completely and for ever cover us and protect us like a peacock. Give the *lawa* to the ginger on the leaf under the shrine, oh yes, give *lawa*, give long life, give wealth and good fortune. Lo! wash your hands and feet; come from your getting up and from your standing place, rest along the way; come as yourselves, and do not imitate the mice! When we call you come, (but) at other times, keep away. Do not ignore the *sikla* words, do not go the way of gossip, follow the *mangpa*, the *yatangpa*, and that way you won't feel shy. We can do everything (for you), we can serve you, do as you request, give you help, *jadau!*

The men relaxed and moved from their haunched positions. Everybody began to move freely again. During the *sikla* everyone was very quiet. No one is allowed to do any kind of work or talk and, in particular, no person or animal should cross the pathway of the house or try to use either of the doorways to the house, which might impede, frighten, or anger one of the *chap*, the spirits of dead ancestors, and stop them from coming to the house:

> this is a time when the *chap* must be persuaded at all costs to come; we cannot see them so we must be very careful not to move or we might by mistake hit their legs, or walk over their legs, or bump into them if we walked aroud as they are called by the *sikla* words.

On one occasion, a chicken was wandering around on the verandah of the house as the *sikla* was in process. A 'brother' of the widow whose *nuagi* was being performed was visibly angry and anxious as the chicken continued unimpeded. Everybody was very still, the women had stopped making leaf plates, the children had been huddled to one side, out of the way, and there was a general hush. But no one dared to move to catch the stray chicken, who looked around startled as if it too was taken aback by what was going on. For me, it was one of the moments which most forcefully convinced me of several things: Lohorung belief in the power of their continued relationship with their ancestors; their conviction that the ancestors were coming to visit; the intensity of Lohorung fear of them, and therefore the need to conform to the correct rules of behaviour.

After the *sikla*, beer is always poured onto the three hearth stones and three portions of water, ginger, rice, gravy, beer, and chicken meat placed near the three hearth stones and four of the same at each doorway of the house, with words to raise their *saya*: To the three stones (*hitchrung tungchrung*):

> oh, you three stones (two stones united by a third) of the house of pillars, the house of beams, of the *lamawa* spring, for twelve months we raise your *saya* with the new rice, with beer, with spirits, with chicken meat, the food and drink offerings way; do not eat up (destroy the pillars, do not eat up the beams, do not play with the wind; protect us from rivals and stay in your right place.

And to the doorways:

> You main doorway, you side doorway of the *lamawa* spring, of the house of pillars, the house of beams, for twelve months we raise your *saya*, with the new rice, with beer, with spirits, with chicken meat, the food and drink offerings way; if we kick you or bump into you by mistake do not let your *niwa* hurt, do not let your head hurt; if a *Lakshmi* (wealth, good fortune) comes, open up, if a witch, evil spirit, bad god comes, go and shut yourself, go and hide!

During the *sokma* ('breath') section of the chant each chicken is killed by a blow on its spine. This releases its breath, which is then said to be carried on the wind to *khammang* and *yimi* and lets them know that the animal has been killed and the offering made. The *saya* of each animal is released along with the breath. Only in return for at least one cock and one hen, as well as the offering of the first crops, will *khammang* and *yimi* keep their side of the agreement and give health, protection, and prosperity.

As we saw in Chapter Three, Lohorung, in their own indigenous rituals, never sacrifice an animal in such a way as to display much blood. The idea is to retain the blood for those to whom it is offered, and pragmatically also for those who consume the meat. Pigs are traditionally shot in the heart with a bow and arrow and the flow of blood is inhibited by a bamboo stopper. The blood taken is drained into a copper container, and divided out later among the participants. Chickens are killed with a blow on the spine unless they are so small that no drops of blood, needed for divinatory purposes and as part of the offering, would come from their mouth, then their heads are chopped off. It's only a minimal amount of blood that is needed to establish the fact that the agreed offering has been made by the living.

In *nuagi* the cock and hen must be large enough for them to be killed with a blow so that a drop of blood can be immediately squeezed from their mouths and dripped onto a leaf: the blood of the cock onto a leaf placed in the right hand section of the shrine, and that of the hen onto the left. According to the Mewahang Rai, the Chicken is regarded as Man's senior in the sense that in the origin myth the Chicken showed Man the way. 'And it is for that reason, that it is in a position to raise *saya* . . . and in a position to show the result and success of the rite by letting the flow of blood. If blood trickles on the leaf, *saya* is strong and has been raised' (Gaenszle 1996: 266). A feather is also plucked from each chicken and placed on the leaf. As the blood is squeezed from the chicken the *yatangpa* watches carefully for any drop of water from the eyes or nose of the chicken. Any sign of water in the eyes of a sacrificial victim means someone in the house will either become ill or die. Water from the eye of the chicken is particularly bad and someone will almost inevitably die. On each occasion that I saw *nuagi* performed only blood came from the chicken, no water. At each divination there are cries of '*syabas*' 'bravo, well done, hurrah!' *Saya* has been raised.The prognosis for the household for the next twelve months is good.

The lack of any very bloody sacrifice among Lohorung Rai[13] is shared by other Kiranti tribes as well as a tribe in Assam (the Minyong Abors), as noted by Fürer-Haimendorf in 1937. He described parallels existing in Arunachal Pradesh (Hill Miris, Daflas and Nagas) and Eastern Tibet (the Amdopa) (1954). Fürer-Haimendorf suggested that the blood plays no significant role 'because the seat of the soul and of life is in the breath and not in the blood' (1954: 603). But the blood drops are clearly important for Lohorung for divinatory purposes, indicating whether the rite has been successful and *saya* raised.

After the chickens have been killed and divination from the blood on the leaf performed, the *yatangpa* places the leaf plates with blood and feather on to the shrine shelves, the one from the cock to the left and that from the hen to the right. The household head, and his 'brother' carefully slit the chickens. The cock is cut in two with the head attached to the right wing, and the hen with the head attached to the left. The left hen portion is always kept for the close daughters and the right-hand portion of the cock for the male household head. The remaining parts of the chicken are cut into tiny portions to be cooked for the rest of the family and guests. More than two chickens should only be killed if the household shrine includes a 'house' for the snakes, the *bongbi*. Such was the view of most people. A few said that more recently it had become permissable to offer more, and some did in practice.The danger was violation of tradition and going against the Lohorung ethos of equality and sharing. Those who sacrificed more were accused of trying to make themselves look important.

The entrails are used for further divination, performed by the main doorway of the house. In order to prevent the anger of *sammang* at *nuagi* four leaf plates with rice, gravy, and beer are also placed in front of the house.

> After the divination the guests sat around and talked, waiting for the food. As at every ritual involving chickens they made yellow chicken rice (*wamik*) burning off the chicken feathers and adding them, with the chopped-up feet and intestines, to the rice. Ram was talking about what he would do the next day. After one's own *nuagi* there should be no work done in the fields, either on that day or the next day. No one else should work there either. Some of the older children were talking about Jit's *nuagi* saying that it was 'big': 'he must have had at least six chickens'. One of the older men commented, 'he's not stupid; it's only his mother who uses the tax money instead of handing it over. He is angry with her'. Prem's aunt, who had offered raksi to drink before the priest had arrived, and had told me not to write down about the ritual, warned me again, saying, 'Don't write.If you follow that path you will be in trouble. *Khammang* and *yimi*, like *sammang*, don't like being talked about'. Prem tried again to persuade his aunt to go to his father's *nuagi*. If she doesn't go then his father will never talk to her again.

During *nuagi* the *saya* of many different objects and people is raised in several different ways. Most important, *saya* is raised in every household. Each household is anxious that their own male household head be revitalized and refreshed by the ritual, so that he can face hostile neighbours, difficulties, and danger with strength and 'his head held high'. So it's usually the cap (*topi* N) of the male household head that is put alongside the offerings under the shrine. Although the *samek*, ritual name, identifying the household head in the ritual, is the same as that for the clan, his individuality is given expression by this piece of cloth, which is said to carry his smell.

I asked why the *saya* of the male head is focused on – after all, the *saya* of all household members, including out-married sisters, is supposed to be raised and strengthened by the ritual. The reply was quite simple: man's *saya* falls most. He has the most to lose, the good name and reputation of the family to bear; he carries the public role, in which he is most likely to receive outside criticism. He is the person most open to attack and it is abuse which commonly causes *saya* to fall. If one of the children, for example, transgresses customary values or badly misbehaves, it's said they are 'throwing away the nose' of their father and risking the possibility that his *saya* will fall. In contrast, the *saya* of the female household head very rarely needs raising, apart from after the birth of a child or after some illnesses. Her *saya* is 'bending', and 'flexible'. It's also said that a woman has the added protection of her natal home. She can still rely on her brothers for their protection, and indeed has her *saya* raised when she visits them at *nuagi*, as well as in her husband's. Daughters too are particularly cared for. When the sacrificed hen is divided, daughters have a special share of meat: the half with the head goes to *yimi*, the other leg, wing, thigh, and shin is called *warang* and is only for daughters.

The head is the seat of a high *saya* so it is important that when the hen is cut, the head should be retained with the left hand portion, and offered to *yimi*. The meaning of the symbolism in the way the hen and the cock are cut is evident to us, as it is to Lohorung. Right is male, left is female and the head of the cock with its life-giving force goes to the male, the head of the hen to the female. The biological asymmetry, however, does not demonstrate as heavy a symbolic weight given to the left–right polarity as in some societies.[14]

The only way a son can have his own *saya* raised, independent of his father, is for him to build a house of his own, with its own household shrine. Only then can he benefit from the status of being *tumgongpa*, meaning 'important person' (its other meaning being 'head of the household') and gain the apotropaic power of being close to a *khammang* of one's own. Only then can he eventually build up prosperity and powerful relations with the ancestors for himself, outside the domain of his father's house. The move to a new house, however, removes the protection from his father's *saya*. His own vulnerable *saya* is now open to rebuke or attack from another *tumgonpa*, household head. It's only possible to guess at the significance of *nuagi* in prior historical times, but given the importance of raising *saya* in the present time, it seems likely that when political autonomy was considerable, when tribal chiefs, called *hang*, for example, were often at war with each other, that *nuagi* had even greater significance in restoring and augmenting the strength of each male household head, each one a potential chief.[15]

So *nuagi* has a lot to do with raising *saya* of household members. That's not so hard to understand. I want now to return to the *saya* in the chant that has to be raised in the house. What are the parts of the house involved in *nuagi* rites? They are the pillars, the beams, the main door, the side door, the three hearth stones, the large bamboo parts of the house, the small cane parts of the house, the woven cane walls, the ladder, the pole at the top of the ladder, as well as the ginger, liquor, bowls, and pitchers laid out under the shrine. All these were said to have *saya* and ritual names so that they could be addressed in ritual.[16] Are these empty forms animated by *saya*? Where is the agency doing the animating? What does it tell us about the Lohorung understanding of life? Such questions about *saya* haunted me throughout fieldwork, as I struggled to understand the concept.

From the ritual chant alone two important points should be made. First, it's clear from the way they are addressed that the house beams, pillars, and objects in the house are 'as if animated' by the presence of the ancestors, who are called to eat.

These objects, particular objects and parts of the house, as mentioned earlier are recognized by the ancestors as belonging to them. 'They are the owners', it was explained to me. The ritual name, by which each object is addressed in the chant, is recognized by the ancestors who know what belongs to them. The ancestors come to the objects and rest on them throughout their visit. Secondly, we can say the ritual deals with these inanimate objects 'as if' they had a consciousness which responds to being called by their ritual name, before the ancestors have arrived. We can see this, for example, when the parts of the house are called upon: *ane chu'ana*, 'you are trusted or held responsible' to protect the family with the strength from a raised *saya*. We can see it also in how they respond to a mere mention in ritual. Simply speaking, the mention of their *samek* name is said to raise their *saya*. So, 'pillars of the house' are addressed as *anglak khim*, and the main door as *nam khetam 'no, sunnali'no lam* (the rising sun one, the golden one) – reflecting the traditional Eastward orientation of the house. From our point of view this might seem to suggest some kind of consciousness, to be able to respond to names and requests. How can we understand this consciousness? I think without understanding *khammang* and *yimi* it is not possible. I've already gone some of the way to answering questions about *saya* in this part of the chapter. I now want to add another strand to the puzzle with a discussion about *khammang* and *yimi*, the ancestral beings at the centre of *nuagi*.

Khammang *and* yimi *(*yumang, yimang)

In Chapter Four (p.94–99), *khammang* and *yimi* were described as being the first incestuous couple as well as being guardians of what is spiritually and morally correct. They relate to all three cosmic zones, with the superhuman beings above, the water serpents below, and the living in between. During *nuagi* itself it was difficult to collect information on the couple *khammang* and *yimi*. From the text of the ritual, we ascertain little about them, except that they are referred to as *hang*, meaning 'king' or 'queen'. We also learn that they are associated with *Khembalung* (the legendary kingdom equivalent to the Tibetan *Shambhala*, a place of peace and prosperity). The couple are linked to Lohorung ideas about protection, prosperity, and the *saya* of all things, which comes across in the ritual text. Moreover, from the talk about Narbong, the man with the swollen cheek, we see an example of *khammang* and *yimi*'s connection with 'knowledge' and 'wisdom'. Narbong's *niwa* was not working well and one explanation was that his household shrine (*mangsuk*) could not work against such a powerful force as the forest ancestor-spirit ritual, *Chawatangma*, performed inside the house.

Khammang and *yimi*'s close connection to the water serpents needs further explanation.The Kulung Rai also have an important series of rituals associated with *Nagi*, the water serpent, and McDougal calls it a pan-Rai deity (1979: 66).17 For Lohorung, the subterranean underworld is conceived of as the abode of the water serpents, the *bongbi*, for whom the ritual is in part performed, and who existed before everything else. *Nuagi* may well come from the Sanskrit *Naga*, the subterranean water deities, or water serpents. Apart from all its other functions, *nuagi* acts to pacify and asks pardon from these water serpents for the activity of humans during the heavy agricultural months, when the soil is disturbed by ploughing, digging, and the removal of stones. The serpents are provoked to ill-humour by this activity and, unless pacified, bring misfortune to households and their property. The very work that Lohorung have to carry out as agriculturalists, and particularly during the agricultural season with the ploughing and digging, is said to lower *saya* – that is, to put each Lohorung individual into a vulnerable psychological state. By these activities they put themselves into a kind of impure state with lowered morale, because the water serpents are angry with them, and when this happens their own protective ancestors begin to hurt and turn away from them. Since they have no time during these months to raise and strengthen their *saya* – that is, renew their links with their close, protective ancestors – their *saya* falls. *Nuagi*, after the agricultural season is over, acts to renew the links with the protective ancestors, raise *saya*, and fundamentally maintain Lohorung society.

Though Lohorung do not make frequent reference to these water serpents, there is a collective conception of snakes encircling and protecting the hearth. *Khimpie*, the house ancestor, is conceived of as being connected to the subterranean region. As mentioned earlier, she disappeared, dragged into a lake by one of the serpents, which is why, so they say, she is sometimes called *sapdewa* (N) 'snake god'. One *yatangpa* told me the origin myth of how Lohorung followed the water serpents, the *bongbi*, in their emergence from the primal lake. In the beginning, when there was only sky and water, he said, the serpents remained in the underworld, but when the sun and moon appeared in the sky, then one of the snakes emerged from the waters and the churning of the serpents pushed up the soil to make the solid earth. And this was how the earth was made. The Mewahang Rai version (Gaenszle 1991: chapter 3: 1) recounts how the snake deity living in the waters made a clod of earth flow downstream from the source to the plains where it burst creating the first human being, explaining why for both Lohorung and Mewahang the place of origin is 'below' and the direction of migration is 'upward'.

The serpents are the ones who still choose the local priests, the *yatangpa*, those who are to work with the *pe-lam*, the myths, rites, and lore of origin. The *yatangpa*, who represent and maintain the ancestral ways, are specifically acknowledged and their role represented on the household shrines at *nuagi*. Their shrine, as mentioned, is different with an extended 'upper houses' and a long lower section. At *nuagi* a plate of offerings is placed for the *bongbi*, the water serpents, on the upper part of the shrine on the right next to *khammang*.

What else do we know about *khammang* and *yimi*? The flowers (*bungkringma*) on the shrine are described as being specifically 'for *khammang* and *yimi*' and as the priest's assistant explained, 'They are like those Tibetan flags on the roofs of their houses'. Reading Stein (1972), we know that the stones and flags on Tibetan houses represent the 'gods of the summits' (*rtse-lha*), 'gods of the country' (*yul-lba*), 'gods of the males' (*pho-lha*), or 'warrior gods' (*dra-lha*) (Stein 1972: 206). Following up what both Stein says about the various *lha* ('gods of the sky') led to some interesting insights into the resemblance of the tradition lying behind the Lohorung deities, *khammang* and *yimi*, and the concept of *saya*, and the *lha* gods of ancient, pre-Buddhist Tibet.

Stein describes the first kings, who became *lha*, as having no tombs, or 'had their "tombs in the sky", since they dissolved into the sky by way of the *dmu* rope, a sort of rainbow' (1972: 203). *Khammang* and *Yimi/Yumang*, 'the oldest (*sabudi*) king and queen' also had no burial: it is said they just disappeared into the sky. The significance of both of these lies in their common belief that there was at one time easy communication between the world above and the earth. This is characterized by Lohorung, for example, in the notion that at one time the living and the dead could intermarry. As we have seen, their household shrine is also similar to the notion of the Tibetan *dmu* rope, a means of communication between the human and the superhuman. Moreover, a rope appears in two Lohorung rituals, and in a third until sacrifice of an ox was prohibited in Nepal. Most Lohorung houses, however, still have a hole in the floor of the house by the hearth (the place in the house that particularly belongs to the ancestors), through which the rope was threaded to join the ox from below the house to the shrine in the house, upon which the horns were hung. And in another ritual to raise *saya*, the shaman uses a rope to join the members of the house to the altar built in the courtyard. The hole is the opening through which the ancestors and 'gods' are understood to pass and through which the *lawa* (soul) of the *yatangpa* or *mangpa* shaman passes when in ecstasy or possessed. To me, the hole and the rope are the clearest concrete expressions of *saya*, representing the link between the ancestors and the living human beings.

An article by Tucci on 'The Secret Characters of the Kings of Ancient Tibet' (1955–6) throws further light on similarities between Lohorung concepts and those of ancient Tibet. First,Tucci writes about new kings taking over from their fathers at the age of thirteen, when they reached not physical maturity but sacred maturity, something quite different 'laden with quite other implications and powers. This maturity indicates the presence of the ancestor in the son, which has ceased in the father' (ibid: 199). The king is thus 'the forefather present among the living by means of a perennial renewed manifestation of his essence' and Tucci emphasizes the point that the perennial renewal and strengthening of the terrestrial manifestation is probably the only way that the forefather can be renewed 'on his ideal plane, and thus escape the fatal exhaustion of the soul, as is not infrequently believed in Asia' (ibid:199). The renewal, the unending event, however, 'was repeated, unending but always new in its temporal localisation'. The new king could not remain in the old paternal palace:

> With his advent a complete renewal took place, a new order was set up. Each king settled into his own palace because the divine presence of the ancestor was reintegrated in him and along with the palace all was reconstituted: *novus incipit ordo* (ibid).

There is an interesting parallel in the Lohorung idea of *saya*, which is also an unending link with the ancestors, the same idea of the forefathers among the living inherent in a power within the person, needing renewal. For all Lohorung, the presence of *khammang* and *yimi* needs strengthening annually, while their terrestrial manifestation in each household head requires a minimum of annual renewal and sometimes more. Moreover, just as the Tibetan king needed his own palace to achieve complete renewal, so too the Lohorung son must be in a different location from his father to take advantage of the powers of *saya*. In general, sons do build their own houses.

Tucci goes on in the same article to describe the 'powers' that were transferrred to the new kings, two of which are operative in each new king, the other two taken over by a shaman and a minister respectively. One of the powers transmitted to the new Tibetan kings was *mnga' t'ang*, 'majesty', a magical power, which constituted their essence, 'the divine presence . . . transcending the vicissitudes of the individuals in whom it descends, as the guardian of the race and of the community' (ibid: 200). It tolerates no contamination or defect:

> This physical soundness is necessary for the group, as only if the sacred person of the king is fresh, intact, rejuvenated, will he be able to perform his function, which is that of keeping off epidemics, causing the rain to fall, assuring fertility, in other words that of maintaining the cosmic and social order intact and in due working order (ibid: 200).

The other power is called the *dbu rmog*, the helmet: beyond this Tucci has to guess at the meaning. He says there is nothing to suggest it is the symbol of military power. Instead, he suggests the word should perhaps be related to the *dmu* rope, the cord connecting earth and heaven,

> and with *rMug*, which denotes magic power, more especially that exercised in relation with the cthonian powers (funeral rites).The helmet . . . is the symbol, the visible emblem of the magic power of the king which is transmitted from father to son . . . It protects the king's head, whence, according to Bonpo tradition, started the luminous rope that bound him to heaven. It should therefore be related to the casque, the bonnet, the turban (ibid: 200).

The ancient Tibetan idea of a continuing majestic, magical power, protecting the race and the community, tolerating no contamination, and transcending individuals, conveys the power and some of the particular characteristics of *saya*, that are symbolized in the turban. Tucci points out that the two powers cannot be separated from each other: 'the one being the essence of power, the other its active symbol' (ibid). Should we interpret *saya* as a magical power, animating *khammang* and *yimi*? *Saya* is for Lohorung also a 'power', one that is essentially in the head, and one that is symbolized by the turban, worn by the household head in some rituals, particularly that in which his fallen *saya* is raised.

In consideration of comparisons with the Lohorung material, we should not forget the Thulung Rai concept of *seor* which is a similar metaphysical concept to the Lohorung Rai *saya*. Though Allen does not deal with the concept of *seor* in any depth, in discussing the problematic nature of translating the term, he writes:

> it would be wrong to think of the *seor* as existing only in the past, in external objects, or in another world, for there are a number of contexts in which the Thulung think of the *seor* as internal to the individual, one informant even defined the term as 'the god within the person'. A further aspect of the concept is brought out by the translation 'fortune', which can be taken either in the neutral sense 'lot, fate' or in the more positive one of 'strength, courage, prosperity'. (DPhil Thesis: 262).

And he comes to the conclusion that:

> The best way for an alien to grasp the unity of the Thulung concept seems to be through some notion such as 'line of continuity'. The ancestors are what constitutes the line of continuity in time and space between the Place of Origin and the here and now, and an individual's fortune inheres in the strength of this continuity. It is because of this that one informant could say that the ancestors' rope simply meant 'life: without it you were dead'(ibid: 263).

The rope referred to is the rope mentioned above, used also in certain Thulung Rai rites.

The pre-Bon Tibetans also conceive of such a rope with protective gods dwelling at one end and man at the other. The Lohorung notion of *saya*, articulated by their ancestors, seems conceptually very close to the notion of these gods at the end of the *mu* rope. Like *saya*,

> These gods relate man to his group in space and time: in space, because identical with those controlling the physical environment, house or country; in time, because they preside over the fortunes of the line, from ancestors to descendants. For man himself, in whom these relationships intersect, his gods guarantee – if all goes well – life-force, power, longevity, and success . . .. Through the man's god (*pho-lha*) males (*pho*) are multiplied and one has a numerous line of descendants; through the woman's god (*mo-lha*) sisters are multiplied, and the female fortune grows; through the god of the maternal uncle, one has good relations with others and prospers; through the warrior god (*dra-lha*) one has much wealth and few enemies; through the life-force god, one obtains long life and steady 'life-force' (Stein 1972: 222).

The similarity of Lohorung *saya* to these Tibetan ideas becomes even more interesting in the light of a further comment from Stein that 'the "souls" (*bla*) are scarcely distinguished from the "gods" (*lha*). The Tibetans often confuse these two words. Just as a man's protecting gods, particularly the warrior god (*dra-lha*) and the man's god (*pho-lha*), residing in his body and born with it, are also represented outside it by objects such as stones, flags, or trees; and moreover, are identical with the protecting deities of the dwelling place' (ibid: 227).

'*Saya* is our *bung*, flower', I was told, *bung* being the complex Lohorung metaphysical concept that I touched on earlier (see p. 79–81), with its broad semantic field, including the meaning 'flower', 'vital spirit', 'essence that is vulnerable'. It can be fresh, strong, assertive and can reflect the household head's self-esteem, good health and prosperity; if high in the head the person can be majestic like the 'kings' (*hang*) of the past, and have the power to ward off attacks, whether from evil spirits or hostile neighbours. This sounds similar to the *mnga' t'ang* power of the Tibetans. Just as the *mnga't'ang* can be extinguished or corrupted, so too *saya* falls if the person is insulted, his morale or pride attacked or criticized, if any member of his household is treated in an insulting fashion or if any member is contaminated by impurity. When *saya* has fallen the person is weak and vulnerable, wide open for attack and everything will go wrong.

There is a comparison to be made, too, in the function of theTibetan kings in maintaining the social and cosmic order, with the function of *Khammang* and *Yimi*. *Khammang* and *Yimi* maintain the physical and psychological good order of each household and maintain adherence to the norms and customs of the *pe-lam*. As we have seen, the Lohorung have no one omnipotent 'god' and no indigenous word which translates the Nepali term *deutā*, 'god' or 'divinity'. Nevertheless, ultimate authority and power combined with notions of moral and spiritual correctness are located in the houshold shrine and the figures of *Khammang* and *Yimi*. Hail and wind, twisted mouths, or distorted, damaged senses are said to be the relationship with *Khammang* and *Yimi* 'going wrong' (*nasi lisa*) and expressing their displeasure for some moral transgression. Whereas the *sammang* generally attack to satisfy their hunger or express their anger at being neglected, *Khammang* and *Yimi* are only said to act if there is a moral or spiritual threat to the society. They are understood by Lohorung to be the 'king and queen', the guardians of the spiritual and moral world, similar to the cosmic and social world over which the ancient Tibetan kings ruled. For Lohorung, however, the terrestrial manifestations of these guardians abide not in one individual, but in each couple who head every household. When a boy and girl marry they are said to 'become' *Khammang* and *Yimi* and in the traditional marriage ceremony the girl is called '*yimi*' and the boy '*khammang*'. However, the role only takes on real significance when the couple achieve a house of their own and when they have their own *nuagi*, that is, when the male household head's *saya* is independent from that of his father and the health and prosperity and strength of their household is said to depend on their own ability to foster relationship with their ancestors and protective gods, as well as those living around them.

Returning to Stein, we can see further similarities in the beliefs of the ancient Tibetan people and Lohorung Rai. Looking at Tibetan ideas about those superhuman beings who gave them protection helped illuminate aspects of Lohorung *nuagi*. Stein writes about the first kings and the sacred mountains. Mountains are *lha*. 'The sacred mountains are "gods of the country" (*yul-lha*) or "masters of the place" (*gxhi-bdag*, *sa bdag*). They are regarded both as "pillars of the sky" (*gnam-gyi ka-ba*) and "pegs of the earth" (*sa-yi phurbu*)' (ibid: 203). *Khammang* and *Yimi*'s mountainous connection is with *Khempalung*, the sacred mountain where the gods of the country live. Yet they also have links with the soil, with the *bongbi*, water snakes, and creator ancestors. *Khammang* and *Yimi*'s association with *Khempalung*, and the 'high path' in the chant, the original migratory journey 'upwards' (and their connection with *saya*, which has to be 'raised' to be strong) are all part of a more general Lohorung reverence for height. Their attitude projects power, strength, health, and prosperity onto that which is 'high', and this is epitomized by *Khempalung*. The ancient Tibetans had a cult of height according to Stein. He writes, for example, about the Tibetan group's or leader's self-assertion as having 'a warlike victorious air, frequently expressed by the idea of height or loftiness, elevation and might, symbolized by the sky . . . The image of sovereignty is the "mighty helmet" (*dbu-rmog btsan*) or "lofty head" (*dbu-'phangs mtho*). So the cult of height is expressed by stones, tree-branches, or flags placed on roofs, passes or one's headgear' (ibid: 204). And he goes on to say,

> Every traveller that crosses the pass lays a stone on the heap or, failing that, a bone, rag, or tuft of wool or hair. At the same time he calls out, 'The gods (of the sky, *lha*) are victorious, the demons are vanquished, *ki-ki so-so*!' The exclamation at the end are war cries. They are accounted for by the warlike nature of the gods (*dgra-lha*) and the idea of passing through a difficult or strategic place. [And then,] the main thing is simply the concept of height, loftiness, or elevation: the actual altitude does not count. The gods associated with sacred mountains and heaps of stones, the 'gods of the summits ' . . . 'gods of the country' . . . 'gods of the males' . . , or 'warrior gods' . . , reign, too, over man's head and shoulders, the mighty helmet, and the roof (ibid: 206).

I am reminded here of the victorious war cry that accompanies the raising of *saya*. We can also understand more clearly what the priest's assistant meant when he compared the 'flowers' on the *Khammang* and *Yimi* shrine with the flags on Tibetan rooves. Just as the stones or the flags celebrate the *lha* gods, and give them respect, the Lohorung *bungkringma* celebrate and worship *Khammang* and *Yimi* as being the ancestral king and queen who reign over the morals of their society, and over the males and over the females of the house. They honour their power and sovereignty or 'lofty heads'. Certainly, in many ways like the *pho lha*, *Khammang* is particularly associated with the males and with the right-hand shoulder and armpit, and with raising the *saya* of the male household head so that he is mighty and proud, in high spirits and without fear. Similarly, *Yimi* or *Yumang*, like the *mo-lha*, the woman's god, is associated with the left and with the protection and *saya* of the females in the house. At *nuagi* when the *yatangpa* stands in front of the shrine, he holds the cock under the right armpit and the hen under the left, the places in which these protective gods reside.

This Tibetan material is also helpful in understanding *saya* that resides in the beams and pillars, the hearth and doorways. We have seen that *saya* is not just an unending link with the ancestors, the link is inherent in a power, a magical power constituting the essence of a person or object. As Lohorung tried to explain, *saya* is our flower, meaning 'essence'.

The Lohorung respect for and closeness to 'nature' and certain objects is based on their recognition and celebration of the fact that individual things have unique powers, their own energy or genius, their own value, either as a species or in their historicity and that, sometimes this made them like humans, in that they are inevitably connnected to the primeval world. We've seen already how everything that has *saya* belongs in reality to the ancestral world and must be viewed with the reality that existed then. Now in the mythical world, at that time, the hearths, the pillars, the beams, and the doorways, as well as other things such as plants and animals, could speak to their ancestors and be understood. It is generally held that they should still be treated in the same way, 'as if' communication was possible, with the same respect and regard, and some might say therefore treating them as animate.[18] But for Lohorung the primary ontological categories of animate and inanimate are not key. Instead they focus on different ways of being in the world. Key categories of existence are, for example 'alive person' *hingkrikpa* or 'dead person' *singkrikpa*; 'forest person' *tapnam ya'mi* or 'civilized person' *khimtangpa*; trees can be 'living' *hingchame*, 'cut but not yet dead' (*hingyampa*) or 'dead, dried up with the sun' (*hengkhempa*). The reason for treating doorways with respect is not because they are seen as animate but because – like everything else – they have their own unique power and value, their own way of being in the world, and Lohorung relate to them within the appropriate framework, that of myth and ritual and respect as for everything owned by ancestors.

It might be said that Lohorung are relational beings involving a relational way of knowing (see Bird-David, 1999) and that they relate to entities associated with the mythical plane in a different way to that of other entities. This is a way of knowing which attacks our assumption that the world is based on a division between animate and inanimate objects, between the human and the non-human, and between the natural and the social. Bamboo in this other way of knowing can be seen as brother. Objects can share special qualities with human beings both filled with ancestral power which has to be refreshed and renewed for it to function properly. If neglected their *saya* can fall. The strength of *saya* in objects and persons is not just to do with the entity alone but in how ancestors and the living *relate* to them.

The concept of *saya*, I think, is as close to our understanding of a 'principle operating in nature' as it is to any 'religious' or 'mystical ' notion. It's clear that the idea of persons, objects, and the spiritual world as being inter–related is opposed to the worldview expressed by Bacon, Hobbes, and Descartes whose mechanistic view has led much of the Western world to see man as against nature or above it, seeing nature as a resource to be exploited (see Morris, 1996, especially Chapters 2 and 21). I can't see, however, that the kind of 'animistic' 'cosmological' aspect of the Lohorung worldview means that, just because not mechanistic, their worldview must therefore be seen as 'a religious worldview' (see Parish's interpretation of Newars, 1991). It rather conceives of the world as a kind of organism, energized by 'primeval vitality'.

In conclusion, what we have seen is that to enter a Lohorung house is to enter Lohorung metaphysics. The implications for our appreciation of Lohorung personhood should be spelled out. The house has a bond in a mystical ancestral strength with humans and with certain parts of nature. To understand what this means to the Lohorung in their relationship with the house I think one has to accept literally the reality that the house is part of the world of the ancestors and that there is some vitality and communication between parts of the house and ancestors, which the Lohorung know they cannot see but they know to have existed, and is therefore a way of being in the world. When women mentioned parts of the house, it was sometimes with a kind of affection and humour because they said they associated them with the ancestral stories. The basket hanging above the hearth (*makdangkha*) reminds them of the story of the stone and *Yechakukpa*, the attic (*talletu*) with the grandmother *Yagangma* and the sisters *Chumling Chongma* who try to kill their brother as he sleeps in the attic, the main pillar with the first couple who lose their child in the hole just as the pillar was being dropped into place, each of the forked pillars with the crow that *Ngagelungma* pointed out was the kind of tree to cut down, when her husband was ignorant of how to build, the hearth is reminiscent of *Khakchrukpa*'s sisters *Tawama Khewama*. The house is the most natural place for Lohorung to relate to their ancestors.

Here let me briefly summarize the importance of *saya* in the house and how the house begins to look for a Lohorung. We saw in the description of *nuagi* how the ancestors identified so closely with the house that they responded to its misuse 'as if' it were directed to themselves. The house and the pillars and objects in the house were also addressed 'as if' they had a consciousness. According to Lohorung, objects with *saya* have an ancestral essence and power. Their ontology is ancestral and relations with them only make sense on the mythical plane in which communication between different species and objects was possible. The *saya*, the link with

Lohorung ancestors and *khammang* and *yimi*, reside in objects they constantly use, such as pitchers and bowls. No wonder, then, they are at pains to protect them and keep them private. We can now understand better why Lohorung place the house-shrine out of the way of harm and contamination from non-Rai visitors. We can now begin to appreciate the appropriateness of the shrine in the form of the house. The house is the place ancestors most identify with. For this reason, 'houses' are always made for the ancestors in the rituals to them.

The individual, the family, and the house, however, are also controlled and protected by the presence of *saya* in the house: *saya* is everywhere; *saya* in the hearth controls the fire, and protects the household from rivals, as requested in the ritual chant; *saya* in the doorways keeps away evil spirits, and encourages good fortune; *saya* is concentrated in the household shrine which has the power to avert misfortune and to protect the household from evil spirits, witches, bad omens, illnesses of all kinds, and even death. It also has the power to bring wealth, and well-being.

To raise *saya*, to give strength to the *saya* of *khammang* and *yimi* and the protective ancestors, as well as raising the strength of the ancestor residing within each household member, is for the Lohorung the most important ritual act he can perform. The house highlights how *saya* is central to the ontological sense of Lohorung personhood, equivalent in many ways to our notion of the individual. The household is the main economic and domestic unit. It is also the most important unit in the relations between the human and the superhuman beings with the ancestral house-shrine as a microcosm of the house. We have seen here how the house acts to order ideas and people. The fundamental need to maintain the high *saya* of households and ancestral beings gives Lohorung society its underlying rationale: it provides the framework for ordering social relations, for maintaining social institutions, and for valuing or disapproving of actions and emotions. Immoral acts are ones which are out of harmony with the Original Beings, behaviour which dishonours and demoralizes *saya*. In this light, *saya* can be seen as an institution in Lohorung society, acting as a symbolic code, a model of behaviour, an experience, a practice of male personhood, and a pattern for tradition.

Notes

1. I use the word 'ceremony' to describe all the activities connected with *nuagi*, and 'ritual' to refer to that part of the ceremony carried out by the priest, ie the 'transformative' as opposed to 'confirmative' part (see V. Turner 1967: 95).
2. Stein describes how the representation of the Tibetan universe 'like that of the human body, was modelled on the dwelling house. Conversely, the human body, the house, and the local environment are so many microcosms nested one inside the other, but of equal valisity' (1972: 204). Sagant in an important article on Limbu notions similar to Lohorung *saya* describes how the Universe, the house, and the body coincide as 'emboxed worlds' (1985: 198).
3. The Lohorung house and self can be understood in terms of embodiment as an existential condition,

as 'an indeterminate methodological field defined by perceptual experience and by mode of presence and engagement in the world' (Csordas, 1999: 182).

4. The organization of space in the house and house symbolism of several other Rai and Limbu groups has been variously described by Allen 1972; McDougal, 1979 :65, and Sagant 1973 and 1984.
5. Allen 1972 gives a detailed account of the significance of the vertical dimension in Thulung society in the expression of motion. In the same article he describes Thulung domestic space and we see here too the importance of the 'uphill'/'downhill' orientation in determining the layout of the house.
6. We can see here how the Western epistemological emphasis on the subject/object divide makes it hard for us to appreciate Lohorung views of reality, and their connectedness to their ancestors. Werner Heisenberg's 'uncertainty principle' (1962) has indicated the extent of the unity and interrelatedness of the universe, which comes closer to the Lohorung view. Gregory Bateson can help us too in his emphasis on relationships, which he saw as being the essence of the living world, so that he looked for the patterns that connect (1972). *Saya* doesn't express a quality or a part of a human being or object (as does 'soul') It expresses a relationship and the health of that relationship.
7. All Rai were understood by Lohorung to perform rites to *nāgi* N. The Kulunge Rai perform rites associated with the water serpent *nāgi* (N), a 'pan-Rai deity . . . relevant for the society as a whole rather than for the household' (McDougal 1979: 66) and Mewahang Rai have rituals to *nāgi* N, the primeval snake from which originated all creation. 'In primordial times nagi caused a lump of mud to flow from here down the waters into the plains to the place 'where all the waters dry up' and there being pierced by a straw (*siru* N, *Imperata arundinaria*) it burst apart – giving rise to the first creature . . . the Primeval Mother Horemma' (Gaenszle 1992: 200). Van Driem describes the na:ghi rites of the Dumi Rai which are clearly similar to Lohorung *nuagi* (1993:42–3).
8. The Limbu concept of *mukumā sām* Sagant translates as 'soul', 'energy','vital force' (1985: 168), *sām phungmā* as 'soul to rise', the Nepalese expression *sir utāaunu* commonly being used (ibid: 167); Allen discusses *sir uthāunu* (see 1976b: 163) and the Thulung concept *seor* in his unpublished D.Phil (1976a: 261–64). He does not relate *sir uthāunu* to *seor*, which he does discuss in terms of its complexity, offering various translations such as 'the god within', 'fortune', 'line of continuity' or'life'. Gaenszle interprets *saya* among the Mewahang (1991: 131) as 'life-soul'; and later *saya* is also the 'vital soul'.
9. Morris (1996: 56) emphasizes that though there is a similarity between shamanic or cosmological thinking there are also dissimilarities in that ecology is combined with positivism. The Lohorung attitude to nature (which we saw in Chapter Five) underlines the relationship between man and nature and conceives of the cosmos as a balanced and integrated whole and nature as something to be respected. This view of nature is often seen as being central to so-called 'shamanistic' religions (see for example Reichel Dolmatoff 1976).
10. 'To throw away someone's nose' may be glossed simply as 'betrayal' or 'to be disloyal to someone', 'to consciously ignore someone's dignity and sense of pride', 'to bring shame upon someone, humiliate, snub someone'. The image of disfigurement may be based on more than mere metaphor. Cutting off noses has been a punishment in Nepal for refusal to conform or surrender (see Kirkpatrick 1985: 164). For Tibetans, too, there is a notion that 'if you sell your house in the village it is like cutting off your own nose, you are certain to lose your centre and betray your own identity' (Gansach- Wilson, personal communication). It is closely connected to effecting someone's *saya*. Lohorung who are insulted, betrayed, shamed, made to lose face, or humiliated have to have their *saya* raised.
11. Sagant 1985 describes an old Limbu man who is tired of living and how he refused to sacrifice to *Nahangma* – a rite similar to *nuagi* – saying 'there is no better means [to bring death] than to refuse to "raise ones head", *sam phungm*' (ibid: 181).

12. In Lohorung there are several names – but covered in general by the Nepali term *balo*, or by the ritual term *surak khim*.
13. The lack of bloody sacrifice is shared with the Thulung Rai (Allen 1976: 135), Mewahang Rai (Gaenszle 1996), and Limbu (Sagant 1981). A small amount of blood is, however, used for divination. Sagant also describes the Limbu notion of a firm relation between blood and prosperity (198: 153), in which the blood plays an essential role in refreshing the soul, *phung sam* 'l'âme-fleur' (ibid: 153). The implication here is a causal connection between blood and prosperity effected by the 'soul flower'. Lohorung said the blood was 'good'. Blood certainly indicated success and a raised *saya*. Though here too there is clearly some relationship between blood and prosperity, I am cautious in drawing inferences about how they are connected (see Needham on Skulls and Causality, 1986).
14. For discussions on dual symbolic classification see Needham 1973.
15. See Sagant's 1981 article 'La Tête Haute' for an in-depth analysis of the political aspect of raising the Limbu equivalent to *saya*.
16. Surprisingly, although the *makdangkha*, the basket store above the fireplace, appears in the *pe-lam* it is not referred to in ritual and it does not appear to have a ritual name. Nevertheless, simply because it does appear in the *pe-lam*, many Lohorung were of the view that it does have *saya*. Generally, if an object is used in ritual, then it has *saya* and if it has *saya* Lohorung are careful about who can come in close contact with it.
17. The belief in the importance of the water serpents is shared by other Rai groups. McDougal talks about the Kulunge *Nāgi* as being a 'pan-Rai deity' (1979: 66), and briefly adds that:

    The Kulunge Rais have an important series of rituals associated with *Nagi*, the water serpent. In front of the house, along the 'lower' wall, are two adjacent stands for placing large earthen pots for beer. When rites are performed for the god *Nagi* during the summer (*ubhauli*), when *Nag*i is up in the mountains, a jar filled with beer (*di*) for ritual offerings is placed on the upstream stand; when rites of the same series are performed during the winter (*udhauli*), when *Nagi* is lower down in the valleys, the jar is placed on the 'downstream' stand. In the corner of the house formed by the 'front' and 'upper' walls, is another beer stand. This is used to hold the offerings of beer made to Purbe, the Household God, and to the personal deities of the householder and his wife (ibid: 66).
18. E.B. Tylor in *Primitive Culture* (1871) described belief in spiritual beings (belief in an impersonal supernatural force) as the simplest form of human religion, and as a failed epistemology. Those beliefs which suggest that spirits inhabit or can be identified with parts of the natural world such as trees, rocks, rivers, mountains he described by the term animism, from the word *anima* 'the soul'. Alan Campbell (1989 and 1995) gives a useful and overdue appreciation and analysis of the term. The idea of 'animism' has been widely discussed in relation to American Indians (and their sacramental vision of nature) and in terms of South-East Asian societies as the need to accumulate life energy as an explanation for headhunting, competitive feasting, and life energy (see Needham 1976). Some have argued, as I would, that the shamanistic outlook of the American Indians is more ecological than religious (see G. Reichel- Dolmatoff 1976) though both are just Western attempts to categorize ways of being in the world which elude us. For a discussion of how animistic ideas are closely related to a relational personhood see Bird-David (1999).

7

The Person and the Cycle of Life

What kinds of view of the person shape, and are given shape by, collectively produced meanings and practices throughout the life cycle? Can we really stereotype the Western view of the person as being egocentric and the non-Western notion of the person as sociocentric? Lohorung conceptions about what constitutes a person and their ideas about the self and emotion lead us to one of the debates that has been prominent in anthropology since the 1980s about cultural views of self and psychological processes.[1] I started to understand these Lohorung ideas as I watched a Lohorung woman give birth. The women gave me their ideas about conception and the capacities of human beings and how they see them developing and changing through the life cycle. As we'll see in this chapter the Lohorung concepts of *niwa* and *lawa*, as well as *saya*, were particularly important in Lohorung discourse about the person.

I want to show in this chapter and the next the importance of distinguishing between a notion of person as a collective representation[2] and persons as social agents when looking at self and emotions cross-culturally. If we view the notion of the person in terms of the dominant publicly accepted conception of the world (that is, cultural knowledge, often expressed in the ritual context) we end up with one view of the person – a cultural category. But if we look at notions of self and emotions in the practices of everyday life, derived from everyday empirical knowledge[3] and in terms of persons as agents in society (Harris 1989), we begin to see how the concepts of the person and emotion actually work and a different view of the person begins to emerge, 'the person as a living being, recognised in everyday life' (Morris 1994: 11). In the description of the Lohorung cycle of life that follows we'll see how there are important connections to be made between the individual self that develops in the process of interaction with others and the notion of the person as a cultural category.

The anthropological argument on personhood has centred on whether those living in non-Western cultures have a conception of the person which might be characterized as 'sociocentric', a socially derived category, whereas those in the West have a conception of the person which should be characterized as essentially individualistic and autonomous, immersed in a mechanistic and dualistic paradigm. Louis Dumont (1970), one of the key figures in the debate, used the term 'individual' to describe the Western concept of the person, arguing there are two different kinds of society each characterized by a particular view of the person. Traditional society is holistic and modern society is individualistic. He argued that 'the perception of ourselves is not innate but learned', and whereas our modern society obliges us to be free, traditional societies lack the two cardinal ideals of modern society and 'know nothing of equality and liberty as values' and 'have basically a collective idea of man' (1970: 8). Geertz similarly has described the Western notion of the person as a 'bounded, unique, more or less integrated motivational and cognitive universe' (1984: 126). From such writings as these has developed a widespread characterization of the Western conception of the person as egocentric and the non-Western conception as sociocentric (Shweder and Bourne 1984), or the Western self as 'independent' as opposed to the non-Western 'interdependent' self (Kitayama, Markus and Lieberman 1995: 524).[4] What many of these influential writings on 'the person' do not emphasise is that very distinction between cultural constructs (views of the self collectively shared in the form of social representations) and views of the self which come from social practice (the self as an agent in society).

Lohorung Rai, as seen in Chapters Five and Six, have an ultimate value of maintaining and recreating the 'natural' order derived from the original order of things. The stories of the *pe-lam*, the origin stories, are the framework for their ideology and that which authenticates the existence of their institutions, the shape of their houses, and the form of their ritual activities. All indigenous rituals aim to 'raise *saya*' – restoring relations with ancestral beings and the original cosmic order. This might lead us to expect a cultural construction of the person which places no value on the individual, a Dumont 'traditional society' stereotype. In examining the concepts of *saya*, *niwa*, and *lawa* in the cycle of life, we'll see that although the Lohorung obsession with maintaining the natural order in society is reflected in the Lohorung notion of personhood, this is far from the whole picture. We'll see how although Lohorung notions of self, gradually learned through their cultural ideas about 'personhood', do indeed emphasize a relational being,[5] we can see how Lohorung individuals work in practice with what appear to outsiders as tensions between autonomy and interdependence, independence and sociality, and how these apparently contradictory Lohorung values in fact work together.

Menstruation, Conception, and Birth

A Lohorung woman's views of self are closely bound up with collectively shared ideas and practices to do with birth and motherhood. Her very essence as a 'person' has to do with menstrual blood (*bung*) and her ability to carry and bear her husband's children. The creative role in the corpus of myths is strikingly undertaken by women; *ninimaremma* in the myth is made pregnant by the wind and *chawatagma* is the one who created the earth, flowers, trees, rivers, and mountains. Yet male discourse ab out how babies are formed is horticultural. Reproduction of human beings is described in the same terms as planting crops or reproduction in flowers and trees.

'The woman is like the earth. If we put seed into the earth, and the earth is good/fertile, it grows. If a man puts his seed into a woman a baby will grow'.[6] The following is a typical view of Lohorung men:

> The woman gives the *khim* or 'house' to keep the seed. The seed in the man's semen are so many. These are the essence of the child. They fight and fight each other and kill each other off, leaving only one. If that one is male, it will be a boy, if female, a girl. If two can't kill each other then twins. That's the way people here say it happens.

One man emphasized the importance of the male role, saying that men were the ones who originally carried the foetus around in the calf of their leg.[7]

Although Lohorung women don't think of themselves as providing a component to the make-up of the child itself in the form of an egg, most talked about their menstrual blood mingling with the man's seed to form the baby. The woman carries the seed and offers a 'house', which contributes to the make-up of the child in the blood that links the child to preceding generations through the maternal line. In South Asian societies generally the essence of a human being is not developed in a single moment of sexual intercourse at which conception takes place – a particularly Western view (Franklin 1991). Rather for Lohorung women the baby develops slowly with the mother's blood in the woman's *thuk*, which I understood to mean 'womb' from their translation of it as the Nepali *pate-ghar* (Turner 1931: 154). They describe it as a 'child-residing place' (*cha-cha-pentham*) different from the *khim*, 'house', the placenta, umbilical cord, and amniotic sac. Whereas the *khim* leaves when the child is born, the *thuk* never leaves. Women liken themselves to sows who also suckle their young, contributing to their young through the milk. Women see children as being related as much to the mother as to the father, each contributing through different substances – the father through his semen offering the 'bones' and the mother contributing through her blood and breast milk.

The essence of 'womanhood' is embodied for Lohorung in one dense concept – her *bung*, a polysemic symbol through which her reproductive role and organs are fused together. *Bung* covers the notions 'flower', 'essence of life', 'genitalia', and 'menstruation'. Menstruation is the 'woman's flowering' *me-nungmam bung* and is considered an essential precursor to conception. One woman's comment explained part of the wide semantic field of *bung*:

> First her *bung* (genitalia) flowers and the blood flows, then it gets its seed, then a baby will grow. Unlike others, those other *singlung* (trees and plants, living things), which seed themselves, as well as the flower *bung* on their own, we *yapmichi* ('people') need someone to get a seed to the *bung* menstruation/genitalia/flower.

Menstruation and genitalia are both referred to as *bung*. The structure of the body and the function are combined. This attitude is similarly present in the fear of diarrhoea when pregnant; they fear they will miscarry along with the flow of excreta.

In its most common form the word *bung*[8] means simply 'flower'. Flowers for Lohorung aren't, however, what we might expect. I came to appreciate this when I innocently picked a flower and was sternly rebuked for picking what belongs to *sammang* ancestors. Just as the ancestors 'own' and visit the hearth, the threshold and various other parts of every Lohorung house, *sammang* ancestors visit certain flowers, stones, trees and sometimes 'linger' or 'sit' (*penuk*) on them. For Lohorung, flowers and these other objects belong to the ancestral reality more than to their own. Drawing no sharp distinction between myth and reality, everything mentioned in the myths of origin, the *mundhum* or *pe-lam*[9] has a vitality and an existence beyond that which ordinary consciousness (*lemmang*) can grasp. This reality is reached by human beings in dreams (*semmang*) and by the shaman or *yatangpa* officiants in their spiritual journeys.

In terms of understanding Lohorung 'personhood' it would be wrong to say then that Lohorung view flowers, stones, and the whole natural world as animate or personalized. An ontological unity, however, binds together the human person, ancestors, and certain animals with certain stones, the hearth and all objects of the *pe- lam/mundhum* cosmos. They are all united in a mythical world whose potency is still experienced in their very essence, their nature, their vital principle (*saya*). There is 'a basic metaphysical unity in the ground of being'[10] and this is central to the Lohorung ideological view of self. Human beings and flowers share an essence. Flowers are not persons but there is a metaphysical sense in which flowers can mirror the state of the relationship between the persons they represent and the ancestral world because there is a direct metaphysical connection between them:[11] persons like certain flowers have *saya*. But more than that, persons and flowers physically show their vulnerability and strength in the way they hold their heads.

We saw in Chapter Four how the *lawa* 'the wandering soul' resides in flowers in the land of the ancestors. If the flower in which it resides is seen by the ritual officiant to be blooming, then the person will be in good health; if the flower is drooping and wilted, then this too is a reflection that the person is dispirited, has been insulted or mistreated, is unwell: all being indications that the relationship with the ancestral world is not harmonious. The flower represents the person but in particular the state of a person's *saya* – the state of the 'ancestral soul' residing within a person – and therefore the state of that person's relationship with the ancestors. When Lohorung say *saya kanim bung* (*saya* is our flower), they are referring to this whole complex of ideas that *saya* is our representation of our personhood in the ancestral world, it is our metaphysical essence which can be strong or weak, grows with metaphysical knowledge. It is also a person's vulnerability, his or her achilles heel, that which ontologically binds a person to another world so that ultimately it is impossible for total freedom to operate. Anything that threatens the harmony of the mythical world is condemned: it is *phenni* (immoral, wrong). Illness and disasters are understood as evidence that something is amiss in the relationship between beings of that world.

Another nuance to the word *bung* pertinent to our understanding of the person relates particularly to its ritual use *phung*. As a concept it is something that is treasured highly, something that is part of growth (*phu:me*) and long life (*phungwa*). *Bung* has to do with the essence of a thing. We might say it has to do with the core of a thing or the concentration of powers from which new energies emerge. In Thulung, *phu(t)* is glossed by Allen as 'accumulate', 'clot' (1975: 229). It's not hard to see how both menstruation and *saya* are easily associated with such notions.[12]

The Lohorung attitude towards menstruation is complex. Lohorung themselves traditionally don't conceive of mentrual blood as polluting, in the way that Brahmin and Chetri neighbours do,[13] which leads Brahmin and Chetri to categorize Lohorung as low-caste and untouchable. Most Lohorung women, however, see the Hindu view as an attempt to constrain women's activities and don't halt their everyday activities of cooking and serving food, beer, and water to others during their menses. Although menstruation is not polluting[14] it is something both men and women are shy about (*ngesima lu*) in each other's company; not only is sexual intercourse during a woman's menses avoided, women who don't avoid it are considered *phenni* ('immoral', 'wrong') because they would show disresepct to their husband, threatening his dignity and his *saya*.

Lohorung see that characteristics and health of the 'self' can be related to conditions of conception including whether the woman was menstruating. They argued that while there is no reason why the man's seed cannot be planted during menstruation, local knowledge has it that the women miscarry if they have intercourse during menstruation. The foetus can grow but it's unlikely to stay in the womb.[15] Moreover, such offspring are *kaise* 'bad'. If they do survive they grow up to be naughty (*e'khemme*), 'they do not work well; such children do not develop their minds (*niwa*). Either their *niwa* is lacking in some way, or they have none and they go "mad" (*nganukmi*); later on they act unpredictably (*dhandhanaunu* N), and their *niwa* does not work well.' Only after the blood has gone are 'nice' *kamnuk* children produced; four or five days after and up to fifteen or sixteen days, then a good, strong child is born. Male children are conceived between the fifth and the sixteenth day.

Whereas a man's metaphysical connection to the ancestral world is firmly linked to *saya*, a woman's metaphysical links are more connected to her *bung* and to her *lawa*, the wandering soul. The *lawa* of every human being comes to it when in the womb, said to be attracted to the woman's *bung* as it is to other *bung*, as it wanders throughout the life of the person. In turn the *lawa* of the child in the womb is particularly attractive to the *lawa* of dead children who have died before the age of two, or to the *lawa* of mothers who have died in childbirth, whose *lawa* never enters the ancestral world but is destined to roam forever. Such *lawa* try to call out to play the *lawa* of the unborn child and they are often blamed for troubles that women incur while pregnant. To avoid these *lawa*, pregnant women noticeably do not sit or linger in doorways, any threshold, for these are known to be their favourite haunts.

The unborn child is not a social being and indeed not yet considered to be a 'person' yet it has powers, much as ancestral beings do, to affect the outside world and be affected by it. The key to its power lies in its immature 'mind' (*niwa*), as yet uncivilized and unsocialized. Lohorung understand the unborn child as possessing *tangpam niwa*, 'own mind' or, as we might say, a personality which is in a person before that person is born, unshaped by society and difficult to control. It might also be thought of as an unconscious self, which later on has to face the conscious mind, *niwa*, that can control its whims and desires. It is this uncontrollable and asocial aspect of tangpan *niwa* in the unborn child which may affect the outside world. For example, the *tangpam niwa* of an unborn child, already innately characterized by an inability to learn right from wrong, will turn *dibu* sour. When beer turns sour as it ferments in the jar women blame some pregnant mother, whose offspring they decide will later lick excreta from their hands. Unborn babies destined to become witches (*boksi* N.) in the eyes of villagers are sometimes blamed for stomach pains, for even as embryos they carry the trait that is inherited by daughters from their mothers.

The unborn child is also affected by what is going on outside and particularly by what the mother and father do. Problems at birth or with the young infant are explained by the behaviour of the mother and father during pregnancy. For example, if the umbilical cord impedes the birth or strangles the child, they say the father must have slaughtered an animal or snake or touched a dead person. If the woman's labour is difficult, and very long, they say her husband must have been making new fences to the kitchen garden (a domain associated with women), which is said to 'lace up his wife's womb'. The husband therefore tries to avoid any such activities and both husband and wife avoid any association with death while the woman is pregnant. If a man kills a chicken or pig while his wife is pregnant, the child they say will have some deformity, usually a deformed lip or nose. This focus on the behaviour of the father may well be compensating for the reality of the emphasis on the woman in labour and birth; it lessens her responsibility, reminds him of his contribution, and continues the ideas of complementarity accepted in conception. But of course metaphysically it also simply expresses Lohorung understanding of the degree of interdependence between beings, the ontologically relational nature of the human being reflecting the inevitable unity that exists between the living and the foetal world as it exists between living and ancestors. When difficult births do occur Lohorung immediately cut the bamboo thongs on any new fences made. If the baby's birth is late, the mother must take responsibility. Did she hit the post or tether of a buffalo into the ground and thereby lengthen her own pregnancy to that of a buffalo? Without wanting to reduce all Lohorung beliefs to emotionalist or intellectualist explanations, in these actions and statements we can surely see experiential attempts, both metaphorical and literal, to bring an element of human control to events in the world that are clearly out of human control.[15] I think Malinowski was also right to see such magical acts or statements as *prima facie* expressions of emotion and derive from natural emotional responses to situations of frustration, to 'impasses' in practical life (1974: 72).

Given this vulnerability of the foetus to the social and spiritual world one might expect Lohorung to perform a preventative ritual before the child is born. They do not. Instead women protect themselves by carrying sprigs of *titepāti* (*Artemisia vulgaris*, 'bitter leaf') or *Mamari bung*, when they walk anywhere away from the safe areas of the compound and the immediate village, and even within the village if they are out at night. They wear the leaves tucked into their wide waist bands and occasionally mutter words commanding the spirits to stick to their own path and not to wander into those of the living.

We can begin to see here how Lohorung concepts of the self and their concepts of the ancestors, whether seen as 'collective representations' (Durkheim 1938) or as 'cultural schemas' (D'Andrade 1994), while most obviously internalized through exposure to knowledge presented verbally, are also passed on to their children non-verbally. The individual is part of culture in more than a cognitive sense and we see here how, as Block pointed out (1991: 193–4), it is as much through knowledge of a non-linguistic kind, through acting, participating, experiencing, and engaging in a world where ancestors and spirts of the dead are a reality, that their particular representation of self is internalized. A woman experiences her blood as life-enhancing and as desirable to spirits, her menses as embarrassing but not polluting. Pregnant, she engages with the world sensitive to the potential dangers of losing her own wandering soul (*lawa*) and the total vulnerability of her unruly, unborn child to her own activities and those of its father. Experiences of the body, knowledge about how to protect it and the emotions attached to it are all contributing features to Lohorung concepts of self.

Late one night in August, Nanda and I were called up to a neighbour's house. Mahili, the woman in labour, crouched in a squatting position, easing her contractions by pulling herself upwards on the long piece of old cloth strung from a house beam, grasping it in much the same way that women cling to a rope for support when grinding rice. She was in considerable pain moaning in the customary way. Warm mustard oil was being rubbed into her belly and back when Nanda and I arrived. If a birth takes a long time, more women are called in to give advice. Soon another woman and her small girl arrived to help.

When a Lohorung woman goes into labour men are supposed to keep away: they shouldn't see the birth – it's woman's work. She usually calls upon her mother-in-law, sister-in-law, or any woman from her own father's clan living near by. These women are the ones to prepare the verandah at the side or back of the house where women commonly wash the dishes, store their pots of fermenting beer and give birth.[17] But sometimes expectant fathers can't keep away and that night Harka, the young husband hovered close by, running in and out of the house bringing oil, hot beer, soap, rags, anything that was called for. And of course, he was much teased afterwards.

A piece of smouldering rag gave off strong-smelling fumes to keep away harmful spirits or ghosts of the dead. Unlike other *chap* the ghosts of women who have died in childbirth wander alone unless they can befriend the spirit of another woman who dies in childbirth, so they hover around labouring women hoping to attack. From time to time one of the women spoke words of warning to the spirits, at the same time circling round the pregnant woman, throwing rice over her, putting some into the pocket of her blouse to feed and appease any approaching spirit (*chap*). According to *kanchhi*, women in labour are particularly vulnerable to attack; their *lawa* (wandering soul) can easily leave when in the midst of labour. Any indication of further weakening of the woman or any desire to sleep is dealt with vigorously: one woman tried to keep her upright, another flapped her skirts in all directions to push away the spirits who must have weakened her. Non-Lohorung ancestral spirits, *bayu* (N.), are said to crave the blood. The women repeat over and over the words, 'the cloth is burning, don't come and give us trouble, you have died, so now you must follow that path, now go.'

The expectant mother from Korunde, sweating profusely with her efforts, kept pulling at her clothes, shifting her waist band to hold up her sarong and pulling at the cloth to cover her body. If she tried to sit or lie down the women pulled her back to that squatting position. That way the baby can come out. The contractions were strong and one old woman helped her shift her position raising her from behind and placing a knee in her back for more support, allowing her to pull herself from the ground with the dangling cloth when the pain was most intense. They gave the woman in labour warm millet beer to give her strength and to hasten the birth. She vomited it immediately.

More and more oil was called for and a bowl of red-hot cinders to keep it hot. And then suddenly soon after midnight the crumpled baby emerged beneath her sarong. And there was great excitement, 'a boy!' But the women's work had not yet finished – they fed the mother hot beer and she herself worked at her belly to push out the afterbirth. The baby was wrapped in a headscarf while the umbilical cord was still attached. The father gingerly emerged from the house and hovered at the edge of the circle of admiring women to peep at his child. Not a glance passed between him and his wife. She was shy of his presence and carefully placed folds of cloth over the cord.

At this point they often give the baby a name. And when the cord has stopped pulsating, the oldest woman present cuts the umbilical cord, an important task for which the woman is given a piece of cloth in appreciation of her assistance. If she is not given cloth, the family is said to remain forever in her debt.

Lohorung view mother and child after birth as being extremely vulnerable. Both are said to be physically weak and spiritually unprotected. The baby, like the foetus, is as yet not a 'person' (*yapmi*) until introduced to the house ancestors, when the baby is named as a Lohorung with a ritual clan name. Before that it does not exist and therefore has no spiritual protection. Moreover, at this point the *saya* of the mother, her link to the protective ancestors, is also weak. They do not say her *saya* falls – she is not anti-social, not demoralized –but it needs raising after birth. Quite simply, during the birth all spiritual beings, including ancestors, are shown by the fumes of the burning rags that they are not welcome. Combined with the stress of childbirth, inevitably, the state of the mother's *saya* is weakened. Birth is the main occasion in a woman's life when her *saya* is at risk.

To improve the physical strength of both mother and child Lohorung women are concerned they consume the right food and drink. The infant is fed only on mother's milk but what mothers eat is said to be passed on to the child through the breast milk. So a mother must eat 'hot' food, such as chicken meat – as much as possible for fifteen days – eggs, honey, and some rice. She must drink hot chicken broth, distilled liquor, and hot millet beer. Hot millet beer is known to make the afterbirth come quickly, make good milk for the child and make breastfeeding easier. A new mother should eat four times a day if possible, or at least three times instead of the normal two. Prohibited 'hot' foods include pork, buffalo meat, chillies, and also hot spicy food that is not easily digested. For a month after the baby is born a woman avoids any cold drink. All the beer is warmed and the liquor (*raksi* N., *et-wa dibu* L.) is only drunk while it is still hot or heated up mixed with butter, a 'hot' food, and mild spices. In part these food rules are a mechanism for delineating the special status of a new mother but they are also a reflection of the Lohorung understanding of the physiology of the body. Lohorung, like others in Nepal, conceptualize food into two categories, 'hot' and 'cold'. Most foods are innately 'hot' or 'cold' though some, like rice or lentils, can be made 'hot' if eaten when made very hot through cooking. Innately hot and cold foods do not refer to temperature but to a symbolic force and a person's strength depends upon maintaining a balance between the two forces and avoiding the type of food innately opposed to some activity. 'Cold' food makes a baby retreat into the womb and after birth women are vulnerable to 'cold' air and food. Hence the importance of eating 'hot' foods before and after the birth. 'Cold' foods are green vegetables, potatoes, bananas, cucumbers, maize beer, and buttermilk. Any incorrect balance between the two kinds of food can produce stomach pains and require 'cool' or 'hot' cures. One 'cool' Lohorung remedy was made by grinding small worms with a white frog, mixed together with water.[18]

A woman experiences her new 'self', her status as a new mother and the collective view of her as weakened, in need of 'raising *saya*', through the special food she eats and in regulations covering her movements and her location in the house. During the first few days mother and child are restricted, a state called *suksi khedu*. They remain on the side verandah of the house or in a corner of the house as far from the household shrine as possible. If the shrine is in the back storeroom, the woman sits on the lower side of the house, near the fire to keep the baby warm. The mother is forbidden to touch the hearth; that is, she is forbidden to have any contact with the ancestors, and kept away from the part of the house with *saya*. The restriction is sometimes talked about in terms of her being *jutho* N 'ritually unclean', or polluting, a Hindu influence. The more indigenous Lohorung attitude at this time is one of extreme care not to arouse the anger or displeasure of any ancestor, especially before the infant has been introduced to the house ancestor. The ceremony, performed five days after the birth if the baby is a girl and six days after the birth if a boy, is regarded as the most important in a person's life. The child's future health and success may rest on it. For this reason no other ancestral, *sammang*, ritual is performed by any other household of the same clan from the time of the new baby's birth, until after the *Khimpie* or *Lataba* ceremony, introducing the child to the house ancestor, has been performed.

The baby's *saya* is raised for the first time in this introduction to the house ancestor.[19] Six days after the birth of a baby boy, a cock is given to *Lataba*. From then on the boy is accepted as a member of the family. Five days after the birth of a baby girl a chicken is given to *Khimpie* and, similarly, the girl is accepted into the household, the lineage, and the clan. On the fifth or sixth day, the mother washes her clothes and cleans with cow dung the areas where she gave birth and subsequently rested. The *yatangpa* priest waves *titepāti* (N) leaves (*Artemisia vulgaris*) dipped in cow's urine[20] over the place of birth, the doorway, the hearth and over the mother and child. The ritual is so important that the house is blocked off or 'cloistered' from any outside intruders, a nepme prohibition as described in Chapter Six. The ancestor *Lataba* or his wife *Khimpie* are then called from their 'place' in Chenge. By repeating the names of the places visited on the initial primeval journey, the ancestors are again 'placed' (*yungmale*) on the same path, the journey is recreated and the *saya* of the ancestor *Lataba* or *Khimpie* is raised. The *saya pokme* rite performed (described in Chapter Eight) raises the *saya* of the mother, and that of the child for the first time. After the completion of the rite the restrictions on the mother touching the hearth or the supply of water in the house is lifted. The mother soon returns to her normal activities.

One woman explained the first *saya pokme* ceremony as being like a person's first marriage – the marriage of the child to the *sammang* ancestors. Another woman put it, 'previous to the *Khimpie* or *Lataba* ceremony, for the *sammang* the child was not in the house'. From now on the baby has a very immature, small *saya*. The infant has begun its relationship with the ancestral world.

The Early Years

A Lohorung child is still not considered to be a complete member of the community even after he or she has been introduced to the house ancestor. The aspect of persons which makes them fully acceptable as members of the community is a mature *niwa*. This is absent in infants and very under-developed in young children. *Niwa* is not born in a person but comes gradually. Like *saya*, *niwa* is at first small and then becomes stronger. *Niwa* is slowly acquired. Lohorung say 'A child when it is born knows nothing; after three days it knows its mother, three months later it knows its father, five years later a little *niwa* comes. Some reach it in four years, others only in seven or twelve.' As one mother put it,

> The younger children's *niwa* hasn't quite come (doesn't quite work). JeTha (the eldest boy) who is twelve, he knows how to *ngesime* ('be shy, modest, respectful'), not to shout, what to eat; he knows and understands when the rice has run out. His younger brother does not. Only when they are twelve or thirteen does *niwa* really come. Jeṭha says 'the rice in the storage basket has run out; mother is always putting out more rice to dry in the sun. We must stop drying the rice. Stop it!' He was worried that we would have no rice. His younger brother cries out 'Rice! Rice!' And Jeṭha says,'Shut up! The rice in the storage basket has run out. We must eat millet mush (*chagkapa*)'. That's his *niwa* talking. Try the younger one with rice gruel, greens or soyabeans, 'I won't eat it,' he says, 'you must clean some rice'. He still has no *niwa*.

FIG 13 Carding Cotton.

The Lohorung view of *niwa* is central to their knowledge of child development and their view of divisions in the life cycle. Moreover, in the attempt to understand *niwa* we confront what might be described as the mental aspect of the Lohorung sense of personhood. *Niwa* classifies a person from most other animals, as a social being. It has the capacity for individual judgement and feelings, it develops knowledge of the social relations in which the self is enmeshed. I have glossed the notion *niwa* as 'mind', though their system for classifying different states of mind is more dependent on this one concept in its various contexts than is our notion, which is more differentiated and reliant on subsidiary categories such as conscience, personality, impulse, or memory. Nevertheless, these meanings are present in the notion of *niwa* and contribute to a complexity which gives it considerable force in Lohorung society. As we shall see, behaviour, opinions, thoughts, and feelings are controlled and ordered by its powers of reference.

Lohorung often say about children, 'children have no *niwa*. They only feel, and have wants, desires; they don't know anything' ('*chachachim niwa ma'a, minukmi te- no; mang so lesuni*'). One could almost say this summarizes their view of young children. They emphasize that children are characterized by their intuitive feelings. They *minukmi* – a verb covering our notion of 'feel', 'want', 'desire' (as in *mantok-lo mi 'ni? essiknga* 'how do you feel? I feel lazy'; or *mang mi:nero? chama minga* 'what do you want? I want to eat'). Children have impulses untrained by social control. *Niwa* is the element of control; to have *niwa* is 'to know' either 'how' or 'that' in order to behave properly. They do not 'know' either the facts or the means involved in behaving and responding to life in accordance with *niwa*. Since young children are considered to experience their environment directly through wants and feelings, they are thought to be in some ways like gods or ancestors. Breast-feeding infants are said to be like ancestors, for example, demanding their needs are met immediately and crying out angrily if they aren't. Having no *niwa* and therefore experiencing life in a totally different way, young children, like ancestors, are conceived of as living in a somewhat different reality from that of adults. And like gods and ancestors, children are considered to have certain powers. Without the interference of *niwa* and the reality of everyday social life it brings with it, the words and actions of children are seen as possessing powers of prediction: 'Children have no *niwa* but they "know". They weed out *niwa*' (*Chachachim niwa ma-a tara lekuchi. Khochi niwa sagukmi*). By this Lohorung mean small children have a natural ability to sort out, and even reject, less important bits of knowledge or behaviour they are expected to learn. They intuitively know what is significant. It is with this trusting attitude that Lohorung expect their children to learn skills throughout the developing years. In this way too Lohorung explain young children's strange comments or actions that later turn out to be significant. For example, if a child unexpectedly speaks *apa*, 'father', before *ama*, 'mother', it is taken seriously as a prediction of the father's imminent death, and the local priest will be called in to diagnose and prevent it. The child who asks why a member of the family must leave, or why they have left, before anyone has even considered or suggested going, is similarly interpreted as predicting their death; if children sleep on their stomachs, something unpleasant will happen to either their father or their mother: the child 'knows' this and doesn't want to see it – the child 'knows' (*leku*) in the sense of intuitively knowing, or 'experiencing' it. The child doesn't know it through his or her *niwa*. From the Lohorung point of view children have some endosomatic quality that can reach future events. Infant teeth chattering in sleep are said to be fear of a future disaster, not a reaction to a past event, as we might interpret it. Lohorung frequently comment on those events that children have correctly predicted and tend to forget the occasions when their unusual behaviour or unexpected affirmations have foretold nothing.

Since children are under the control of their wants and feelings, Lohorung emphasize they must be treated with patience and tolerance. The society's attitude to child development is characterized by extreme tolerance and indulgence. Children in the beginning should be allowed to live according to whim, like ancestors; according to the impulses and desires which are said to come from them, from their natural state and not from society. Small children up to the age of about five are allowed to be selfish, demanding, unrestrained in all their behaviour. Whatever small children want they should be given. Adults took this for granted and the following is an illustration of how they saw denial of wants as being outside the small child's capabilities.

Early on in my stay in Loke Pangma, it became well-known that I made cups of hot, sweet, milky tea in the early morning. They were very attractive to adults and children of all ages – a luxury never found elsewhere in the village. Weak, thick beer is the local beverage even in the morning. Sometimes so many adults and children came to visit, and so early, that I was overwhelmed with tea-making and infants. Though it was a good way of learning the language and collecting information from the adults, I asked two women I knew well if they could restrain the children from coming over too early (to give me time to wake up and have a few moments on my own). My request was misinterpreted. The adults came less and when they came they brought with them liquor or eggs in exchange for the tea. The ethos of reciprocity is very strong. The older children barely came at all, while the younger ones came as much and as early as ever. 'You don't have to give them much' said my neighbour, 'just give them a little. They don't understand *ma-a* ('there is none'), or *e'khe:ma* ('don't go')'. When I later explained the misunderstanding and that my problem was not shortage of tea, Anumpa, my assistant, smiled, 'You can't stop them coming. If you can give them a little tea, then they'll go off. We try to stop them coming but they don't hear if we say "Don't go!" They have no *niwa*'. From the Lohorung point of view there is no point in not giving young children what they want for they have no *niwa* to understand anything else.

Capacities developing in the young child, such as walking and talking, are not considered to be demonstrations of *niwa*; nor are crying, sleeping, eating, or defecating. They are said to be more like hunger, in that they just happen to one. They are said to be inborn, internal to a child from the beginning, merely some of the inexplicable abilities of children which encourage Lohorung to refer to them as 'gods' (*deutā* N). It's only because mankind was cursed that children cannot walk from the beginning like animals can. As the story goes, a woman who wanted a child saw a cow with its calf. She was jealous and took the calf. The cow cried and cried and cursed whoever had taken her calf, 'may the offspring of the one who took my child not walk for the first year of its life'.

Lohorung lack of concern for obedience in the very young and their constant attempts to comfort and amuse children make sense in the light of their view that children have no *niwa* and therefore no understanding but many, many feelings and desires. Parents cuddle and dandle their children, put up with all kinds of behaviour, and in general give them considerable attention.

One day I watched *Māhili* wash her child's hair with warmed water and soap as she sat enjoying the sun. She then sat for what seemed a long time smoothing out the emerging curls with butter. She let him play for a long time, calling to him occasionally to come to be dressed and tempting him by raising her blouse and offering her breast. But she was patient and willing to watch his antics as he played in the fine earth and laughed at his expressions. In the end, eager to leave, she managed to attract his attention by calling out '*dudu, dudu*' ('milk, milk') and lifting her blouse again. He saw the breast and lost all interest in the sandy ground crawling with amazing speed to his mother. And she didn't trick him; she gave him a long drink of milk before she left.

Mothers have close relationships with their babies: they are offered the breast whenever needed, picked up by any nearby adult or child to play with them if there is any sign of distress. And babies are carried, if not on the back of their mother then on the back of an elder sibling, sometimes on the back of a grandparent. They are taken to the fields, to the kitchen garden, to fetch water, to wherever work has to be done. They are carried in stretches of material which tie at the front of the person's body, thus allowing considerable contact between baby and carrier. They are constantly rocked, jogged, and rhythmically patted on the bottom. Men, women, and children can be seen doing this patting and jogging as they walk or stand about talking. If the child is very young the mother is never far away. If a baby cries he or she is offered either the breast or some other distraction. Babies are never simply left alone to cry.

There are two important reasons young children are not left alone. The first is that adults themselves hate to be alone. Their lives are intricately intertwined with networks of kin. Their identity is bound up wth the household, village, and neighbouring villages. Exchanges, hospitality, working in the fields in groups – this is the social and cultural reality not just for Lohorung but for many in Nepal.[21] Lohorung understand themselves as reliant on close reciprocity for their survival and have an image of themselves as living in villages closely huddled together so that noone ever need be alone. To be without family is to lose part of oneself and hence their incomprehension about how I could leave my own family in England. Given this image of an interdependent self that is embedded in social relations, to leave a child alone would be inhuman. Happiness, warmth, security come from being with others. Mothers who died a bad death in childbirth are destined to one of the worst fates – to wander alone forever. Fear accompanies those who walk alone and women almost never do.

This links to the second reason children are never left alone. From the Lohorung point of view it is not only abilities such as walking and talking that are inborn and internally derived; certain feelings, such as anger and fear, are said to be spontaneous in children before *niwa* has come. And, whereas under the influence of *niwa* such feelings can be directed and controlled, in the earlier impulse form these emotions are considered by the Lohorung to be irrepressible and dangerous. Children's uncontrolled emotions are like those of the ancestors. Lohorung have a special term for children's anger, *yik'bok'kheda*, the same kind of anger manifesed by ancestors and described earlier, that is, an emotion, mood or tantrum which takes a great deal of time and energy to counteract. Without *niwa*, children are said to be at the mercy of their emotions and therefore need a great deal of support in dealing with them and this is particularly the case concerning fear. Having no *niwa*, children are characterized by the ease with which they are frightened or tricked, for example, by mischievous ancestors, such as *Chawatangma*.

The vulnerable part of the child is its *lawa*, the soul that can leave the child's body and wander around. The *lawa* may be frightened or stolen from the child's body and the loss of it means the loss of consciousness, and eventually means death to the child concerned, though the *lawa* itself continues to survive.[22] The *lawa* of an adult is more used to its abode and hence wanders less, though its loss is as fatal to an adult as it is to a child. Throughout life Lohorung, therefore, avoid frightening situations and protect their *lawa* with *saya*, made strong, by strengthening their links with the protective ancestors. The *lawa* is seen as growing stronger and `more clever' as the person gets older: in a child the *lawa* is as fragile, as helpless and exposed as the child itself. For a child everything is new and anything may seem frightening. The *lawa* can be lost when the child accidentally trips or is startled by a noise. With this understanding of the nature of infants and children, their mothers keep them as close as possible. If a child falls or starts to cry someone is quick to pick it up.

Night is even more dangerous than day. At night the child's *lawa* may wander from the body to explore. If the child has been frightened or startled in its sleep, or the child's body becomes somehow unrecognizable to the *lawa*, it refuses to return. It will only return to a peacefully sleeping body. In adults the *lawa* has had time to get attached to the body it belongs to, and 'knows' how to return to it when it has roamed: when I asked how the *lawa* 'knows', I was told that *lawa* also have *niwa*. The child's *lawa*, however, like the child, has no *niwa* and is also unaccustomed to the body it inhabits. Thus, it often becomes attached to places and things apart from the child; places, for example, visited by the child, which it refuses to leave when the child leaves. Mothers carrying their infants can sometimes be heard saying, in semi-ritual style yet using baby talk;

> *lawa*, let's go, *lawa* let's go;
> child's *lawa* let's not stay in the forest (house/by the river);
> let's go home; come eat meat
> eat rice, drink tongba, eat egg,
> drink milk, let's go!
> let's go to the clan's spring (Lohorung version in Appendix 3).

Anumma, the wife of my assistant, came to stay for a short time with me in Kathmandu, and brought with her her youngest son aged three. In the moments before leaving the house in Kathmandu, she made sure she went to every place her son had been to in the house and garden calling out '*lawa khe:mayo* etc.'

In spite of the precautions taken by mothers, children are sometimes frightened, their *lawa* leaves their bodies, and it has to be called back. This is done by either the local priest, *yatangpa*, or, if the child is still suckling at the breast, by its mother. Once the child has given up its dependence on the breast, the mother no longer has any control over the child's *lawa*. The most common way for a mother to recall her child's lost *lawa* is to perform a brief ritual, which she can do herself. The mother takes thread she has woven herself and makes seven knots in the thread, saying *pak pak puk puk* words over each of the knots to keep away malevolent spirits. The seven knots are to catch the soul. The number seven is mystical and appears, for example, in the number of fronds on the household shrine, in the number of generations necessary before a clan may split, and the number of sisters associated with the ancestor *Waya*. More generally, it is an identifying feature of shamanic ideology (Eliade 1972). The mother colours the thread with turmeric, which protects the mother from all Lohorung evil spirits as well as pan-Nepal ones, like *bhut*, *pret*, *daini* and also from *bokshi*, witches. She colours some more knotted thread and ties it round her wrists making bracelets (*seng*), and ties some more round her ankles making anklets (*langkong*), and some more round her neck. At dawn, when nobody else is awake, she goes to the spring, either the clan's ritual spring, where clan ancestors first found water, or to a spring in the yard, or to a nearby pond. She must be sure to meet noone or her rite won't be successful. She goes to the spring with a pitcher which has the knotted piece of thread laid over its mouth, collects some water from the spring and while returning to the house, she holds the pitcher in her left hand and a small knife (*katche*), thought of as a woman's protective weapon, in her right. She waves the knife in her right hand from left to right, as if pulling something from the air towards her; and dips the end of the knife into the water to drop in the *lawa*, if she has caught it. Waving her arms she speaks using a combination of ritual and baby talk (Lohorung in Appendix 3):

> today may the *lawa* of a *chiksaba/dekhama* of the *lamawa* spring,
> Come back; be you at the foot of a tree, be you at the top of a tree,
> be you at the base of a bamboo, at the top of bamboo, be you under a stone, inside some water, a little up from the path, a little down from the path, under the wing of a chicken, whichever, come back!
> Come back! even if you have gone off to play by the river, to play from hilltop to hilltop, even so, come, that *lawa* which is the right length to your inside, come; too small, too short don't come,
> We call for a longer, the right size *lawa* of my child come!
> Let's go to our *lamawa* spring! let's go eat rice, go and eat meat,
> go and drink *tongba*, drink milk, eat eggs, let's go let's go!

When she reaches the house another adult must be waiting for her at the door of the house with the child in his or her arms. As the mother approaches she throws some cold water from the spring, flicking some out of the pitcher onto the child, who usually wakes up with a start. As the infant awakes the mother calls out:

> The child's *lawa* has come back, come back,
> settle yourself down, come sit in my lap, there, there;
> its all right the child's *lawa* has come back;
> Stay lying down, lie down, lie down.

The mother then gives some of the water to the child to drink, and the thread which had been carried across the mouth of the pitcher is tied around the child's neck. The *lawa* is said to come to the child's liver, though some say that it goes first to the *niwa* and then travels through the body to the leg, passing the liver on the way. It's said if the *lawa* is in the *lungma* (liver, but may also mean heart as well) when a child is frightened, it is at such times that the *lawa* is lost. If it's in some other part of the body it's far less likely to disappear.

The *lawa* of children is sometimes also enticed away by the *sammang* ancestor *Chawatangma*. One of her favourite games is known to be that of stealing the *lawa* of some young boy or girl and hiding it under the wing of a chicken. When this is thought to have happened a piece of the child's clothing is tied to a chicken, which is then let loose among the others. At the end of the day the same chicken is caught and the mother waves the piece of the child's clothing saying *'lawa ta'ayo'* etc. (as above).

The danger of a child losing its *lawa* is taken seriously and Lohorung act to protect children from potentially harmful situations.[23] They avoid taking children through forests where all kinds of spirits linger. During the planting season when people often cover their faces with paint or mud, they are warned not to go near a baby; those under ten aren't permitted to attend the *pappamama'chi* ritual because their *saya* is small and *niphero* 'pliable, bending, soft'. The *saya* within the child is said to be small and vulnerable when the child is young, and just like the child it is easily frightened. If it is overwhelmed or frightened by the power of the *pappamamma* ancestors, the *lawa* of the child leaves. In ancestral rituals when children are allowed to attend, they are kept as far as possible from the shrines, and near to women, whose *saya* always remains somewhat soft and weak, 'easily persuaded' (*okningbak*) in contrast to the *saya* of men which gradually becomes stronger and more crafty.

If we look at how Lohorung characterize children in their early years we can see the extent to which Lohorung representations of the person are tied to the concept of a social being in a very basic way. Lohorung thought about the person concerns itself primarily with the *relationship* of the person with others both in their understanding of the being of the person (ontologically) and developmentally. Ontologically persons only come into existence when they begin their relationship with ancestors and, since uncontrollable emotions like fear and anger are in the very nature of their being and are life-threatening, their survival depends upon protection obtained by their relationships with adults and ancestors. This dependency does not just relate to children: it is fundamental to all human beings. The need not to be alone is fundamental. In children intuitive feelings and desires, uncontrolled emotions, and a weak *saya*, as we will now see, develop naturally and through social relations with adults into abilities to relate to others, listen to others, relate to others, and co-operate with others, not into capacities to cope with being alone. The concepts of *lawa*, *niwa*, and *saya* are important in differentiating children from adults and men from women but also in articulating the Lohorung view of the intrinsic relatedness of infants with other human beings, with ancestral beings and with the natural world. Noone can escape this ontological unity.

If we understand this view of the child, it is totally consistent that Lohorung behaviour towards children is very protective, caring, tolerant, and full of attempts to keep them in the sight of others and away from frightening situations. We can begin to see here how Lohorung protectiveness creates a milieu in which the fearful takes on its frightening proportions, how Lohorung behaviour constructs some of the *kisime* 'fear' which is experienced. Rather than learning how to face fearful situations, infants are taught to avoid them, at the same time as experiencing their own parents' or siblings' avoidance and fear of those situations.

In the next section we shall see how children learn about *kisime* and how its meaning begins to be connected not just with what we call 'fear' but how this overlaps too with 'shame' and 'respect'. We shall also see how children's development of *niwa* enables them to control at least some of the flightiness of their infant *lawa*.

The Years of Developing Niwa

From talk about *niwa* and from social experiences in which *niwa* is involved, children learn what is approved of, what is expected, and what will bring them a 'good' way of life, health and prosperity. Lohorung children understand about themselves from two kinds of knowledge; one is from the way other people talk about their *niwa*, and thus their desire to acquire skills. Their sense of self and how to relate to others greatly depends on their understanding and application of *niwa* and all that it stands for. The second derives from moral bonds that hold together parent and child in Lohorung society, brother and sister, and husband and wife, which are perpetuated by children learning about *niwa* and experiencing its application in everyday life.

Lohorung often sum up their notion *niwa* as if it had two main facets. As one informant said, 'When people have *niwa*, they understand conversations, the heart begins to itch, they recognize the desire to fight for others, or for themselves, they see jealousy and compassion'. Here, then, we have two main aspects of *niwa*, one being the capacity for comprehension, the awareness or awakening of interest in society, acquiring skills and traditional ways; and the other the arousal and acquisition of feelings which relate to other people; to feel for and against others, a sensitivity which includes the potential to hurt others and be hurt by others. These are the characteristics that distinguish a mature adult from the being who is still a child. It is recognized, however, that these develop slowly. At first *niwa* is 'small and closed', traditionally indicated by the thumb and forefinger pressed tightly together. 'As a child gets older it opens a little, all people's *niwa* open a little, some open wide. But some quickly go back small: they close up again.'

One of the core aspects of *niwa*, as we can see from the above informant's statement, is its association with the development of social, as opposed to selfish, attitudes. It is thought to be the awakening of children's interest in what is going around that encourages them to be social, 'to understand conversations', and to try to perform activities that adults carry out. *Niwa* arouses the desire to imitate. *Niwa* is beginning to emerge when, as early as age four, children ask for a small basket for themselves so that they can carry small amounts of fodder for the animals, wood for the fire, and small pitchers of water. They sneak off with a small friend and whittle away at a piece of wood, try to husk and thresh with a small winnowing tray, and are eager to go off with their elder siblings to guard the seeds from the birds and monkeys. This behaviour is all seen as the emergence of *niwa*. It also shows in young children's play, when they pour water into leaf cups, playing drinking alcohol (*raksi*), or cooking earth into millet mush. By watching and doing is how *niwa* is said to learn; knowledge is gained by participating in the world as operated by *niwa*. And adults do not tease children if they cannot perform some skill properly; children find out most of their mistakes from siblings. Children suddenly do or say things that demonstrate the emergence of this social *niwa*. For example, the child who notices that the rice in the storage basket has run out shows that he has developed his social *niwa*, a sense of responsibility when he tries to stop his mother from preparing more rice to eat, by saying 'we must eat millet mush'. When children start to talk about 'our fields, our cattle', or fetch water without being asked, they are said to be demonstrating social *niwa*.

From what Lohorung say about *niwa*, it is apparent that it also has the sense of 'memory'. When children can 'remember' (*mittokme*) social duties or everyday tasks, it's said that they begin to show *niwa*. It's said that if *niwa* 'sees', then it remembers. At first children 'hear' but without *niwa* they do not understand, do not 'see' for themselves and so do not 'remember'. For the Lohorung this explains why young children only do things when told. They do not 'see' that the fire needs more wood, that more water has to be collected from the spring, that the rice fields need weeding. *Niwa* is the store of those duties, experiences, and the knowledge which should be remembered. Painful experiences on the other hand are not stored in *niwa* but in the heart. When recalling the death of a child, for example, a woman expressed it as 'my heart remembers it, my heart hurts'. It was explained that *niwa* does not ache for such events. *Niwa* is only necessary to 'know' and understand the aching of the heart.

What *niwa* has to remember are socially accepted behaviour, attitudes, skills, duties, and some traditional knowledge. Adults scold children for not performing their duties by saying, 'You are not making your *niwa* see it'. One night my host in Gairi Pangma returned complaining and shouting at his thirteen-year-old son, 'You are no better than an infant. You go out to cut grass, and return with enough to feed a pigeon not a buffalo. We might as well sell them, and we will have to sell if you don't watch your *niwa*. You might as well stay away from home, you are like a dog wandering from one house to another. Go on, be off from us, you *imtikhekhuba* (one who always sleeps). Can't your *niwa* see that the grass is suffocating the millet?'

The Lohorung term for this kind of 'telling off' is *losime*, 'to tell, rebuke': *niwa* sometimes has to be 'told' for it to grow. Teasing is also used to encourage the growth and application of *niwa*. Walking to the fields we passed a young girl carrying a basket half full of grass. 'Where are you going? Can your goat only eat that much? It must be ill', said my companion, peering into the basket.

The combination of memory, adult duties and skills in *niwa* are almost inseparable in Lohorung way of thought. As one boy put it: 'I left the cattle down in the field and I came home. My *niwa* did not see the cattle at all while I was talking to my friends. Where my *niwa* went, it went. I did not see my *niwa*'. Here the use of *niwa* as subect or object is the only distinction between memory and duty. A further example of this can be seen in the exclamation of a mother to her daughter, 'You put the grain out to dry just over there. Now it's about to pour with rain, can't you see your *niwa*, don't you remember the grain? Where has your *niwa* gone?' *Niwa* is associated with local knowledge, and traditional skills. Nevertheless, from the way it is used in the following phrases, as well as those mentioned in this chapter, its semantic field includes our notion of 'mind', 'judgement'. 'If people's *niwa* (mental attitudes) do not agree then no work gets done, the work is ruined'. (*Yapmim niwa tongni anke yompok-no lini so nasi li*). 'She has such a light *niwa* (mind, head for thoughts) that it flaps in the wind like a leaf' (*khom niwa ettano sope le, hiwa-ba singbak rokno khe*). 'The boy has land, he shows respect, but my *niwa* (mind, judgement) will not accept him, I do not want to give my daughter to him' (*watangpa kamnuke le, ropa chuk, ngesimalu, khom niwa khasini, kam pisa pima mingani*).

The 'duties' that Lohorung children have to remember are their initial contributions to economic activities, and children themselves often see them as being opposed to *tangpam niwa* 'their own *niwa*', that is, their own desires and wishes – and to 'play', *wapchame*. Just as Western children, when rebuked, cry out, 'I'm never allowed to do anything' so too Lohorung children in response to requests from parents to attend to their *niwa* and their duties, complain 'Our own *niwa* (*tangpam niwa*) is never allowed'. Adults looking back at their childhood often vividly remember the crucial time when *niwa* and work (*yompok*) began to take over from play, whether the time was stretched over a few months, or years, or whether the time was notified by a sudden event like the death of a parent or an elder sibling, for example, which necessitated an early acceptance of responsibilities. This memory of the interplay between play and work, *tangpam niwa* and *niwa* in childhood is perhaps best illustrated by an excerpt from a description that Nanda, the woman in whose house I first lived, gave me in her life story.

> I sometimes used to play with *nana* (elder sister), going to the village to play with other friends, to play 'brides' or 'weddings'. We two together used to go far to friends; she was bigger and so I was allowed to go too. When she got bigger our friends were different. And of course *jeṭha* (elder brother) and *kanchha*'s were different. *Jeṭha* was hardly ever at home if he wasn't looking after the cattle or the water buffalo with friends he was off with them fishing or catching birds. Sometimes friends came to our house, sometimes we went to their house to play. While father was alive it was easy; just play all the time. Father was so pleasant. Not once did he hit us. He was never angry with us. If we refused to 'hear' what was said to us mother sometimes used to hit us. But he would say 'No, don't hit them. Don't hit them; it's not necessary, they don't need it. Look at your own *niwa*; you don't know anything it seems, what then can you expect young children to know?' One day mother said to me, 'pick up that brush!' I said 'I'm not going to! just like our Sancar does'. Mother picked up the brush and hit me. Father, who was in the yard splitting cane, came quickly up the house ladder, 'if you hit a child there must be something wrong with you' and he picked up the brush and hit mother. Mother disappeared into the house. They got on well together usually. Father used to say, 'Don't worry, everything will be alright' when anything went wrong. Then *mamma* (grandma) died. And the next year father died. After father died it was work, all work. While he was alive we all went off to play. Afterwards mother and *nana* (elder sister) went off to the fields. I stayed at home to cook rice, make the *dibu* beer, fetch the water, feed the pigs, look after the chickens; I had *niwa* then; I knew

> what had to be done. There was also *kanchha* to look after, and our house is so isolated, the rest of the village so far up or so far down, he refused to stay alone. I used to have to carry him to the spring, then he would refuse to walk back; I had to try and persuade him. I was hardly twelve. The spring was far away – very far, far to get back home. Once I'd got the water pot back home, I'd make sure the door was shut, pick up *kanchha* again and go to the village to friends; but only for a bit, then quickly, quickly I had to go and let the goats loose, feed the pigs and as quickly as possible set the fire going, put the rice on to cook, see to the goats and pigs and chickens again and so everything was just right, for when mother came back, she would say 'and what have you two been up to?' 'We've done everything' we used to say.

There is a difference in the years of a girl's developing *niwa* and that of a boy, which is alluded to in the above description. Nanda learns many of her skills by performing her duties in and around the house: her elder brother is hardly ever at home – always away with the other boys, or it could be with an uncle.

Location is one difference. Another difference is that boys learn most of their skills away from the family with their peers, whereas girls develop their *niwa* working alongside their mothers, other women as well as other girls. Nevertheless, what is similar in the case of both boys and girls is that they are left to show their *niwa* at their own pace. Skills are picked up rather than being taught directly: the Lohorung attitude is that *niwa* comes on its own. Thus, they watch others and when their *niwa* is ready they join in, and if they make mistakes they are gently put right. 'Boys, first they never hear, then if you tell them off their *niwa* is so hurt, they can't work, *saya* falls.' This explained why boys are often left to go off on their own, though occasionally sharply rebuked for not fulfilling the tasks their *niwa* should see. Soon *niwa* comes and they assume responsibility; without apparently being taught anything they know what to do.

Nanda had to give up much of her time for play when she was about twelve years old and this is not at all unusual among Lohorung. A young daughter is often left at home to carry out domestic chores with perhaps the exception of the household beer-making, considered to need a 'clever *niwa*' and experience. Girls usually start by making their own and selling it at market. There are many reasons why daughters as young as twelve are left with such responsibilities – to free a healthier or older strong-bodied female to assist in the farm labour; sometimes, as in Nanda's case, it is the loss of a parent which suddenly reduces the labour force. Apart from death, the man of the house may also be absent for months or years working in Assam or in the army, leaving the rest of the family to carry out the work on the land at home. More significantly, however, a daughter of that age is simply expected to have enough *niwa* to 'see' and carry out domestic duties; her *niwa* sees her responsibilities and she fulfills them. In return she is treated like an adult.

The Lohorung child's life is not all work. As we've seen, play is considered to be important for the development of *niwa*, and for the first six or seven years, sometimes even more, Lohorung allow and even indulge *tangpam niwa* 'own *niwa*', children's own wishes and desires. Infants follow their mothers, elder brothers and sisters and other children of the village, or sit with them near the house. Nanda remembers playing 'brides' and 'weddings' still the favourite play of young Lohrung girls.They make small dolls from cloth remnants of old skirts or scraps begged from the tailors. One doll is 'the bride' (*dangma*) and another 'the groom' (*dangpa*). Smaller dolls are the 'children' and they play what we would call 'mothers and fathers'. Boys may join in part of these games but very soon they want to go off and trap insects or join the older boys looking after the goats or cattle, where the games are tests of physical strength, such as hopping and trying to knock over the opponent or games of endurance, such as 'scratching hands until the blood comes'. Lohorung adults encourage games of 'trapping', and 'cooking', or 'ploughing' by making toy bows and arrows, tiny wooden ploughs, foot-mills, and grinding stones. Moreover, they respect the secrecy often surrounding children's play. Some of the play is interesting as adaptions of the culture's own customs, such as ritual shrines made of grass and mud, or as adoptions of the customs of a neighbouring group, such as playing 'Sherpa burials' using a pile of stones to bury a dead insect. For Lohorung, play of children is seen as an encouragement to the development of *niwa*.

Niwa *and Social Development*

Niwa must not only remember and keep a watchful eye on duties, but also on respectful behaviour and posture. Ways of walking, sitting, or eating, for example, can be the expression of the extent to which a person is showing awareness and application of socially expected *niwa*, as opposed to *tangpam niwa* (own personal inclinations). The girl who sits on her toes or feet in a squatting position (*chom chom toke*), in which her hands are free and she is ready for action, is said to have *niwa*. The one who sits with her arms and legs crossed, on the other hand, is lilable to be teased or rebuked, 'Where has your *chakunima*[24] *niwa* gone? You sit like a lazy one. Don't you feel any sense of shame (*ngesime*)?'

The kind of behaviour that demonstrates the application of social *niwa* is less scrutinized in boys than in girls. Girls and women face innumerable injunctions and interdictions. Men must watch their *niwa* in the home of their wives' parents and brothers, women in the home of husbands' parents and elder brothers. Since residence is patrilocal and couples usually spend the first few years of married life in the man's parental home, it is inevitable that women confront more people and localities demanding the correct, established rules of respectful *niwa* than men. Women should not smoke in front of respected kinsmen, or laugh or talk too much; they should always cover their heads in their presence, and should offer the traditional hospitality to them. Newly married couples avoid talking to one another. The woman keeps, as much as possible, apart from her husband; she serves him food and eats her own afterwards; she spends as much time as possible occupied in work. If she follows such behaviour, she is considered to have *niwa*. Even if she has spent many nights singing with her husband and his friends previous to marriage, she is expected to show modesty and respect during the period between marriage and the birth of her first child. Although details of all the different kinds of respectful behaviour need not be mentioned here, I add one colloquial phrase which expresses the complexity of repectful *niwa*; `A fully grown adult has ten *niwa*: one for spouse, one for son-in-law, one for children, one for guests, one for parental home, one for work . . ..'

The number ten is not meant literally: it has a mystical significance as in the phrase 'ten Kiranti brothers' *Das Bhai Kiranti*. What is important is that those who adhere to all the various traditional codes are said to have *niwa*. A civilized person is the one who remembers the discipline laid down by the ancestors.

We can begin to see how personal life takes shape in Lohorung culture and how much the sense of self is constructed from their notion of *niwa*, which tells people how they should act, how they should feel, and how they can be happy and successful, so long as they are willing to follow the traditional way of life. *Niwa* explains to children the behaviour of adults around them, it explains to them why they have to perform duties and behave in certain prescribed ways, for if they did not they would be considered to have 'no *niwa*' which means to be an infant, or totally anti-social, or mad. Moreover, it is in terms of *niwa* that many personality judgements are made and these too encourage children to develop certain attributes and to suppress others.

Lohorung value most highly the *niwa* that is 'giving', or 'giving with love founded on esteem' – the giving with affectionate regard – almost like the Chritian caritas. The Lohorung language has no noun meaning 'love': the emotion is expressed in the terms of giving. A 'big *niwa*' is a charitable one. Someone with a 'little *niwa*' esteems only himself.[25] The stomach of 'little *niwa*' is never full: it never admits to have eaten'. When Lohorung say 'he or she has *niwa*' they often simply mean they are giving – of either sympathy or hospitality. Whatever pain, misfortune, sorrow a 'big *niwa*' has to cope with, it always gives. The *niwa* that gives with affectionate regard is expected towards parents, elders, and ancestors, a giving *niwa* to those of the same age or younger. Children are encouraged to share with siblings and friends. The giving *niwa* is not, however, by definition advantageous as Lohorung proverbs illustrate: '*niwa Chuksima* (the giving person) should be restrained, or there's nothing left for one self, or 'The one who has *niwa* has nothing at all; the one without *niwa* is prosperous'. Indiscriminate exaggerated generosity is undesirable. The law of *niwa* requires a general disposition for altruism up to the point where it can please both receiver and giver: beyond that point it would be a burden. *Niwa* acts to moderate behaviour. The controlling factor or agent of the 'giving *niwa*' is the 'frugal *niwa*' (*hamchame niwa*). This one restrains a woman, reminds her not to give in to the demands for more beer for each visitor; it encourages her to eke out the remaining household supply of rice by occasionally preparing some other grain. The skilful adult is the one who can co-ordinate all the different *niwa*, and cope with all the expectations of the community. If a girl or woman gives too much, she is called careless, or ignorant (she has no *niwa*), or has forgotten her 'frugal *niwa*'. If she gives too little she is liable to be judged as miserly. A man who gives a loan of rice interest free to a lineage member is said to have a 'big *niwa*'. About the one who refuses, it may be said, 'Well, a stone never cooks' (that is, you can't turn a hard man into a soft-hearted one); the 'little *niwa*' never sees beyond itself'.

These judgements in part function to control and direct children towards the values of the community, for the very continuity of the group depends upon the way in which the notion of *niwa* pervades its members. The phrases emphasise the morality of the collectivity. As personality judgements they should be seen in the main as public character classifications. When Lohorung comment on children's or other adults characters they are usually referring to their social *niwa*. They describe an apparent predominant quality in *niwa*, that is then taken as being their type of *niwa*, manifesting itself in their actions, behaviour and decisions. 'Big *niwa*' and 'little *niwa*' are both examples of character or personality types. People are also said to have 'soft *niwa*', meaning they tend to be compassionate and easily moved; or a 'cold *niwa*', which describes someone who does not talk and is unfriendly. Some other adjectives Lohorung use to sum up a person's *niwa* character are 'crafty', 'lazy', 'shy', 'hard- working', 'brave', 'boastful', 'jealous', 'clever', 'undecided' and 'self-important'. The number of *niwa* character types is extensive, but not unlimited. Lohorung do not conceive of a range of individual, heterogeneous personalities as varied as we do in the west, for each Lohorung identifies to some extent with the collective community he belongs to.

Lohorung children want to emulate and please adults. They also want to comply with what their elders expect them to do and to demonstrate *niwa* types that are approved. But they also have their own *niwa* and this is where the conflicts begin, particularly in the ages between twelve and eighteen or so, when they marry. When Lohorung children find that their own *niwa* leads them to receive negative personality judgements they almost always become shy and ashamed, or as the Lohorung say, *ngesmalu*. Parents say if children show too much of their own *niwa* they must be scolded (*losikma*) with words, to make them feel shame, *ngesime*, usually achieved by applying some personality judgement `What a lazy one! You sit *penchampa* 'one knee up, one down, like a man', 'You dog! Why do you go again and again to other people's homes just like a dog: well you must be a dog and not a person (*yapmi*). To stay at home is to be a person: to wander around is to be just like a dog'.

The 'scolding' *losikma* is often as much teasing as rebuking, or angry remonstrations. The first time I saw a scene of *losikma*, I interpreted the words (above) of the two parents as playfully irritating their son, likening him to a dog and making comments about his night-time ventures and homeless drifting from one house to another. I was surprised how shaken the son looked. His mother explained that he was spending most nights away from home, sleeping as many youths do in each others houses. He was never at home and he was not looking after the cattle, coming back home late in the morning expecting to be fed. Ganesh, she said, was upset (*niwa yamuk*) by the words they used and that was what they wanted – to make his *niwa* look at what he was doing. From then on he began to behave as a member of the family, who had responsibilities to fulfill. He began to listen to his *niwa*. For many days, however, as he went around without a smile, people commented, 'It's okay, he is ashamed, he has become a bit clever'. . (*kho negesimalu, nuk, kho ichhuba lisa*).

The same strategy of 'scolding' *losikme* to make someone feel ashamed *ngesime* is also applied to more serious crimes. The following is an extract from my diary describing such an event:

> Last night Bhimal's elder brother had been stealing rice from people's fields –leaving the stems and removing the heads. Tambe realized someone was tampering with his rice and waited for the person to return last night. He caught Likpa redhanded. He was led off to the main part of the village and was questioned by Tambe and Gumbe Then he was led off to Ganga Prasad's house the *Rai* and *sadasye* ('ward member') where the whole incident was recorded including the thumb print of Likpa. He was scolded (*losikme*) but given forgiveness this time so long as he did not repeat the act. If he did he would be handed over to the Khandbari police. In all he had taken about twelve pathi of paddy (about 48 lbs.).

A few days later I wrote:

> The comments during the past few days have been harsh enough to make Likpa run away, what usually happens, I am told, if someone steals. People have been saying things like, 'he has no nose'; 'instead of doing a little work, stealing is easier but self-respect, honour (they used the term *ijjat* N) disappears'; 'there are no old people in his house, no babies, his life is so easy, so why be lazy?'; 'if he were my son I would cut off his hands'; 'he is worthless (*phenni*); people have told him to watch his *niwa* and everyone avoids him'.

Adults and children over the age of twelve or thirteen are generally held responsible for their behaviour, since they all are directed by a consciousness of what the community expects – i.e. *niwa*, for Lohorung as we have seen, also talk about *niwa* in the sense of 'conscience'. Those who ignore their social *niwa* bring upon themselves the possibility of a wide number of sanctions. One of these is the pain from *niwa* itself. Breach of injunctions in those who have *niwa* brings about the pain of *niwa*. *Niwa* is said 'to hurt' when knowledge of what should be done is not done, `When *niwa* hurts it talks at night, people cannot sleep, they tell lies, and they are frightened'. *Niwa* as 'conscience' is the source of certain dreams and nightmares. The guiding line for conscience, *niwa* is the established way represented by those older than oneself. 'If an older person scolds, *niwa* aches: if someone younger tells one off, *niwa* only feels contempt.' The painful *niwa* talking internally to a person is the Lohorung way of describing conscience. Whereas those who have consciously done wrong bring upon themselves a hurting *niwa*, those who inadvertently transgress the principles of social *niwa* may cause the anger of the ancestors, bringing misfortune and disease. Worst of all, breach of the law of social *niwa*, the injunctions it includes, and the ways of behaviour prescribed may bring about the loss of *niwa* itself, that is, madness.

In every Lohorung adult and in a child over a certain age, *niwa* lies as a watchdog over his or her behaviour and activities, controlling them to conform with the traditional and normal way. The character types and personality judgements expressed in terms of a person's *niwa* restrain the antisocial and encourage the personality which can make a positive contribution to the continuity of order within the community. 'If people's *niwa* does not agree, then no work gets done, the work is ruined' goes the saying. Lohorung also pass on the dogma:

> People whose *niwa* is nice to see, they get on with everyone. That one, all people like. An ugly *niwa* person no-one gets on with, and they call him dishonest.

A 'nice-to-see' *niwa* is one which knows open, social behaviour and shows desire for collective interdependence and co-operation. Individual privacy has no place. Far from being accepted, the person who seeks privacy or solitude is considered to be suffering, afflicted by a fallen *saya* (ancestral essence), and must be brought back to health. Attempts to raise one's own status, out of line with one's age, are frowned upon. Differences in wealth are explained as much by strong links with the ancestors (high *saya*) or private rites to *chawatangma* as by individual endeavours. Status is achieved with age and the *niwa* that accompanies it, and not from personal efforts. Traditionally roles are ascribed and a person waits to be invited to perform special roles: noone offers his or her skills. Elders are invited to calm and settle a quarrel, a man becomes 'Rai' when his elder brother wants to join the army.[26] Roles are not achieved by competition. All these factors act to produce a particular kind of person – co-operative, uncompetitive, accustomed to fluid status and the consensus of the community.

The introduction of schooling has introduced to those Lohorung children attending a new way of learning, foreign to traditional *niwa* development, and this is rote-learning. To those who cannot attend it is an attractive alternative to work and more like play. There is, moreover, a growing attitude that the capacities of a person must include the ability to read and write. The inability to read and write is talked about as a mark of 'dumbness', since it has so clearly led many people into trouble, to lose land for example (see Caplan 1970). As one woman put it, 'we older ones, we can't read and write, we are no better than the cows and oxen we feed'. For many, however, the practical considerations, the need for girls' and boys' labour at home and in the fields keeps children out of school. If anyone goes, it is the boys, for it is generally stated that boys need to read and write more than girls. Their *niwa* is different.

The reality is that in Pangma most girls of school-going age[27] under fifteen had had no schooling. Girls should develop traditional *niwa* rather than literacy. When it comes to choosing a wife for their sons both men and women say they want a girl who demonstrates she has *niwa*, that is, knowledge of Lohorung customs, competence in agricultural activities, domestic skills, the experiences of running a house, some ability to weave, the ability to look after, respect and obey her in-laws and her husband, and demonstrate the knowledge of how to behave. Literacy was almost never mentioned as a positive attribute desirable in a daughter-in-law.

School offers children an insight into a world which presents a direct conflict to the duties of *niwa*. It gives children time to be with Brahmin and Chetri, Newar and Gurung children, a time when they solidify their Nepali identity as opposed to their Lohorung identity. In many ways it presents a world from which Lohorung adults are excluded.

Although ideologically literacy is not valued precisely because it undermines what traditionally constitutes a 'person' and encourages personal autonomy, the reality is that the younger generation and some of the older generation recognize its significance. A few of the youths and girls denied the opportunity to go to school (parents couldn't afford to pay for hired labour to replace them) began to congregate and learn the alphabet with some of the younger ones who went to school. They could be heard at night chanting the alphabet. Nowadays youths agreed you have to read and write: without literacy, you can be tricked , as they have been in the past over land by educated Brahmins and Chetri.[28] During fieldwork the undercurrents of dissatisfaction with traditional attitudes to education began to manifest themselves. The motivation was undoubtedly self-improvement of various kinds. Two girls revealed they wanted to learn to write secret love letters. There was much demand for this new form of communication with the opposite sex and one literate girl was in much demand reading and writing the correspondance between amorous couples.

We can see here clearly the difference between 'person' as a collective representation, as a 'cultural schema' (D'Andrade), and 'the person' as an agent in society. What is striking, however, is that the ethos of interdependence and co- operation remained even in this demonstration of group independence. Literacy, like anything else, must be shared. Not to do so would be seen as mean. In this example, although individuals acted on their own initiative to create schooling for themselves, the idiom is collective.

There is more to *niwa* than the development of individual discipline, memory, and capacities that we have seen so far. It also explains how people act as independent agents, its frame of reference including many personality judgements while at the same time, almost in contradiction, playing that key role in developing and maintaining the ideal nature of man and woman.

The key point here is that whereas the ideological notion of person reflects what is most highly valued in the society, namely ideas of honour and respect, and maintaining traditional ways, the person as social agent, is distinct. Looking at work on the person in South Asia we could, like some authors (e.g. Dumont 1970; Marriott 1976, Kakar 1978, Östör, Fruzzetti and Barnett 1982) follow the individual, egocentric/ holistic, sociocentric opposition. For Sudhir Kakar, for example (1978), individual and personal identity is regarded as of minor importance in comparison with kin and caste concerns and the person in India is bound up with a Hindu world image allowing little possibility for individuation (Kakar 1978). Similarly, according to Marriott, if one looks at persons in South Asia from a transactional and medical approach they are not like the Western 'indivisible bounded units' but 'divisible' or 'dividual' persons. 'To exist dividual persons absorb heterogeneous material influences (1976a:111); the South Asian person is 'permeable, composite, partly divisible and partly transmissible' (1976b:194).

In trying to understand the notion of the person in Nepal, I find Kakar's work useful. The significance of the network of kin, the 'relational self', the sense of personhood conceived and experienced through social relations is pre-eminent and has been observed in several comunities.[29] Illness in Nepal could not be understood unless we drop the Western notion of the indivisible unit. My own initial view of Lohorung Rai personhood, however, was that although the concept of the person is understood in a particularly social manner, emphasising the significance of kin ties and 'relatedness', we also have to recognise that notions of 'self' and 'personality' are not denied (Hardman 1981:161). Later, McHugh (1989) writing about the Gurungs took a similar view; 'while relatedness is of central importance in South Asia, this does not eliminate the concept of the individual' (ibid:77). This lead her to reject Dumont's assertions which talk of India lacking 'the conceptual reality of the individual being (1960:431); and those which claimed that whereas in the West the 'ontological unit is the human indivisible being [in] traditional India it is always a whole . . . an entirety embodying relations, a multiplicity ordered by its inner, most hierarchical, oppositions, into a single whole' (1965:99). It seems to me, however, that we don't need to reject Dumont to understand the notion of the person among the Lohorung or the Gurung. In these traditional societies the notion of the person as 'collective representation' and as valued in the 'conscience collective' is one that is embodied in the whole. This is the culturally constructed ideology of personhood. Even the 'individual body, the lived experience of the body-self'(Scheper-Hughes and Lock 1987:6) for the Lohorung,as we see in this chapter, has to a large degree to submit to the social body. I think Dumont is correct in his assessment of the difference in values between India and the West. In his view the difficulty modern society has in understanding Indian society lies in our individualistic world view and in the value that we place on the individual, on freedom and liberty (Dumont 1970:20). In contrast in India, and in Nepal, the highest *value* is on the idea of society. Modern and traditional societies 'differ in their ultimate *values*'.[30]

Returning to Lohorung values, certainly what we have seen so far is the extent to which Lohorung value the social. There is no doubt that the self that maintains society, the self that shows honour and respect to traditional ways is most highly esteemed. But more than that, the person is deeply embedded in family and wider kin, their bodies, emotions, minds, and senses part of a 'living body' (German Leib,see Ots 1994) in which exchange, charitable giving and frugality, feelings of shame and conscience are emphasized. At the level of the *habitus* (Bourdieu's sense of bodily dispositions) to be alone day or night is to be lacking in a fundamental sense.

The Lohorung self *should* be subordinated to ancestral ways as an ideological notion and the self is embodied in a similar sociality. However, this doesn't prevent Lohorung from accepting human individuation. As Leach says, 'In all viable systems there must be an area where the individual is free to make choices so as to manipulate the system to his own advantage'(Leach 1962: 133). Let me explore this a little further.

Niwa and Individual Variation

From my description so far of different characters and the extent to which social *niwa* pervades individuals, requiring them to conform, it might seem that a Lohorung child has little possibility of developing a personally derived identity. This is not the case. Lohorung recognize that everyone also has 'own *niwa*' (*tangpam niwa*) and this includes those personal inclinations and impulses which are expected to be brought under the control of *niwa* as it develops ('I have a sleeping *niwa* but I must not sleep, I still have to pound the rice.') The control, however, mainly applies to the formal, public sphere and that is naturally the focal area of talk about *niwa* as a socializing force. Control or discipline to be learned has to be emphasized. But Lohorung take it for granted that social *niwa* will not predominate all the time. A girl, for example, within the private sphere of her own home, or with other women, would not be expected to adhere to all the restraints, the interdictions expected from her social *niwa*. She must 'know' them, but she also knows when she can live according to her 'own' *niwa*. People in informal situations can sit in any manner they please, in whatever manner their individual *niwa* chooses. When girls and women are sitting together and see or hear the approach of some respected male kin, there is a commotion to find scarves, rearrange dress, hide cigarettes and the butts, and find some means of showing that they are busy. Children do something similar when they hear parents coming. Everyone knows about the discrepancies in behaviour of social *niwa* and 'own *niwa*'. Wives and husbands who have lived long together, forget many of the injunctions imposed by social *niwa* and individual personalities are not brought under control. Intimate and friend relationships are relaxed. Perhaps one could say that they can in some ways be even more relaxed than in the west. Knowing the strict rules of prescribed behaviour means first that behaviour in public situations does not have to be a matter of individual concern, and secondly that if one generally conforms to social *niwa*, one's own individual *niwa*, personal desires, and ways of behaviour are not seen as a threat to the community. An example of this is the case of two sisters who annually plough their fields themselves, since there are no men in the household. In terms of traditional ways these women are going against their social *niwa* and they are often teased; but the practical situation is accepted and they are not judged or rebuked for submitting to this idiosyncratic behaviour.

Lohorung recognition of individual *niwa* emerges in such phrases as 'I feel like letting my own *niwa* do what it wants (take its own course). If you could do what your *niwa* wanted now, what would you do?' or when a mother in reply to her daughter's inquiry about what job to do next says 'It's too hot for work. Whatever happens to please your *niwa* do that. I'm going to sleep'. I have heard children in reply to their parents' request to work in the fields and stop playing use phrases like, 'Our own *niwa* (*tangpam niwa*) is never allowed, elder brother is doing nothing, tell him to go!' Individual *niwa* is allowed free expression in the sense of 'opinions' and certain feelings. Social *niwa* is more concerned with action and behaviour. There is no objection to men or women stating their opinions even if they contradict social expectation. For example, a woman may object to a prospective son-in-law: 'The boy has land, he shows respect, but my own *niwa* will not accept him. My *niwa* will not eat it (trust him). I don't feel like giving my child.' Since personal opinions are not restrained, individual *niwa* at times comes into contact with social *niwa*, 'I didn't feel like being guilty in my own *niwa*, but later (social) *niwa* would not accept it, and after a while my *niwa* began talking (conscience). All night long I couldn't sleep'.

Although 'own *niwa*', meaning own desires and wishes, is generally not allowed in public behaviour, it should be said there is an increasing modern expression of own initiative of a kind that is not frowned upon. Examples of this initiative are to be seen in the local market in Khandbari. One couple, for example, own little land but every week they reach market early and buy eggs, chickens, ghee, vegetables, etc. These they sell along with the baskets, mats, winnowing trays woven by him and the paper cigarettes and beer made by her. They are described as having 'clever *niwa*' and respected for their efforts.

Selling beer and liquor is increasingly an area in which women are demonstrating initiative, their sense of agency and their 'own *niwa*'.[31] The profits are used to accumulate money for their store of private property (*pewa* N) as well as adding weight to women's opinions and decision-making power within the household.[32] Some women take full advantage of the role of selling alcohol, which is highly valued,[33] and use it to increase their power and voice their opinions in village affairs and even in wider local issues. They acquire a clientele, who visit regularly on market days and sit around them drinking and talking. Some of these women are 'clever', say the Lohorung; they develop a reputation for producing the best liquor, so that their patrons always return. Others, who sometimes water down their *saruwa* (wine-like drink made particularly by the Lohorung) 'show to everyone their small *niwa*'. Some women accumulate such a reputation for good beer and *saruwa* that people seek them out in the village when travelling through, or those in the village, finding themselves short, look to them for a loan. By simply extending the scope of a traditional commodity such women show enterprise that is not a threat to the community.

The fact that there are so many Lohorung terms for people who show individual, and often socially unacceptable, personalities or characters illustrates how Lohorung, in spite of the controlling force of social *niwa*, are not subjugated totally to conforming stereotypes. To mention a few of them: Lohrung talk of the irritator, the one with the fishing-hook heart, who fishes for play or disturbance, (*khechimawa*), the gossip (*bokmawa*), the flirt or coxcomb, and in particular the narcissistic person in terms of dress (*chorekpa* or *chorekma*), the trouble-maker (*mangkhekla*), the volatile, easily roused to anger one (*somkhewa*), a nonsense- talker (*somtrekpa*), the energetic character (*pannukha*), the jealous character, (*lamthing lamukhuba*), the pliable, easy going one, (*okningbak*), as well as all those mentioned previously as adjectives describing people's *niwa*-character.

Lohorung accept that own *niwa* (*tangpam niwa*) can have considerable freedom of expression in private spheres, so long as it does not go too far. The principles of social public *niwa* must always be kept in mind. Children must learn how to control 'own *niwa*', their own impulses, desires, so that under the controlling capacity of social *niwa*, individual, own *niwa*, may be given recognition.

Marriage and Tangpam niwa

Marriage is one of the main areas in which both Lohorung men and women express *tangpam niwa* and talk about themselves as active agents. The issue of marriage leads household heads to use strategies and the subordinates to use tactics each one to maximie his or her *tangpam niwa* (own wishes).

An arranged marriage is the form of marriage most parents would like their children to accept, and about two thirds of Lohorung marriages are arranged and take place with full-scale ritual and ceremonial exchanges.[34] These are either first- time marriages or men's second marriages. The second marriages of men are mostly of widowers, who want to offer the most formal kind of marriage to their new wives, in spite of the cost. First-time marriages are carefully planned by parents. Negotiations take place late in the evening or very early in the morning: no one else should know about them, in case an agreement cannot be reached. Too many rejections, known by everyone, would 'throw away the nose' and threaten the *saya* of the boy's parents.

But rejections are also bad for the girl and her parents, who can gather a reputation for being self-interested, not really wanting to marry off their daughter. The secrecy of the negotiations firmly places the decision in the hands of the parents, lessening the possible control of 'public images'. This is significant for the Lohorung notion of the person in three ways. First, it is the public face of the house/family that is here the 'person', as if it were acting for the boy or girl, and decreasing emphasis on the individual. Second, the secrecy emphasizes the importance of the parents' choice, that is, their responsibility and agency without any interference from outside elders or the children involved. The relatives of the boy try to convince the girl's parents of his worth, and it is the girl's mother and father alone who decide if the boy is right for her, thus placing the emphasis on the parents not the girl. Third, the lack of self-reflection or personal motivation concerning many of such marriage is reflected in the number of people who have been through them without their own consent; this does not mean that they were carried out by force, merely that consent was not considered a necessary prerequisite. In the same sample research about half said they had been married without their specific consent.

In matters of marriage it is thought that the 'will', 'wishes and desires' (*tangpam niwa*) of sons and daughters may not at first agree with the 'wisdom' (*niwa*) of their elders, but eventually it is said they will understand the choice, and a great deal of persuasion may be needed to get through the most difficult initial stages of 'marriage' which is more of a process than an event. In fact, when boys express a preference for or particular dislike of the chosen partner parents tend to listen, whereas girls are thought to be generally more unwilling to marry and therefore need more guidance. The case of Heluwa *sahili* is typical.

> Sahili's elder sister refused to marry the husband from Heluwa chosen for her by her parents. She ran away with a Dekhim man to avoid the marriage. All sahili's uncles and aunts and parents, then we all said to her, 'look now you must marry him. We have promised your sister but she has gone, you should go. See, there he is with so much paddy, maize, fields, buffaloes, cows and no one there to look after him. His two elder sisters have married and left, he has no brothers only one old, old mother. He can make you happy, whereas with others you do not know; you will be miserable trying hard to scrape a living'. She cried and refused for many days. But in the end we persuaded her to go. And now she is happy. She has a beautiful son, she has stayed ten years and she is happy. We were right.

The opportunity for self-expression begins when youths and girls are in their teens. They join up with others, sometimes just a few others, some maybe already in their early twenties, or some recently married though at the stage when husband and wife do not live permanently with each other. They meet regularly in small or large groups at night, and sometimes join together from several neighbouring villages, thus establishing a perfect opportunity to get to know possible potential marriage partners. They enjoy the freedom of boisterous games, flirtations, singing, laughter, and gaiety, without any of the normal constraints imposed by those to whom they must show respect. They gather in the fields or hills, in an empty hut or cattle-shed. They make up their own rules, those who arrive last have to sing first. They can be seen grouping together at the larger annual fairs held on the hilltops or river valleys. In larger gatherings the amusement and high spirits are encouraged by liquor, sold or given away to those the girls happen to favour. Frequently the time is spent singing songs which involve exchanges between groups of girls and groups of boys, girls on one side boys on the other. The contents of the songs are superficially innocuous but to the initiated are full of amorous innuendos. They add what they like to the basic song. The following is a close translation of one of the songs always sung in Nepali:

The girls begin:

> The wall of the mountain is knocked down when the yaks had a fight;
> the day has gone, the night has gone, explaining the sinning mind.
> The wind and again the wind, the Sunday market takes place at Dolaha,
> the Saturday market at Silani. The cotton of the cotton tree, we two poor people
> say today we will lament.

The youths reply:

> From over there what sort of bird came down and stayed filling
> the tree? The hard walnut, this is our trouble and will remain forever.
> The creeper of the river crossed the ford, we must go, having weighed the
> tola [measure] of gold, father will probably be angry, oh sister oh but . . .

The markets held weekly in several different places in the locality offer good meeting grounds, as indeed is mentioned in the song. Kanchhi told me this is how she met A. She told me how they met first at market. 'He offered me a cigarette but I refused, "*dungani*" ("I don't smoke"). Then later friends told me he wanted to meet me again. I couldn't remember who he was. And they told me he was the one who offered me a cigarette. We met again the next week at the next market. He came up and offered me biscuits and eggs, so many things. We sat side by side on one of the benches by the side of the market but I was too shy to say or do anything. He bought me tea. I had to throw it away when he wasn't looking; my heart was going *tuk tuk* I couldn't drink anything. He wanted to meet again.' At first she refused but was later persuaded by friends who were a little older; she was only fourteen at the time. She agreed to meet in one of the cattle huts in the field's below and between their two villages. At first they were never alone. He sat in one corner of the hut, sometimes with a friend and she and her companions sat in the other corner. 'He sang me songs, telling me how much he liked me and calling me *iksama kānchi*. I sang back that I didn't know what to say until I became a bit more clever at replying. And when he asked to see me in seven days, I sang back "no, in fourteen". I gave in though and agreed to seven. We met again and again in different places. It must always be in different places to sing together.' It was only later that they stopped going with the one or two companions who had kept on going with them. They went to sing to each other in the forest. Then there was more talking than singing, planning on how they could stay together. His elder brother had not yet married and A. should wait for him to marry first.

In this particular case, the kin of both the girl and the boy used strategies to prevent any continuation of their relationship; heavy pressure was put on kanchi and A. to conform to their parents' wishes. Without A. or *kānchi*'s knowledge, throughout the twelve months that she and A. had been seeing each other, messengers from A's family had been trying to persuade her mother to marry her to A's elder brother. *Kānchi*'s father was sick at the time and her mother kept refusing. The brideprice was high, however, and the groom's spokesmen reassured the mother that *kānchi*-would not be expected to leave her natal home until she was ready. Her mother finally agreed. When A. and *kānchi* found out, kanchhi pleaded with her mother to stop the agreement. A. tried to persuade her to go with him. As she told me the story she confided that if only she had been older she would have known how to push for what she wanted: she would have gone with A. – either eloped or agreed to a 'capture' marriage, if A. could arrange it. As it was, she gave in to her mother with all the offers of new clothes and gold. She was formally married to the elder brother, with whom she still lives.

This case shows the strength needed to fight against the desires of parents and kin and social pressures to conform. In general, the Lohorung rule is that if a girl is told by her parents to marry a particular man, then she must obey, even if her own mind *tangpam niwa* is against it; yet some do follow their own wishes and survive the condemnations which ensue. Minnu, for example, was nineteen when her parents began to receive two lots of suitors asking for her. Her case ended somewhat differently from *Kānchi*'s above:

All those involved in the secret negotiations, except her mother, said Minnu's father and mother should give her to the *Biksik* clan family from Dhupu village. Although it was not as close as some villages, there were relatives there; if she didn't marry soon she'd go with the *Lumben* man she sung with, and he was already married and had children, *phenni* ('no good') – if she went with him she couldn't come near the village; if she went to Dhupu, that other family in Dhupu might give their daughter to Dache who had to marry soon; they wouldn't give her to many of the other villages, which are harder, further away, and anyway, maybe nobody else would come to ask for her and she would end up like Rekhu – she refused so many they stopped coming. But Minnu's mother was uncertain and worried. She was not just saying 'no' because parents always say no at first. She said Minnu should follow the old Lohorung custom and marry the one chosen by her parents, yet they should make the right choice. When young she had heard talk about a *mangpa* (shaman) in

Dhupu whose wife was a *bokshi* (witch); could they assure her that this was not the boy's parents; moreover, they had looked at the horoscope and it had said that Minnu shouldn't be married before she was twenty. Also, he was Kartik month and that doesn't mix with Minnu's sign – their *ghan* (N) do not mix; they had no surplus rice or millet this year . . .. The secret talks continued. Minnu knew what was going on although the talks took place either late into the night or before dawn. She had stopped eating and working properly. She was very unhappy and deeply loved her Lumben man, whom she has known for over a year. She knew that he has no land and many brothers, and that it would be hard for her, especially since he already has a wife. She knew she would be unhappy if they married her to Dhupu – it was so far. Two weeks later Minnu ran off at night with her Lumben. She went to his house and refused to return home. Her mother tried to persuade her father to fetch her back but he refused. 'She has gone of her own will (*tangpam niwa*). She must stay. She is not my daughter.' Her mother was distressed: 'How will she eat? She cannot eat millet mush but what else can they afford? What kind of life will she have working in others' fields just to get enough to eat?' Other adults in the village were far from sympathetic. They said she had 'thrown away her father's nose' (*apam nabuk we-lan-pitu*), that she was worthless, good for nothing (*phenni*); many were angry and insulted her to her face. One said 'Minnu's eyes are damaged: her eyes can't see anymore' (i.e. she is blind to the situations she has let herself in for). Another commented 'she has gone to lie on top of the first one, taken properly: there will be trouble'. People said 'she has become a leaf', the way of saying that she has fallen to the worst possible condition – one in which she will have to eat off leaf plates and eat what others leave. Brothers, aunts, uncles, younger siblings are all angry. The *saya* of her father inevitably falls in such situations, putting at risk his well-being and the prosperity of the household. Relatives know they should shun her. Many are sorry for the older wife. One day this earlier wife lost her temper with Minnu, but for this she was 'thoroughly beaten' by her husband. Minnu, however, was not totally alone. There were those who talked about others who had done the same, who had followed their own mind, *tangpam niwa*, and were still happy, and those that criticized her family for making too much fuss. A few months later Minnu and her husband formally 'changed relationships' (*saino phernu* N) with the relatives of both sides.[35] This means that they formally altered the kinship terminology used between both sides; this also gives acceptance to the union as marriage and meant Minnu could return to her natal home. From then on the couple began to spend considerable time assisting with the work to be done in Minnu's natal home. Minnu would go there about four times a week to work and brew her beer there; her husband about once or twice a week.

About a quarter of marriages in Pangma are marriages by elopement or 'theft', that is, with the partner of their choice, without their parent's consent[36] The form of marriage, known as *kusubang*, 'theft' marriage, is striking in that it is a legitimate transgression of the normal rules and a powerful tactic, in which sons can try to obtain the wife of their own choice. In brief, it goes against the usual Lohorung rules concerning correct behaviour towards the bride's parents, and yet, it is traditional and totally accepted. With this form of 'own choice' the couple do not have to leave the village in disgrace for a short time, as they often do in elopement. Normally, it is the bride's parents who are the first to know about a suitor for their daughter and the ones who make the decision. In the case of 'theft' they are completely powerless and find out only when their daughter has agreed. It allows total disregard of the expected respect of a son for his father and mother, and permits a strongly selfish orientation of the groom. It requires the groom to 'know his own mind', to follow *tangpam niwa*, and to ignore parental authority, to demonstrate considerable planning capabilities and the organization and co-operation of certain kinsmen. It can only work if the groom achieves emancipation from expected behaviour, and arouses the enthusiasm of his peer group, and sometimes members of the older generation to assist him in his plans. This remains the case even if the girl who is captured is in fact also involved in the plot and is a willing collaborator.

My neighbour gave me this brief description of a 'theft'. 'It happened like this. People from Pawa and Pangma were coming to R's wedding in Dhupu and they intrigued. *Māhila* had seen a girl from Pawa and knowing that she would be going to the wedding he got ready. "You should take her", said the other youths. So off everyone went to the wedding. But those who knew about the "theft" disappeared. They went the lower path which comes out near Maruwa. Many youths were involved and that was where they captured the girl from Pawa. Here and there the youths emerged. She began to fight, and first with Nargate's father because *Māhila* had been held up and hadn't arrived yet. He was late. But Nargate's father had agreed to help and he knew what was fitting, and in addition he was becoming an old man. He had no male children and was well known by everyone in Pawa and in Pangma, and Dhupu was the home of his father-in-law, so stopping to talk to him, the girl thought nothing of it, but Nargate's father realizing the groom *Māhila* was late saw what had to be done. He caught hold of her hand first. Usually it is only after the groom has caught hold of the girl's hand that the other youths can catch hold of her. But all the accompanying boys had arrived, some down below, some on the path like this when the groom was still late. So when Nargate's father caught hold of her and the groom wasn't there, she began to shout, "I'm not going to live with you, you donkey. I'm not going to stay with some knowing old man, some insect-ridden yak's tail, I will not live with such a one. I will not. I will not live next to a first wife with so many children. I will not", and she fought and fought. And then suddenly a boy wearing a black topi (traditional hat) arrived. He was about nineteen or twenty and everyone looked at him. She stopped and asked, "which is the groom?" "The one wearing the black topi, that one who has just appeared", they answered. Then she agreed to go along. The youths caught hold of her and accompanied her along the path. I was there on the ladder to the house. But at the ladder she stopped and refused to come up any further. She fought and the youths holding her shouted to her, "go up, go up!" But she firmly refused. She refused to climb the ladder that would be the ladder to her own house – the ladder of the groom's house. So then all the youths surrounded the bottom of the ladder. "How much money do you want?" they asked. "Whatever you want we will give". And she insisted on the pledge [the mutual promise made by the groom and bride]. They agreed and they were able to tie some money into her shawl and then she immediately went up the ladder to the house. That's what we do in "theft"; whatever she wants as pledge, we must give. Whatever makes her happy we must give. Some of those over the Arun river, that side they cheat: they don't give what they promise. We must give what she asks. If she wants gold, we give gold, if she wants silver, we give silver, if she wants money we give the amount she wants and that makes them stay. If she doesn't want to stay even when we agree to give everything then we tell her that the *yatangpa* knows a spell (*mantra*). We tell her that he will throw red powder over her, will say the spell and she will immediately have love (*maya* N) for the boy. *Really*, it works. They will like (*nenchame*) only that boy and nobody else. We tell her, "you will lose all wish to go to your natal home, you will feel nothing for your own family, only for the one here. You will forget your natal home, your mother and father, you will like only this boy and you will only want to stay with him, to look after him". After this when a girl is captured her family, mostly her brothers come to see if she is happy. If she is, then the brothers tell the groom how much meat her family require as the first gift. They exchange kinship terms in the yard of the groom'.

We can see clearly here how the boy is given advantage over and above everybody else. Most significantly he chooses the girl and has to persuade her to stay, so that her father and brothers have no option but to accept the accomplished deed. The girl has the right to refuse, though everything in a theft marriage works against it. This is summed up by the belief expressed above that she can be charmed to fall in love with her suitor. It could be said that the institution of 'theft' marriage is the society's way of dealing with potential father/son conflict. It offers a rebellious son with a mind of his own, *tangpam niwa*, the chance to make an important decision and to make a public statement concerning his independence.[37] 'Theft marriage' also demonstrates an institutional acceptance of *tangpam niwa*, or as we might put it, an affirmation of an 'inner self' in their notion of the 'person' and the need (in boys at least) to express it.

Before looking at death and *niwa*, it might be helpful to sum up what has been gathered about *niwa* so far. It shows that the Lohorung view about child development is closely related to their understanding of *niwa* and how it works. From talk about *niwa*, children learn that they have to follow traditional ways, that they must respect their parents, and brothers and sisters, and indeed all senior kin. They begin to learn that what is important about themselves is not what they want but what their *niwa* tells them to do. What is important is not personal authenticity or their unique identity, but the ability to follow formally prescribed behaviour. In public the norms of this behaviour are quite rigid. Their emotions too have to be controlled by *niwa*. By the age of ten or so they should have enough *niwa* in the stomach to restrain their anger. By then too, children have been taught to listen to their *niwa* as a controlling force in respect of two different kinds of fear; first the fear that startles and causes their *lawa* to leave, and secondly the fear that is connected with feelings of awe and respect. With the development of *niwa* they learn to understand situations or events which previously would have startled them. They learn to be less frightened of strangers and to transform the sense of helpless impotence in the face of adults into feelings of respect and shyness. Both feelings warn a child internally, but the knowledge which reduces or transforms them is derived externally, taught by adults in the form of words and threats about *niwa*.

Thus, *niwa* acts as self-control in physical, mental, and emotional terms. *Niwa* in some ways might well be called the Superego.[38] What we have seen here is how Lohorung children are expected to internalize the formal norms, the value standards, with few offers of explanations. Skills and knowledge they learn and pick up largely through imitation, combined with the inculcated desire to emulate adults and be treated like an adult.

Niwa is frequently conceptualized in terms that might be construed as an indication of conceptual realism.[39] When Lohorung talk about *niwa* as being, for example, 'at first small and closed' they are, however, talking metaphorically in the same way that in English we might talk about people being big-hearted and small-minded. If we compare the Lohorung conception of mind with our own, there are several ways in which they differ. The main difference lies in their use of one *niwa* concept where we would use several different concepts, such as conscience, personality, impulse, memory. The Lohorung system is less differentiated than ours. Second and contiguous with this lack of differentiation are *niwa*'s encompassing powers of reference, greater than our notion of mind, such as the close relation of *niwa* to feelings and to metaphysical aspects of the body. Lacking our Western mind–body dichotomy, *niwa* is both affected by and can affect *lawa* and *saya*. When *niwa* hurts, *saya* falls; if *niwa* is not strong and big, *lawa* leaves. Third, mind is treated anthropomorphically – that is, *niwa* is treated as a person, who accepts, speaks, is pleased, agrees, is there, is crafty. In the West we have adopted a more mechanical metaphor.

Death, Niwa, *Lawa and* Saya

It is fitting that a section on death should end a chapter on concepts of *niwa*, *saya*, and *lawa* and the cycle of life, for 'life' ends for the Lohorung at death: the 'person' (*yapmi*) is no longer 'flourishing, alive' (*hinkrikpa*) but 'dead' (*sinkrikpa*) with its *bungpi lawa* no longer sitting on a flourishing flower. At death the person becomes a spirit of the dead (*chap*) eating only wind and breath *sokma*.

When I asked about the old I was told 'they are like gods' (*deutā* N), expecting the kind of respect that *sammang* ancestors receive and allowed to live their lives according to whim. They are allowed to be selfish, and though their bodies are weak, their *saya* and *lawa* are resilient. Their *niwa*, by the time they reach about seventy, has begun to fade: '*Niwa* becomes smaller. Old people begin one conversation, and the next moment they forget what they were talking about: they put belongings in one place, and search for them later in another. *Niwa* begins to die.' At some point the old say, 'I'm old: now I need new clothes.' This is also said to be a warning of their imminent death. All the spirits of the dead are conceived as wearing the clothes that they die in.

The following description of the rites surrounding death are from informants and not first-hand. I did not see any funerary rites in their entirety and I found it difficult to obtain detailed information about them. This in itself is significant. People avoided conversations about death, saying if you talk about it someone will die – benevolent and malevolent spirits can hear and are attracted to talk about themselves. After death the *lawa* of the dead person remains attached to the children of the house and the rest of the family, and tries to entice away their *lawa*.

Prior to death the person's *lawa* is understood as wanting to join the dead and leaves the living body as frequently as it can, mostly in dreams in which the person about to die begins to see the dead more than the living. They see and meet their deceased relatives and in particular their dead father just as if they were awake (*lemmang-pi*) not as if dreaming (*semmang-pi*). Eventually, the *lawa* stays away so long that not even a skilful *yatangpa* officiant can return it to the body. The *lawa* is said then to go first to the person's left hand and then to the household shrine. The breath (*sokma*) stops and the person dies.

As soon as someone has died, the corpse, dressed in new or clean clothes, is placed in front of the main door with legs pointing towards the inside of the house.[40] The body is taken to the grave as soon as possible. The hair and nails of the person are cut and later put into the grave with the body. The bier made from green bamboo (*yongbaphu*) is much like a stretcher, with two long poles and small horizontal poles. The corpse is wrapped in a white cloth, leaving the face uncovered. Once placed on the bier, white cloth screens are placed over upright bamboo sticks stuck into the two long poles on either side of the body. To understand the white cloth we need to refer back to the story (in Chapter Four) of how the dead ended any possibility of further marriage with the living by erecting a white cloth to act as a screen between the two worlds of the dead and the living. To emphasize this separation a stone and a white flag are hung by the grave and for the same reason the body is wrapped in white cloth.[41]

Flowers are placed all over the sides of the bier and one particular kind of flower is placed between the toes and in the ears of the dead person – a flower called *michiremma bung*. This flower is known to cry when a person dies. The explanation was that the flesh and body of the flower is seen as the same as that of the person, both born together.[42] On the outside of the bier are placed thorns as well as flowers to keep away the *lawa* and any *chap* who might be near. The *niwa* of any *chap* is said to see the thorns and the *michiremma bung* and 'knows' from these symbols that someone has died and that it should keep away.

Daughters unbraid their hair and it was said they usually cry. The procession to take the body is led by the eldest son carrying the white flag and a sword tarawar. Another son, or close male relative, follows behind with a leaf-bowl containing small coins, vermilion, and one *mana* of husked rice, the dead man's 'ration', *chasak*, for his journey to the land of the dead. Occasionally the procession stops to offer these to the deceased, attaching them to the forehead. Each time the procession stops people come from their houses and offer money to add to the face of the corpse. 'Classificatory' daughters and sisters are the ones supposed to offer the money, also for the dead person's journey. Some women accompany the procession including any daughters, but only those who are not fearful (*ekisikhubachi*) may go. Two men at a time, changing with others as they become tired, carry the corpse feet first. No officiant accompanies the group and the funeral party is quiet except for the sound of instructions. They go to the graveyard, usually on a small hill on the outskirts of the villages.

At the burial ground a grave is dug, and a fire made out of dried bushes. The deceased is fed with alcohol *raksi* (N) and beer (fermented millet) in a bamboo vessel *tongba*. The beer is dripped into the mouth with a bamboo pipe. Sons and grandsons walk around the grave three times, in a counterclockwise direction, preceded by the white flag, the sword, and a plate of food. The corpse is untied and any ornaments removed. It is guarded carefully for if touched by any animal, the person becomes the kind of spirit (*chap*) that is excluded from the fully integrated dead. The bamboo bier is dismantled. The corpse is lowered into the grave and buried face upwards.

The son carries an unlit twig torch three times around. He touches the four corners two at each end and then lights the torch and puts it in the corpse's mouth and then throws away the torch. This is the 'last fire' known as *dhagwati* in Nepali. One son gives the body fire, the rest give earth. People around the grave and those sitting some distance away offer soil with their left hand. Soil is placed on the dead person's mouth.The cloth which wrapped the corpse is used to cover the face in the grave. The corpse is covered with stones, soil and then more stones. Finally a stone is erected by the heap of smaller stones.

Below the burial site, the sons, sons-in-law, and sister's sons are shaved; they wash and put on new white turbans and loin cloths, which is all they wear. Subsequent to this no one touches them, and they touch no one until after the rite on the third day. As they return toward the village they are met by women bearing beer and snacks, contributed by as many houses as possible in the village. After the snack they walk nearer to the village where a fire is burning and everybody who has been to the funeral throws onto it a green branch of thorns and steps over the smoking fire, expressing the crossing of the boundary, the departure from one state to another. From the state in which they have related to the dead person, in which all actions are in reverse (the corpse is placed in the opposite direction to how people sleep; the left hand and not the right is used to throw soil; they walk counterclockwise round the grave,) they cross the boundary back into normal village life. By throwing thorny bushes into the fire, they keep away any *chap* that might want to follow.

During this first part of the rite, the corpse is put into a new ritual position and given a new identity, thereby separating the person from the living. Lohorung say the *niwa* of the *chap* knows it is dead when it sees the *michiremma* flowers in its toes, the thorns, the particular kind of bamboo used only for the dead, the white cloth surrounding it, and from the fact that when they drink their *tongba* beer from a container they see in the water the reflection of their faces covered with money and vermilion. Because of this, guests are respectfully offered beer in bamboo containers covered by a leaf to ensure that they cannot see their reflection and to make it different from the offering at the grave. If someone uses the left hand to pour, he or she risks being teased for treating relatives as if they were dead and being accused of disrespectful and potentially dangerous behaviour.

So far we have seen that when the person is dead, the *lawa* goes to the shrine and *saya* becomes the spirit of the dead ancestor; it becomes either a wandering *chap* or a *chap* that is one of the *pappamama'chi*, depending on the way the person dies. *Saya*, the link with the ancestors, is liberated to become itself an ancestor. With the *saya* goes the *niwa*, thus explaining why ancestors still have *niwa*, though more like the *niwa* of a child. If a child dies before the age of eight, or rather before the loss of his or her first teeth, Lohorung say the *saya* has not developed enough: 'the *saya* which is like a *deutā* seeks another person'. Thus if a child dies young, it will not become *chap*. The loss of the first 'milk' teeth is for the Lohorung the indication that the child has a developed *saya*. Only then is the child a 'real' *pukka* adult man or woman.

No member of the clan of the dead person may eat spices, *ghiu* (clarified butter), chutney, millet, chilli, or salt for three days after the death and then a small rite is performed at night, sometime after midnight, to finally send away the *chap* that has been allowed to wander for three days. This ensures that the *lawa* has been separated from those it loves:

> we give the chap to eat and drink but there should be no fire or they won't speak. We must be very still and musn't say a word or be afraid or we ourselves will die. They would notice us and take us as well, especially if they see you're frightened. The chap of the one who

> just died goes to collect the others. Then we feed them in every direction, up, down, sun setting, sun rising. These chap never put people in trouble; they are fed without having to, not like the *sammang* who give trouble and then get food.

In this small rite, after the 'liminal period' (see Van Gennep 1960 and V. Turner 1967) of three days, the family place in the four corners of the house bananas (from which they later divine the form of death) and beer in plates, put onto *miksremma* leaves. When the dead person's *niwa* sees the banana and the *miksremma* leaves he is supposed to be reminded yet again that he is dead and now *chap*. After midnight the *lawa* and *saya* are warned again to separate from their family and possessions. Waving a thorny *chiching* branch over the body, the elders speak together:

> From now on, you *bubu/nana* [whatever the relation is] you must go to the heavens, go to the side [area between hip and ribs] of a very very rich man, keep away from here, do not mimic the mice, do not take the frustrating path, keep peace with the others, stay with the others, make your talk and actions agree [with theirs], make your legs agree, make your hands agree; give up your attachment to your cattle, your fields, your garden, all the utensils, pots and pans, your relatives, stop loving them all; do not interfere with the *lawa* of our children, stop loving them, do not interfere with their lives; now go from now on, go to the side of the 'ancestors', now go.

This is spoken twice, once in the house and once at the graveside, with the waving of a thorny branch. The thorny branch is said to 'catch hold and not let go' (*khek-bungkhe*) of the *lawa* to make it listen, and also makes the body of the deceased look less attractive to it so that it 'lets go of its love' (*chenchamimpa chumimpe*). In this way a chap becomes integrated into the world of the *pappamamma'chi*.

Van Gennep's classic work on rites of passage suggested that a funeral involves a transition that begins with the separation of the deceased from life and ends with incorporation of the dead person into the world of the dead (1960: 28). Van Gennep also noted that funerals, of all *rites de passage*, express the core values sacred to the society.

What we see emphasized here in the funerary rites are Lohorung values and ideas developing from their relationship of trust with the superhuman world. We see the care taken to feed the dead, in return for the new *chap* adhering to their altered status. We see too the compassionate way in which the spirit is requested to separate itself from the living, addressed with paternal firmness but gently, so as not to hurt their *niwa*. It is striking the extent to which relations with the dead resemble those with the living, as if the Lohorung at times extend their social world to include the dead. The dividing cloth between the two worlds is so fine we can appreciate the interdiction against showing fear in such rites lest someone's *saya* is not strong enough to prevent his or her *lawa* being swept into the other world. It makes sense that the main aims of the rite are to educate *niwa* about its new host, to ensure that the ancestor within (*saya*) becomes *chap*, and that the life-principle *lawa* separates from the body.

Between Person and Actor

Given the significance of kin, sociability, and control of the self through *niwa*, it is all too easy to emphasize the social as opposed to the more egocentric orientation of the Lohorung concept of the person. The social whole is ontologically clearly more important than any individual actor. However, although a Lohorung individual is expected to conform to traditional ways of behaviour, give in to the *niwa* of the household head, and accept that social *niwa* should prevail over *tangpam niwa*, that individual can still develop and express a personality of his or her own and make individual choices.[43] Although fighting against society, a woman can marry the man she wants, and she can leave the husband she dislikes. A man can accumulate money to buy land and live away from the village. A Lohorung can stand apart from a social role in order to laugh or comment about how others are performing their social role, whether the role is that of marriage intermediary, shaman, or 'father'. Individuals are not merely figures in a social pattern in the way they are in some societies. Read's pioneering work (1959) suggested that for the Gahuku Gama there is 'no essential separation of the individual from the social pattern' (1959: 276). In contrast Lohorung, see individual characteristics and a tendency for egocentrism and the expression of *tangpam niwa* as being innate as well as essentially asocial: sociability and the control of self have to be learned. Inevitably, then, the proliferation of Lohorung ideas concerning the nature of men and women and what has to be developed focuses on why a person should be social and how he or she can be social. This is the only way for their society to survive.

Lohorung personal identity is thus in part learned through these ideas about personhood and through cultural institutions. Just as I've suggested that *saya* can be seen as an institution, so can the concept of *niwa*, acting as a symbolic code, a model of behaviour and a pattern for tradition. I suggest that key institutions in Lohorung lives are to be found in the concepts of *saya*, *niwa*, *tangpam niwa*, and *lawa*. Lohorung individuals work with what appear to outsiders as tensions between autonomy and interdependence, independence and sociality. Looking more closely, however, we have seen how in fact apparently contradictory Lohorung values work together.

The approach of interpreting a culture through its own self-conceptions, as we have done here, owes much to people like Hallowell, Geertz, Rosaldo, Harris, and Lutz, who have shown how effective it can be. Geertz (1973) showed how the Balinese notion of the person, which accentuates anonymity or depersonalization, is linked to their symbolic structures for characterizing time and for organising social conduct.

> As the various symbolic orders of person-definition conceal the biological, psychological, and historical foundation of that changing pattern of gifts and inclinations we call personality behind a dense screen of ready-made identities, iconic selves, so the calendar, blunts the sense of dissolving days and evaporating years that those foundations and that pattern

> inevitably suggest by pulverizing the flow of time into disconnected, dimensionless, motionless particles . . . [so too to] maintain the (relative) anonymization of individuals with whom one is in daily contact, to dampen the intimacy implicit in face-to-face relationships . . . it is necessary to formalize relations with them to a fairly high degree, to confront them in a sociological middle distance where they are close enough to be identified but not so close as to be grasped (1973: 399).

Indigenous concepts of the person, as Geertz views them, are part of the cultural system and as such are analytically distinct from social structure and individual psychology. As part of the cultural system they contribute to the fabric of meanings in terms of which human beings interpret their experience and guide their actions, while social structure is the form those actions take. 'Culture patterns provide a template or blueprint for the organization of social and psychological processes, much as genetic systems provide such a template for the organization of organic processes' (1973:216). Geertz showed how indigenous notions about self may be used to explore and analyse cultural patterns, symbolic structures, that is, the cultural system. As other anthropologists (for example Michelle Rosaldo,[44] or Catherine Lutz) have shown, they may also be used to make sense of two other distinct domains, that of social institutions, marriage, ritual, socialization, social life, age-sets; and the domain of individual motivation and experience. Lohorung indigenous notions and theories are helping us to understand phenomena in all three domains.

Notes

1. Interest in the person as a cultural category of course precedes the 1980s, e.g. Mauss's classic essay 'A Category of the Human Mind, the Notion of Person, the Notion of Self' (1938). Hallowell's work on the Ojibwa Indians (1955, 1976) showed how their conception of the person was not equivalent to the Western conception, largely because the Ojibwa view was based on the assumption of a basic metaphysical unity in the ground of being and a personal rather than mechanistic theory of causation (1976). In a pioneering article, Read suggested that the Gahuku-Gama of Papua New Guinea do not separate the individual from the social status which he occupies and hence do not see the person as an ethical category (1955: 199). Fortes's work on the Tallensi also shows how limited 'individuality' is understood to be in some societies. He makes a comparison between Tallensi notions of Prenatal Destiny and Oedipal Fate and suggests that in this context the individual has no choice. Submission to his ancestors is 'symbolic of his encapsulation in a social order which permits of no voluntary alteration of his status and social capacities. It is the common interest, the collective purposes that prevail' (1959: 33). See also Shweder and Bourne (1984) who discuss the terms by which we should try to understand the concepts of 'person' among other peoples to compare them with our own.
2. Also known as 'cultural frames' (Holland and Quinn 1987).
3. See Bourdieu 1977; Rosaldo 1980; Lutz 1988; Abu-Lughod 1986.
4. According to Kitayama, Markus and Lieberman the self is made meaningful by 'a set of internal attributes such as goals, desires, abilities, talents, or personality traits and the major cultural task is to discover, actualize, and confirm these internal attributes of the self'. This is in contrast to those cultures where there is no such emphasis on the separation or independence of self, stressing instead

a `fundamental interdependence and interconnectedness' (1995: 524).

5. Dumont demonstrated in *Homo Hierarchicus* (1970) how whereas our notion of person is connected to our obsession with equality and status, in India in contrast the obsession is with maintaining society itself. And it is this which gives the caste system its rationale (ibid., chapter one; and Quigley 1995: 30–1).
6. This is similar to some Indian ideas about conception, such as in Bengal (see Fruzzetti, Östör and Barnett 1982: 19; Dube 1986).
7. The desire of men to reproduce without women is noted too in Onians (1954: 178–80) and how the head and the knees are understood as the seat and source of life and the life fluid, often associated with the sap of plants. Zeus engenders a child in his head and a folk-tale of Zakythos has a beautiful maiden springing from the king's calf, while the Nilotic Masai tell of a old man giving birth to twins from his knee. Onians suggests the association of the knee with generation may be linked to the growth of shoots from the 'knees' of plants and explains the widespread superstition that an enemy by interlocking his fingers can hinder childbirth.
8. *Bung* has the alternatives *phung* or *pung* and all three of these are closely related to the word for 'flower' in other Kiranti languages; in Limbu *phung*, in Bahing *phung*, in Dungmali *pung*, in Sam pang *bung*wa, in Dummi *pumma*, in Khaling *pungma*, in Thulung *bung*ma. It is also perhaps related to the Lohorung verb for 'grow' which has the stem *phu:* as in *phu:me* to grow; *phu:da* 'grown up' or 'has grown'; *phu:rino* 'everything grown tall' (as in the monsoon). A conception of flowers similar to the Lohorung exists amongst the Tamang (e.g. Höfer 1981), who says, 'There is a mystic linkage betwen a particular kind of flower, a particular kind of *cen* and the genitalia of a female – the latter being also called flower. Once the shaman has discovered which flower corresponds to his patient's 'flower' he can identify and placate the cen held responsible for the woman's barrenness or menstruation trouble' (ibid: 15). According to Peters (1981: 90) flowers in Nepal are associated with health and vitality.
9. As mentioned in Chapter Five the myths are referred to either by the term mundhum or *pe-lam*.
10. See Hallowell's description of the Ojibwa Indians (1976)
11. Spielberg's film *E.T.* uses a similar notion to express the relationship between an extraterrestrial and a human boy. When the relationship is fading the flower droops.
12. It should be added that the association of menstruation with *bung* may have a wider cultural relevance or have been reaffirmed or influenced by the Nepali term for the menstrual flow, which is *phul*, also the Nepali for 'flower'.
13. In Brahman-Chetri culture a woman becomes polluted and untouchable during the first three days of her menstruation: ''or these three days a woman must not enter the kitchen, touch food or water that others will eat or drink, or even worship the gods or the ancestor spirits. She may not comb her hair or oil it, and she sleeps separately in a downstairs room. Also she may not touch the adult man' (Bennett 1983: 215).
14. A few women deliberately adopt the Hindu idea of ritual cleanliness and refuse to cook while menstruating. I knew of only one woman, however, who took pollution ideas to the extreme of performing the *Rishi Panchami* rituals of purification – purifying herself of the possible sin of having touched a man whilst menstruating.
15. Infant mortality is high. Miscarriages are frequent. The following demonstrates how miscarriage and infant deaths can affect a household. KB lived for sixteen years with his first wife who had seven children but all died of dysentery within one month. She died in the same month and the following year he married another woman from Danda Pangma. She, however, eloped with another man from Loke Pangma after one month with KB. The same year, he married a widow from Angla, who already had a son from her first marriage. She still lives with KB. Sadly, though she conceived frequently and had eleven children, six sons and five daughters, all died at birth or when very small, while other conceptions miscarried. In spite of the many births there were no children alive.

A woman who worked for the couple as a cowherd was persuaded to act as a wife in the hope of getting a son. She stayed as a wife for over a year and bore a daughter who still lives with her father but the mother eloped with a sarki (one of the cobbler caste) from Chandanpur. A year later the couple persuaded a Khambu (Chamlinge Rai) woman from Majhuwa to join as a co-wife. She died childless two years later.

16. For a detailed analysis of the 'intellectualist' and 'symbolist' approaches to religion see Skorupski (1976). According to anthropological theory and in particular what is called the rationality debate, statements which for example explain difficult labour in terms of the activity of the father, often referred to as odd beliefs, must either be seen as instrumental (the 'intellectualist' view) or communicative (the 'symbolists' view). For 'intellectualists' they are magical statements based upon natural observations which have led to explanations of the physical world but are at the same time mistaken beliefs because not fitting with science; or they must be seen as symbolic statements having little to do with belief. Tylor and Frazer, two key intellectualists, saw magical thinking as a way of explaining the natural world just as science does for the Westerner. Frazer saw the analogy between magical and scientific conceptions of the word as being close. 'In both of them, the succession of events is assumed to be perfectly regular and . . .determined by immutable laws' (1922: 56). Symbolists, such as Durkheim 1965; Leach 1961, 1969; or Douglas 1966 all emphasize that religion and magic are different from science in being symbolic. Magico-religious statements such as the ones here are not to be taken literally but are aesthetic, metaphorical, and not literal. To understand these Lohorung statements neither interpretation seems satisfactory. Both ignore how beliefs can develop a momentum of their own in particular circumstances; both ignore the role of the imagination and the power of emotional involvement. Such statements are not necessarily entirely pseudo-scientific nor purely metaphorical and expressive. Neither can, for example, explain the beliefs of modern Pagan witches.
17. For comparative purposes see Bennett's 'Sex and Motherhood' (1976) that includes a description of birth among the Brahmin-Chetri.
18. The 'hot' 'cold' view of the physiology of the body is shared by many groups in Nepal (see for example Stone 1976) and may also be compared to the Indian Ayurvedic system of health which also equates health with balance.
19. Gaenszle (1996) analyses the Mewahang Rai oral ritual text – a *saya pokma* ritual performed after the birth of a child. Gaenszle translates *saya* among the Mewahang as 'head soul' and 'vital soul'.
20. Gaenszle says that among the Mewahang the mother and the rest of the household drink the urine of a calf (1996).
21. For example Ortner (1978) on Sherpa life or Holmberg on the Tamang (1989), McDougal on the Kulunge Rai (1979).
22. The notion of wandering souls is prevalent in societies all over Central and North Asia, in Tibet, China, and the Far East. See Eliade, 1972: 215–20; Watters 1975; see also Desjarlais 1992, Chapter 5.
23. In a chapter on soul loss Desjarlais makes the important comment that although there is 'one "illness" category ("spirit loss"), there are at least two "diseases".'(1992: 145), and notably whereas emotional distress lies at the root of much adult soul loss, children's soul loss has more specifically to do with fear, producing a 'precise behavioral patterning: the child becomes silent, withdrawn, numb' (ibid: 145).
24. This is a play on words: *nammi rokno chak*, 'she eats like a daughter-in-law', that is, she is modest, hard-working and sensitive to others' needs.
25. As Holmberg says about the Tamang 'Not to exchange and share stifles well- being. To hoard, to leave out, to be tightfisted or closemouthed, to crave wealth or to exploit without return for personal enrichment all are violations of the principles of exchange . . . One cannot overemphasise the pervasiveness of this ethos *even in the contradictions of it in practice*' (1989: 54)

26. Allen has some interesting comments on the new sorts of role and decision-making processes that now confront the Thulung Rai. 'So the new role is exercised in a new social unit, is concerned with new sorts of social activities, is exercised for abruptly delimited periods, is gained and lost by competition, is isolable from the totality of an individual in an unaccustomed way. The decision-making process is equally untraditional. Formerly the presupposition was that a discussion would lead to gradual emergence of a consensus, whereas nowadays the institution of voting admits the possibility and increases the likelihood of, overt unreconcilable differences of opinion' (1972b: 161)
27. From a Pangma sample of 35 households 87.5 per cent of girls had had no schooling. 82.6 per cent of women in the sample population were illiterate compared to 32.6 per cent of men. For some, schooling for girls is 'wrong' (*phenni*). There is an old saying, 'if girls have schooling, then the home of our wife's father will come to an end'. The meaning of this goes somewhat as follows: school makes girls 'clever', but they forget all other work. They no longer see their *niwa*, when they come home they don't want to do housework; they want to be like their brothers. Then no man wants them for a wife: they are known to be lazy in the fields. Alternatively, they do not want to marry, or want to marry a Brahmin/Chetri. Whichever way it is, if they do not marry, or marry a Brahmin/Chetri, they reduce the likelihood of boys from other clans finding wives and hence having children. Though many laugh at the saying, they nevertheless mention it.
28. See Caplan 1970 who describes what has happened to land ownership among the Limbu.
29. See Hardman 1981 on Lohorung Rai; Desjarlais on the Yolmo 1991; McHugh on the Gurung 1989; Parish on the Newar 1991.
30. See Declan Quigley(1995: 24–5; 31) for his analysis of Durkheim.
31. A comparison of the Rai with the Tallensi (Fortes 1983) and other West African social psychologies (Horton 1983) is interesting in showing how relatively full of initiative Rai are allowed to be in comparison to these cultures. Horton comments that people share a strong collectivist element, 'an element most strikingly exemplified by the idea that the successful individual, even in his most idiosyncratic moments, is sustained and constrained by a delegation from the "forces of society" ' (Horton 1983: 72).
32. Liquor sales in one year brought in between Rs.1000–2000 (at the time, £1=Rs.24.00) into the households of quite a few enterprising women. One woman made as much as Rs.3,456 profit (£1,486).
33. Alcohol is valued and regarded as powerful, as the following story shows:

'At the time when there was no rice, there was a dog, a snake, and a bear who were fighting, and all died; people put them into a hole in the ground. From that hole grew a plant, a creeper, (what they later called *habektangma*) grew out of the hole. People tasted the plant and it was very spicy and they began to act very strangely; they were very drunk and unable to talk or walk properly, so they threw it away. Later they thought it must be useful somehow, and they said, "let's eat it with water". They dried the leaves and crumbled them to dust and put it in the water and drank it. They found this time that they became a little drunk and they were very strong. They did much work and felt good "Our bodies are good now", they said. They tried adding it to maize, then to millet, and later on to rice and it tasted good'. But they say, 'drink fairly, the right amount and everything is good, if you drink just a little too much, then people cry like a dog, if they drink more than that they fight like a bear. If they drink even more they they lose their mind, forget everything and wherever they are, they sleep like a snake.' The making of alcohol is restricted to women, who keep part of the process secret and exclusive. Yeast cakes, for example, needed for brewing any liquor, are only made by the oldest women in the community, and are made secrectly and then distributed to those they please. They can also be bought in the market but most women 'swear by' a particular old woman's yeast cakes for making good beer.

34. The figure is derived from research done twenty years ago but from what I can gather the number

of arranged marriages is still high. For a description of Lohorung arranged marriages see Hardman 1999.

35. Those who said others had followed their own *niwa* were reflecting what research also showed, that is, that about about a quarter of marriages in Pangma were marriages by elopement or 'theft', the partner of their choice, without their parent's consent, and about half of these were people in their first marriage. Many elopements take place when the boy or girl are away from the village.
36. All Lohorung marriage forms emphasize the transfer of jural authority over a woman. The full marriage is, however, only complete after the last rite. If this rite has been completed it is hard for a woman to leave, especially if she wants to marry someone else. If a widow wants to remarry, she first has to persuade her husband's younger brother to give up his rights over her. If he wants to claim her, then her suitor may try to capture the widow and pay compensation. If her husband is still alive, she can still desert him, using some tactic to do so. Many simply return to their natal home. Others who want to marry again are 'captured', or re-marry in *jari biha* (N) 'fine marriage', or 'elopement', in which the new husband pays the former husband a fine of about Rs.1000. The sum is less if the woman has married in this way before, and decreases each time she remarries. Previously, the first husband had the right to take his revenge on his successor with 'a cutting (i.e. sharp) knife', *boktam dabe,* allowing him to mutilate or even kill him. Even now the new couple keep out of the way of a previous husband. Those who are determined to follow their 'own mind', *tangpam niwa*, do so even knowing that this 'throws away the nose' of a father, a whole household, possibly a husband. They keep away until the 'hurt *niwa*' is strong again.
37. Sagant (1970) discusses 'theft marriage' and makes the point that Limbu sons usually acquire their independence slowly, indirectly, never head-on; they take liberties and the father feigns ignorance; they stay out all night, they make their first trip to Assam on their own and their father watches. Only in 'theft marriage' is the rebellion overt. The father's authority is totally undermined and yet in the end he has to give the couple a *tika*, the mark of his acceptance.
38. In an article on teaching ethnopsychology Barry Michrina describes using my early article on *niwa*, *saya*, and *lawa* (Hardman 1981) to help encourage understanding the worldviews of others. One student suggested the tripartite could be seen as 'the Id, Ego and Superego' and went on to explore the similarities and differences, '*Niwa* is not like the Superego because when it involves antisocial behaviour it is like the Id' and so on (1996: 5). Comparing Western and local theories is a key process in translating other cultures. Were there time and space, Lohorung theories of child development could be compared to those of Piaget.
39. A term of Piaget used for example by Hallpike (1976) to argue that 'primitives' have a different mentality to Westerners.
40. This takes us back to the beginning of the chapter where I described the complex Lohorung notion of *bung*, and to the belief that every person has a flower representing his or her life in the world of the dead and to the notion of multiple souls. There is also a flower representing the person in the world of the living.
41. See Sagant 1976: 168 and McDougal 1979: chapter VII for descriptions of Limbu and Kulunge Rai funerary rites. Among the Kulunge Rai the white flags are given by the out-married women of the local clan group as an expression of 'sisterly' love for their 'brother' (McDougal 1979: 126).
42. The following is one man's explanation to me of what happens to the body at death. In his view there are not just two 'souls' (*lawa* and *saya*) in a person, there are many. This reflects a principle lying behind the Lohorung understanding of the person, of the existence of a multiplicity of souls. These act as a kind of 'mutuality of consciousness' with various parts of the natural environment. The following is an attempt to translate what he said, 'Ours, you know in our bodies, in people's bodies there are those, those *chap*, let's call them. For all of us, so they say, our "talking one" goes to *Naralok* (our place up there), and there it stays. Suppose I die, mine, yours too, just like that our "talking one" goes to *Naralok*. As for the "body one" (the flesh), that one goes in the earth and

stays with the soil; it goes to be friends with the soil – all that concerns the flesh is the soil's share. And now, "the fire one", yes let's call it the fire – it's like that, our inside, our *hongsiu* (deepest inside). We living ones we eat mandarines, berries, maize, all those things we eat, don't we? Deep inside fire exists, they say, and all those things the fire cooks. That one, our *hongsiu* (deepest inside) when we die goes to meet the fire. So that one goes. Now, our *hangsa* (N "main body, soul") one goes to *Indra lok* (heaven). *Jema Raj*, our enemy, takes it, so they say, first six months before death, so that one goes to *Jema lok*, let's call it that, or *Indra lok*. The "breath one", that one goes to catch up with the wind. Then the other one, our *lawa* it goes to seek a dwelling place so they say in your women's bellies, that *lawa*, that *jiphangsa* (N "life-heart") goes to look for a dwelling place and goes to women's bellies – like that a child is made. Then, those mocking ones, those are different; four brothers of one, eight brothers. What are they? Well, they made the bones. Those *sekowa-mekowa* (*sekowa*, "bone" in L) bones ones – the grave watchers, those ones they call the *chap*. Those are the teasing, haunting kind, those are *chap* indeed. They come to nine brothers; that means these, this and this eye, that makes two, this three, this four [the nostrils], this five [mouth], this six and seven [the ears], and below, at the other end, there are two, eight and nine. So in all there are nine brothers. So it is those we chase away, the mockers and teasers, when they threaten us, the *sikla* (the *chap* called at *nuagi* and at the funeral). We call them, "*aluatham, beluatham, pakpoktae*" (rise up from the shady places, the eartb places, come etc. as in *nuagi*).'

43. Mines (1988) points out that despite the common consensus that individualism is devalued in India, in private Indians are active agents 'pursuing private goals and making personal decisions that affect the outcome of their lives' (ibid: 568). Similarly Lohorung Rai are able to act as spontaneous idiosyncratic individuals in what might be seen as a predominantly supra-individual ethnopsychology (see Heelas and Lock's 1981 model, in which societies can be plotted depending on whether the concept of the 'self' is idealist or passiones.)
44. Rosaldo in her book *Knowledge and Passion* shows how the institutions of marriage and headhunting, among others, become comprehensible through language of the heart, and in particular the notion of *liget* 'anger, energy, passion', which develops in complementarity with *beya* 'knowledge', 'suggests the passionate energy that leads young men to labor hard, to marry, to kill, and reproduce; but also if ungoverned by the "knowledge" of mature adults, to engage in wild violence' (1980: 27). Ilongot youths seek the *liget* which can be achieved in headhunting exploits in order to gain social and psychological maturity. The *liget* of headhunting stands 'as a symbol of his autonomy and freedom from constraint, his ability to engage in the cooperative enterprises of adults without fear of a humiliating domination' (ibid: 230).Throughout the book Rosaldo shows how the Ilongots' views of experience, knowledge, emotions, and actions (their indigenous psychology) provide the images, patterns, rules, and meaning of activities such as marriage and tossing heads. Rosaldo also looks at the domain of individual motivations and individual psychology and experiences, as they are seen by the Ilongot and as they are bound up with the social world. She looks at how their indigenous psychology provides models for the self, and interpretations of action (see ibid: 23).

8

Emotions and Concepts of Mind: Understanding Lohorung Behaviour and Social Institutions

Introduction

Until recently, there were two extremes in anthropology concerning the study of mental processes. On the one hand, there was the radical position of Hallpike (1976), who argued that primitives conceptualize mind and psychological processes in a totally different way from that of adults in the West; and that, for example, they have no elaborate terminology to express any of the finer shades of experience. On the other hand, there was and still are those anthropologists who rely on an assumption that other people share our Western ideas about emotions and other mental states to such an extent that we can uncritically apply our own terms without examining the indigenous concepts. More recently, some anthropologists, linguists and psychologists have emphasized the significance of the socially constructed 'person' and have included emotions as part of that social construction (Rosaldo 1980; Heelas 1986; Lutz 1988, Averill 1990).[1] The acceptance of emotions as universals has been attacked with arguments that the meaning of emotions varies considerably across cultures (Shweder 1991). On the other hand, there is growing support for the notion of some kind of universality of emotions.[2] Some researchers reveal a complex interplay of the biological, the self and society so that even romantic love can be seen as a universal (Jankowiak,1995). This chapter will, add to the evidence that neither of the first two viewpoints is acceptable and will argue against any strong constructivist view of emotions. I also want to expand on my argument, already emphasized in this book, that if we want to understand a particular culture, their behaviour, thought, and meaning systems, we have to look closely at people's indigenous concepts.

The aim of this chapter is largely ethnographic. It does not intend to survey the ever-increasing literature on the anthropology of emotions or enter in depth into the debate as summarized by Lutz and White (1986). It will, on the other hand, explain my response to the debate, and my position in it, based on my understanding of Lohorung concepts of emotion, their meaning and significance. In the first section I will give examples of emotion terms within detailed specific contexts to show how

Lohorung talk about emotions, and to show how these concepts can help us understand Lohorung behaviour and institutions. Emotions have to be understood in their socio-cultural context. Lohorung ideas about emotions – how, when, and why they occur – are part of their implicit cultural knowledge from which they make inferences about the behaviour and activities of their fellow men and women. This emotion knowledge also 'fits', as we shall see, with their general philosophy of life, their theories about the unity of the human and superhuman worlds, their values of co-operation and compassion. The importance of studying the emotions has been succinctly expressed by Catherine Lutz in several articles. One of her clearest statements goes as follows:

> emotions are assumed here to be the primary source of human motivation. If emotions are simultaneously viewed as cultural concepts, they become important as statements about, and motivations for the enactment of cultural values. If motivation is seen as culturally constituted (Hallowell, 1955 p.100–106), study of the emotions and their development becomes crucial for understanding the psychosocial origins of behaviour. Thus, emotion in the individual may be said to have its parallel, on the cultural level, in values: the concept of emotion, then, can provide a critical nexus for understanding the individual's creation of, and participation in, social institutions. (1983: 247).

My aim in this chapter is to see how Lohorung emotions and their cultural values replicate each other. Though my position is not that emotions are necessary determinants, I do claim that the frameworks expressed in emotion or mental-state terms reveal those features of social life that are essential for its structure, its general theory and its cultural values.

I should emphasize two caveats. The first is that my intention throughout has been to discover how the Lohorung themselves view and evaluate emotions and other mental states, how they handle them, and how they relate them to more general ideas about the nature of human beings (such as the concept of *niwa*). The aim has not been to understand the actual nature of their inner feelings, such as whether they feel exactly the same way as I feel when experiencing a particular emotion. Since, as philosophers have pointed out, I cannot be sure that I feel the same pain or fear as anyone else in my own culture, how could I possibly do so in another? I am therefore not talking about mental states as such but about Lohorung conceptions of those states.

The second point concerns the slippery nature of emotions as a category even within our own culture. Emotions do not form a natural class; they cannot be linked together under one set of classifications nor be sharply divided from moods, motives, attitudes, or character traits. Nevertheless, even though they do not form a class in the way that we normally conceive of such classes, they do, I think, form a polythetic class.[3] From the descriptions that follow it will be clear that Lohorung concepts discussed in this chapter do fall under the rubric of 'emotions', or more generally 'mental states'. From the beginning of fieldwork, I adopted a tentative stance and tried to resist the temptation to make an immediate gloss on every word, expecting some concepts to be as culturally specific perhaps as our 'Monday morning blues'.

Lohorung Conception of Mental States

In this section I want to look at the Lohorung conception of mental states in general, a category which encompasses more than 'emotions'. It includes expressive feelings, ethical feelings, (feelings of obligation and shame), perceptual states, cognitive states, and personality traits. The Lohorung have no general category term for 'mental states' or 'emotions'. The Lohorung concept *minukme*, 'feel' is the most general abstract term used. It's used in such contexts as 'how do you feel?' (*manthoklo min'ne?*) or 'how did he feel when he did/said that?' (*manthoklo mimpoku hanke akro lete/kase?*) or in conjunction with some activity, such as 'I feel like eating/going' (*chama/khema mi'nga*). Another concept, *som kheruk*, 'heart itches' is also close to the term 'feelings'. An example of its use goes as follows: 'Once mind has developed, children can understand conversations; and their heart itches', that is, the part of them in which many feelings are located has become active, they begin to feel. (*niwa puse khema hang pisachi khanawa wabukmi; som so kherukmi*).

These are the mental states I was able to find as being recognized by Lohorung:

Indigenous words	**English gloss**
apikhuba	stingy, mean
bongsime, bongsik, bongchame	to lie, to be lied to, hence disappointed
chemlangme, chemlangsung	ignore
chenchame, chen chen minuk	elated, pleased, like
chenchabokme	happy, content
chiksime, chiksik	disapprove,feel disgusted
chime	learn (a skill)
chung'lu	cold
chung niwa	cold-hearted
chungme	worship
diha lengme	proud
essime, essik	lazy
ha'chak'wa minuk	excited, impatient
hangme	respect
hapme, habukmi	cry, weep
hekme, heku	be able
heme	hear

Indigenous words	English gloss
herem herem minuk	hungry, empty
hingchame, hingkrikpa	alive
hoprek' pikhedu	empty
hoptiwa'lu	hot, sweaty
huk'bekme	worship, pray
kamnuro mikuchini	feel unhappy, sad, uncomfortable
kanga yongpa	proud
khechimawa	irritable, itchy
khimtibungme	hold in mind, remember
kima lu'e	fearful
kisime	fear
kubrowa	foolish
labukme	respect
lamthing lamuk	jealous
langhangme	hope, wish for
lawa kisik	shocked, terrified, soul loss
leeme, leeku	know, he knows
lemmang	awake
letokme	learn (a fact)
lungchame	like, love
lungma diha'l'le	feel brave
mehangkheda	sulky
mi'bungdame, mi'bungdu	remember
mi'chame/mi'lame	homesickness, lovesick, sadness of separation, heart yearning for someone far away[4]
mi-dhangme	be attentive
mi-k'wa'ruru leme	feel like crying
minchame	hope
mingkheme, mikheme	forget
minseme,(minse, minse)	wonder, curious
minukme, minuk	feel
mitokme, mitoku	remember
mukungnga mingkhuba	brave
nabuk we'langdu	hurt pride
nenchame	like, feel kind
ngenukme, ngenukmi	quarrelsome, irritable
ngesime	shy, ashamed, shame
ningbak' mesikme	homesick, nostalgic
nisasi' lik	fear (of water)

Indigenous words	English gloss
niwa chai'kheme	feel hurt
niwa chuk'e'le	feel generous, unselfish
niwa chume	believe, trust
niwa entae	feel relieved
niwa i'i	feel moody
niwa kaise	discontent
niwa kamnuk	content
niwa kisik	respect, awe
niwa makhara	mad
niwa mi'chak'nga, huk yoktokni	homesick, lovesick, sadness of separation
niwa meding	irresponsible
niwa mak'chame	dizzy
niwa pime	trust, have faith
niwa tuguk	hurt, upset, sad
niwa yamuk	anxious, guilty, worried
naksubang	insane
panukha	energetic
pima mikhuba	generous, giving
pudung	awake
sak/sage lubokme	hungry
sapthame, sapthak	satisfied
saya dashi kheda	depressed, melancholic, demoralized, dispirited, (see *saya* in text)
semmang makme	dream
sengkhara	drunk
sichame, sichak	dislike, hate, feel cruel
sinti'khema, sinti'kheda	angry, bitter
sirda yakchame	get angry
siri ledhangme	jealous
siri phongme	humble
siri tangpa	suddenly angry
sokma	breath
som'chai'khenga	pity, compassion, sorrow, eat heart away
som'khepokme, som'khepok	angry (heart)
som'kheruk	feel, heart itches, feel jealous
som tuguk, tukung	heart hurts,compassion/love for someone close
temuku	frightened away
thamsik (thamsitingmi)	jealous

Indigenous words	English gloss
tokma nenchame	feel grateful
tukchanie	sane
tungkheme	fainting with hunger
wai'mesime	thirsty
waptokme, waptok	understand
yakta'khema, yaktampa	worn out, tired
yangsime, yangsima lu	fear (of height)
yik'bok'kheme	feel angry
yik'kheme, yik'ti'kheme	very unhappy
yin'keng	dejected
yongnukme	feel munificent
yongukme	possessed

This list conveys something of the variety and extent of Lohorung inner-state terms. And there are more. My list can't be exhaustive for two reasons. First, it omits the Nepali words in use, terms which are increasingly used as Lohorung society absorbs pan-Nepalese culture. For example, the Nepali term for 'love', *maya* N, is now in common use to describe 'romantic love'. Girls and boys use it freely especially in the songs they sing to each other, some of whom marry for 'love'. Other emotion terms frequently used in the Nepali songs sung by the young – including the Nepali for 'pity' (*daya*), 'jealous' (*daha*), 'unhappy' (*bekhushi*), and 'happy' (*khushi*) – are also, for example, part of everyday vocabulary as are such Nepali concepts as *dukha* 'distress' or 'grief', *dikka* 'trouble', 'worry', and *doshi* 'guilty'.

Secondly, Lohorung frequently describe the experience of an emotion with a phrase, a metaphor, or a proverb, whereas English and Nepali often have a single term. Asking for Lohorung words which translated Nepali ones was at times hopeless. Puzzled by the lack of a term, yet knowing they had the concept, Lohorung sometimes searched in vain for one word equivalences. Instead, Lohorung terms emerged in everyday situations or in trying to translate stories. Sometimes not one word but several appeared. For example, for the Nepali *surta* 'worry' we realized Lohorung use *niwa yamuk* 'mind is talking'. But in order to express concern or generalized worry they also often use a proverb drawn from one of the *pe-lam* stories. They might say to indicate worry or concern, *siksikwara lam*, *bekbekwara lam*, which translates 'the main, wide and easy path, the dangerous path': in other words it says, 'I'm worried that you might take the wrong path, as did the two children in the myth. Be careful'.

English also has numerous similar proverbs, such as, 'it's a long road that has no turnings', 'don't put all your eggs in one basket', 'a bird in the hand is worth two in the bush'; and indeed concepts such as 'caution', 'timidity', or 'over-confidence', are defined and understood by us in part with proverbs and metaphors (see Lakoff and Johnson 1980). To express 'anger' Lohorung have several verbs and phrases such as, 'with that person my mind is cold, I don't want to talk' (*'ako ya-pmi nung kam niwa chiso'le yamuma mingani'*). Or, when talking about people being 'angry', instead of using an adjective 'angry', Lohorung use verbs, vividly describing the form the anger is taking, 'they are fighting, quarrelling, wrestling, hitting each other, not talking to each other, refusing to bring rice'. Their understanding of 'brave' came in the form *mukungnga minkhuka* , literally 'a person feeling I can do' or *lungma diha'le* 'heart/liver is big' (and will not cry). The phrase 'I feel as if my *lawa* has disappeared' (*lawa makhemparole'nga*) expresses for them the feeling of 'shock', feeling lifeless, the shaken, upset feeling after a severe fright. As Lohorung words and phrases became comprehensible to me it became increasingly clear that the complexity of their verbs, including the use of eleven pronouns with their different verb formations, and rich metaphors enable them to express many of their abstract ideas including emotions without necessarily using abstract nouns. Perhaps it was in part this difficulty of obtaining abstract equivalences which led Hodgson to note in 1857 that the Lohorung have 'a total absence of any term for nearly every operation of the intellect or will, whether virtuous or vicious, and lastly for almost every abstract idea' (1880).[5]

Anger: Lohorung Concepts

Psychological stereotypes of cultures in terms of personality types have little to recommend them. To me the characterization in Nepal of Rai men as people with quick tempers, famous for their outbursts of violence and their sensitivity or readiness to take offence, was a vast oversimplification.[6] Yet for some years the British Army did not recruit Rais and Limbus because of this reputation. There are stories told by Newars, Brahmins, and Rai of the Pangma area, describing Lohorung aggressions and extended feuds with violent outbreaks on market days which do corroborate the stereotype. Until recently, for example, the Chetri/Brahmin population of Chandanpur greatly feared Lohorung. They told me how they used to race past Pangma on their way to Khandbari to avoid meeting them. Their image of the Lohorung was of 'strong and volatile men, ready to fight with any non-Lohorung, if somehow provoked or drunk on local alcohol; men who had little or no idea of law and order'. At that time many Chetri or Brahmin would not consider friendship with a Lohorung and contact with them was kept to a minimum. The stereotype, is a clear distortion of their general nature, but it does pinpoint a central feature of Lohorung culture – the significance of 'anger' and 'rage', in particular in response to insult. In this section I want to explore this significance and the meanings of Lohorung concepts of anger, what it means for them to feel angry; how such feelings are expressed, socially regulated and managed.

The Lohorung concepts which fall under the English notion 'anger' can be divided into two categories. The first includes those concepts which describe sudden eruptions and changes in mood, exemplified by Lohorung descriptions of children literally 'going sour', *sinti'kheme*. They are moods which in their severe form we would describe as temper tantrums. The Lohorung verb seems particularly apt to describe the internal fermentation (or frustration as we see it) that becomes too potent for the child to bear. One description of *sinti'kheme* went as follows:

> when infants want to go to a place a bit far away but they don't manage to reach it they 'become frustrated' (*sinti'khemi*); if they cannot have more good things to eat and drink they 'get frustrated'; when they're a bit older and if they don't get to wear nice clothes, or nice bracelets, nose rings or gold jewellery they 'get angry with frustration'.

This mood of frustration is theoretically ascribed only to children and ancestors, but I've heard it used about women as well. Though the 'anger' of the ancestors is also conceived as being like the 'frustrated anger' or 'temper tantrums' of children, Lohorung refer to it with the more polite concept of *yik'bok'kheme* (also applied to children). When describing ancestors the implication is that the ancestors are not being offered what they want and are now in a tantrum. And just as children, in such a mood, are placated with enormous effort so too are ancestors. Ancestors require lavish food offerings to counteract this mood; the sourness of the mood foiled by tempting morsels . . . so perhaps it's not pure chance that the verb includes the belly '*bok*'. The interpretation of the concept of 'anger' as 'goals blocked', as Harris does, (1989) is useful in understanding this Lohorung category. Lohorung would also agree with developmental psychologists that children are born with the capacity to experience this emotion.

The second category of Lohorung concepts, which fall under our notion 'anger', differ from the first in that they rely on the presence of *niwa* (mind) for their emergence and therefore for Lohorung are not simply innate capacities. Our notions of consciousness, will, conscious desire, determination, and sensibility are all included in the complex meaning of *niwa* and the adult forms of Lohorung 'anger'. *Niwa* only appears when the child begins to respond to the social world. In young children *niwa* has not yet developed and their emotional outbursts are seen as being undirected and totally spontaneous. The concepts we are dealing with here are *sirda yakcha'bokme* (or simply *yakchame*), *siri khangme* and *som khepok*. Lohorung understand the concept *sirda yakcha'bokme* or simply *yak'chame* to express the same experience as the Nepali *risaunu*, which Turner defines as 'to be angry' (1931: 538).

If we look at these concepts in use, they include what we would call 'justifiable anger'. For example, asked about the occasions when people experienced *sirda yakcha'bokme*, children of ages varying from six to fourteen years old suggested the following kinds of situation: (in each case I have glossed the term using 'angry' to show how it seems to 'fit' the semantic field of *sirda yakcha'bokme*) :

- When you haven't done good work parents 'get angry'; they wave a stick at you like they want to hit you; people's faces go red if you don't do work well and they 'get angry'.
- When you do something wrong, others 'get angry', like if the rice isn't ready when they come home from working. If I go to fetch water and break the pot, then my parents 'get angry'. In the evening when they come home from the field and find you've done something wrong or stupid they 'get angry' . If somebody killed someone else's dog or pig the owner would 'get angry'.
- If I don't do as I'm told my mother 'gets angry'.
- When a cow or pig goes into a field and starts to eat your crops, then you 'get angry'.
- If one person hits another person and shouts at them then the other person 'gets angry'. If my brother hits me then I 'get angry'. People who hit each other 'are angry'.
- When people shout and fight and quarrel they 'are angry'.
- If you get too big-headed other people 'get angry'.
- When people are drunk they easily 'get angry'. They have different *niwa* (mind); if you don't know someone is drunk and they do something wrong, then you 'get angry' and the drunk person acts even more 'angrily'.

Many of these examples emphasize the moral 'ought' role of *yak'chame* and in this sense 'justifiable anger' is within the semantic range of the concept. It expresses what people feel when someone has done something wrong; it makes people want to punish someone else either physically or verbally, and facially it has the same reddening effect as does 'anger' for many of us. However, both justified and unjustified aggression are implied in the examples, and it is unjustified aggression, 'when people shout and fight and quarrel' or 'when people are drunk' which indicates the other semantic slant to *sirda yakcha'bokme*. The concept, thus, also conveys our understanding of 'uncontrolled anger, rage, fury'.

The concept *siri khangme* conveys the same kind of uncontrollable anger or rage as does *sirda yakcha'bokme* but without any positive component. We might simply want to gloss it as 'rage'. *Som khepok*, literally 'heart erupts', describes an 'anger' similar to the 'rage' of the other two concepts but it is understood as physiologically developing along with *niwa* (mind). It implies an uncontrollable aspect which comes along with a deeper understanding of morality and the knowledge of what is right - what we might call spontaneous indignation. The truly adult person always 'has a desire to fight for self or others'. This is said to be an increasingly important feeling that one naturally has as one grows up. As *niwa* develops so too people develop this rage. But adults should be able to control it. Those who can't are called *som khewa*.

Someone described to me a person who couldn't control his anger, showing how the concepts are used. 'Today he was "angry" (*yakcha'bokdu*) and he didn't speak; his work didn't go well and so he was "angry" (*yakcha'bokdu*); yesterday he was very "angry" (*saro yakcha'bokdu*) with me. He asked me over to give me something, and what did he give me?– it's not right – as the conversation went on it was clear he was just very angry with me. Those people – whatever you give them, do for them, it always ends in "anger"/ "rage" (*som khepok*). If they're told to work, and they don't feel like it, they immediately get into a rage (*som khepok*); if something doesn't work and they're told off or told it hasn't been done well, they fly into a rage (*som khempok*). If something goes wrong with the ploughing they get angry (*yakchama lu*) and they start to hit the oxen. At home if the work hasn't been done well, they fly into a rage (*som khepok*) and they're the ones who start the shouting, and the quarrelling begins.They always end up in a rage (*som khepok*). Whatever you give them to eat or drink they're angry (*som khepok*); if the children don't listen to them they get angry (*yakchama lu*)'.

How 'Anger' is Expressed

Lohorung take anger for granted. They recognize its positive role in their lives which they learn from their understanding of the lives of their ancestors and the rules about its expression which they have inherited.

Hitting in Lohorung society has a significance as a form of punishment and as an expression of righteous anger when something wrong has been done: it is acceptable for parents to hit their children; for a wronged husband to beat a rival; for a man to respond to an insult that attacks his honour. On the other hand, there is a negative side to hitting: for children to hit their elders is traditionally 'wrong' (*phenni*); to hit one's sister would also be 'wrong'; and physical violence between men of one's own tribe is acceptable only under exceptional circumstances.

The adult form of anger, controlled by reason (*niwa*), is more directed and calculated than the diffuse anger of children. It is often expressed by 'telling off, commanding' (*losikme*), by 'beating, hitting' (*rokme*), or by 'the desire to fight, pick a quarrel, or argue' (*hibokme or hime yoguk*) with those who offend or provoke. The number of words for expressing anger are indicative of the ways in which adult anger is expressed: *hekme* to cut, *semchame* to tease, mock, scorn, drag someone's name in the mud, *sechame*, to insult behind their back, *chungme* or *chung bungme* to wrestle, *nakme* to scratch, *kime* to kick, *bokme* to cut, *dupme* to hit with fist, *rukme* to punch, *pektangme* to smack with stick, *phektangme* to smack with hand, *boktangme* to cut, *duplangpime*, to hit and wound. Anger is often then specified in terms of interpersonal relations with others, and is talked about in terms of its social manifestations.

To give you some examples, when two friends, each with one ox, agreed to plough together, and one of them did not turn up, the expression of anger by loudly insulting the man behind his back (*sechame*) was considered justified. A man who was angry with his wife expressed it by 'going to fetch water' (*yowa lakhuba pikheda*), that is, by performing an activity rarely allocated to men, so that the 'anger' is known to the whole community and is considered appropriate. A woman may best

FIG 14. Men ploughing with oxen.

express, it by 'refusing to make beer' (*dibu e'pikhuba*) for her husband. Since it's an activity forbidden to men, she forces him to go to other houses to quench his thirst and lets her anger be known 'socially'. Provoking the anger of the suitor of one's sister is acceptable because it draws the attention of the community to the relationship and discourages flippant flirting. By means of these deliberately 'social' expressions of anger, the community can also maintain some control and may even interfere. It's *niwa* which is said to enable these techniques for expressing anger; it's supposed to 'know' when anger can be given full vent. Until recent Nepal government laws were introduced, a Lohorung cuckold, for example, who sought to kill the lover of his wife was not considered 'mad' or out of control of his *niwa*. On the contrary, he would have been expressing a traditional Lohorung right.

On market days or days of co-operative harvesting, when considerable quantities of local beer were consumed and there is much merrymaking tempers were often aroused, conflicts surfaced, and insults began: 'you arsehole!' said Tindule to his eldest son, in an argument about the timing of the harvest. 'You know nothing' said the son. 'You ass, trying to teach your father. You know everything and would have done it a long time ago I suppose!' shouted the father. And so they went on quarrelling. 'Enough! Okay, from now on you can do everything' said the father. 'And so I shall!' After the pause for some beer and a snack, the eldest son turned to do the work of bundling the straw. He climbed onto the high platform for storing the hay.

Then Tindule started to give away the hay, selling it to whoever would have it. 'Rather than store this, better to die' the father shouted out. 'It's only the rice, so what!' shouted the son.'I'm going to sell the land too,' retorted Tindule aiming a stone missile at his son on the platform. And it hit. He climbed up onto the platform and they began fighting. Only then did the others interfere. They separated them and some took the father back to his house. The eldest son then exploded 'How much do I have to listen quietly to his noise (*chen chen khemdhangme*)? My father has really given me great pain, much anguish. Up until now I've never had any help. I feel as if I don't know anything: everything I do is wrong, in our fields, at home, eating, going to meet people. Today it went badly wrong. I feel bad that I did it. But he goes too far when he hits mother. When he has drunk something he gets so angry (*yakcha'bokheku*), he hits even her . . .'. Each side was listened to. They commiserated with the son about the difficulty of his father but he was told he must obey his father. The display of anger on such public occasions is not, however, coincidental or merely alcohol-induced, for the 'social' expression of anger was acceptable and even encouraged.

Tindule and his son kept to the rules by making their conflict public, manifesting their anger by picking a heated and dramatic fight (*hime yoguku*) at harvest time. They dealt with anger in an open way which most Lohorung consider better for the person than silent warfare: 'those that have *niwa* words get angry outside, those with no words to be angry stay silent and remain angry and it gets bigger. No one can help.' In their case, the community was able to maintain some control and give what we would call therapeutic advice. We can see here the positive aspects of anger as controlled or guided by the rules.

Although rules are recognized and although *niwa* is supposed to be in control, as we can see, individual differences in the way that anger is expressed are accepted as being a reflection on the different types of *niwa* that exist, or as we might say they accept that different people use different strategies to deal with anger. Anger can be expressed in different ways. Some say when they're angry they just want to hit something and then it goes, whereas some just laugh if they're angry, and the more they laugh the more angry they are. 'There's one in Heluwa village like that. She has a soft voice but inside she's so angry and nobody realizes at first. Downstairs she's laughing but in the attic she beats the children.' Some people show their anger by sleeping and avoiding their work, so everyone gets to know about it. Some people complain loudly especially if work has not been done: 'Ganesh and the others do no work: they go out to cut grass and return with enough to feed a pigeon not the buffalo. We might as well sell the buffaloes. And the grass is suffocating the millet it is so long. Do you want to starve? How can the millet grow if you boys do not cut the grass?'

In general, a person who refuses to speak at all when angry is seen as holding onto his or her anger so that it lasts longer, while a person who explodes in quick angry bursts and then returns to normal is considered to be someone who can overcome his or her anger quickly: '*ichok sirda yacha'boka, chitto siri makhe*' ('if they can be angry for a moment, then quickly the anger dies'). However, if anger is mixed with another emotion, fear or jealousy, then they say *siri ledhangme*, and being angry for a moment may not be enough: The relationship between co-wives is known as being particularly difficult.'If a woman gets pregnant her relatives will quickly force her to go to the man's house and settle as the younger wife. Normally the situation gets very tense with the eldest wife doing her best to get rid of the younger, by physically hurting her, pulling her hair, spoiling her clothes, or whatever. Ram's uncle's wife, she was very angry and jealous; she shouted and pulled the younger wife's hair whenever she could. She was so angry she constantly used words to turn her husband and the village against *kanchi*. At first, he was on *kanchi*'s side. But the elder wife needled (*ngnenuk*) him. She worked on his trust/belief (*niwa chume*) until he too went into a rage (*som khepok*) with *kanchi*. Just as if I went on telling you bad things about Anumpa (my assistant), how he was worthless and what bad things he said about you, so you would not want to work with him. She did that to her husband. And he then began to hate the younger wife so in the end they were both violent with her; they hit her arms and face. The older wife has powerful relatives in the village whereas *kanchi* had no brothers to be angry for her. In the end he had to build her a separate house and give her some fields. The two families are still angry. They do not talk to each other.'

The variety of expression, or strategies, is captured by one man's view of couples who get angry with each other, 'Some husbands and wives tend to turn their backs on each other, some reduce each other to tears, some people weep, some become "mouth narcissists" *yaba choekma*, some people walk out, some close their ears, some feign innocence with a look of "what have I done?", some just don't talk, some people look as if their eyes get really big, some get tiny eyes, some cry out scattering abuse like a destructive person; some cry out "arsehole!" to everyone; men sometimes throw things around and hit their wives, sleep and stop working and some stop going home and stop eating; women refuse to give food and drink; that's about it unless they go off to the Terai or Assam but if they go somewhere else then they always come back.'

Social Regulation and Anger Management

The rules about anger have little to do with the form of its expression. The rules have to do with the appropriateness of its display and this is connected with the attitudes of respect expected between certain categories of kin. Respect towards elders and one's father and mother means anger towards them should be tightly under control. The appropriate feelings for kin are traditional and are changed, for example, when someone marries in a rite called *saino pheraleme* N. Explanations for some of these expected emotions refer to myths. For example, when a man marries, it's said his brothers must never be angry with his wife. 'They must think of her like a sister; she is a girl and because she comes to be a wife to me she is *Tawama Khewama*. After she has come my brothers must be good to her – anger is forbidden. Although she comes from another clan she is now ours and to be angry with her is *phenni* (wrong)'. *Tawama Khewama*, it may be remembered, were *Khakchrukpa*'s elder sisters. They 'come' (*ta'me*) to the clan of their husbands and leave their natal home. After every marriage those women who have been cooks throughout the ceremony on the groom's side bang their pots and pans and sing: 'Oh, *Tawama Khewama* has come! Today oh, pillars of the house, oh, beams of the house, front door of the house, and side door of the house, oh, three hearth stones, the *Tawama Khewama* of the *lamawa* spring clans has come!' (see Appendix 3 for Lohorung text).

Brothers are, therefore, rarely angry with a sister-in-law. They fear her brothers' anger and protective protective attitudes.[7] If she were treated unjustly or with anger they would have to contend with her brothers. As the traditional rules go, brothers are expected to be 'very angry' (*saro sirda yakcha'bokmi*) with anyone who offends or hurts a sister. And Lohorung say they used to be more angry than they are now in such situations. In the past they fought far more than they do now. Young boys especially were angry (*sirda yachabokhe*) and fought with each other. 'What used to happen – if another young boy made a promised meeting with one's own sister, then of course you became angry: 'why have you made a meeting with my sister?' and they would start to hit the other boy. 'What! Is it forbidden (*phenni*) for your sister to talk to me?' they used to say and then they would start wrestling and fighting. Now they don't do it so much. But some people still do: it's the tradition and brothers should do that for their sisters.'[8]

In fact anger to any close female relative, mother, sister, or daughter or to a cow is considered to be a 'sin' *hiwa*, or *pap* in Nepali. When someone has become lame, or a limb stiffens, for a Lohorung some close relative must have hit his or her mother; and that mother is now taking her revenge (*umam papolagaliki*) – it's said the impact of such violent behaviour occurs almost always two or three generations later. This explains, I was told, why certain clans such as *Dekhim* and *Yangkhrung* were no longer wealthy – in both clans either people's limbs stiffened, wounds developed, or people in the clan died young.

We can see then that there are traditional expectations concerning the suppression as well as the expression of anger. By the age of about ten, Lohorung children, as we've seen in Chapter Seven, are expected to have enough *niwa* to control some of their emotions. Demonstrations of extreme rage are no longer excusable. By this age they should have enough *niwa* inside the stomach to control the stomach anger; words of reason should make sense and an adult form of anger, one that 'comes with' *niwa*, should emerge, either the one located in the heart *som khepok*,or the one of words, that of the mouth, *sirda yacha'bok*.

Anger has its rules because all behaviour in the ideal adult is bound to *niwa* and therefore must be controllable, unless that person is possessed by some ancestor or evil spirit. Some anger, Lohorung say, may be controlled simply by exercising the muscles in the nape of the neck. The elders always say, 'rage never does any good to anyone or anything. See that it does not happen.' ('*Siri mangpiso kam lagalinie*', *kakmi pasingchi, 'siri akhangmume kakmi*'). However, Lohorung sometimes explain someone's inexplicable, exaggerated anger as being caused by the mischievous spirit of someone who has died by accident, or as the mischievous act of the ancestor *chawatangma*, but they have no specific name for a spirit provoking anger.[7]

The 'Anger' of the Ancestors

That anger can be dangerous and has to be managed is particularly clear to the Lohorung from their experience of the anger of the ancestors. Is their understanding of 'ancestral anger' the same as that of their own? In trying to answer this question I want to compare one suggested English prototype of English 'anger' with two possible schemas for Lohorung 'anger'. We can see where the two models differ. The following is the model suggested by (Lakoff and Kovecses 1987):

1. **Offending Event**

   Wrongdoer offends self
   Wrongdoer is at fault
   The offending event displeases self
   The intensity of the offence outweighs the intensity of the retribution (which equals zero at this point), thus creating an imbalance
   The offense causes anger to come into existence

2. **Anger**

   Anger exists
   Self experiences physiological effects (heat, pressure,agitation).
   Anger exerts force on the self to attempt an act of retribution

3. **Attempt to control anger**

   Self exerts a counterforce in an attempt to control anger.

4. **Loss of control**

   The intensity of anger goes above the limit.
   Anger takes control of self
   S. exhibits angry behaviour (loss of judgement, aggressive actions).
   There is damage to self
   There is danger to the target of anger, in this case, the wrongdoer.

5. **Retribution**

Self performs retributive act against wrongdoer (usually angry behavior)
The intensity of retribution balances the intensity of offensce.
The intensity of anger drops to zero.
Anger ceases to exist.

The Lohorung model is very similar to this but with crucial differences, the first difference being that in Lohorung, like in Chinese (King 1989 in Kövecses 1995), there are two prototypical models operating:[10]

1. Offending event/violation of rule
violation noticed and offends *niwa* or *saya* sensitive to tradition, and insults.
offending event arouses *niwa*, *som*, and *siri*.
imbalance in the body

2. Anger
Body experiences body changes; heart itches, *niwa* hurts, belly sour, face red,

3. Tension
Decision by *niwa* to control body (n.b. not for ancestors) or act responsibly against violation

4.Release anger
body lets go with behavior hitting, fighting, shouting, silence, not brewing beer.

5. *Niwa* no longer hurts
expression restores equilibrium

The other model differing in stage 4 and 5.

4. Diversion
anger diverted to various parts of the body
somatisation (headaches, ecstatic shaking, stomach aches etc.)

5. Compensation
Response to diversion from community and rituals compensates and balances offence.
Responsibility dispersed.

The significance of the Lohorung model is that I suggest it helps to explain both ecstatic illness discussed in Chapter Four and how Lohorung often understand illness as the anger of ancestors. Let me explain. First, the ancestors' anger is understood to work on the same model as that of the living but ancestors, as the ultimate respected beings, are not restricted in the expression of their anger. Control for them is not an issue. They are 'like children' and allowed to express their spontaneous emotions. The ancestral model would therefore jump from 2.Anger to 4.Loss of Control. However, the outlet for these beings obviously cannot be the physical contact of 'hitting' or verbal abuse. The force of the arousal[11], however, must be given an outlet. As guardians of tradition they are even more offended by violations than any living beings. But the second model indicates the solution. According to Lohorung understanding of anger the explosion can be diverted. For the living the diverted anger manifests itself in somatisation, which can take the form of ecstatic shaking. For the ancestors, the force of their anger is diverted to the living.

This brings me to my second point – how can the emotions of a person be diverted to give someone else bodily symptoms? According to Lohorung the anger of a living person can adhere to another's body. Without a 'bounded' body and with a more organic view of the 'person', the 'souls' that make up a person can, for example, move within the body and are not contained by it. *Lawa* can leave its host. Emotions, though contained in the body can also touch others. Anger, like the jealousy of witches, can produce bodily symptoms in someone else and its impact can be lethal. Witches, *boksi* (N) carry anger and jealousy. Though witches are never openly accused, it's general knowledge in any village who the *boksi* are, and people avoid them for fear of arousing their jealousy or anger. If aroused, they are said to give poison, *nas* (N) or they can poison with looks. This causes stomach-aches and smarting eyes; then nails fall off, teeth fall out, the skin goes yellow, and the body dries out. Even if a witch is considered to have brought misfortune, Lohorung react passively and without malice for as with the ancestors, boksi cannot help causing the harm they do.[12]

Anger adheres to people in other ways. It can also touch someone because, as you may remember, the vital aspect of a person, *saya*, is highly sensitive to expressions of anger in the form of insult or harsh words. A person's *saya* may fall if his or her mind (*niwa*) has been hurt or insulted. Unless a person's *saya* can be raised by one of the local officiants, whether *yatangpa* or *mangpa*, he or she will die. To be angry and to hurt someone else's *niwa* is not surprisingly classified as *phenni* 'wrong', even though, as we've seen, it is also expected and even encouraged in some circumstances. People say *niwa tukmipe chuma phenni* ('to hurt someone's *niwa* is wrong'). There is, however, an overtone in this – in the verb *chuma* – of 'to persist in hurting is wrong'. If the dispute is over and done with quickly and people make up, it is acceptable. If two people are fighting (angry with each other), someone else will say 'don't be angry with each other, stop hurting each other's *niwa*; to do that is wrong, *saya* will fall, make it up!' The danger of anger here lies then in how it affects *saya*, the vulnerable aspect of man: his achilles heel. There is a close relationship between *saya* and *niwa*, the former responding to the hurt mind. Since the impact of the anger can be lessened if the mind no longer hurts, institutionalized compensation is part of the remedy. After a quarrel home-brewed spirits are always given, since sharing the alcohol indicates that things are back the way they should be (see Sagant 1985: 187). Even if the *saya* of individuals can be raised, anger can leave long-lasting rifts between families, as, for example, between the families of the older and younger wives of Ram's uncle.

Let's now return to the ancestors. Every Lohorung knows about the sudden anger of the *sammang* ancestors. The logic of their anger and tantrums provides the Lohorung with a natural philosophy that explains all kinds of misfortune and sickness such as loss of appetite, acute pain in the 'heart, liver, kidney' (*lungma*) area, headaches, earaches, sweating, stomach aches, limb and chest aches, difficulty with breathing, shaking, cramp, sudden blindness or deafness, boils, paralysis, severe burns, or sudden blood from the nose or mouth. If someone suddenly runs off into the jungle, jumps into the river, or falls off a precipice, the house ancestor *khimpie sammang* must be angry. If people burn themselves or their house burns down, *khimpie* is angry. If people become 'mad' – that is, their *niwa* stops working properly – if they act in an antisocial manner, or if they suddenly cannot speak, it could be *khimpie* or the mischievous forest ancestor *chawatangma* who is angry. If someone feels giddy it is the anger of *chawatangma*. If the crops are not plentiful it could be that the *pappamamma'chi* are angry, or it could be that someone has promised *chawatangma* extra offerings and she is angry because they have failed to do so. As we have seen in Chapter Two the Lohorung spend much time and energy placating the endless anger of the ancestors.

The anger of *sammang* and the offerings made can only be understood if we conceive of the ancestral anger in the human terms we have discussed. Although the *sammang* have left the world of the living in one sense, in Lohorung thought they still live much as humans do and though in a different zone they are still interlinked with them in a unified cosmos. The anger of the ancestors is understood as the indication that something has to be repaired in the system of trust between living and non-living. The logic of their anger makes more sense in terms of this trust. The relationship is reciprocal. There is an expectation and a trust that the living will look after the society in the traditional way, that they will look after those who can no longer enjoy its produce by making the requisite offerings and will refrain from transgressions of behaviour, such as incorrect kinship behaviour. In return, the living expect protection from outside superhuman forces, and trust the *sammang* to respond when favours are requested and the appropriate offerings made. They expect to be able to negotiate with their ancestors, and communicate, through their priests and shamans. The expectations of each are based on the experience of generations. If a particular ancestor feels let down he expresses his anger by afflicting the humans with pain or misfortune until the humans have shown their reliability again with offerings. The ancestors are in control and never wrong; it's humans who are fallible, especially since they live in a world which includes non-Lohorung, full of modern attractions competing with the traditions of the ancestors.

Further reasoning behind the anger and tantrums of the ancestors lies in their particular temperaments and in the Lohorung understanding of a connection between hunger and anger. The ill-humour of ancestors is perceived at times to be related to their appetite, whether for food, attention, or obedience and indeed in almost all contexts the Lohorung may talk about the anger and the hunger of the ancestors interchangeably, as equivalent notions. When someone is ill people say 'X *sammang* ancestor is angry' or they may equally well say 'X *sammang* ancestor is hungry' (for example *chawatangma sagesi'boka*). This makes sense when we realize that for Lohorung the mind is principally physical, and mental states, such as anger, have their physical manifestations. Hunger of the ancestors, their strong physical desire for something, is understood as the physical aspect of their anger and their anger is associated with the mental aspect of their hunger. It also makes sense, therefore, that both their minds and their bodies must be satisfied before they can be pacified and that the only way they can be satisfied is with offerings of particular kinds of food and talk from the priest who offers words of reassurance.

The Lohorung notion of satiety is *sapthame* which they say means 'to have enough of what you want', that is, to have enough food and drink and clothes. When someone has had enough food or drink and is offered more, he or she says '*sabu, sabu*'. Nevertheless, he or she will then be pressed to have more; the way that the person says '*sabu, sabu*' and whether it is accompanied by a gesture of the hand covering the cup or plate usually conveys whether he or she really have had enough; if not, then the phrase '*chaibano, sapthanga eremo*' ('truly, I have really had enough') conveys that the individual is really satisfied. The term is connected to having enough food and drink and sometimes clothes, though for the Lohorung (as indeed for us) it is only with food and drink that one becomes fully satisfied with no room for more. With clothes, as with money or material objects, someone may well not be satisfied with what is offered: appetites for these are harder to measure. Accordingly, when the Lohorung offer food and drink to their ancestors to appease their anger they have a measure of what is needed. Given the values of the Lohorung, they know they must offer meat and millet beer to satisfy, just as they would offer to a respected guest. Chicken meat may be enough, but as we have seen in Chapter Two the appetites of the ancestors differ so that the specific offerings made to each vary according to their particular likes and dislikes. Offering food and drink to pacify the anger of the ancestors makes sense for two reasons: first, the anger is closely linked to hunger and secondly, the kind of feasts offered are more likely to truly satisfy than any other kind of offering. When the normal offerings do not satisfy and pacify the ancestor and the pain or sickness continues, it's clear to Lohorung that the anger has developed to a tantrum, the stage of the *yibok'kheda* anger (the anger of frustration) and the ancestor must be pampered with chickens and pigs to swing his or her mood. But just as children in a tantrum may not be satisfied with rice, sweet things, or the breast, so too the offerings to the ancestors may be a provocation to an increased tantrum: both 'know' with the kind of god-like intuition they both possess, just how much they can get, and if the offering is not adequate to the mood, it is rejected.

So, to summarize the main features of anger, we've seen that Lohorung understanding of this emotion is intimately bound up with their experience of the ancestors and their understanding of the body. They are embraced by a system of values dominated by the ancestors, and *saya*. But we can also see that anger and its outward manifestations are for Lohorung in some ways desirable, insofar as it provides opportunity for social control, education, and public expression of personal distress. Moreover, some say that individuals at times take advantage of *sammang* to express physically what they otherwise could not. Remember the mother of the girl who eloped – she was able to shake and bare her breasts and at last demonstrate the anger and frustrations she had kept to herself. She explained her condition as *sammang*. Others saw it as her anger and we have seen here how anger, if controlled, can be diverted to bodily symptoms. If she had been openly angry about her daughter, she might have received some, but not much, sympathy because 'officially' Lohorung say anger should not be felt for long. In contrast, her bodily symptoms brought her compensatory rituals and community support. In this way her anger did eventually disappear.

As a human emotion, anger is not considered to be something that must always be suppressed, nor something to be expressed in whatever way one feels like. The strong sense of justice and morality which acts to maintain the ideal co-operative and egalitarian nature of Lohorung society goes along with a ready anger to guard and enforce it. If people are not co-operative and socially minded, they will encounter the anger of those older than themselves. The adult form of anger is often socially desirable. Just as the ancestors are regarded as watching over the values, behaviour, and manners of those who perpetuate the society they originally created, and become angry with those who flout the rules, so too do living adults watch out for right and wrong behaviour and express their legitimate anger. Moreover, anger makes public the conflicts that may be related to one or a few households but which are inevitably relevant to the community as a whole. In general the Lohorung are good-natured and tolerant; anger has its place and its rules.

Fear

The word *kisime* which I glossed as 'fear' occurred daily in Lohorung conversation. The word was used in a kind of dyadic relationship with anger, to describe their feelings toward someone who is angry; it is an emotion term which was used to describe attitudes towards ancestors, elders, parents, and as a response to illness or troubles. The emotion term, however, needs to be understood in its varying contexts so that its meanings of 'respect', and 'feel in awe of'emerge as fully as that of 'fear'. Moreover, as might be expected there is no one noun in the Lohorung language to describe what we collectively classify as 'fear'. Instead, they use several verbs to describe the kinds of fear that need to be differentiated one from another.

The verbs *yangsime* and *nisasilime* cover very specific situations. *Yangsime* is used to describe what someone feels when confronted by a precipice, a sharp cliff, a narrow path looking down into a deep valley below, or the sensations of the *rotiping* – a small, wooden version of a fairground Ferris-wheel, put up locally all over Nepal on certain national holidays. As I watched the seats whirl around, several of my companions explained their look of horror when I suggested a ride: *yangsima'lu* (you feel *yangsime*), they said, *abui! saro lungma tuk tuk khe* ('oh! no, it makes the heart/liver go "tuk tuk"') and some thumped on their chests with a clenched fist. *Yangsime* seemed to produce the main symptom of a thumping heart, and was sometimes accompanied by dizziness, feeling faint, or feeling hot and cold. But the word cannot be translated as 'vertigo', as might be indicated by these situations and symptoms, since it is also used to refer to experiences of extreme cold. For Lohorung, however, extreme cold is generally experienced in higher altitutes, where indeed the symptom of a thumping heart is common as it is with fear. Thus, *yangsime* seemed to have three components: being high up, and being cold, and having a thumping heart. Lohorung do not have much experience of extreme cold or very high altitude, since they mostly live in the middle hills of Nepal in a relatively mild climate. On journeys, however, or when shepherding the sheep and goats on the upper pasture-land, they do face bitter cold, snow, ice, and wind as well as the narrow paths, sheer cliffs, deep valleys, and dizzy heights. It is with this environment that the *yangsime* fear is associated. *Yangsime* expresses fear that is immediately felt physically; the fear that starts what Lohorung call the lungma, the liver/heart thumping.

The verb nisasilime is like yangsime but refers to the feeling that is experienced when water is involved, such as when crossing deep rivers. I first encountered the word as part of the explanation for why the Lohorung do not marry those Rai who live to the West of the swirling waters of the river Arun, a river which is crossed by what is called a 'twin'. This is a bamboo basket tied to a steel cable, securely attached to both sides of the river. A person sits in the basket and races to the centre of the rope with the force of his own weight, and then has to pull himself and the basket to the other side. Since the Lohorung do not swim and since the spirits of those people who regularly drown in these rivers haunt them, it is not surprising that these large rivers present a formidable problem for them. The 'river spirits', *hongma chap*, make the body shiver and cold if they attack. These spirits are yet another reason for *nisasilime* – a word we can perhaps gloss as 'fearing the water'.

Turning now to the more general term *kisime*, the situations which provoke this emotion cluster around the following:

- at night
- when alone
- in the forest
- when far away from home
- when someone has died and the rites for the dead have not yet been performed

- when confronted by leopards, bears, monkeys
- when surprised by water buffalo, sheep, or jackals at nigh
- when seeing somebody like an elder brother, in the company of elders
- when work has not been done well and you have to face father
- when people are fighting and quarreling
- when a dog gets angry and goes mad
- when someone comes home from market drunk and acts like a madman (*ngaksubang*) or drunk and acts as if he might hit you
- when passing the house of a witch (*boksi*)
- after certain dreams which indicate someone in the family will die
- when the crops have been planted and still the rains don't come
- a little bit when *apa*, father, comes from work
- in many rituals concerning the ancestors
- in marriage talks
- also when we go to our in-laws
- when you first see the man you are going to marry

From situations such as these, it's clear that *kisime* has a range of reference which covers our notions of 'awe', 'panic' or 'terror', 'fear', and 'respect'. It could also be said that the Lohorung conception of 'respect' incorporates more 'fear' than ours does. When the Lohorung talk of situations in which *kisime* comes close to our 'respect', such as visiting in-laws, there is an element of dread as well as esteem. The Lohorung talk of 'having to *kisime*', *kisimale* (gloss 'having to respect') when in the presence of in-laws, but they also talk of how severely they feel *kisime 'saro kisimalu'*, (gloss 'how intensely I feel fear') after someone has died or when with in-laws, so much so that most men go out of their way to avoid meetings. The *kisime* women talk about feeling for their husbands has a strong sense of 'fear' in the first few years and it then becomes closer to our 'respect' as the couple grow older. This initial emotion, close to our 'fear', is expressed in the intransitive form of the verb *kisime*. The later 'respect' meaning is expressed in the imperative form of the verb. The semantic range seems valid since the Lohorung consider some situations should be avoided if at all possible, because they might even encourage the *lawa* of a person to leave.

After death when new *chap*, 'spirits of the dead', join others to eat and drink and are called to the house, the Lohorung say: 'we should be quiet and musn't be frightened or we ourselves will die. If someone calls you in the night at this time you mustn't answer: it's very frightening (*saro kisimalu*) but if you show your fear you will die'.The risk is that the person might be 'startled', so that risk is that the person's *lawa*, 'soul', will be frightened and may leave his or her body causing death unless the *yatangpa* can find it and return it.

By contrast, *kisime* is socially required in other situations; either the person should *kisime* or *niwa* (gloss 'mind') should *kisime*. Without appreciating the 'respect' aspect of the verb *kisime*, one might have concluded that *kisime* was a physiological term, and that, for example, the Lohorung felt considerable physiological fear of their elders and ancestors. It became clear, however, that Lohorung do not make the mind/body division and the term referred as much to a mental state that should accompany certain contexts. In such contexts *kisime* is often linked to the influence of *niwa* (gloss 'mind'); insofar as *niwa* involves the development of sensibility, knowing the correct feelings for people and when they may be expressed, it is intimately bound up with this aspect of *kisime*. The Lohorung often talk of *niwa kisik* meaning the 'awe' or 'respect' due to elders and ancestors. They make statements like, 'Everybody fears the father-in-law; nobody dares to disobey him. He gets what he wants.' It would be misleading, however, to say that the Lohorung go constantly in 'fear' of their elders, ancestors, and the recently dead. Yet at times they clearly do 'fear' them, in ways that were surprising to me at first.

On many occasions I was taken aback by the behaviour of Lohorung companions. Their behaviour was often eventually explained in terms of their fear of the spiritual and ancestral world. I soon learned that no one goes out and about alone anywhere near the outskirts of the village after dark when the spiritual world is especially active, and most people avoid it altogether. On one occasion I had to go with Nanda to the other end of the village at night, as she had to go urgently up to the blind man's house which is on the outskirts of the upper part of the village on the far side of a small wood. She needed someone to go with her: women never walk alone outside of the village and particularly not at night. I thought her fear was to do with fear of the dark. As we climbed our way up through the village I realized her fear had more to do with the spirits of the dead. She picked some *titepāti* leaves and tucked them under her long cloth cummerbund. She told me to tuck some under my belt. We had to pass the ridge where some of the dead are buried and she grasped my hand. She pointed out the place where Chok Sing's grandmother had been buried but clearly wanted to hurry away. The 'spirit' of Chok Sing's grandmother had been tormenting the family with cramps and stomach-aches, even though they thought they had given her drowned body a good burial. On the *mangpa*, shaman's, advice a few weeks ago they dug up her grave on the ridge. Everything had rotted away except for one shin bone. They threw that bone in the river Arun and so far there have been no more aches. Nanda didn't want to talk about it. She dipped her finger into the pot of beer we had taken with us and flicked some drops in all directions for the *chap* who might try to attach themselves to us, and said *khema-yo, kisimalu* ('come on, let's go, it's frightening').

From this it would be misleading to imply that the Lohorung have a psychic disposition similar to that of the Tibetans characterized by Tucci as being in 'a permanent state of anxious uneasiness' (1980: 173). 'Every physical or spiritual disturbance', he explains, 'each illness, every uncertain or threatening situation leads him to embark upon a feverish search for the cause of the event and the appropriate means to ward it off' (ibid: 173).

Lohorung fear is more occasion-bound and their disposition more relaxed. The Lohorung are afraid at times of illness, the dark, death, and the most unpredictable and uncontrollable elements of the superhuman world, yet I could never describe their search for causes as being 'feverish'. They readily consult their local priests or shamans and have great faith in their analyses and prognoses. If an illness is particularly intractable they also seek out *bijuwa* or *ojah*, the Nepali healers. Lohorung also talk about having less to fear than their other Nepali neighbours who have to contend with the anger of the Lohorung superhuman world, without the extra protection of *sammang* ancestors or officiants who know how to deal with them. Moreover, they have strategies for coping with fear and they may avoid especially threatening situations by altering their plans. Like Nanda, for example, they perform actions, such as stuffing *titepāti* into waistbands to ward off frightening spirits. If they have to walk at night outside the village they carry flaming bamboo torches, which they say lights the way and keeps away the evil spirits of the dead. Women are almost always in groups if out late and they invariably make a lot of noise singing, laughing, and shouting to each other. 'If we sing and laugh, a little bit, we do not fear.' Very often, of course, the Lohorung are in situations where they cannot sing and shout. They cannot do this, for example, in the frightening moments in *nuagi* or 'when someone calls out to you in the night and you mustn't answer: if you answer you may die'. Some frightening situations are also too protracted for such measures. After the death of someone in the village, the spirit of the person, *chap*, is allowed to roam freely for two nights before it is attracted once more to the house with offerings, and then given entreaties to leave forever and find peace with the other well-integrated dead. Children are so afraid during this period that many of them refuse to sleep for fear of the spirit of the dead person. Moreover, none of the children and many adults refuse to go out in the dark alone, even within the village. Every cry of a jackal, every stone which trips them or the creak of a wooden post, any unexpected sound is the dead person's *chap*.

These frightening invasions into everyday life are hard for many of us to imagine. Nevertheless, I did not receive the impression that the Lohorung were in constant fear. We have to remember that, as we saw in Chapter Four, there is trust in the relationship with ancestors as well as fear, and as we can see from the contexts of what they say and their behaviour there is also considerable respect.

The Lohorung Concept Ngesime

The Lohorung concept of *kisime* can be glossed as 'fear' and also as 'respect tinged with fear'. Here, we shall see how it has a 'family resemblance' to the emotion ngesime, a verb with a meaning much like our 'sense of shame', which the *Concise Oxford Dictionary* defines as 'feeling of humiliation excited by consciousness of guilt or shortcoming, of having made oneself or been made ridiculous, or of having offended against propriety, modesty or decency'. It is close too to 'being shame-faced' or 'feeling shy or embarrassed'. There is a strong social expectation of *ngesime* and *kisime* in certain circumstances that induces respect and culturally acceptable behaviour. The concepts are both expressions of the Lohorung philosophy of life which is characterized by the domination of the ancestors, *pe-lam*, and *saya*.

Ngesime, in one sense, is a less severe form of *kisime*: both express the Lohorung principle that in relationships age deserves respect and deference. So, for example, one feels *kisime* (respect tinged with awe) in the presence of a father's elder brother but *ngesime* (shy, modest respect) with a wife's brother and a husband's mother. Nanda, for example, when talking about her life history talks of the arrival of her husband's marriage 'party' and the gathering of relatives who arrived all at once. She expressed confusion about what emotion she was feeling in the face of these relatives, 'Was I afraid (*kisingnge*) or was I feeling shy (*ngesingnge*)? I don't know. I felt afraid and then shy and then afraid. In the end, I was crying. And they asked me if I was not ashamed (*ngesinanihe*) to cry'. The Lohorung recognize that the emotion *ngesime* is one which is innate and yet one which can and must also be developed for behaviour to be culturally acceptable.

To understand the meaning of *ngesime* let us look at some of the situations in which the word is used. You are expected to feel *ngesime*:

- with new people or people not seen for a long time
- at Dasain (the Hindu festival): when you have to go to other people's houses
- at a home you don't know as a guest, especially if you're required to eat or do something
- with some relatives: with father, with uncle, with *dema* (Father's elder brother's wife) and *sima* (Fyb's W);with wife's brothers.
- when arriving home at the same time as your husband.
- if you're wearing old and ragged clothes and you meet someone from another village
- when you go to shit or piss and someone sees you; you both feel *ngesime*.
- if you shit on the path you feel *ngesime* because you don't know where to look
- if you're naked and someone sees you
- if you don't work properly and people tell you off
- if you're no good, if you've done wrong, especially with those who are good, and important.
- if you steal and friends ask why you steal
- if others talk with knowledge and you have nothing to say and you feel stupid

From these situations, we can see that the meaning of *ngesime* is close to our 'shy', 'ashamed', 'sense of shame', 'sense of modesty', 'loss of face', 'embarrassment' although with one main difference – they treat impropriety as being as important as guilt. They also stress the awkwardness that goes with the emotion for us, reflected in gestures such as putting up the scarf to hide part of one's face, looking at the ground, shuffling feet, hanging the head low, having restless eyes and body, and not knowing where to look or what to do.

There is a moral component to *ngesime* as there is in 'shame'. Just as children learn to listen to their *niwa* so they have to learn *ngesime*. Some of the prescribed aspects of the emotion became clear in this incident. The mother of Lumpe *mangpa* (shaman) and her new daughter-in-law are quarreling. It was not an arranged marriage: Lumpe used to meet her at the market in Khandbari on Saturdays. She is from Diding. They used to stay out all night together and had a sexual relationship. Now she has come to Pangma to his home. But he has gone now to Daran (military camp) and will maybe go to India for two to three years. Mother and daughter-in-law have been quarreling more and more. On Saturday the girl went to market and returned late to the house with her own mother. Mamma, her mother-in-law, had as usual prepared rice for only four people and by the time the daughter-in-law returned they had all eaten leaving only a little for her. When the girl and her mother arrived she told her mamma that a guest had arrived. When she found out there wasn't enough rice for her mother she was insolent, 'What! You, you are worthless; aren't you ashamed (*ngesnanie?*) Here is a guest and there is no rice for her'. The insolence irritated the old lady especially when the girl continued to show no respect. Her lack of respect and lack of shame (*ngesime*) was shown by the fact that she never offered to sweep if the older woman was sweeping, nor offered to carry water if the older woman started to go for water, and in general did as little work about the house as possible. Yesterday mamma was grinding maize. There was no offer of help from her daughter-in-law. Later on mamma returned to do some more grinding and the girl commented, 'oh! there is some maize to grind is there!' and she sat and watched. Mamma, apparently, became like a ripe bean in the face and exploded, 'You got your teeth into my son's shirt tails, you *mujinina*! ('woman who is sexually enjoyed',: i.e. you took my son by sexual skill). You misled my son and cheated us. You are long in the tooth so you came on your own account. Now you do no work at all. You have no sense of shame, modesty' (*ane ngesinanie?*).

This episode speaks for itself, but how should we understand the suggestion that one feels *ngesime* 'with certain categories of kin' and 'when you arrive home at the same time as your husband'. In terms of classificatory relationships, there is a range of expected attitudes or feelings stretching from 'fear' (*kisime*), and 'deference' (*ngesime*) at one end to 'teasing' and 'joking' (*sechame*) at the other. At the easy and relaxed end, men and women tease each other and joke about sex and excreta, sometimes mildly, sometimes in the most bawdy and provocative way. As the relationships move away from this pole such topics become watered down until they reach the other pole where any such topic would be forbidden and avoided at all costs and any mention or hint of sex or bodily functions would provoke *ngesime*, 'embarrassment' or 'sense of shame'. Guiding these attitudes are two principles – first that age has a higher social position than youth and should therefore receive respect and deference; and secondly, that any woman who is a possible potential spouse can be teased and treated unceremoniously. We can see this clearly in the following, which gives examples of those females a man feels relaxed with and can tease and those with whom he feels *ngesime*.

ngesime	**relaxed**
Sister, classificatory 'sisters' (own generation)	Brother's wife's sister, sister's husband's sister
Wife's elder sisters	Wife's younger sister
Younger brother's wife	Elder brother's wife
Mother's elder sisters	Mother's younger sister
Father's elder brother's wife	Father's younger brother's wife
Mother's elder brother's wife	Mother's younger brother's wife
Father's elder sisters	Father's younger sisters

(For kinship chart and terminology, see Appendix 2).

A man especially feels *ngesime*, respectful restraint, deferential and polite with women older than his mother and father, who are all classified as *dema*, and with affines who are older and not potential wives. With his wife's elder sister, *nanama*, he must *ngesime*; she must have been married before her younger sister and thus belongs to another man's clan. A man's younger brother's wife is classified as being like a son's wife, *nammi*, or a brother's son's wife, also *nammi*, and is thus sexually taboo and she like her husband's elder brother will *ngesime* when together. In contrast, a man has no restraints on his relationship with his wife's younger sister, *ngetengma*, a possible second wife, and can be sexually flirtatious with her. Indeed, with all affines in the same generation who are potential spouses there is a particularly easy relationship and the opposite of *ngesime* is almost expected. Both parties may be cheeky and joke without restraint.

The second incomprehensible case mentioned above is that of feeling *ngesime* 'if you arrive at home at the same time as your husband'. This makes sense if we understand the Lohorung's attitude to sex and relations between married couples. Young couples who are unmarried are free and easy. Though careful not to imply actual sexual relations, they freely refer to or imply sex quite openly in bawdy jokes and songs. However, once a couple has married and are actively involved in a sexual relationship, they begin to *ngesime* in relation with each other when alone and in the way they treat their spouse in the company of others. There is a general rule that any man or woman, boy or girl who is involved in sexual relations must *ngesime* (show modesty and shyness) in their relationship to the rest of society, and to each other. They should never flaunt their relationship. So, those newly married avoid each other in public, including within the home. They do not sit together. The aim is to make sure that they are not found out, exposed, in any position or proximity which might have sexual connotations. If they were found near each other or indeed found in the act they would 'feel very much shame, and shyness', *saro ngesima lu*. It should be said, however, that any feelings of 'guilt', married or not, would not be felt, for there is no moral disgrace in discreet sexual relations whereas, for example, there is for stealing.

Newars have a term similar to *ngesime*, namely *lajyā*. 'Being a moral person means regulating the self through *sensitivity* to the emotion *lajyā*. Self-control requires the capacity to experience *lajyā* (Parish 1991: 324). As with Lohorung so too among the Newar to have *ngesime/lajyā* means to behave in the correct fashion.

If women arrived empty-handed, people would say,'Why send her empty-handed? It seems this woman has no shame, look she has really come empty-handed!' or they would say, 'walking about without a *huksok* gift: she has no nose and no shame'.[13] When visiting her natal home a woman must carry enough for the main parental home and for the house of each brother who has split off. If a woman doesn't take to the brother's houses as well as to the parental house, the wives will comment: *kho ngesini*? ('has she no shame?').

Although it is incumbent on a woman to bring *huksok* when she visits, it would be shameful (*ngesima lu*) if the mother or father asked their daughter for substantial gifts – say of money or rice – however rich her husband is. As wife-givers a woman's parents have the right to ask both their daughter and their son-in-law to work for them in the initial period of the marriage, but to ask them for money or rice would be seen as wrong and 'big-headed' or vain, inflating the imbalance in the relationship between the two families. When a woman asked her daughter from Gairi Pangma for rice, for example, people from her mother's village said they felt ashamed (*ngesima lusa*). One woman said, 'That narcissistic woman, she takes away everything that is her own child's (*um pasamim chopno sabitu*), has she no shame (*ngesini*) narcissistic woman?! We affines (in-laws) should be shy to go to our son-in-law's home.' Since most marriages are within the locality and with clans that continue a pattern of exchanging women, it would also be counter- productive for any one family to overplay their advantage as a wife-giver: they are more likely to find a wife for their son if they too show modesty (*ngesime*). And to show their modesty, recipients of *huksok* gifts always offer some small gift of food or drink for the woman to carry back to her husband's home. To follow *ngesime* is to behave in the proper way.

We can see how important it is that girls and boys learn to *ngesime*. In particular, the Lohorung say, girls must be taught to *ngesime* so that they obey and marry the boys they are told to marry. Boys are given more choice in part because it is their nature to *ngesime* less and to assert themselves more. Some children are recognized as being especially 'shy' by nature (they *ngesime* a lot) which is said to be the gods within them, while some have almost none by nature and have to be encouraged and taught.

'Love' and 'Happiness'

I have looked at some of the more fundamental elements of Lohorung emotion theory, such as their concepts of 'fear', 'anger', and *ngesime*. I look now briefly at how the Lohorung conceive of the emotions 'love' and 'happiness', concepts for which, at first, I thought Lohorung had no direct equivalence. When given the Nepali terms *maya* 'love', *khushi* 'happy' or 'happiness', and *bekhushi* 'sad' or 'sadness', my informants found it hard to find Lohorung parallels.[14]

The Lohorung language has no abstract word for 'love' or the Nepali *maya*. Only the Nepali word *maya* can be used to describe 'romantic love' and the romantic form of marriage, 'love marriage', which is contrasted to the traditional form described as 'capturing by hand and foot' (*lang huk tukmale*). Yet, there are numerous examples to show that the Lohorung fully recognize the emotion maya or 'romantic love': for example, in the way kanchi talked about her feelings for her husband's younger brother or Ritu's love for a married man which led to her elopement and parental disfavour. Moreover, Lohorung have ways in which they can express emotions similar to 'romantic love' such as, *ettano nen'chakung* 'I like very much', *namnam pisikung, mi'chakung*, 'all day long I want to give, I (literally) eat the distance', 'I feel for him'. Often the emotion is expressed metaphorically, and includes images of 'heart hurting' or 'giving'. There is also an old word lung'chame meaning 'to like', the opposite of 'to dislike something'. It has a modern equivalent, *nen'chame*, again meaning 'to like, enjoy something or someone', but it has no sexual or passionate connotations. The *lung* of the old word refers to the *lungma* 'heart and liver' (organs they do not separate in emotional terms) and which is still an organ conceived as being an organ affected by emotions: for example parents, when they lose a daughter in marriage, say they feel they are losing their 'heart and liver' and their *lungma* hurts.

The emotion expressed by *maya* or 'love' has only recently been given emphasis. Within the Lohorung's own indigenous concepts all the terms near to our notion 'love' have components of 'compassion', 'pity', and 'affection' or 'nostalgia' rather than the sexual attachment and passion that the terms 'love' and *maya* evoke. For the Lohorung it is not 'romantic love' but 'compassion' and 'nostalgia' that are the important emotions. These are the emotions emphasized by their cultural institutions and everyday attitudes. Certainly the traditional lifestyle has little room for romantic love. Arranged marriages in which the couple barely know each other is the expected beginning of stable relationships betwen men and women. The prevalence of love marriages, *maya biha*, is said to be new. Traditional 'theft' marriages offered a similar escape. The culture allows teasing, laughing, and bawdy relations among the young which must always have produced couples who fell in 'love'. Such relationships, however, though accepted, are not viewed in a positive way. 'Cultures differ in the way they encourage or discourage the expression of romantic passion . . . [in some] it is tolerated but not celebrated or asserted' (Jankowiak 1995: 17). Traditionally a Lohorung daughter must marry the husband chosen by her parents and she should stay with him. Officially, this is what parents still want for their children. However, I have heard two fathers talk in favour of love marriage. They knew it was time their daughters married, but did not have what they considered to be a sufficient crop to support the correct kind of wedding. They talked as if they hoped their daughters would 'fall in love' and elope. After Minnu's elopement too, some of the older women made no critical comments. My neighbour said, 'Why so much fuss? Many people do it these days. If she does it herself, if it goes wrong she has only herself to blame'.

On one of my trips away from the village a European couple, hoping to meet me in the field, arrived in Pangma and stayed in my house for two or three nights. On my return my next-door neighbour asked me with some curiosity and disapproval about the couple, the kind of people they were and whether they were in general 'worthless', (*phenni*), 'lacking in modesty' 'no shame' (*ngesikmini*). She joked and nudged; she was shy (*ngesima lusa*) about raising the topic. She talked quietly so others could not hear, and told me about the loudness and openness of their sexual behaviour and the lack of 'modesty' (*ngesime*) they showed in the way they related to each other in public. How could they be always entwined in each others bodies? Was this normal? Did they have no shame (*ngesime*)? Was this behaviour allowed in my country?

Romantic love as we know it in the West goes along with overt physical contact, often flamboyant sexuality. In contrast, the Lohorung are traditionally restrained in their gestures. Lohorung adults do not kiss for example. Kissing is restricted to small pecks on the heads of children. This fits with what we have seen in the previous section about the modesty of sexual couples.

Traditionally, therefore, Lohorung culture emphasizes that a woman should subdue feelings of romantic love: whereas 'sadness' (*som-chai-khenga*) is accepted as part of life's pain (*dukha*), 'love' (*maya*) is disruptive. Indeed, for the Lohorung *maya* is something that cattle share with human beings, while only human beings feel what in Nepali is called *daya*, that is 'compassion', 'kindness', 'charity', and 'pity'. Cattle live only for themselves, whereas humans have the emotion which attaches them to others, that is 'pity', 'compassion', 'wanting to give'. It is this mental state – expressed by the Lohorung in such notions as *mi-chame* and *som-tukme* – which is important in their culture, not the 'love' which our own culture cultivates and which the Lohorung subdue.[15]

The 'love' that the Lohorung emphasize is the feeling of affection and concern for loved ones who are sick or for those from whom they are separated either through death or marriage. It is this compassionate, kind 'love' which we see in their ritual dealing with the ancestors and the spirits of the dead, such as in the care to feed them with the food and drink they especially like. Giving to ancestors is to show devotion to treat them with affectionate regard. It is this 'love' which we also see in the treatment of out-married sisters, the gifts given at her final marriage rite, (L. *sangsawa*) and the gifts given by her brothers to her sons 'because she cannot inherit the immovable goods and they (the brothers) can'. The Lohorung love for their children and for siblings, in particular brothers to their sisters and sisters for other sisters is most typically expressed by gifts; giving food and drink is the Lohorung way of showing affection. I am reminded of the caritas kind of 'love' in the new testament: that is, love for people in general rather than for a specific individual. 'Romantic love' is seen as a possible destructive force, though one that is structurally crucial for the society. As we have seen in Chapter Five, the structure of Lohorung society needs either a marriage by capture or a 'love marriage' to 'break the bones' and divide up a clan into two, so that marriage within the clan can take place. Nevertheless, *maya* 'love', though sometimes convenient, is not valued.

The two concepts which express this 'compassionate love' are *mi'chame* and *som'tukme*. Both could be glossed as 'love and compassion' or 'love and sadness'; *mi'chame*, however, is felt for someone who is far away and som'tukme for those who are near. *Mi'chame* is used to describe the emotion felt for a child who has died for example, or the emotion a woman feels when she thinks of her mother and father and siblings when she has left them to live with her husband; the feeling too a young girl may feel for a boy who has left the village to join the army or to make a trip to Assam or the Terai. The term is often used with *niwa* (mind) as if the mind is working in the distance, much as it does for us in what we call 'homesickness'. The term *som'tukme* 'heart-hurting' is used to express the feelings for people who are close, for one's child who is sick, for one's grandchildren who have just been orphaned, for someone, a relative perhaps, who has just travelled a long way, for anyone who needs help or kindness. *Mi'chame* or *som'tukme*, emphasized by the Lohorung, are part of the Lohorung moral ideal that people should have 'compassionate love'.

'Happiness' for most Lohorung has largely to do with the external state of things and one's proximity to other people. The Lohorung term which seems most close is *chenchame* (literally 'to eat strength') 'to like, be pleased'. Asked when they felt *chenchame*, children aged between five and fourteen pinpointed these events: *chenchame* happens when

- you see or are given good things to eat or wear, when you get gifts of clothes from the bazaar; at Tihar or Desain when you get good things to eat; if I can drink milk
- children cry and then their mothers come and they *chenchame*
- when other people have done all your work for you; when we've finished work and can go and play; when they're able to play; when people go to the local bazaar • if you own a lot of cattle, chickens, pigeons, ducks, and fields; when people get rich; if someone gives you a lot of money.

FIG 15 *Mangmani* and her granddaughter.

Adults described *chenchame* in much the same terms. Thus 'happiness' has to do with nice clothes to wear, good food to eat, being rich, having no work to do and therefore time to go to the bazaar with friends, drink and eat with them and sing songs. From these definitions the term *chenchame* has a similar semantic range to 'happy', which to us conveys ideas of being 'lucky', 'fortunate', 'content', and 'glad'.

One woman defined the term *chenchame* as being similar to the term saptanga meaning 'to have enough': to have enough food or clothes to get by on, that is 'to suffice', but she said 'you use *chenchame* when you have a bit more, when you have nice food or nice things, something good *kamnuk* happening to you'. As we might do, the Lohorung define 'happiness' in terms of the situations that elicit it. We might in addition refer to some subjective, physiological state that accompanies it. For the Lohorung 'happiness' is related to a condition of *niwa* that is then reflected in the face: 'he is happy in his *niwa*, I know it in his face' (*niwa-bi chenchak, ngachik-bi letukung*).

Happiness' also has to do with being near other people. This became more clear to me when I talked to the Lohorung about 'unhappiness'. Being too far from other people is frightening and makes people unhappy. One man talked to me about how 'unhappy' (*kamnuro minukmini*) he was as a child, having to look after the goats and sheep in the hills and often quite alone. Usually Lohorung children who do this work go off in groups. Lohorung too find it hard to understand how some of the other Khambu Rai groups live in stretched-out villages with fields in between the houses. They said they would be 'frightened' and 'unhappy' to live like that. When I talked to women about where they would like their daughters to live when married, many mentioned the area of Pangma for the reason that it has five dense villages all close together and close to the bazaar. Going to the bazaar makes people happy because they can meet and be with other people, as well as because on market day they can eat and drink well, and possibly buy new clothes. The Lohorung always walk in groups and find walking alone, as I sometimes did, very strange.

The opposite of 'happiness' for the Lohorung is *dukha*, Nepali for 'trouble', 'sorrow', 'pain' or *som'chai'khenga*, their own word for 'pity, compassion, sorrow', as well as their expression for 'unhappiness' or 'sadness', which they express as 'not to feel good', *kamnuro minukmini*. Extreme grief, rather than sadness, can be an unnatural emotion not accepted as being part of the person but dissasociated from the person and seen as an angry ancestor, as in the case of Rituama, the woman who shook as if possessed after her daughter eloped with a married man. 'Sadness' for the Lohorung, as for us, can be regrets or deep stirrings; for them as for us it also involves a lack, linked with sorrow, grief, and not feeling good.[16] The cause of it could be the loss of the company of a person or the lack of desired clothing.[17]

Since Lohorung notions of happiness and sadness express the pain of privation and the pleasures of gain they also highlight certain cultural features of Lohorung society. On the one hand, the prevalence of death, illness, poverty, and the lack of interesting food was portrayed in the notion of 'sadness'; and on the other hand, the delight of anything to vary the boring staple diet of rice, maize, millet, and lentils, and the pleasure of the company of others, songs, and something new to wear was vividly clear in their understanding of 'happiness'.

Saya Pokme, 'Raise *Saya*'

I have been looking at Lohorung concepts that are distinctly emotion terms. They clearly relate to individual emotions. I now discuss the concept of *saya* which is a more general concept, more complex and pervasive than the individual emotions I have been discussing so far.

As we've already seen, the Lohorung word *saya* is not easy to translate. It could be glossed as 'soul' to convey its metaphysical aspect. *Saya*, however is more than a 'soul ' and one Lohorung trying to explain it said *saya* comes from the 'soul' (he used the word *hangsa*)

Saya endows everyone, and some more than others, with a vitality and a 'power', almost like a magical energy. It can be powerful or weak. The words used to describe it are 'small', 'fierce', 'hard', 'strong', 'limp, bending', 'weak, fragile', or 'skillful'. The power of *saya* derives from its link with the ancestral past, and ancestral traditions, conventions, and sacred words. It is like an ancestral spirit or a powerful principle infusing all persons and some natural and material objects with an energy. It has a psycho-physical impact on an individual that is as forceful as the Freudian notion of id, or the Greek idea of destiny, for unless a person's *saya* is flourishing he or she loses all vitality and all will to live. *Saya*, they say, 'is our *bung*', which means that *saya* is our 'essence, fertility, life-force, lifeblood'.

Saya is also 'power' in the sense of resistance to misfortune and disease, an inner strength (*chen chen*) and an inner resource to face the world with head held high, deriving from and depending upon good relations with the ancestors. Raising *saya* (*saya pokme*) has to do with reaffirming this power and returning a person to his or her ideal emotional and moral state. The beliefs to do with returning the strength of *saya* are complex. The inner state seems to be concentrated in the head, for it is the head that the *yatangpa* concentrates on in the rituals to raise *saya* and the Lohorung describe it as situated 'in the head'. The Nepali equivalent, *sir uthaunu*, translates literally as 'to raise the head'. The head itself is associated with the whole person as the main locus of *niwa* and therefore of consciousness, knowledge, and memory, and also of disturbance in madness. If *saya* occupies a high position, then ancestral powers are strong within the body. If *saya* falls, a man or any member of his family is liable to become weak, apathetic, unsociable and may fall ill. It is as if *saya* were an ancestral consciousness, or as we might put it an unconscious realization of relations with the ancestors. If our ancestral consciousness is strong, then we can be confident, strong, and assertive. We are well-grounded. In the West we think of self-confidence, high self-esteem as coming from our 'selves': the Lohorung conceive of if it as coming from a high *saya* – that is, from a good relationship with the ancestral world. *Saya* is also a person's vulnerability, for if it is 'small' it may fall, or even if strong, harsh criticism or insult from another person can make it fall. If it falls, the typical symptoms are depression and the inability to resist fatigue or attack from enemies. The person whose *saya* is low has no wish for companionship: he or she withdraws from as many social activities as possible. Moreover, such a person's body becomes an inhospitable site for the essence or breath of life, namely the *lawa* 'wandering spirit or soul'. The person whose *saya* has fallen and whose *lawa* has found another resting place in the natural environment will die unless the *saya* is raised and the *lawa* returned. It is clear that the 'high' and the 'low' refer to attitude as much as location.

The notion that the position and state of a person's *saya* can be the indication of his or her psychological and physiological health can be further illuminated by the Lohorung concrete metaphorical descriptions of *saya*. For example, the conditions of a person's *saya* is often conceived of in term of the flower that represents that person in the world of the ancestors. A person whose *saya* is high is represented by a blooming flower. The flower representing one whose *saya* has fallen is wilting and drooping.

From these descriptions of *saya* a 'low *saya*' could perhaps be called depression. Depressive illness can after all take culturally distinct forms (Kleinman and Good 1986: 6). This translation is, however, misleading for three reasons. In the first place, whereas the fallen *saya* or 'low' *saya* is the opposite of 'high' *saya*, the one bad and the other good, 'depression' in English is not usually thought of as having a polar opposite. Our notion of 'depression' is a state of aberration from the normally expected psychological condition which requires no active effort to maintain it. *Saya*, on the other hand, is in constant need of attention, revitalization, and lifting: all Lohorung indigenous rites act to raise *saya* (*saya pokme*) and, as we saw in Chapter Six, *saya* is specifically renewed and revitalized in the special acts performed at *nuagi*. The ideal moral and emotional state of every Lohorung individual has to be annually restored in these rites, as though everyone becomes a little emotionally and morally run down over the year.

As a second objection, whereas depression is the responsibility of the individual, low *saya* is as much the reponsibility of the ancestors as of the individual. This emphasis on the role of the ancestors detracts from the idea of low *saya* as a mental state. From the description of the state of the person as a result of low *saya* (such as lassitude, unsociability) it sounds to us like an internal state. But for the Lohorung the power of *saya* is as much outside the person as inside and to raise it the ritual has to deal with the superhuman forces involved as well as the living ones. For the Lohorung the person is thus distanced from responsibility for the emotion.

This brings me to my third hesitation in translating low *saya* as depression. *Saya* as a potential source of feelings such as melancholy, lethargy, hopelessness, hurt pride, and inadequacy is certainly similar to our notion of depression. Yet, for us the condition is mainly psychological (though also often manifesting physical symptoms), whereas a 'low' *saya* for the Lohorung is inevitably linked with a person's material state of affairs. We can be depressed and prosperous; Lohorung find it hard to conceive of this. For them, high spirits, health, and prosperity are almost inevitably connected, and so are low spirits, illness, and financial hardship. With the one concept of *saya* the Lohorung can express the state of a person's health, fortune, and relations with the ancestors.

How *Saya* Falls

The high *saya* is related to the natural order of things which is good and strong and connected to the way things originated – that is, with the ideal ancestral past. *Saya* is known to fall when the ancestors, either those upholding the ancestral traditions or personal ancestors, are insulted or when *niwa tuguk* 'mind hurts'. This happens when respect is not given, when the traditional order or morality is flouted, in situations of severe grief or feeling insulted, such as when someone runs off with one's own daughter. The following are some examples of situations which make *saya* fall, given by some Lohorung children aged between six and fourteen:

- if older people tell you off, or get angry with you
- if somebody hits you and beats you
- when somebody says they're going to die and they say they feel ill and that's all they say (then you know their *saya* has gone down)
- if you fail an exam at school, especially if everybody else passes
- if my mother and father tell me off for doing something wrong (then I feel 'low *saya*' and go away from the house. I want to be alone and my *niwa* (mind) hurts.)
- if someone insults you
- if other people have a lot to eat and drink and you have nothing
- if there's no rice in the house
- if one only always has nasty, horrible clothes to wear; if you get caught cooking unripe maize over the fire and they tell you off
- if you're feeling ill and somebody says you're not going to get better
- if somebody brings clothes or presents for somebody else but not for me
- if friends go on a journey and people at home say you can't go
- if people give money to others but not to you

We can see from these examples how similar in some ways the mental state is to our 'feeling hurt' or 'feeling depressed'. It is also similar to 'feeling demoralized' or to our notion of 'hurt pride'. In another context, a Lohorung Gurkha talked about how his *saya* had to be raised when he heard he was not to be given an expected promotion. He thought *saya* would fall if he did not do well in the particular course exams that he thought he should do well on. His *saya* would fall if in general he didn't get what he hoped for, if his pride was hurt, or if he felt insulted. Thus, we can see that the contexts of depression and 'low' *saya* are similar, the expression of them is similar, but the way that they are conceived to affect the individual is different. For Lohorung *saya* is linked to ancestral morality and dictates certain standards of behaviour. Actions or behaviour which go against convention and 'throw away the nose' (*nabak we'langme*) or insult (*suphangme*) the good name of the head of the household, of the clan, or family, or treat the house itself with less than respect, all lessen the potency of *saya* as do acts or events considered to defile someone, such as the birth of a child for the mother.

So far I have emphasized the notion of *saya* as a powerful ancestral principle, almost an ancestral substance infusing all persons and some natural and material objects with an ancestral heritage. This essential nature of *saya* is similar in all things.

However, *saya* falls more often in some people than in others. It is said to differ in intensity from person to person, according to their status, responsibilities, sex, and knowledge. Those who are mature males and females have most pride in their ancestral past and are expected to show contempt for those who do not respect it. The source of pride and contempt is *saya*. A translation of *saya*, therefore, might be 'ancestral pride' or 'ancestral dignity'. Those who particularly attend to the ancestors and their lore, such as the local priest, the 'Rai' chief, and heads of households, are said to have especially vulnerable, sensitive *saya* that easily fall. They are the ones who hold ultimate responsibility for the dignity and strength of the community as a whole. Men's *saya* are more sensitive than women's because they have to deal with the world outside of the home where insults and disrespect abound and they also carry responsibility for the rest of the household. To the degree that a person's *saya* is intense it is at the same time increasingly liable to humiliation. Since aggression and contempt are the main weakening influences on the exalted position of *saya*, it appears to be similar to our notion of pride. However, Lohorung 'pride' is not connected with high opinions regarding one's personal qualities, but with those derived from the ancestors. The great responsibility of all men in the public sphere, in debates, ritual, fighting, and traditional knowledge accounts for the conception of men as having more *saya* than women, and similarly women more than children.

How to Raise *Saya*

We have seen in Chapter Six how *saya* is raised in the *nuagi* rite. Apart from this annual ritual, *saya* is raised incidentally by all other ancestral *sammang* rites but also by small specific rites performed either by the local priest, the *yatangpa*, or by the shaman, the *mangpa*. The following rite performed by the priest exemplifies the extent to which *saya* is linked to the ancestors and how it has to do with returning some vitality to the 'sick' person whose *saya* has fallen.[18]

The ritual requires two bamboo containers, *tongpa*, full of matured and fermented millet, and two gourds containing the strong, thin beer which is squeezed from similar millet; one *mana* of husked rice grown in one's own fields; one crowing cock; ginger; a turban, which is tied around the head of the person whose *saya* needs raising; a *kukri* knife placed in the same person's hand. When the elders of the village arrive they sit to the left and the right of the 'sick' person and in a small earthen oil lamp some *siwali* (a water plant, *Blyxa octandra*) or *titepati* (*Artemisia vulgaris*) flowers are placed before the lamp is lit. The lamp is placed on top of the husked rice. The priest takes the cock under his right arm, and begins to shake a little as he recites. The elders join in at the end,

> O raise the *saya* of this kechaba of the *lamawa* spring. If an enemy has lowered his *saya*, if his father, mother, wife, children, brothers or sisters, have lowered his *saya*, today you raise it; on the right and on the left we elders are sitting so you raise his *saya*; from today make his *saya* strong and walk close to your enemies, make them wander and run away. (See Appendix 3 for Lohorung text)

As the priest says *mechirayo meruku*, the priest's assistant, the *peguang*, kills the cock by striking it on its back with a stick and as the drops of blood come out, everyone shouts, '*saya* has been raised!' (*saya pogayo!*). Everyone present then has to jump up and make the 'patient' jump up as well, shouting as they do so. If no blood comes from the mouth but water instead from the eyes or nose, the rite has failed.

The shaman examines the chicken's blood to foresee the fortune of the family. The ritual tradition that symbolically links blood wi th the good state of *saya* links blood with the ancestors and with success, prosperity, and a healthy life. This perhaps makes more sense if we refer to the significance of blood in a *pe-lam* myth, in which two of the primal ancestors, the two younger brothers, are led to offer blood from their sister's finger to get them out of the primal lake, while the eldest brother came out by sacrificing a cock. Some kind of blood offering was needed to get them out of the primal lake. Though I have expressed my hesitations about the form of the relationship, there does seem to be some conceptual link between blood, prosperity, success, and health. In the rite to raise *saya* the drops of blood are necessary to show that *saya* has been raised, to show that it has been reinvigorated. It is perhaps not coincidental that both *saya* and menstruation are symbolised as *bung* 'flower', and flowers are symbols of life. The moment at which the blood of the cock or hen flows or does not flow is tense. Sagant (1991) found the same intensity in a similar rite among the neighbouring Limbu and he suggests the relationship between blood and prosperity and raising the vital force of the head of the Limbu household can be compared to the Nagas' head- hunting. He writes that it is blood which allows the 'flower-soul' to be refreshed

> To hold one's head up high is to make blood flow in order to ensure the prosperity of the household. . . . . .The capacity to spill blood appears to be the expression of the vital force. It is apparently highly valued in Limbu culture. As far as I was able to judge, the act always seemed to be accompanied by a very strong emotion. And this feeling, according to me, is neither an accident nor passively submitted to. On the contrary, it is perhaps thought of as positive and actually sought after. But, at the same time, this violence, deeply ingrained in the cultural fabric, is closely controlled by society (1991: 136, 147)

Those who purposefully cause someone else's *saya* to fall are called upon by the elders to offer compensation. A decision is made about how much money should be given to the aggrieved party. The sum is then given along with a bottle of home-brewed spirits. When the money has been handed over and both parties have drunk together it is equivalent to raising *saya* by ritual means and the two groups in conflict should again be at peace. Until recently, the offended party used to capture the culprit and put him into the *thyangro* N, similar to the stocks, and he would only be released when the compensation had been paid.

Everyone, both Man and Ancestor, needs high *saya* for well-being and from the very beginning of the order of the world the force of vitality could be conveyed to ancestors and balance restored simply on the sight of a drop of blood. The transmissibility of substances, qualities, and emotions is a key difference between Western and Asian notions of the person. Just as the jealous evil eye of the witch brings about acute diarrhoea in the victim and the anger of *khimpie*, the house ancestor, is not just a feeling but communicates in the form of paralysis or wounds, so the quality of the drop of blood is transmitted to *sammang*. The Lohorung notion of person is close to the Hindu in which persons are not fixed, bounded entities but 'permeable, composite, partly divisible, and transmissible'. 'Processes internal to the person are . . . continuous with processes of exchange between and among persons' (Marriott 1976: 194). The force of the blood can enter the bodies of the ancestors as easily as blood is spilled, whether from a bird, a sister's finger, a chicken, or a pig, just a drop is enough to raise the vital connections between living and *sammang*, to raise the source of energy, courage, and self-respect so that balance is restored to the order of the world.

Saya in material objects

One further aspect of *saya*, which is important in terms of understanding Lohorung knowledge of mental states, is the presence of *saya* in material objects. As we saw in Chapter Six, it's not restricted to human beings. It's present in some kinds of rice, maize, millet, ginger, liquor, some plants and trees, and certain parts of the house; indeed in all material objects connected with the original order of things as established by the primeval ancestors, and duly recorded in their ritual language. Everything that has *saya* has great potential energy and power. It's also vulnerable to the loss of that vitality. Plants, for example, containing the principle of *saya* within them, will eventually shrivel and die or decay unless they are given appropriate attention in ritual and their *saya* constantly raised. Lohorung say that if bamboo strips are dissected before the growth of the maize crop, an activity which would flout traditional ways, the growth of the maize will be spindly and sparse, reflecting the low state of their *saya*, or as we might say, reflecting a sense of neglect, humiliation or demoralization. This bond between nature and human nature in some mystical ancestral strength is hard for us to appreciate, though Wordsworth comes close to describing:

> 'I have felt /
> A presence that disturbs me with the joy /
> Of elevated thoughts: a sense sublime /
> Of something far more deeply interfused.'
>
> (*The Prelude*, Book II).

In order to understand the meaning of *saya* and thus the Lohorung experience of 'shame', 'depression', 'honour', 'dignity', 'humiliation', and 'demoralization', one has to accept literally the reality of the relationships between men and ancestors, and between men and nature. Lohorung perceive physical phenomena as part of the social and psychological world and the handiwork of ancestors from whom they are descended. To remove stones from another man's wall, for example, could well mean he would need his *saya* raising. Lack of respect for the reality of ancestral time when for example springs, stones, and crops could talk can affect a person either emotionally or physically and can be fatal. There is a strong social pressure to avoid inducing this state in others, which means avoiding insulting, disrespectful, unconventional behaviour. As we have seen, those who directly cause someone else's *saya* to fall have to pay the consequential compensation.

Saya and *Lawa*

Some Lohorung say *saya* is like *lawa*, the essence of life, the internal life-giving force which at the same time is out of the control of the individual it belongs to. With a consciousness and will of their own, they are what we might nowadays call a 'subconscious' element of man, putting its host into involuntary states. Both concepts are particularly associated with the head, and are sometimes used synonymously to describe the state of someone who lacks strength, vitality, and the stamina to persevere with his sometimes harsh way of life. The two notions are, however, different and the difference can be summarized in terms of their essential nature: *saya* is conceived as being essentially strong whereas *lawa* is essentially timid. The combination of the two concepts functions to explain two fundamental and accepted characteristics of human nature: the need for strength, and the inevitability of certain weaknesses.

Saya and 'Honour'

An emphasis on respect and shame that we have seen to exist among the Lohorung is often associated with cultures in which 'honour' is important, such as in Mediterranean cultures or in the Middle East. How does Lohorung *ngesime* 'shame', 'shyness', 'modesty' fit with the Lohorung notion closest to 'honour', which is *saya*? For the Lohorung *saya* to fall – that is, for a person to be dishonoured – the person will necessarily feel more than just *ngesime*, 'shame', but will feel personally 'shamed', which the Lohorung conceive as 'having one's nose thrown away', *nabak we'langme*. This is one reason why the Lohorung *ngesime* does not stand as a pair with 'dishonour', whereas low *saya* and 'nose thrown away' do stand as a pair. In any case, Lohorung honour, or high *saya*, is not identical to the 'honour' in Mediterranean cultures. In the Mediterranean and Middle Eastern countries 'honour' has to do particularly with 'the value of a person in his own eyes . . . [and] also in the eyes of his society. It is his estimation of his own worth, his claim to pride, but it is also the acknowledgement of that claim, his excellence recognized by society, his right to pride' (Pitt-Rivers 1965: 21). For Lohorung, high *saya* or honour has little to do with justifiable pride, for pride is conceived narrowly as someone 'acting big' – the literal translation of *diha lenguk*. The Lohorung notion of 'pride' is closer to our idea of arrogance, or self-importance, an unduly high opinion of one's own qualities than to any idea of dignity. For the Lohorung high *saya* (honour) has to do with maintaining good relations with their ancestors, maintaining the ideal nature of man which emphasizes a person's social, co-operative capacities, his status as a member of the community and as an adherent to traditional ways rather than as a unique individual, with much self-worth. Whereas the Mediterranean 'honour' implies a right to pride, the Lohorung high *saya* implies a person's physical, psychological, and material well-being as well as a good relationship with his ancestors.

What we see here in *saya*, then, is a complex notion similar to some other Himalayan concepts, and fairly difficult for us to comprehend. Unlike the other emotions I have discussed, *saya* is a much broader psychological and material state that has strong links with Lohorung institutions, particularly the ancestors and the political power of the head of the household. The significance of *saya* must have been even greater prior to the introduction of 'Rai' chiefs. We can still see the significance of *saya* in the Lohorung's relations with their ancestors, reflected in all their rituals. At some time it must have had similar significance in everyday political life as an indicator of power, material success, and strength to hunt. The Lohorung still talk of the way that slaves, *yungsa*, were captured in raids. Rich men employed 'slaves', gave them clothes, food, lodging, whatever was agreed upon, in return for work and little freedom, though they had to be well looked-after. The slaves were sometimes those who refused to pay the compensation for causing someone's *saya* to fall, often because they had captured a woman without the permission of the family. Even now, as we have seen, the frequency with which persons perform rituals to raise their *saya* is an indication of their position of power. The 'Rai' chief has his *saya* raised most frequently of all.

Universalism vs Relativism

One of the reasons for looking at Lohorung ethnopsychology and concepts of self and emotions in other societies is that in their variety they may give insights into our own, ethnocentric vision of what constitutes psychological life. It has been argued that common sense, part of our indigenous or folk psychology, is highly influential in the formation of academic psychology and that in the West language and culture and the common sense embedded in them are heavily influenced by the language of psychology (Heelas and Lock 1981; Lutz and Levine 1983).

In the light of what I have described in this chapter, what can we learn about our bias, what do I make of the main debate that continues between the 'relativists' and 'universalists?' Are emotions culturally relative? Can we say that 'self' and 'emotions' are linguistic and cultural creations, that all mental and metaphysical states are constituted by culture?

If we look at positions in the West, what do they contribute? Taken to an extreme we have the position adopted by Winch in the 1960s that our idea of what belongs to the realm of reality 'is given for us in the language that we use. The concepts we have settle for us the form of the experience we have of the world' (Winch 1963: 15) At times Winch argues that indigenous notions can only then be understood in their own terms, implying that there are no universal criteria. The Western anthropologist can describe how ritual magic is 'true' for a particular people; she cannot resort to any notions of scientific truth to look for alternative explanations, or declare their 'truth' as 'untrue'. If we follow Winch then our problem is that any kind of analysis or interpretation becomes inappropriate, and we can only report and try to understand emotions in their context, but as the Lohorung material has shown, there are some clear similarities in emotional models as well as differences, so can't we do more than this?

There are, I would however argue, important reasons for treating cultural beliefs, including religious beliefs and beliefs about the self and emotion, as constituting their own reality. Blindly accepting universals can lose the force of cultural meaning systems which have been shown to be of prime importance in, for example, determining emotional experience (Rosaldo 1980; Levy 1973; White and Kirkpatrick 1985; Lynch 1990). I hope this book will contribute to that understanding. In terms of identifying content – that is, establishing the meaning of key concepts, how a society understands the meaning of emotions, how they are classified, how they are understood in the dynamics of everyday life – we need to report what participants' say and view these phenomena in their own context, from the participants own point of view. As this book has tried to show, people do live their lives according to cultural frames of reference, including self and emotion terms, and we can find out from participants what these are. But in the very process of saying this, I am presuming the existence of a common reality. Otherwise I would not have been able to learn the

Lohorung language, nor what their behavior, concepts or institutions meant. Much of what the anthropologist does is a matter of translation. The very process of disentangling and translating necessarily implies accepting some universal criteria.[19]

So, although in my approach to the Lohorung I have been influenced by Rosaldo's approach (1980), her emphasis on translation, the importance of interpreting the common sense, and the questioning of the tendency of anthropologists 'to assume that underneath a culture's nets of problematic and distinctive rituals, rules and myths [there are] our homely, but in some sense universal, next-door neighbours' (1980: 22), I have also tended to be more cautious. First, when it comes to her view of culture, she argues that instead of seeing culture as an 'arbitrary' source of 'contents' that are processed by our universal minds, it becomes necessary to see how 'contents' may themselves affect the 'form' of mental process' (1984: 137). I am unconvinced that there are differences in the fundamental mental processes of different cultures, though I would accept there are different ways of thinking, (such as the logical, imaginative, metaphorical, and intuitive) and that we can think with very different concepts. She expresses her views most succinctly in an article `Toward an anthropology of self and feeling' (1984). She here rejects the view that culture simply provides the content that is processed by a universal mind. The 'form' of mental processes in her view may be affected by the contents. As she says, 'Just as thought does not exist in isolation from effective life, so affect is culturally ordered and does not exist apart from thought.' I would argue that although concepts can alter the way we experience and understand processes, it does not alter the processes themselves.

Secondly, I have some reservations about the work of both Rosaldo and Lutz and their strong constructivist position on emotions. The strong constructivist position (that is, the idea that concepts are constitutive of reality) works best when there would be no reality in the absence of the concepts. If Lohorung had no concepts of *sammang* who intrude into their lives when they are angry, then there is no way in which angry ancestors could intrude into their lives. God cannot have an impact on an atheist. In terms of emotions a baby of twelve months does not have a *concept* of being happy or upset, yet does express very clearly to others what it feels, and this certainly looks like contentment/happiness at times and being upset at others. When the baby eventually acquires a concept of being happy or upset, it makes sense of pre-existing experiences or entities and is not simply following experiences that depend for their existence on collective concepts (see Harris, P. 1989). Lutz applies her strong constructivist position to metaphysical domains and the emotional domain. The problem is particularly difficult when we find emotions like *saya* or *ngesime* which cut across both kinds of domain connecting up with ancestors and metaphysical notions as well as states that we might want to describe as psychological.

What is important for the study of emotions is that Lutz and Rosaldo have encouraged anthropologists to look closely at how people understand themselves and to see their concepts and actions as *in some ways* the creations of those understandings. But, although I argue in favour of relativism I am also advocating caution. Radical relativism could lead to the position that people's emotions are simply determined by the culture they belong to.

What I would argue is that relativism might be considered as a kind of methodological device to understand material from another culture, similar to Dilthey's *verstehen*, his emphasis on 'interpretation' in which 'meaning does not lie in some focal point outside our experience but is contained in them and constitutes the connections between them'. (Dilthey 1976: 239). This resonates with the interpretive-performative approach in anthropology.

My inclination to adopt a more relativist, and at least a modified constructivist, approach in terms of understanding the frames of reference within which concepts of self and emotion are embedded is in part a reaction to the dominant universalist approach previously applied, in particular to emotions. Prior to 1980 most work looking at emotions simply accepted the Western psychological view that emotions are psychobiological processes 'that respond to cross-cultural environmental differences but retain a robust essence untouched by the social or cultural' (Abu-Lughod and Lutz 1990: 2). These psychobiological processes, as understood by Western scientists, were treated as universals.[20] Emotions such as fear and anger were *assumed* to be universal emotions and some anthropologists were all too aware of the neglect of the social, 'and while emotions are often seen as *evoked* in communal life, they are rarely presented as an *index* of social relationship rather than a sign of a personal state' (Lutz 1988: 4). The biological underpinnings of emotion emphasized by Charles Darwin were instead accepted. Emotions were seen as part of the child's learning experiences, so that rage, fear, and love could be viewed as innate reactions which then develop into an array of emotional responses. In spite of an increased acceptance by many theorists of the interaction of biological and environmental factors in explaining the complexity of emotions, many psychologists continue to stress the biological. Paul Ekman's cross-cultural research , for example, has concluded that happiness, sadness, fear, anger, surprise, and disgust are universal emotions, largely on the basis of responses to facial expressions of emotion in the US, Chile, Japan, Argentina, and Brazil. Ekman (1972) found a high degree of agreement in the identification of emotions portrayed.[21] Psychologists are reluctant to give up a long tradition based on the Darwinian universalist view of emotions.

The universalist vs relativist debate led to a rupture between the two disciplines of anthropology and psychology concerning the study of emotions, the anthropologists declaring that emotions belong to culture while most psychologists took the view that they belong to our nature and are universal. Melford Spiro stands out, remaining an anti-constructivist in favour of universal pan-cultural psycho-dynamics: 'I believe, the processes that characterize the working of the human mind are the same everywhere – even though human cultures are different – then there are certain psychological criteria by which such judgements can be made' (1984: 327).

In a more convincing fashion, the psychologist Paul Harris argues that although we need to acknowledge the important role of society in children's developing grasp of the more complex emotions of pride, shame, and guilt, we also need to accept that this understanding is based on children's grasp of the basic emotions of happiness, sadness, and anger which are innate. Children are born with a capacity to experience these basic emotions and in an interactive process with others come to appreciate that others also experience these basic emotions. From this understanding children learn to incorporate more complex emotions through a process of 'imaginative construction' (1989: 103). The argument is persuasive. If Darwin's biologically based universal emotions have become 'capacities' to experience happiness, sadness, and anger, this can be taken to a further stage to say that the innate capacity is to sense merely feelings of displeasure or pleasure (or upset/content) rather than anything as semantically specific as 'anger' or 'happiness'. Wierzbicka (1986, 1999) takes this view, arguing that emotion words can be defined in terms of universal semantic primitives If, however, Schachter and Singer (1962) are right in saying that there is nothing intrinsic to feeling that distinguishes fear from anger, then these capacities to sense negatively or positively are developed or restricted in an interactive process with others to produce specific emotions. It is those with whom the infant interacts, i.e. members of a particular culture, who develop these negative and positive feelings into emotions of happiness, sadness, *ngesime*, *som khepok* or anger. If this is the case then to understand the emotional world of a culture the stress has to be placed on how the emotional life of children is constructed from the very earliest moments.

In these debates on the universality of emotions raised by writers such as Rosaldo, Lutz, Geertz, and Shweder and Levine, most anthropologists sided with the social constructivists. In the social or cultural construction of emotions – emotions are in part an idiom for defining and negotiating social relations in a moral order; emotions are socially shaped; they are 'embodied thoughts' (Rosaldo 1984: 143) or 'culturally constructed judgements' (Lutz 1985: 64); 'moral appraisals . . . grounded in the nature of our bodily selves' (Lynch 1990: 14). This has led to a useful questioning of those Western assumptions which shape Western notions of self and emotions and those assumptions that shape concepts in other cultures (Lutz 1988; Lutz and Abu-Lughod 1990). Notions of self and emotions reflect values, conflicts, struggles; notions of self and emotions intertwine with notions about social relations, moralit,y and moral responsibility. I suggest that there are universal 'processes' or 'capacities', the basis of emotions, but emotions themselves also take shape from the world one lives in, from interaction with others, from one's conceptions, and these in turn help to create that world. So my position is that emotions are not generated by innate biological processes which can be identified by the English categories of 'fear', 'anger' etc.. Emotions emerge from some universal capacities but the form these capacities take depends on interactions and relationships with others, that is from the social context. Hence, emotions also have to be understood as culturally constructed concepts. In order to appreciate how people understand the meaning of particular emotions, we have to explore how people talk about and explain emotions as we have tried to do in this chapter.

We have looked in detail in this chapter at Lohorung indigenous concepts of emotion. So my final response to those initial questions about the universality of emotions is to reflect on what Lohorung taught me about emotions. As we've seen in this book Lohorung understanding of emotions emphasizes that for them emotions can be rational and socially constructed (such as those connected to *niwa*, *saya*, and *ngesime*) and at the same time embodied emotions, located in organs (*som*, heart; b*ok*, belly; and in *lungma*, the heart/liver complex) and therefore grounded in the physiological. They appreciate a clear connection between their own ontology, their ancestral heritage and their emotional health. There is no division between thought (*niwa*), emotions and physical states, since in their experiences, of anger for example, all three are intricately entailed. Similarly, *niwa* should be kept deep inside the belly so that the emotions can be a mixture of what is culturally expected and what is innate. For Lohorung, then, emotions are both cultural and grounded in the bio-physiological. There is enough that is universal for us to be able to recognize the similarities and differences in our ideas of self and in our emotions. There are clearly some variations as we saw in analysing the prototype models of anger. These similarities and differences are also clearly exemplified in the concept of *niwa*, how it develops in a child, how it relates to *tangpam niwa* and in the necessity to develop the emotion of *ngesime*.

Seeing how emotions are embedded in their cultural context reveals how significant they are as idioms for defining and understanding social relations and the moral order. We've seen how Lohorung emotions and cultural values replicate each other. Their conceptualization and understanding of anger and fear need to be appreciated as a pair working as an institution of control, which is so highly valued. Fear acts as the rudder of anger directing anger towards appropriate kin. Anger guards and enforces morality and justice. Justified anger should be expresssed, but only appropriately since the anger of a son could lead to the fall of his father's *saya* (and ultimately his death). *Kisime* the 'fear' that is close to 'respect tinged with fear' is regarded as essential to human relations, and to maintaining order. The form of 'fear' that is close to 'fright' is undesirable and should be controlled by *niwa* and suppressed, particularly in relations with the superhuman beings. The moral emotion of *ngesime* 'shyness, shame' is, on the other hand, positively encouraged since it shows the proper way to behave. Emotions that have to be managed are thought of as being managed by *niwa*. Lohorung interest in emotions and mental states is expressed mostly in moral terms; they should be controlled or listened to in terms of their relationship with the superhuman beings and with the living.

Lohorung ideas about emotions can help us understand their institutions, such as marriage and why theft marriage is still so acceptable, their kinship system and how sisters are protected through their husband's fear of their brothers, the treatment of their ancestors through understanding their 'anger'. Lohorung emotions are also institutions in themselves, 'codes of communication, according to the rules of which one can express, form and simulate feelings, deny them, impute them to others, and be prepared to face up to all the consequences which enacting such a communication may bring with it' (Luhman 1986). As we've seen the concept of *saya* is related to an inner state, a psycho-physiological state, a state that should reflect 'uplifted vitality', 'dignity' and 'self-respect'. When it falls we might want to call it 'depression', 'humiliation' or 'shame'. Lohorung explain how they feel about a wide number of situations in terms of the symbolism surrounding *saya* and much of Lohorung behavior is organised according to the rules of *saya*. More generally a person's mental and feeling states also have a consequence for the person's prosperity, health, and position as head of the household; *saya* and the correct application of *som khepok*, *ngesime* and *kisime* are also sources of prosperity, sociality and physical well-being. These emotions relate the behavior of human beings to the values, morality and institutions created by the ancestors. We've seen here how their force as authoritative statements or 'codes of communication' extend widely into Lohorung society.

Notes

1. Harré (1986) gives a basic introduction to the social construction of emotions. Recent ethnographic works on the emotions can be found in Abu-Lughod (1986),Desjarlais (1992), Harris (1978), Jankowiak (1995), Lutz (1983, 1988), Lutz and Abu-Lughod (1990), Rosaldo (1980, 1984), Schief-flin (1983), White and Kirkpatrick (1985), Wikan (1990).
2. See Wierzbicka (1999: 1-48); Lakoff and Kövecses (1987) and Kövecses 1995. They argue that the structure of emotions can be described best by 'prototypes' or sequences of events. This method is applied on page 237–8 in this Chapter.
3. The term 'polythetic' is applied in contrast to 'monothetic' used in biology, zoology and bacteriology for 'a class defined conventionally by the common possession of at least one feature by all of its members. . .polythetic came to be applied to a class whose features shared no single feature in common' (Needham 1979: 65) yet they share a class. Wittgenstein uses the example of games. There may not be one feature common to all games yet it is possible for each game to have four out of five defining features.
4. This could be compared to the notion of *tsher ka*, 'pain, pain of separation' among Yolmo people, described in *Body and Emotion* (Desjarlais 1991: 393). It is not to do with worry or anxiety nor the sadness or feeling s of rejection of the West but to do with isolation, 'a depressive melancholy'. He compares it to the Hindu *viraha*,'the "longing in separation" in the absence of the beloved and typically strikes the "heartmind" when a daughter leaves her parents' hearth in marriage' (ibid: 103).
5. Hodgson's comment is inspired no doubt by the nineteenth century evolutionary theory that primitive people think concretely, prelogically, etc. and that civilized people think abstractly, logically, and scientifically, rather than by what he found in Nepal.
6. After the Falklands war Argentine propaganda made out that it was 'the cannibal Gurkhas [who] were the sole reason for their defeat'. The *Observer* article which reported this (29 January 1989)

also described Gurkhas as being 'a gentle people most of the time', going on to describe how Gurkhas beat up a British major and a Gurkha officer after a party in Hawaii. Their anger, it stated had been roused when the major told Americans that the Gurkhas came from a" primitive, underdeveloped country and were basically in it for the money' (ibid: 29). The implication is clear: when roused the Gurkha can be violent.

7. See McDougal 1979 on the close relationship between Rai brothers and sisters.
8. In traditional Lohorung marriage talks, the old men from the girl's side ask the groom's father if they will pick a fight and similarly the groom's side invite the girl's side to eat and drink and not to pick a fight (see Hardman 1999).]
9. The Limbu conceive of anger as having life as a spirit. One of their *mundum* contains, as Chemjong tells us, 'the stories of creation of the universe, the beginning of mankind, the cause and effect of their sin, the creation of evil spirits such as the evil spirits of Envy, Jealousy and Anger and the cause and effect of death in childhood' (1967: 21), and later he explains how the sinful souls of the dead trouble the living after their accidental deaths and that the evil spirit of envy, jealousy, and anger is called '*Nahe*n' (ibid: 25).]
10. See B.King's Chinese model in Kovecses 1995: 52, which helped me draw up the Lohorung model
11. Lakoff and Kövecses understand emotions in physicalist terms and anger specifically in terms of a hydraulic metaphor. Forces well up and have to explode. This is a Western view. However, I think it is shared by Lohorung They talk metaphorically of anger filling the belly, and of the need to express anger for it to wane. It grows inside along with *niwa*.
12. Aware of how anger and misfortune or bodily symptoms can be connected, Lohorung talk about being careful to avoid anger. Women explained to me the courtesy and hospitality given to guests partly in terms of compassion and partly in terms of avoiding their anger. Food satiates and alcohol pacifies; the Lohorung guest is given plenty of both. And there are lots of half-beliefs about what will provoke anger in a guest; 'you mustn't give a person either an egg or a chilli by handing it to him or her direct by hand or the two people will be angry with each other and fight. Instead, you must place it on the floor or on a dish. Anger figures in dreams too as an inauspicious omen. If you dream of fire, anger will follow; if you see oxen fighting, you will have a quarrel over land; if you see an old woman and she's angry, you'll get sick, whereas if she's in good humour you'll be healthy.
13. The Lohorung for these two phrases are: *manthalo khoprek pangangme? igo me'nungma ngesini e'raichha khoprek le ta'dae emo!* and *huksok meding lamdumti: nabuk ma'a ngessini*.
14. Increasingly anthropologists argue there are culturally diverse emotions (e.g. Levy 1973, 1984). More generally, writers emphasizing the role of culture in shaping emotions anticipate differences in the emotion categories of different cultures (see Heelas and Lock 1981, Lutz 1980). Lutz for example describes how *song* covers what in English would be described as 'anger' and sometimes 'sadness'.
15. Jankowiak (1995: 5) argues that anthropologists have tended to ignore romantic love. His edited volume aims to show the 'near' universality of the emotion finding it in 148 out of 166 sampled cultures.
16. Lutz describes sadness among Americans as being connected to feelings of rejection, personal failure, and lack of control (1988: 148).
17. see Desjarlais 1992: 90–134 on Yolmo grief and the songs sung to help people work through their feelings of grief.
18. See Sagant's (1990) article and his description of 'losing face', *sam mumma* in Limbu and *sir tolinu* in Nepali, and the various forms of compensation. According to Sagant for Limbu 'Losing face can occur in various circumstances: dishonour, impurity, offence, wrong or indignities incurred' (1990: 137–42). Compensation is also discussed in Sagant 1978. See also Gaenszle (1996) – an article on 'Raising the Vital Soul'.

19. It is important that these universal criteria are not confused with our own Western classification and beliefs (Lukes 1973).
20. Paul Heelas, taking the constructivist line, and showing the degree to which emotions vary across cultures (1986) also emphasizes the extent to which psychologists in fact accept a cultural component on top of the biophysical; 'those supporting the endogenous approach have also found it necessary to introduce exogenous determinants...biologically generated elements have to be 'enriched' by meanings before becoming emotional experiences' (ibid 1986: 235). If we accept the argument put forward by Heelas, then meanings are essential for the construction of emotions and 'differences in knowledge (this situation means "anger", this "euphoria") are crucial in determining which emotions are experienced [and] emotion talk, providing the linguistic distinctions, lies at the heart of the matter' (ibid: 237).
21. Carol Izard similarly argues that because newborn infants display certain emotional expressions, they are innate (Izard 1978). When infants show disgust when tasting an unpleasant substance like quinine, they are said to be experiencing the emotion that is the automatic corollary of the facial expression. That is, wrinkling the face produces the feeling of disgust. Though both Ekman and Izard emphasize that emotions are genetic, they do also acknowledge that learning is significant in emotional development, such as in controlling emotions. Other psychologists support this suggestion. Harris et al. 1986 demonstrate the extent to which children learn how to mask or 'fake' an emotional state.

9

Personhood, Emotions and Ethnopsychology: Concluding Remarks

The Lohorung relationship with the ancestors and other superhuman beings and their beliefs concerning the *pe-lam*, form a philosophy of life that upholds certain principles, such as the unity of nature, the superhuman, and the human, and the significance of the recreation of the 'natural' ancestral order to avoid chaos. We have seen how these are paralleled in the social structure. The fission of clans maintains the unity of the tribe; the separation of brothers repeats the separation of the initial brothers Tiger, Bear etc; and the emphasis on the household as the main structural unit recognizes the essential equality and unity of all men, each a king, *hang*, in his own house, with its hole to receive the symbolic rope joining the human and superhuman worlds. We have examined certain key concepts of this philosophy and we have seen how they define and orient the person. Protected by *saya*, strengthened by renewed links with the ancestors, the person is still vulnerable to such natural emotions as fear and anger that could affect *lawa* or *saya* and be fatal. *Niwa* acts to control emotions and behaviour, stressing the need to conform to traditional ways, yet allowing self-expression. Certain core emotions have been examined in this final chapter to show how they fit into the predominant system of thought or philosophy and reveal Lohorung knowledge of mental/feeling states. By looking at these mental states and seeing how they relate to other aspects of the ethnography, we can begin to understand what it means to be a Lohorung.

The emphasis in Lohorung philosophy is on the ancestors who are easily angered, on the vulnerability of human beings who are easily frightened, and on the inevitable closeness between them, in the form of *saya*, that is present in both the human and the superhuman, and acts as a link. The delicate relationship between them is based on trust. Each has a strong dependence on the other and has confidence that the other will provide what they mutually need. The Lohorung philosophy does not involve an omnipotent god and passive worship, but humans and superhumans, both active in gaining their ends. The ancestors directly experience the living, mentally and physically, in the form of hurting mind (*niwa*) and lowered *saya*, when the world they created and lived in is abused, their possessions mistreated, or they themselves are ignored. The living directly experience the ancestors in the form of sickness, pain, and misfortune. These two principles of experience act as the basis for Lohorung morality and their classification of misfortune and sickness. The mental states of *ngesime*, *kisime*, and some anger are emphasized by the Lohorung in their attempts to meet the moral standards of their ancestors: freshness and vigour in individuals (both human and superhuman), groups, and material objects is conceived as being reduced by breaches of moral interdictions. All rituals, and myths when spoken, reinvigorate the relationship between the ancestors and the living; but *nuagi*, above all, is the essential ritual that renews and re-establishes order where disorder may have occurred. It restores the strength of the vital and impersonal force of *saya*. Such are the bare bones of Lohorung philosophy.

In these concluding remarks, I shall examine first the Lohorung sense of personhood that emerges from what has been described in this book and then outline the theoretical implications of the knowledge about Lohorung emotions and mental states in terms of their ethnopsychology. We shall hence see further the importance of these mental states and emotion concepts in terms of understanding the rest of the ethnography.

The Person

In trying to assess the Lohorung 'individual' and their sense of personhood, we have seen that the Lohorung at times define an individual according to his or her kin status, and according to such roles as household head, husband, wife, brother, mother. Each individual is, however, much more than this. Unlike some peoples (see Read 1955 on the Gahuku-Gama), the Lohorung do distinguish individuals from the social roles and social statuses they enact. Individuals are not merely figures in a social pattern (i.e. living in a society where there is 'no essential separation of the individual from the social pattern' Read ibid: 276). Lohorung accept that separate individuals can perform the same 'Rai' duties differently; shamans and local priests can carry out the same rituals with considerable variation in content and style; and it is well known that each household head has a particular way of organizing his or her own household, some better than others. For Lohorung, there is a 'social' aspect of personhood, defined by roles and status, and there is a 'private' aspect of personhood, what we call the inner self, that has to be controlled by social *niwa*. A 'person' for the Lohorung is unique as well as having a social position. This is reflected in one man's remark, 'There are as many different *niwa* as there are faces. Some you can reach easier than others'.

Given the significance of kin, sociability, and control of the self, it is all too easy to over-emphasize the social as opposed to the more egocentric and hidden orientation of the Lohorung sense of personhood.

The element in Lohorung society that most seems to constrain the individual, however, is the connection of the 'person' with the ancestors. All Lohorung are caught up in a set of beliefs concerning the ancestors. Their own physical make-up, that renders them vulnerable through *saya* and *lawa*, inevitably links them to their ancestors, and makes journeys to areas without similar beliefs more difficult. They can go to Assam, to the Terai, where there are shamans, either Lohorung ones or local varieties. These beliefs limit their sense of agency and some try to reject the beliefs, to take on instead other beliefs, such as Christianity. But, often, as many recount, it does not work. Prem, as we have seen, became ill and the medicine only worked when he came back to the village and found a *yatangpa* priest. It is noticeable how few Gurkha make use of their pensions in other ways than bringing their money back to the village. Is it this fundamental way of thinking about themselves in relation to the ancestors that prevents them? Those Lohorung who were concerned about my future in a country without mediums to communicate with the superhuman beings were also reflecting their own difficulties of separating from such a world. Prosperity, health, and general well-being in this way of thinking can only prevail if constant attention is given to the ancestral world.

If we consider Lohorung ideas about the legal and moral personality, the Lohorung sense of personhood is closely connected to his or her status, family, and clan. The 'person' is, moreover, restrained by collective ideas about the power of the ancestors. The Lohorung individual, nevertheless, skilfully maintains a sense of agency and expresses his or her 'own wishes, opinions' *tangpam niwa*. Moreover, although a Lohorung individual is expected to conform to traditional ways of behaviour, to the *niwa* of the household head, and to the way in which social *niwa* is expected to pervade an individual, yet he or she can still develop and express an individual personality and make individual choices, such as marriage partners; and can stand apart from a social role in order to laugh at how one particular individual is performing a social role – of shaman, for example; or can be angry with another's performance of the 'father' role. In the arena where formal relationships are maintained, individual idiosyncracies are frowned upon. In private, informal, daily relationships, however, as we have seen in Chapter Seven, individuals are far from inhibited with friends or close relatives, not requiring respectful behaviour. The diversity of their personalities is evident to the Westerner and is obviously also recognized by the society itself in the number of phrases available to describe personality, and in the number of situations where idiosyncratic decisions or ways of behaving are not described as being antisocial, but are accepted as being just an expression of the person's particular character, his or her *tangpam niwa* – that is, 'own, personal *niwa*' – or inner capacities independent of society.

Individual characteristics and a tendency for egocentrism and the expression of *tangpam niwa* are thought of as being innate: sociability and the control of self have to be learned. Inevitably, then, the proliferation of Lohorung ideas concerning the psychological and physiological nature of man focus on why a person should be social, how he or she can be social and how he or she can come to be in control of that which is individual for one's own sake. While a person's identity is constrained by the community and forces of control outside of the self, such as parental strategies to control, and the force of ancestors, individuals also use tactics to overcome them such as by marrying men they want, leaving those they dislike, accumulating money to buy land away from the village, or to exist on their own initiative.

Theoretical Implication of Lohorung 'Emotion' Knowledge

Let me now outline the theoretical implications of what I have said about Lohorung 'emotions' and mental states. We should firstly consider what components of emotion the Lohorung emphasize. There are various components to the experience and expression of emotions, which include:

1. the context or the situation of the emotion (for example a person's death, a daughter's elopement);
2. the mental state (for example grief or depression);
3. its behavioural expression (for example crying, a hanging lowered head, wringing hands, lack of sociability);
4. its physiological accompaniments (for example low body temperature, sleeplessness, no appetite);
5. linguistic and paralinguistic expression (for example wailing).

These components may be variously emphasized by different cultures. The first element, the situation or context, is clearly very important to Lohorung, and I would say central to their experience of emotion.[1] When asked to define emotion terms, as we have seen in Chapter Eight, they do so by offering a range of situations. Moreover, when describing their feelings in daily life they focus on what has happened, they talk mainly about the surrounding event. They rarely talk about physiological accompaniments. The Lohorung logic of emotions is based on the shared understanding of the natural response to the particular or the everyday common situations. However, although Lohorung think of the situation as the initial cause of an emotion, they can and do distinguish between the situation and the emotion. They recognize that anger or grief, for example, can last for a long time, well after the insult or the death has taken place, so that they conceive of the emotion as distinct from and persisting well beyond whatever precipitated it. Moreover, they also recognize that thoughts about the situation, as much as the situation itself, will rekindle or exacerbate an emotion.

Lohorung, therefore, recognize that an emotion is not triggered in some automatic way, simply by encountering some situation. Fear (*kisime*), for example, is first of all apprehended by mind (*niwa*). As one woman put it:

> If one fears (*kisik*) in the mind then the heart/liver (*lungma*) fears (*yangsik*). If the mind retains it, only then does it come into the liver/heart. If at first the mind doesn't hold onto it, then nothing happens. First of all the mind goes cold, later the liver/heart starts to thump boom boom.

The 'mind' (*niwa*) is indeed involved in many other emotions, such as anger, relief, sadness, anxiety, or feeling hurt. This is close to the Aristotelian view of emotions in which an intelligent way of looking at situations is dominated by a particular desire. From the description of the Lohorung concepts of 'anger' and 'fear' we can clearly see that the Lohorung conceive of the rationality of emotions. Emotions are part of thought, close to *niwa*, with only a few experienced in the heart and the liver. Lohorung believe emotions can and should be controlled insofar as *niwa* can either hold onto them or let them go. Thus it makes sense that the main Lohorung theory for coping with fear is to occupy the mind with something other than the frightening situation, such as with singing or with looking for mugwort (*titepāti* leaves) Cogitation is important for the Lohorung as well as the situation.

The Lohorung's emphasis on situation or context in their understanding of emotion is close to one aspect of our own Western view. We constantly engage in an analysis of our emotions by linking feelings of anger, fear, hurt, for example, back to situations that caused or might have caused them. We rarely confine an analysis of our emotions to an analysis of some internal, subjective feeling. When people explain and analyse how they feel, they usually include some consideration of the situation that made them feel the way they do. Free-floating anger or anxiety seem to us odd rather than natural. The difference between the Lohorung attitude and our own lies in the way that the Lohorung sometimes expand the context of an emotion beyond the boundaries that we would usually impose. What we would call the 'real' context is enlarged to include the ancestral and the metaphysical aspects of their lives. The extreme grief of a woman is seen as being unnatural, affecting her so unbearably that the emotion is reconceptualized and seen instead as being the anger of one of the ancestors. The state of Narbong is one that both we and the Lohorung describe as 'mad' (*ngaksubang*). However, the context of Narbong's madness is conceptualized by the Lohorung as being the anger of *Chawatangma*: 'At Narbong's home his grandmother used to keep the secret kind of *Chawatangma* . . . but they don't do it anymore and Narbong's *niwa* has stopped working properly'. Another person described the following context:

> In front of their house there is a mango tree. Narbong cut all the branches off the tree. His brother told him not to cut them. Narbong said it prevented the sun from coming in and made the land barren. So he cut it. Since then he is mad (*ngaksubang*) perhaps because there was a *deutā* (N god) in the tree.

In this conceptualization, the 'madness' is no longer assumed to have an exclusively psychological origin. The state is not seen as coming from the person but from an external force, and actions that the Lohorung direct to that state (that is, offerings to *Chawatangma*) are quite unrelated to it in our eyes.

From what has been said about Lohorung emotions in Chapter Eight, we can say that Lohorung share two of our Western theories of emotion, indicating the degree to which their indigenous understanding of emotion is not alien to our own. The first, the psycho-dynamic theory or cathartic/expressive theory, for us includes theories of repression, and the mechanisms in which repressed emotions and motives find disguised expression. Typically, this theory says, 'Do it!' 'Express it!' Similarly Lohorung say, 'show your anger about an adulterer!' 'It's good to show anger quickly rather than holding on to it'. The second theory, the socio-dynamic theory, prescribes changing activity to lessen the potency of an emotion. A Western prescription might be, 'if you're angry go and listen to Mozart'. (The meanings to which the anger is attached are altered.) The Lohorung similarly prescribe, for example, fully occupying a girl who has just come to live with her in-laws with routine chores, so that she does not have time to feel homesick thinking about her parental home. In a recent article Spiro (1984: 330f) takes up Rosaldo's claim (1984: 137) that the Ilongot understanding of emotion is alien to the Western one, lacking the dominant psycho-dynamic model. Spiro analyses the Ilongot head-hunting material and shows how well in fact the 'Western' psycho-dynamic theory fits the evidence. From what I have learned about the Lohorung, it is clear that they have a theory of emotions similar to that of ours in the West.

Looking at the Lohorung's conceptualization of most emotions, moreover, their ethno-psychology seems similar to our own. There is nothing, for example, particularly sociocentric about their view. In whatever way the term 'sociocentric' is unpicked, the Lohorung seem no more or less sociocentric than us. First, the Lohorung do not have any surprising emotions which are only induced when with an audience. They feel *ngesime* (to feel shy, embarrassed, ashamed) mainly in social situations but equally, shyness or embarrassment are for us almost inconceivable outside a social context. We do not feel embarrassed or shy when totally alone, or if we do, it is because we are remembering some previous social situation. Moreover, the Lohorung are not lacking in feeling guilty as opposed to shame. Their concept of 'guilt' is *niwa yamuk* (literally 'mind talking') and the Lohorung freely admit to feeling bad or *niwa yamuk* about things they know they have done wrong, even if nobody knows about them or criticizes them for them. 'Guilt' for them is sometimes a private emotion, not a public or sociocentric one. People also said they often felt privately 'proud' (*diha lengme*), because to be publicly proud might provoke criticism of excessive grandiosity. Secondly, although the Lohorung see a social situation (or rather something in a social situation) as the main cause of an emotion in a situation and therefore defining it, this is no reason for calling the Lohorung view particularly sociocentric. As I have already argued above, we also consider the situation of an emotion to be essential in its definition and find free-floating emotions odd rather than natural. Lastly, there is nothing particularly sociocentric about the Lohorung view of emotions as having a social cause since they have the notion of emotions as mental states as well. They see both the social and the mental aspects of emotion. In looking at any of these three possibly sociocentric views of emotion, there in fact seems to be no real difference between the Lohorung notion of emotion and ours.

Lohorung ethnopsychology does, however, depart from ours in at least four ways, and these emerge most clearly when we begin to understand the concept of *saya*. First, the Lohorung do not separate material well-being, bodily well-being, and psychological well-being as much as we do. For them low spirits, illness, and financial hardship are almost inevitably connected, and so are high spirits, health, and prosperity. Of course, this tendency to run together the material, the bodily, and the psychological does sometimes occur in the West. For example, people who feel 'down' try to cheer themselves up by buying new trousers or try to encourage a positive attitude to gain health or to be successful. This difference between the Lohorung and the West is a matter of degree. When less tractable problems arise we in the West seek out specialists.

This leads me to the second point of departure. Whereas Lohorung view ill-health and misfortune in the same way as those who are called upon to deal with them, we seek out specialists who practice modern scientific medicine and form a group apart. They have their own knowledge and scientific theories of disease which emphasize the physical and biochemical. The lay person trusts this knowledge but may have his or her own lay understanding of ill-health and misfortune. Moreover, whereas we would seek out separate specialists to deal with material, bodily, and psychological disorders, Lohorung tend to go for a common solution – a ritual that raises *saya*. We see the doctor as dealing with our bodies and the psychiatrist as dealing with mental problems.The doctor understands our fever and we certainly don't take our psychological problems to the bank manager. For Lohorung, emotions as well as illness, or failure of crops, are part of the field of action of the *yatangpa* and mangpa. Of course part of the difference lies in the number of experts to whom we have recourse – the doctors, opticians, financial advisors, psychotherapists – who separate out our material, physical, and psychological experiences, but it also has to do with the fact that we work with a mind/body divide. Lohorung have a more 'organic' conception of the person.

Thirdly, their remedies are not non-spiritual, as are the remedies of the crop specialist, doctor, psychologist, but involve at all times the superhuman beings.

Fourthly, whereas for us political strength is non-spiritual, for the Lohorung someone who has political power, as well as anyone who wants to become a household head, also has to have strong and good relations with the superhuman world.

All of these are linked to the central metaphysical notion, which dominates Lohorung life, that states of well-being are connected to one's relation with the ancestors.

In this sense their ethnopsychology and their metaphysics are much more closely bound together than are ours. The ancestral *sammang* rites, the *nuagi* rite, the structure of the house, and the emphasis on the household head, the Lohorung concern with the mythical *pe-lam* and the local *yatangpa* priest, as well as traditional marriages, are all related to this primary concern with their relationship with the ancestors. Their states of emotional well-being and prosperity depend upon it.

Looking at Lohorung ethnopsychology[2] as a whole we can perhaps make the following points about emotions that might have relevance cross-culturally.

On the one hand, perhaps there are certain commonsense notions[3] that will be universally acknowledged in the ethnopsychology of all cultures. With respect to emotion, such notions would be that:

1. Emotions are usually precipitated by external events and many of these (but not all of them) will be interpersonal events.
2. The event causes the emotion but the event and emotion are distinct; the event is usually something that happens in the external world whereas the emotion is a psychological state that has a cluster of subjective, physiological, and expressive features; the emotion can endure well beyond the occurrence of such a precipitating external situation.
3. Nevertheless, most emotions wane and disappear over time. There are, no doubt, some emotional states, such as depression, that wax and wane but do not disappear. However, the very persistence of depression or of pathological grief renders the emotional state abnormal in Lohorung and our eyes. We expect normal states of sadness and grief to eventually dissipate.
4. To speed up their disappearance, one can either confront the situation that causes the person's emotion (if the situation is recurrent) or one can confront the person's appraisal of the situation (if the situation cannot be altered).
5. A person's appraisal of a situation – and hence the emotion he or she feels towards it – can be altered by getting the person to view the situation in a different perspective, to avoid thinking so much about it, to think deeply about other things, to control the mind not to think at all etc. using whatever strategies are current. There will be occasions when a person lacks insight into the reason for an emotion. He or she may suddenly feel angry towards another person without knowing why. But such inexplicable emotional states tend to be regarded as anomalous rather than standard.
6. Emotions are often overtly expressed in behaviour and speech, but they can be concealed from others.
7. Free-floating emotions (with no apparent external cause) are anomalous.4

On the other hand, there are also culture-specific notions that are not to be found universally, or to be universally acknowledged. These are likely to be elaborated when the person's emotional state is too intense, persistent, or disruptive for normal social relations to continue or when conventional strategies for dealing with the emotions break down – that is, when strategies 4 and 5 above do not work. At this point, members of different cultures will seek different remedies; there may even be uncertainty within the culture about the most appropriate remedy so that several may be tried, particularly if the situation is irregular and problematic. They may try to mend relations with the ancestors by means of a shaman or several other officiants, and seek out Western medicine as well, and at the same time suspect a neighbour of witchcraft. Some, moreover, will try to make themselves 'better' with pills, and see a psychotherapist, an acupuncturist, and a faith healer, and will see their local general practitioner.

In this book we've seen how folk models of personality, thinking, and feeling or ethnopsychologies may be used to explore and analyse three distinct domains: that of cultural patterns and symbolic structures (i.e., the cultural system); that of social institutions, marriage, ritual, socialization, and social life; and the domain of individual motivation, individual psychology, and experience. Lohorung indigenous psychological notions and theories help us to understand phenomena in all three domains. Moreover, notions of 'self' or 'emotion' have been seen to serve as quasi-institutions. Looking at the alternative frames of reference, the 'other worlds' within which Lohorung notions of 'self' and emotion are embedded, we can see how they are constructed and perpetuated by the interactions of everyday life, by Lohorung interpretations of events and phenomena, and by their interpretations of their own experiences.

Notes

1. Lutz discusses the significance of situation for the Ifaluk in their construction of emotion in her 1981 article.
2. As mentioned in Chapter One, strictly speaking the Lohorung do not have anything as narrow as a 'psychology' with its connotations of professional boundaries. I have been concentrating on those aspects of culture which have to do with psychological matters, with what the participants consider to be the nature of people, their motivations, with such concepts as mind, memory, and their understanding of mental and emotion states.
3. We do acknowledge certain free-floating emotional states such as depression or as in 'the "blues" are gonna get you'; these need not have any particular object. However, these states are perhaps best thought of as moods: certainly they do not constitute the standard example of an emotional state, about which we can legitimately enquire, what are you sad, angry, or upset, etc. about?
4. Horton (1982) makes a useful distinction between two distinct and complementary levels of thought and discourse. The first he names 'primary theory' which is the thought and discourse of 'everyday' or 'commonsense', and which 'does not differ very much from community to community or from culture to culture'. (ibid: 228). The other he names 'secondary theory' where differences are not 'differences of emphasis and degree', they are 'startling differences in kind as between community and community, culture and culture' (ibid: 228).

APPENDIX 1

Characteristic Features of the Lohorung Language

Phonology

1a. Consonants

	Bilabial	*Dental*	*Alveolar*	*Palatal*	*Velar*	*Glottal*
Stops	p	t		T	k	-k
	ph	th		D	kh	
	b	d			g	
	bh	dh			gh	
Affricates			c			
			ch			
Fricatives			ts	x h		
			s			
Liquids			r			
			l			
Nasals	m		n	ng		
Semi-Vowels	w			y		

1b. Some examples of contrast

bene!	tear it!	*tense!*	hold it!
bhene!	go first!	*there!*	lift it up!
pene!	sit down!	*dene*	put it in!
phene!	use it!	*dhokop*	tonsil
keng	tooth	*cenchame*	to like
xen	soup	*chenkue*	strong
ge'tong	a bit higher	*tse*	clothes
ghekchiwa	a small black bird	*sensen*	all night
		hensen	somehow
		rekma	to hammer
metong	a bit up from X	*lenlen*	all day
wenda	tomorrow		

nentang	near	*yemkue*	sharp
		ngachik	face

2a. Vowels

	Front	*Central*	*Back*
Closed	i iu		u
Half closed	e		o
Half open	ea	a	
Open	ai		

All vowels can be either long or short.

2b. Some examples of contrast

mi	fire	*ma*	mother
mik	eye	*mākme*	to dream
mīu	up there	*maitu*	lost
muwa	eagle	*lea*	don't know
mūme	to do	*lokling*	traditional shirt
mechuk	chilli	*lōme*	to say

3. Verbal Morphology

Verbs in Lohorung have two different verb stems, one derived from the infinite form and the other from a third-person non-future form, which can be referred to as the finite form. From these two all verb forms can be derived by the addition of two kinds of affix, either suffixes or enclitics. The relationship between the stem and the affix in the Lohorung verb is not simple: I was able to distinguish several different classes identified on the basis of the relationship between the finite form and the infinite. The classes in part depend on the final consonant of the base. Thus, for example, many have a single eliding final consonant as in:

Finite form	*Infinite*
lō:s-u (he said)	*lō:ma* (to say)
sei:t-u (he killed)	*sei:ma* (to kill)

whereas others have a final consonant cluster with eliding consonant as in

Finite form	*Infinite*
sabd:u (he wrote)	*sāp:ma* (to write)
hāngd:-u (he saw)	*hāng:ma* (to see)

Some examples of the many suffixes and enclitics which can be attached to either the finite or the infinite base can be seen in the following:

With the finite base

yungs is used to express a habitual action in the past. *ka khe-yungsing* I always used to go. *eru* either indicates a lack of certainty as in *kange ana rok-neru* I am going to hit you (though I may do something else like it).or that an apparent question is not really a question but asked as an indication of politeness and therefore requires no answer, *as in ane wenda hāta khe-neru?* Are you going to market tomorrow?

ro is used to describe an action that is interrupted by another action. *im-chaing-ro kaise semmang magung* While I was asleep I dreamt a bad dream.

With the infinitive base

male indicates necessity: *Khe-male-nga (*I must go.)
ese is an enclitic linking two clauses, the first explaining the reason for the second: *ning-tok-wa tug-u-ese kho khimpi men-ta* (Because his head was hurting he did not come home.)

The complexity of the Lohorung verb, which includes the use of eleven pronouns all requiring different verb formations, enables them to express many of their abstract ideas in verbs rather than nouns. Their concepts of love, hate, anger sense of shame, fear, will and marriage for example can only be expressed in verbs.

Apart from the every day language sketched here, Lohorung also have a ritual language, that appears in Appendix 3 in the ritual chants. (See also Allen, 1978, an article on Thulung Rai ritual language.)

APPENDIX 2

Kinship Terminology

Father's Father	*Pappa*
Father's Mother	*Mamma*
Mother's Mother	*Mamma*
Mother's Mother's Brother	*Pappa*
Mother's Father	*Pappa*
Father's elder Brother	*Deppa*
Father's younger Brother	*Ba:bang*
Father's elder Brother's Wife	*Dema*
Father's younger Brother's Wife	*Sima*
Father's elder Sister	*Dema*
Father's younger Sister	*Nana*
Father's elder Sister's Husband	*Depp*a (*Ki:bu* if younger than Father)
Father's younger Sister's	*Ki:bu* (*Deppa* if older Husband than Father)
Mother's elder Brother	*Koyeng Deppa*
Mother's younger Brother	*Koyeng Koyeng*
Mother's elder Brother's Wife	*Dema*
Mother's younger Brother's Wife	*Angni*
Mother's elder Sister	*Dema*
Mother's younger Sister	*Sengma*
Mother's elder Sister's Husband	*Deppa*
Mother's younger Sister's Husband	*Ba:bang*
Father's Sister's Son	*Bubu* or *Nusa*, depending whether older or younger than ego.
Father's Sister's Son's Wife	*Nammi* or *Ki:na* depending on whether spouse older or younger than ego
Father's Brother's Son	*Bubu* or *usa* depending on whether older or younger than ego
Father's Brother's Son's Wife	*Nammi* or *Ki:na* depending on spouse's age, as above
Father's Brother's Daughter	*Nana* or *Nusa* depending on age as above
Father's Brother's Daughter's Husband	*Ki:bu* or *Maksa* as above
Father's Sister's Daughter	*Nana* or *Nusa* as above
Father's Sister's Daughter's Husband	*Ki:bu* or *Maksa* as above

Elder Brother	*Bubu*
Younger Brother	*Nusa*
Elder Brother's Wife	*Ki:na*
Younger Brother's Wife	*Nammi*
Mother's Brother's Son	*Yesa*
Mother's Brother's Son's Wife	*Ki:na* or *Nammi*, depending as above
Mother's Brother's Daughter	*Nana* or *Nusa*, as above
Mother's Brother's Daughter's Husband	*Ki:bu* or *Maksa*, as above
Mother's Sister's Son	*Bubu* or *Nusa*
Mother's Sister's Son's Wife	*Ki:na* or *Nammi*
Mother's Sister's Daughter	*Nana* or *Nusa* (also for Wife's Brother's Wife)
Mother's Sister's Daughter's Husband	*Ki:bu* or *Maksa*
Elder Sister	*Nana*
Younger Sister	*Nusa*
Elder Sister's Husband	*Ki:bu*
Younger Sister's Husband	*Maksa*
Son's Wife's Father	*Ngap*, (also for Daughter's Husband's Father)
Son's Wife's Mother	*Ngamma* (also for Daughter's Husband's Mother)
Son	*Pasa*, *thukpa*
Son's Wife	*Nammi*
Brother's Son	*Yesa*,(also for Mother's Brother'sSon's Son)
Brother's Son's Wife	*Nammi*
Brother's Daughter	*Yesama* (also for Mother's Brother's Son's Daughter)
Brother's Daughter's Husband	*Maksa*
Daughter	*Pasa*, *Samsawama*
Daughter's Husband	*Maksa*
Sister's Son	*Hanglisa* (also for Husband's Sister's Son)
Sister's Daughter	*Hangnusa* (also for Husband's Sister's Daughter)
Son's & Daughter's Son, & Son's & Daughter's Daughter	*Yangmin*
Wife's Father	*Nampa*
Wife's Mother	*Mamma*
Wife's/Husband's elder Brother	*Bunampa*
Wife's/Husband younger Brother	*Ngap*

APPENDIX 2: KINSHIP TERMINOLOGY

Wife's/Husband's elder Sister	*Nanama*
Wife's/Husband's younger Sister	*Ngetengma*
Wife's Sister' Daughter	*Yesama*
Wife's Sister's Son	*Yesa*
Wife's Sister's Husband	*Yongniba* (addressed as *Bubu* or *Nusa* depending on age)
Wife's Brother's Son	*Yesa*
Wife' Brother's Daughter	*Yesama*

APPENDIX 3

Lohorung Texts

Nuagi chant (see Chapter Six)

anglak khim, surak khim, hiti khim, miti khimpie, ane chu:ana.
sabudi hang o! chong chi hang o!
khasukma'no lam ye , khayama'no lam ye.
nara'no lam yo, malewa'no lam yo.
ha:y! tella'no lam yo. chayuma'no lam yo,
ha:y! khembalung'no lam yo. lasachi'no lam yo.
a:y! a:y! khongma lam ye. namdama'no lam ye.
a:y! a:y! nam khetam'no lam ye. sunnali'no lam ye. rupali'no lam ye.
a:y!!!! anglak khim, surak khim miti khim hiti khim
a:y!!!! sakbali yo khim khim yo. o'mali yo khim yo. thupmali'no khim yo.
a:y!ha:y! waiphu'no lam ye.
ha:y! ha:y! e phekurie'no pentange nam, tella'so phesa, lasu'so phesa.
a:y!ha:y! kaso'no dam ye. sunna'no dam ye. ropa'no dam ye.
ha:y! kisa, yasa'no dam ye.
ha:y! biksa'no dam ye.
a:y! ha:y! chawa'no dam ye.
ha:y! a:y! diwa'no dam ye. lawa'no dam ye. Khammang mim mui'no dam.
ha:y! khahi 'no dam, yakham 'pi so, mukham 'pi so, wekhamam igo.
ha:y! yulamba lam'pi go. igo wekhama lam igo.
ha:y! muino lam'pi, nekha khi'no lam pi.
ha:y! a:y! sechi'no. hense'no.
semmang lam ise, hanse'no nukok'no pise.
huwa'no pise. wekhamam igo.
lawa'no pise, puwa'no pise'mo. charawa'no pise, chasum'no pise. khe'miknge
ha:y! wekhamam igo. o! nanglakha'ro, saya'no pokse.
ha:y! la! wekhamam igo, narano saya, kubono saya
ha:y! saya'ni, hang'mo.
ha:y! wekhamam igo. bhuta'no, bhayu, bharmangsi, choran'no tense'no ye.
a:y! wekhamam igo, sero'no, subi'no tense'no ye.
jori'no pari lano tense ye. mikwama'no, nakwama'no tense ye.
a:y! anna mi'go. wekhamam igo.
heh! nak hiwa'no, dek hiwa'no tense ye. wekhamam igo. wekhamam igo.
lasawa'no, hechima'no tense ye. wekhamam igo.
tokchama'no tense, yokchama'tense ye. wekhamam igo.

hitchama'no tense, pichama 'no tense ye. wekhamam igo.
somekla'no tense, tomekla'no tense.
khomkhomna'no tense, tingtingna'no tense. wekhamam igo.
hurepta'no tense, pereptu'no tense ye. wekhamam igo.
sukmawa'no tense, simawa'no tense. lambawa'no tense, khokwa'no tense.
a:y! siwama'no tense. tense'no ye.
lahari kong'no tense ye.
jhiu jhiri'no tense, sunali kong, rupali kong'no tense ye.
phekuri'no, phaksang'gi ro; tarawaro miriwaro.
kobing ana bangse heh! gopala tarawaro miriwaro
kopse, bengse, sen hinse ye, baba heh! baba heh!
lasu'no saya, tella'no saya na lase'no saya ye..
kisa'no saya, yasa'no saya, biksa'no saya ye.
chawa'no saya, diwa'no saya ye.
ha:y! puwama'mi saya go, koptetu, doptetu oh! asen'no.
namchiliwa nampa'no, sapdimpa'no, khopdimpa'no bopdimpa'no,
phekuri'no chuptangi huge go.

SOKMA

merokma wa'go rogue. puwamami hiwa'go, chawa nenuye!
labok! hiwa laso, puwa laso:
yulamba lampi'go ta'ang, wekhamam igo ta'ang.ayu banke''go ta'ang,
sensi hendame, semmang hendame,
nukok'no pise, nuwa'no pise, charawa'no pise, chasum'no pise, ta'ang. wekhamam igo ta'ang.

UMCHA

bhuta 'no tense, bayu'no tense, ta'ang.
bharmangsi'no tense ta'ang.
sehe'no tense, sindi'no tense ta'ang,
ayu ba ta'ang, mi-:kwa'no tense, nakwa 'no tense,
tarawa mirikwaro, ko:pme, bengme.,sahe! bakha'no tempa sahe!
baluwa'no tempa sahe! maiyuma'no lampa sahe!
anglak'no khimpi, surak'no khimpie, tella'no dampi sahe!
lasu'no dam, kasu'no dakpi, sahe!
sunna'no dampi sahe!, pacha'no lumpi sahe!
chupting, bengsing sahe! pasing, desing sahe! sachep'no ngachep'no sahe!
dichowa, chachawa bi sahe! tongtemma cham ye, sahe!

mikwama tense sahe! nuyak'no tense sahe!
sechino tense, nuwano hense sahe!
lawa'no hinse'no sahe! puwa'no hinse'no, jadau!!

enna lamawabia chawabie, pappa sikla, ma'ma sikla, tuba, laba sikla, kitna, dema sikla, bu'nusa sikla, cheli bheti sikla, chero mero sikla chuk'aniha! ennam pentam talo banke poktam yeptam panke aluatam, baluatam, singtam lang lingtang lam pok'karane, yepkarane. Hiwaba lam banke, toklungtok'bi sokma nense, perere nense, oba tampang panke charawa hinse, khelawa hinse; tamaniha, lawa hense, puwa hense, sense hense, makse hense; anglak khimpi, surak khimpie, sunna doka, ropa doka, hitchrung tungchrung khimpi kakdakune; langre sokdakme, hukre sokdakme, lasudampi, telladampi, men'ngesire, mentaksire, yeptamaniha,pentamaniha; bara mahina bia tongtema cham, hatekma cham, sakbak'tam, pi'mali'tam, phulu'tam, bumbulu'tam, khambulu'tam, subila'tam, wengbila'tam, pichili'wami, sachep dam, ngachep dam, chechime dam, khenchime dam, buktimpa cham, songtimpa cham, timpimpa cham, kaso dam, yowa dam, diwa dam, chawa dam; enna, pappa sikla, ma'ma sikla'go saksiro, wepmasiro, chaane, dungane, annem chero mero songko chabakamchine, dungbakamchine, le'no'ledamni, kha'no khangdakdamni, niwa etugane, taunwa etugane. kange lamawa chawabiha chiksaba'go, chigi saya, nara saya, saya're pi'me, lawa're pi'me, puwa're pidamne.
khomkhomtu khenso, pereptu khenso, boktukma khenso, chohen khense, tak;lo tempi'me; boksi, bayu, brahmangsi, chora, desana, masana, sehe, sindi, tak'lo tempi'me!
Raja daino, kaji daino, ista daino!
saturso tangpam ledeme, supamaro ongpumaro, luluwaro, sapden nepme khorekwaro, tanglo khupme, tatawaro kopdame, bengdame, tella lasubi'no lawa elipime, lawa're pidame, puware pidame, chaware pidame: lo!
langhuk sok'khetane, annamim poktam yeptam'pi kharane, tauntekanabi pempime, deu pitra langpi'me
siduma wayengma elengma, kerukchimro tamaniha, aru bela atamaniha, sikla wamla eluchamaniha, i'chama lam akhmaniha, mangpa're tikchim, yatangpa're tikchim, akrok'lo ngesik e'khemani'ha.
Hali lekingka, sewa lekingka, binti lekingka, guhar lekingka, ba jadua!

angla khimpie, surak khimpie, hitchrung tungmarung lamawa chawabie chuane; anna bara mahina tongtemma cham, khatemma cham, diwa chawa, pichili wa mi sachep ngachep, chechime dam, khenchime dam saya pokdachimme. angla e'chabimme, sura e'chabimme, hiwa'ba nung e'wapchame, jori tempimme, pari tempimme, taun tekanabi pempimme.

anna lamawa chawabie angla khim, sura khimpie,
sunna doka, ropa doka, chuane;
bara mahina tongtemma cham, khatemma cham,
sachep ngachep, chechime dam, khenchime dam, diwa chawa,
saya pokdachimme;
sigachim,kagachim, hangso, niwa etukme, taunwa etukme,
Lakshmi taklo, hembokmane,
boksi, dahini brahmangsi taklo sektikhemane!

Words to recall the infant's lawa (see Chapter Seven)

lawa khe'mayo, lawa khe'mayo
chacham lawa tapnampi epayako
khimpi keh'mayo; cheche chasi
maman chasi, totung dungsi, meding chasi
dudu dungsi khe'mayo!
lamawa chawablie khe'mayo!

ayu'go ta'ang lamawa chawabie chiksaba/dekhama mim lawa
ta'ang ke'mayo, singlangbi chu'ana, singsokpi chu'ana angso,
baphum langpi chuanna angso, baphum sokpi, chu'ana angso
lingkowa langpi chu'ana angso, yowa hongsiu, mamphu metarent,
lamphu memarent chu'ana kamgso, wa'mi laprengbi chu'ana angso,
ke'mayo ta'ang!;
hongma pangpheduna angso, dara kada pangpheduna angso, tak;
ako hongma rokno bhe lawa tae mi'chu'ma, chhoto a'tae,
lahamo ngagune tokbe'kero, kero, kero-bhe chacham lawa tao!
lamawa chawabi ke'mayo ta'ang!
mamam chasi, cheche chasiu,
totang dungsi, dudu dungsi, me'din chasi ke'mayo, ke'mayo!

chacham lawa ta'ayo, ta'ayo
sisi'lo, pompola, logo, logo, logo
chacham lawa ta'ayo; kolak, kolak, kolak.

Chant of the Women after Marriage (see Chapter Eight)

Tawama Khewama ta'ayo!
ayu anglak khimpie, surak khimpie, sunnalie dokha, rupali dokha,
hitchrungpi, tungchrungpi, lamawa chawabi tawama khewama ta'ayo!

To Raise saya

lamawa chawabie kechabam'go ayu'go saye pogayo!
Jori parichie saya dashitami hangso,
ape ame khimtangme pasachiechie, bu-nusachie nanuse'chie saya dashitami hangso ayugo anago saya pogdachime!
chupthing, bengsing pasing desing, masing machi pendingka hanke
anago saya pokdachime!
aie banke saya cheng cheng lema nung anam jori pari chim kekpi lamdum timane waiti-mane, pintimaneyo

Bibliography

Abu-Lughod, L. (1986), *Veiled Sentiments: Honour and Poetry in a Bedouin Society*, Berkeley: University of California Press.

Acharya, M and Bennett, L. (1981) *The Rural Women of Nepal: An Aggregate Analysis and Summary of Eight Village Studies*, CEDA Kathmandu, Nepal: Tribhuvan University Press..

Ahern, E.M. (1973), *The Cult of the Dead in a Chinese Village*, Stanford: Stanford University Press.

Allen, N.J. (1972a), 'The Vertical dimension in Thulung Classification' in *Journal of the Anthropological*. Society of Oxford, 3:81–94.

Allen, N.J. (1972b), 'Social and economic change among the Thulung Rai', *Report to the SSRC on Social Change in Rural Nepal*, organized by C. von Fürer-Haimendorf.

Allen, N.J. (1974), 'The ritual journey: a pattern underlying certain Nepalese rituals' C. von F¸rer-Haimendorf, (ed.), *Contributions to the Anthropology of Nepal*, Warminster: Aris and Phillips.

Allen, N.J.(1975), *Sketch of Thulung Grammar*, New York: Cornell University Press.

Allen, N.J.(1976a), *Studies in the Myths and Oral Traditions of the Thulung Rai of East Nepal*, unpublished DPhil.Thesis: Oxford.

Allen, N.J.(1976b), 'Shamanism among the Thulung Rai', J.T. Hitchcock and R. Jones (eds), *Spirit Possession in the Nepal Himalayas*, Warminster: Aris and Phillips Ltd.

Allen, N.J.(1976c), 'Approaches to illness in the Nepalese hills',J. Loudon (ed.), *Social Anthropology and Medicine*,, London: Academic Press.

Allen, N.J. (1978), 'Sewali Puja Bintila Puja: Notes on Thulung ritual language', *Kailash*, Vol. VI, No.4.

Allen, N.J.(1987), 'Thulung weddings: the Hinduisation of a ritual cycle in East Nepal', *L'Ethnographie*, LXXXIII, Nos.100 – 101.

Ardener, E. (1972), 'Belief and the Problem of Women',J. La Fontaine (ed.),*The Interpretation of Ritual*, London: Tavistock.

Averill, J.R. (1980), 'A constructivist view of emotion', R. Plutchik and H. Hellerman (eds) *Theories of Emotion*, Vol 1, 305 –340, San Diego, CA: Academic Press.

Averill, J.R. (1990), 'Inner feelings, works of the flesh, the beast within, diseases of the mind, driving force, and putting on a show: six metaphors of emotion and their theoretical extensions', D. Leary (ed) *Metaphor in the History of Psychology*, Cambridge: Cambridge University Press.

Bateson, G. (1958) *Naven*, Stanford: Stanford University Press.

Bateson, G. and Mead, M.(1942), *Balinese Character: A Photographic Analysis*, Special Publications of the New York Academy of Sciences, II. The New York Academy of Sciences.

Beattie, J. (1966) 'Ritual and social change', *Man* (n.s.) 1: 60 –74.

Bennett, L. (1976), 'Sex and Motherhood among the Brahmins and Chhetris of East Central Nepal, *Contributions to Nepalese Studies*, Kirtipur, Nepal: Tribhuvan University Press.

Bennett, L.(1983), *Dangerous Wives and Sacred Sisters: Social and Symbolic Roles of High-Caste Women in Nepal*, New York: Columbia University Press.

Berger, P.L. and T.Luckman, (1967) *The Social Construction of Reality: A Treatise in the Sociology of Knowledge*, London: the Penguin Press.

Bird-David, Nurit. (1999), 'Animism revisited: personhood, environment, and relational epistemology', *Current Anthropology*, Vol 40, Supplement Feb.

Bista, Dor.Bahadur. (1967), *People of Nepal*, Kathmandu: Ratna Pustak Bhandar.

Blacker, C. (([1975] 1986) *The Catalpa Bow: A Study of Shamanistic Practices in Japan*, London: George Allen and Unwin.

Bloch, M. (1991), 'Language, anthropology and cognitive science', *Man*, 26, 2.183–198.

Bloch, M. (1992) *Prey into Hunter: The Politics of Religious Experience*, Cambridge: Cambridge University Press.

Bock, P.K. (1988) *Rethinking Psychological Anthropology*, New York: W.H. Freeman and Co.

Boddy, J. (1989) *Wombs and Alien Spirits: Women, Men and the Zar Cult in Northern Sudan*, Wisconsin: University of Wisconsin Press

Bourdieu, P. (1977), *Outline of a Theory of Practice*, Cambridge: Cambridge University Press.

Bourguignon, E. (1973) *Religion, Altered States of Consciousness and Social Change*, Ohio: Columbia State University Press.

Boyer, P. (1994) *The Naturalness of Religious Ideas: A Cognitive Theory of Religion*, Berkeley: University of California Press.

Brain, J. (1973) 'Ancestors and elders in Africa - further thoughts' in *Africa* 43 (2) 122–133.

Briggs, J.(1970) *Never in Anger: Portrait of an Eskimo Family* , Cambridge, MA:Harvard University Press.

Burkert, W.(1983) *Homo Necans: The Anthropology of Ancient Greek Sacrificial Ritual and Myth*, trans. P.Bing, Berkeley: University of California Press.

Busby, C.J. (1997) 'Permeable andpartible persons: a comparative analysis of gender and body in South India and Melanesia', *Journal of the Royal Anthropological Institute*, 3 (2): 261–77.

Campbell, A. (1840) 'Note on the Limboos and other hill tribeshitherto undescribed', *Journal of the Asiatic Society of Begal*, 9 (102), part 1, pp 595–615.

Campbell, A. (1989), *To Square with Genesis. Causal statements and Shamanic ideas in Wayapi*, Edinburgh: Polygon.

Campbell, A.(1995), *Getting to Know Wai Wai*, London: Routledge.

Caplan, L. (1970), *Land and Social Change in East Nepal: A Study of Hindu Tribal Relations*, Berkeley/Los Angeles: University of California Press.

Carrithers, M., Collins, S. and Lukes, S. (eds) (1985) *The Category of the Person: Anthropology, Philosophy, History*, Oxford: Oxford University Press.

Chatterji, S.K. (1950) 'Kirta-Jana-Kti, the Indo-Mongoloids: Their Contribution to the History and Culture of India', *Journal of the Royal Asiatic Society of Bengal*, Letters Vol XVI, No 2. Vol XVI, pp 143–235.

Chemjong, I.S. 1961, *Limbu–Nepali–English Dictionary*. Kathmandu: Nepal Akademia.

Chemjong, I.S. (1967), *The History and Culture of the Kirat People*. Phidim: Tumeng Hang.

Csordas,T.J. (1994), *Embodiment and Experience: The existential ground of culture and self*, Cambridge: Cambridge University Press.

Csordas,T.J. (1999), 'The Body's Career in Anthropology', H.L. Moore (ed), *Anthropological Theory Today*, Cambridge/Oxford: Polity Press.

Csordas, T. and Kleinman, A. (1990), 'The Therapeutic Process', T.Johnson and C. Sargent (eds), Medical Anthropology: *A Handbook of Theory and Method*, New York: Greenwood Press.

D'Andrade R.G. (1987), 'A Folk Model of the Mind', D.Holland and N.Quinn (eds), *Cultural Models in Language and Thought*, Cambridge: Cambridge University Press,112–50.

D'Andrade R.G. (1994), 'Cultural meaning systems', R.A. Shweder, R.A. Levine (eds.), *Culture Theory*. Cambridge: Cambridge University Press

Desjarlais, R. (1989), 'Healing through images: the magical flight and healing geography of Nepali shamans', *Ethos*, 17, 289–307

Desjarlais, R. (1991) 'Poetic transformations of Yolmo "sadness", *Culture, Medicine and Psychiatry* 15: 387–420

Desjarlais, R. (1992), *Body and Emotion: the Aesthetics of Illness and Healing in the Nepal Himalayas*, Philadelphia: University of Pennsylvania Press.

Desjarlais, R. (1996), 'Presence' C. Laderman and M. Roseman (eds), *The Performance of Healing*, London/New York: Routledge , 143–64.

Dilthey, W.(1976) *Selected Writings*, H.P. Rickman (ed with introduction), Cambridge: Cambridge

University Press.

Doore, G. (1988) *Shaman's Path,* London: Shambhala.

Douglas, M. (1966), *Purity and Danger*, Harmondsworth: Penguin.

Driberg, J.H. 1936 'The secular aspect of ancestor worship', *Journal of the Royal African Society,* 35 (138) (supplement).

Dube, L. (1986) 'Seed and earth: the symbolism of biological reproduction and sexual relations of production', L. Dube, S. Ardener and E.Leacock.(eds), *Visibility and Power:essays on women in society and development*, Delhi: Oxford University Press

Dumont, L. (1960), 'World renunciation in Indian religion', *Contributions to Indian Sociology*, 4:33–62.

Dumont, L. (1965), 'The modern conception of the individual:notes on its genesis', *Contributions to Indian Sociology*, 8, 13–61.

Dumont, L.(1970) *Homo Hierarchicus: The Caste Sytem and its Implications*, London: Weidenfeld and Nicolson.

Dunsmore, S. (1985), *The Nettle in Nepal: A Cottage Industry*, Surbiton: Land Resources Development Centre.

Durkheim, E.(1938) *Rules of Sociological Method*, New York:The Free Press.

Durkheim, E. (1964 [1915]) *The Elementary Forms of the Religious Life*, London: George Allen and Unwin.

Eagleton, T.(1998) 'Edible Ecriture', S. Griffiths and J.Wallace (eds), *Consuming Passions: Food in The Age of Anxiety* , Manchester: Mandolin – Manchester University Press.

Ekman, P. (1984), 'Expression and the nature of emotion', K.Scherer and P. Ekman (eds), *Approaches to Emotion*. Hillsdale, NJ: Lawrence Erlbaum.

Eliade, M. (1957), *The Sacred and the Profane:the Nature of Religion*, trans.W. Trask, New York: Harcourt, Brace and World.

Eliade, M. ([1951]1972), *Shamanism: Archaic Techniques of Ecstasy*, trans. W. Trask, Princeton: Princeton University Press.

Elwin, V. (1958) *Myths of the North-East Frontier of India*, Shillong: North-east Frontier Agency.

Etter, M. (n.d.), *Marriage by Capture in Shing Sa*. Unpublished article

Evans-Pritchard, E.E.(1937), *Witchcraft, Oracles and Magic among the Azande*. London: Oxford University Press.

Evans-Pritchard, E.E. (1951), *Social Anthropology*, London: Cohen and West.

Evans-Pritchard, E.E. (1956), *Nuer Religion*, London: Oxford University Press.

Firth, R. (1964), 'Shaman, spirit mediumship and spirit possession', J. Gould and W.L.Kolb (eds), *A Dictionary of the Social Sciences*, London: Tavistock.

Firth, R. (1996), *Religion: A Humanist Interpretation*, London and New York, Routledge.

Fortes, M.(1973), 'On the concept of the person among the Tallensi', G. Dieterlen (ed), *La Notion de la Personne en Afrique Noire*, Paris: Editions du Centre.

Fortes, M.[1959 (1983)], *Oedipus and Job in West African religion*. Cambridge: Cambridge University Press.

Fournier, A.(1974), 'Notes préliminaires sur des populations Sunuwar dans l'est du Népal', C. Von Fürer-Haimendorf (ed), *Contributions to the Anthropology of Nepal*,Warminster: Aris and Phillips.

Franklin, S.(1991) 'Fetal fascinations: new dimensions to the medical-scientific construction of fetal personhood', S.Franklin, et al (eds) *Off-Centre: feminism and Cultural Studies*. London:Harper Collins Academic, 190–205.

Freeman, D. (1983) *Margaret Mead and Samoa: The Making and Unmaking of an Anthropological Myth*, Cambridge, MA: Harvard University Press.

Fürer-Haimendorf, C. von, 1954, 'Religious belief and ritual practices of the Myniong Abors', *Anthropos*, Vol 49, p588–604.

Fürer-Haimendorf, C. von (1973), (ed.), *Contributions to the Anthropology of Nepal*, Warminster, Aris and Phillips.

Fürer-Haimendorf, C. von (1975), *Himalayan Traders: Life in Highland Nepal*. London : John Murray.

Gaenszle, M. (1991), *Verwandschaft und Mythologie bei den Mewahang Rai in Ostnepal. Eine ethnographische Studie zum Problem der 'ethnischen Identität'*. Wiesbaden-Stuttgart: Franz Steiner Verlag.

Gaenszle, M.(1993), 'Interactions of an Oral Tradition: Changes in the *muddum* of the Mewahang Rai of East Nepal', Gérard Toffin (ed.), *Nepal: Past and Present*, New Delhi: Sterling Publishers Private.

Gaenszle, M. (1996) 'Raising the head soul - a ritual text of the Mewahang Rai', *Journal of the Nepal Research Centre*, 10, 256–268.

Geertz, C. (1973), 'Person, time and conduct in Bali', C. Geertz *The Interpretation of Cultures*, New York: Basic Books.

Geertz, C. (1973), 'Thick description: Toward an interpretive theory of Culture', C. Geertz, *The Interpretation of Cultures*, New York: Basic Books.

Geertz, C. (1984), 'From the native's point of view: on the nature of anthropological understanding', R.A.Shweder and R.A. Levine (eds.), *Culture Theory*. Cambridge: Cambridge University Press

Geertz, C. [1983](1993), *Local Knowledge*, London:Fontana Press.

Girard, R. (1972) *La Violence et le sacré*. Paris: Gallimard.

Gomm, R. (1975) 'Bargaining from weakness: spirit possession of the South Kenya Coast, *Man*, 10, 530–543.

Good, B.J.(1994), *Medicine , Rationality and Experience*, Cambridge: Cambridge University Press.

Granet, M., ([1922]1975), transl. M.Freedman, *The Religion of the Chinese People*, Oxford: Basil Blackwell.

Hallowell, A.I. (1950) 'Personality structure and the evolution of man', *American Anthropologist*, 52, 159–75.

Hallowell, A.I. (1955), *Culture and Experience*, Philadelphia:University of Pennsylvania Press.

Hallowell, A.I. (1976), *Contributions to Anthropology,* Introduction, R.D. Fogelson, Chicago:University of Chicago Press

Hallowell, A.I. (1992),*The Ojibwa of Berens River, Manitoba*, J.S.H. Brown (ed with preface), Orlando, Florida:Brace Jovanovitch.

Hallpike, C.R. (1976), 'Is there a primitive mentality?', *Man*, 11:2,253–270.

Hamerton-Kelly, R.G. (ed.) (1987) Violent Origins: Walter Burkert, René Girard, and Jonathon Z. Smith on *Ritual Killing and Cultural Formation*. Stanford: Stanford University Press.

Hampshire, S. (1959), *Thought and Action*. London: Chatto & Windus.

Hardman, C. E. (1981), 'The psychology of conformity and self-expression among the Lohorung Rai of East Nepal', P. Heelas and A. Lock (eds), *Indigenous Psychologies*, London: Academic Press.

Hardman, C. E. (1990), PhD, London, *Conformity and Self-Expression: a Study of the Lohorung Rai*

Hardman, C. E. (nd), 'Lohorung Women of the Arun Valley', Paper submitted to US AID.

Hardman, C. E. (1996), 'Vitality and depression: the concept of *saya* as an institution in East Nepa, *Religion* 26, 1–14.

Hardman, C. E. (1999) 'Rites of passage among the Lohorung Rai',G. Harvey (ed) *Indigenous Religions*, London: Cassell.

Harner, M. (1990), *The Way of the Shaman*, San Francisco: Harper.

Harris, G. 'Possession "hysteria" in a Kenyan tribe', *American Anthropologist*, 59, 1046–66.

Harris, G. (1978), *Casting out Anger*. Cambridge: Cambridge University Press.

Harris, P. (1989), *Children and Emotion: The Development of Psychological Understanding*, Oxford: Basil Blackwell.

Hastrup K.and P.Hervik, (eds), (1994) *Social Experience and Anthropological Knowledge*.

London/New York: Routledge.

Heelas, P. and A.Lock,(eds), (1981), *Indigenous Psychologies: the Anthropoloy of the self*. London: Academic Press.

Heelas, Paul. (1986), 'Emotion Talk across Cultures', R. Harré (ed.), *The Social Construction of Emotion*, Oxford: Basil Blackwell.

Heisenberg, W. (1962), *Physics and Philosophy*, New York:Harper & Row.

Helman, C. G [1984(1994)] *Culture, Health and Illness*, Oxford: Butterworth- Heinemann.

Herrenschmidt, O. (1982) 'Sacrifice: symbolic or effective?' M. Izard and P. Smith (eds), *Between Belief and Transgression: Structuralist Essays in Religion, History and Myth*, Chicago: University of Chicago Press.

Hitchcock, J. (1973), 'A Shaman's song and some implications for Himalayan Research' C. von Fürer-Haimendorf, (ed.), *Contributions to the Anthropology of Nepal*, Warminster: Aris and Phillips.

Hitchcock, J. and Jones, R. (eds.) (1976), *Spirit Possession in the Nepal Himalayas*. Delhi: Vikas Publishing House.

Höfer, A. (1973), 'A note on possession in South Asia', C. von Fürer-Haimendorf, (ed.) in *Contributions to the Anthropology of Nepal*, Warminster: Aris and Phillips.

Höfer, A. (1981), *Tamang Ritual Texts 1*. Wiesbaden: Franz Steiner

Holland, D. and Quinn N. (1987) *Cultural Models in Language and Thought*, Cambridge: Cambridge University Press.

Holmberg, David H. (1989) *Order in Paradox:Myth, Ritual and Exchange among Nepal's Tamang*, Ithaca/London: Cornell University Press.

Horton, R. (1961), 'Destiny and the unconscious in West Africa', *Africa*, 31, (2).

Horton, R. (1967), 'African traditional thought and Western science', *Africa*, 37, 1–2.

Horton, R. (1982), 'Tradition and modernity revisited', M Hollis and S Lukes (eds), *Rationality and Relativism*, Oxford: Basil Blackwell.

Horton, R. (1983), 'Social psychologies: African and Western', M. Fortes (ed), *Oedipus and Job in West African Religion*, Cambridge: Cambridge University Press.

Howes, D. (1991), *The Varieties of Sensory Experience: A Sourcebook in the Anthropology of the Senses*, Toronto: University of Toronto Press.

Hsu, F.L.J. (1949), *Under the Ancestors' Shadow: Chinese Culture and Personality*, New York: Columbia University Press

Hubert, H. and Mauss, M. ([1899]1964), *Sacrifice: Its Nature and Function*, trans. W.D. Halls, Chicago: University of Chicago Press.

Hultkrantz, Å. (1978) 'Ecological and phenomenological aspects of shamanism', V.Diózegi and M. Hopp·l (eds), *Shamanism in Siberia*, Akadémiai Kiadó, Budapest.

Hultkrantz, Å. (1988), 'Shamanism: a religious phenomenon', G. Doore (ed), *Shaman's Path*, London: Shambhala.

Humphrey, C. (1996), *Shamans and Elders: Experience, Knowledge, and Power among the Daur Mongols*, Oxford: Oxford University Press.

Hutton, J.H. (1921), *The Angami Nagas*, London: Macmillan and Co.

Jankowiak, W. (1995), *Romantic Passiion: A Universal Experience*, New York: Columbia University Press.

Jäschke, H.A. (1975), *A Tibetan-English Dictionary*. Delhi: Motilal Banarsidass.

Jones, R. (1974) 'Religious symbolism in Limbu death-by-violence', *Omega*, 5, 257–66.

Jones, R. and Jones, S.(1976), *The Himalayan Woman*. California: Mayfield Publishing Co.

Jones, R. (1976), 'Spirit possession and society in Nepal', J. Hitchcock and R. Jones (eds.), *Spirit Possession in the Nepal Himalayas*, Delhi: Vikas Publishing House.

Kakar, S. (1978) *The Inner World; A Psychoanalytic Study of Childhood and Society in India*, Oxford: Oxford University Press.

Kardiner, A. and Linton R.(1939) *The Individual and His Society*, New York: Columbia University Press.

Kitayama, S. Markus, H.R. and Lieberman, C. (1995) 'The collective construction of self esteem: implications for culture, self and emotion', Russell, J. et al (eds) *Everyday Conceptions of Emotions: An Introduction to the Psychology, Anthropology and Linguistics of Emotion*, Dordrecht/ Boston/ London: Kluwer Academic Publishers.

Kleinman, A. (1980), *Patients and Healers in in the Context of Culture*, Berkeley: University of California Press.

Kleinman A. and Good, B.J. (eds.), (1985) *Culture and Depression: Studies in the Anthropology and Cross-Cultural Psychiatry of Affect and Disorder*. Berkeley: University of California Press.

Kluckhohn, C. (1953), 'Universal Categories of Culture', A.L. Kroeber *Anthropology Today*, Chicago: Chicago University Press.

Kopytoff, I. (1971) 'Ancestors and elders in Africa' *Africa* 42(2): 129–142.

Kövecses , Z. (1995) 'Metaphor and the folk understanding of anger',J. Russell, J. Fernandez-Dols, A. Manstead and J. Wellenkamp, J. (eds), *Everyday Conceptions of Emotions: An Introduction to the Psychology, Anthropology and Linguistics of Emotion*, Dordrecht/Boston/ London, Kluwer Academic Publishers

Kroeber A.L. (1955) *Anthropology Today*, Chicago: Chicago University Press.

Laderman, C. and Roseman,M. (1996), *The Performance of Healing*, London/ New York: Routledge.

La Fontaine, J.S. (1985), 'Person and individual: some anthropological reflections', M. Carrithers, S. Collins and S. Lukes (eds), *The Category of the Person*, Cambridge: Cambridge University Press.

Lakoff, G. and Johnson, M. (1980) *Metaphors We Live By*, Chicago and London: University of Chicago Press.

Lakoff G. and K^vecses, Z. (1987) 'The cognitive model of anger inherent in American English' in D.Holland and N.Quinn (eds), *Cultural Models in Language and Thought*, Cambridge: Cambridge University Press.

Leach, E.(1961), *Rethinking Anthropology*, London: Athlone Press.

Leach, E. (1969), *Genesis as Myth and Other Essays*, London: Cape, 1965.

Leach, E. (1962), 'On certain unconsidered aspects of double descent systems', *Man* 62:130–134.

Lévi-Strauss, C. (1968), 'The effectiveness of symbols', *Structural Anthropology*, London:Allen Lane, the Penguin Press

Levy, R. I. (1973) *The Tahitians: Mind and Experience in the Society Islands*, Chiacago:University of Chicago Press.

Lewis, I.M. [1971(1989)], *Ecstatc Religion: a study of Shamanism and Spirit Possession*, London: Routledge.

Lienhardt, G.(1961), *Divinity and Experience*. Oxford University Press.

Lienhardt, G.(1985), 'Self: public, private. African representations',Carrithers, M., Collins, S. and Lukes, S. (eds), *The Category of the Person*, Cambridge: Cambridge University Press.

Lindquist, G. (1997) *Shamanic Performances on the Urban Scene: Neo- Shamanism in Contemporary Sweden, Stockholm*, Doctoral Dissertation, Stockholm University.

Linton, R. (1945) *The Cultural Background of Personality*, New York: Appleton-Century.

Niklas Luhman, (1986) *Love as Passion: The Codification of Intimacy*, trans. J. Gaines and D. L. Jones, Cambridge: Polity Press Appleton.

Lukes, S. (1973) 'On the social determination of thought', R. Horton and R. Finnegan (eds) *Modes of Thought*, London: Faber & Faber.

Lutz, C.(1983), 'Parental Goals, Ethnopsychology, and the Development of Emotional Meaning' in *Ethos*, 11(4):246–261.

Lutz, C.(1987) 'Goals, events and understanding in Ifaluk emotion theory', D.Holland and N.Quinn (eds), *Cultural Models in Language and Thought*, Cambridge: Cambridge University Press.

Lutz, C. (1985) 'Ethnopsychology compared to what? Explaining behaviour and consciousness among the Ifaluk', G. M. White and J. Kirkpatrick (eds.), *Person, Self and Experience. Exploring Pacific Ethnopsychologies*, 35–79, California: University of California Press.

Lutz, C. (1988) *Unnatural Emotions*. Chicago: University of Chicago Press.

Lutz, C. and L. Abu-Lughod (1990) *Language and the Politics of Emotion*, Cambridge: Cambridge University Press.

Lutz, C. and R.A. Levine (1983) 'Culture and intelligence in infancy: an ethnopsychological view', M. Lewis (ed) *Origins of Intelligence*, New York: Plenum.

Lutz, C. and G. White (1986), 'The Anthropology of Emotions', *Annual Review of Anthropology*, 15:405–36.

Lynch, O., (ed) (1990), *Divine Passions: The Social Construction of Emotions in India*, Berkeley:University of California Press.

Macdonald, A.W. (1957), 'Notes sur la claustration villageoise dans l'Asie de Sud-Est', *Journal Asiatique*, Paris: Imprimerie Nationale.

Macdonald, A.W. (1975), *Essays on the Ethnology of Nepal and South Asia*. Kathmandu: Ratna Pustak Bhandhar.

McDougal, C. (1979), *The Kulunge Rai: a Study in Kinship and Marriage Exchange*. Kathmandu: Ratna Pustak Bhandhar.

Macfarlane, A.(1976), *Resources and Population. A Study of the Gurungs of Nepal*. Cambridge: Cambridge University Press.

Macfarlane, A.(1978), *The Origins of English Individualism*. Oxford: Basil Blackwell.

MacLellan, G. (1995), 'Dancing on the edge: shamanism in modern Britain', C.Hardman, and G.Harvey (eds), *Paganism Today*, London: Thorsons.

McHugh, E. (1989), 'Conceptions of the person among the Gurungs of Nepal', *American Ethnologist* 16 (1) : 75–86.

Malinowski, B.(1927), *Sex and Repression in a Savage Society*, London: Routledge & Kegan Paul.

Marriott, McKim (1976a),'Hindu Transactions: Diversity without Dualism', B. Kapferer (ed.), *Transaction and Meaning*, Philadelphia: Institute for the Study of Human Issues.

Marriott, McKim (1976b), 'Interpreting Indian society': A monistic alternative to Dumont's dualism', *Journal of Asian Studies*, 36(3), 189–195.

Mauss, M. [1938(1985)], 'A category of the human mind: the notion of person; the notion of self', trans. W.D.Halls, M. Carrithers, S. Collins, and S.Lukes, (eds), *The Category of the Person*, Cambridge: Cambridge University Press.

Mead, M. (1930), *Growing up in New Guinea*, New York: William Morrow.

Mead, M. (1935), *Sex and Temperament in Three Primitive Societies*, New York: William Morrow.

Mead, M. (1939), *From the South Seas*, New York:William Morrow.

Messerschmidt, D.A. (1976), *The Gurungs of Nepal*, Warminster: Aris & Phillips.

Messing, S.D. (1958), 'Group therapy and social status in the Zar cult of Ethiopia', *American Anthropologist*, 60, 1120–6.

Michrina, B. (1996), 'The Challenge of Teaching Ethnopsychology', *Anthropology of Consciousness*, 7(1),4–9.

Mines, M (1988), 'Conceptualising the person: hierarchical society and individual autonomy in India', *American Anthropologist*, 90, 568–79

Ministry of Defence, (1965), *Nepal and the Gurkhas*. London.

Morris, Brian, (1996), *Ecology and Anarchism: Essays and Reviews on Contemporary Thought*, Malvern, Worcestershire: Images Publishing.

Myers, F. (1986), *Pintupi Country, Pintupi Self: Sentiment, Place and Politics among Western Desert Aboriginals*, Washington: Smithsonian Institution Press.

Myers, F. (1979), 'Emotions and the Self: a theory of personhood and political order among Pintupi

Aborigines', *Ethnos*, 7(4), 343–70.

Needham, R.(ed.) (1973), *Right and Left:Essays in Dual Symbolic Classification*, Chicago: University of Chicago Press.

Needham, R. (1976), 'Skulls and Causality', *Man*, 11(1),71–88.

Newell, W.H. (1976), *Ancestors,* The Hague/ Paris: Mouton.

Noll, R. (1985), 'Mental imagery cultivation as a cultural phenomenon: the role of visions in shamanism', *Current Anthropology*, 26, 443–61.

Noll, R. (1988) 'Shamanism and schizophrenia: state-specific approach to the "schizophrenic metaphor" of shamanic states', *American Ethnologist* 10(3), 443–59.

Nourse, J. (1996), 'The voice of the winds versus the masters of cure: contested notions of spirit possession among the Laujé of Sulawesi', *The Journal of the Royal Anthropological Institute*, 2(3), 425–42.

Okely, J. and H. Callaway, (eds) (1992), *Anthropology and Autobiography*, London: Routledge.

Onians, R.B.(1954), *Origins of Europe*, Basingstoke: Macmillan.

Oppitz, M. (1968), *Geschichte und Sozialordnung der Sberpa* , Innsbruck/Munich: Wagner University Press.

Ortner, S, (1978), *Sherpas Through their Rituals*, New York: Cambridge University Press.

Östör, A., Fruzzetti, L., and Barnett, S.(eds) (1982), *Concepts of Person: Kinship, Caste and Marriage in India*, Cambridge, MA: Harvard University Press.

Ots, Thomas (1994) 'The silenced body – the expressive leib: on the dialectic of mind and life in Chinese cathartic healing', T. Csordas (ed), *Embodiment and experience: The existential ground of culture and self*,Cambridge/New York:Cambridge University Press.

Parry, J. (1982), 'Sacrificial Death and the Necrophagus Ascetic'in M.Bloch and J.Parry (eds.), *Death and the Regeneration of Life* ,74–110, Cambridge: Cambridge University Press.

Parish, S. (1991), 'The sacred mind: Newar cultural representations of mental life and the production of moral conscousness', *Ethos* 19(3):313–351

Peters, Larry (1981) *Ecstasy and Healing in Nepal: An Ethnopsychiatric Study of Tamang Shamanism*.Malibu, CA : Undena Publications.

Peters, Larry and Douglas Price-Williams (1980) 'Towards an Experimental Analysis of Shamanism', *American Ethnologist*, 7.

Pignéde, B. (1966), *Les Gurungs*.The Hague: Mouton.

Pike, K.L. (1954), *Language in relation to a Unified Theory of the Structure of Human Behaviour*, 3 vols, Glendale Summer Institute of Linguistics.

Pitt-Rivers, J. (1965), 'Honour and Social Status', in J.G. Peristiany (ed.) *Honour and Shame*, London: Weidenfeld & Nicolson.

Proust, M. (1972), *Time Regained*. Vol. XII, (trans. A. Mayor). London: Chatto & Windus.

Quigley, D. (1995) *The Interpretation of Caste*, Oxford: Oxford University Press.

Rana, J.B. & Malla, K.P. (1973), *Nepal in Perspective*. Kathmandu: Ratna Pustak Bhandar.

Read, K.E. (1955), 'Morality and the concept of the Person among the Gahuku-Gama', *Oceania*, Vol. XXV, No. 4.

Reichel-Dolmatoff, G. (1971) *Amazonian Cosmos: The Sexual and Religious Symbolism of the Tukano Indians*, Chicago: University of Chicago Press.

Reichel-Dolmatoff, G. (1976) 'Cosmology as ecological analysis: a view from the rain forest', *Man*, 11(3), 307–18.

Reinhard, J.(1976), 'Shamanism and Spirit Possession: the Definition Problem', in J.Hitchcock and R. Jones, (eds.), *Spirit Possession in the Nepal Himalayas*, Delhi: Vikas Publishing House.

Robertson-Smith, W. (1889), *Lectures on the Religion of the Semites*, Edinburgh: Black.

Rosaldo, M.Z.(1980), *Knowledge and Passion, Ilongot Notions of Self and Social Life*. Cambridge: Cambridge University Press.

Rosaldo, M.Z. (1984), 'Toward an anthropology of self and feeling', in R.A.Shweder and R.A. Levine (eds.) *Culture Theory*. Cambridge: Cambridge University Press.

Sagant, P. (1969), 'Tampungma, divinité limbu de la forêt' *Objets et Mondes*, IX.

Sagant, P. (1970), 'Mariage "par enlèvement" chez les Limbus, Népal, *Cahiers Internationaux Sociologique*. XLVIII., 71-98.

Sagant, P. (1973), 'Prêtres limbu et catégories domestiques' in *Kailash*, I,(1).51- 75.

Sagant, P. (1976a), 'Becoming a Limbu Priest: Ethnographic Notes', J.Hitchcock and R.Jones (eds.), *Spirit Posession in the Nepal Himalayas*, Delhi: Vikas Publishing House.

Sagant, P.(1976b), *Le Paysan limbu – sa maison et ses champs*. Paris/La Haye, Mouton.

Sagant, P. (1978), 'Les Pouvoirs des chefs limbu au Népal oriental' *L'Homme*, Paris, XVIII, 69–107.

Sagant, P. (1981), 'La Tête Haute – Maison, Rituel at Politique au Népal Oriental', G. Toffin (ed.), *L'Homme et la Maison dans l'Himalaya*. Paris: Meudon C.N.R.S..

Sagant, P. (1985) 'Head Held High', *Kailash*, XII,(3-4), 161–221.

Sagant, P. (1987), 'La cure du chamane et l'interprétation des laïcs', *Ethnographie*, LXXXIII.

Sagant, P. (1991), 'With head held high: the house, ritual and politics in East Nepal', in *Man and His House in the Himalayas: Ecology of Nepal*, New Delhi:Sterling Publishers Pvt.

Samuel, G., (1993), *Civilised Shamans: Buddhism in Tibetan Societies*, Washington: Smithsonian.

Sapir, E. (1927) 'The Unconscious Patterning of Behaviour in Society', in (ed.)E.S. Dummer *The Unconscious: A Symposium*. New York: Alfred Knopf. 114–142.

Scheper-Hughes, N. and Lock, M.(1987), 'The Mindful Body: A Prolegomenon to Future Work in Medical Anthropology', *Medical Anthropology Quarterly,* 1:6–41.

Schiffelin, E.L. (1985), 'Performance and the cultural construction of reality', *American Ethnologist*, 12, 707-24).

Seeland, K. (1980), *Ein nicht zu entwickelndes Tal, Traditionelle Bambustechnologie und Subsistenzwirtschaft in Ost-Nepal*. Diessenhofen, Verlag Rüegger.

Shaffer, Robert, (1955) 'Classification of the Sino-Tibetan languages', *Word*, 111:94–111.

Shirokogoroff, S.M. [1935(1982)], *Psychomental Complex of the Tungus*, London: Kegan Paul, Trench Trubner & Co.

Shweder, R.A. (1985), 'Menstrual Pollution, Soul Loss and the Comparative Study of Emotions', A. Kleinman, *Culture and Depression* 182-215, Berkeley: University of California Press.

Shweder, R.A. (1991), *Thinking Through Cultures: Expeditions in Cultural Psychology*, Cambridge, MA: Harvard University Press.

Shweder, R.A. Levine,R.A.(eds.) (1984) *Culture Theory*. Cambridge University Press

Skorupski, J.(1976), *Symbol and Theory: a philosophical study of theories of religion in social anthropology*, Cambridge, Cambrideg University Press.

Spiro, M. (1966) 'Religion: Problems of Definition and Explanation', *Anthropological Approaches to the Study of Religion*, ed. by M. Banton, London: Tavistock.

Spiro, M. (1982) 'Collective repesentations and mental Representations in Religious Symbol Systems', *On Symbols in Anthropology:Essays in Honour of Harry Hoijer*, ed. by J. Maquet, Malibu: Udena Publications.pp 45–72

Spiro, M. (1984), 'Some reflections on cultural determinism and relativism with special reference to emotion and reason', R. Shweder and R. Levine (eds), *Culture Theory*, Cambridge University Press.

Stein, R.A. [1962(1972)], *Tibetan Civilisation*, trans. J.E. Stapleton Driver, London: Faber and Faber.

Stein, R.A. (l957), 'L'Habitat, Le Monde et Le Corps Humain en Extreme-Orient et en Haute Asie', *Journal Asiatique*, 245.

Stone, L. (1976), 'Concepts of Illness and Curing in a Central Nepal Village', *Contributions to Nepalese Studies*, 6, 55-80, Kathmandu: Tribhuvan University Press.

Toba, Sueyoshi, (1983), *Khaling Texts*, Yak 7.Tokyo: Institute for the Study of Languages and Cultures of Asia and Africa.

Tucci, G. (1955), 'The Secret Characters of the Kings of Ancient Tibet' in *East and West*, 1955–1956, 6.

Tucci, G. [1970(1980)], *The Religions of Tibet*, trans.G. Samuel, London: Routledge Kegan Paul.

Turner, R.L. (1931), *A Comparative and Etymological Dictionary of the Nepali Language*. London: Routledge and Kegan Paul.

Turner, V. (1967), 'Betwixt and Between: the liminal period', *Rites de Passage*', W.A.Lessa and E.von Z. Vogt (eds), *Reader in Comparative Religion: An Anthropological Approach*. New York: Harper-Collins, pp234–43.

Turner, V. and Bruner, E.M. (eds), (1986) *The Anthropology of Experience*, Urbana and Chicago: University of Illinois Press.

Tylor, E.B. (1871), *Primitive Culture*, London: Murray.

Van Gennep, A. [1909(1960)], *The Rites of Passage*, trans.M.B.Vizadren and G.I. Caffee, London: Routledge and Kegan Paul,(first pub 1909).

van Driem, G. (1992), 'Le Proto-Kiranti Revisité: Morphologie Verbale du Lohorung', *Acta Linguistica Hafniensa*, Vol 24, Copenhagen: C.A. Reitzel.

Vitebsy, P. (1995) *The Shaman*, London:Macmillan.

Waddel, L.A. (1899), *Among the Himlayas*. London: Constable and Co.

Watters, D. (1975), 'Siberian Shamanistic Traditions among the Kham-Magars', *Contributions to Nepalese Studies*, II, 123–68.

White, G and Kirkpatrick, J. (1985) *Person, Self and Experience: Exploring Pacific Ethnopsychologies*, Berkeley: University of California Press.

Wikan, U.(1990), *Managing Turbulent Hearts: A Balinese Formula for Living*, Chicago: University of Chicago Press.

Wikan, U. (1991), 'Toward an Experience-Near Anthropology', *Cultural Anthropology*, 6: 285–305.

Wikan, U. (1992), 'Beyond the words: the power of resonance', *American Ethnologist*, 19(3).

Wierzbicka, A. (1999) *Emotions Across Languages and Cultures*, Cambridge: Cambridge University Press.

Winch, P. (1963) 'Understanding a Primitive Society', Wilson,B.R. *Rationality*, Oxford: Blackwell Publications.

Young, D. E. and Guy Goulet J.(1994), *Being Changed by Cross-Cultural Encounters: the Anthropology of Extraordinary Experience*, Ontario: Broadview Press.